# UNSEALED

## THE TIME OF THE END

### Today in the Prophecies
### of Daniel and Revelation

MELISSA HANSON

# UNSEALED: The Time of the End

ISBN: 979-8-9879277-2-4

Library of Congress: 2023913583

Printed in the United States of America

*Visit www.unsealedthetimeoftheend.com for more information.*

Dedicated to all who will receive this
word with "readiness of mind"
and search "the scriptures daily"
to find out if these things are so.

Acts 17:11 KJV

# Contents

# Preface

*Unsealed: The Time of the End* is written from a layperson's perspective and offers a simple, biblical explanation of the prophecies found in Daniel 2, 7-12, and each chapter in the book of Revelation. It is the compilation of over ten years of intensive research comparing the Bible and the Spirit of Prophecy to current events, accompanied by regular periods of prayer and fasting. Most importantly, it is an urgent call for sincere Christians, "… knowing the time, that now it is high time to awake out of sleep: for now our salvation is nearer than when we first believed" (Rom. 13:11). Its purpose is to give the reader a systematic overview of Bible prophecy and how it applies today, thus preventing deception and instilling an urgency to share these messages with others. Because the Lord speaks to His people individually through His Word, the author's objective is to share her research and encourage all to study God's prophecies for themselves, comparing scripture with scripture. It is written so that readers can discover each presented premise by looking up the biblical references in the parentheses found inside the chapters and in the discussion questions at the end. All scriptures are taken from the KJV or NKJV, and each chapter begins with the accompanying Bible prophecy.

Moreover, the Hebrew and Greek meanings of words are taken from the Strongs Concordance, using the KJV of the Touch Bible Loaded Study App. Also, the appendix lists the definitions of the prophetic symbols with supporting Bible texts for easy reference, as well as the confirmation of modern repeated prophecy. Through the use of these simple tools and an abundance of child-like faith, one may unseal a deeper understanding of the prophecies of Daniel and Revelation and how they apply to life today.

May the Lord grant us wisdom liberally in studying His truth! (James 1:5). He promises, "I will pour out my Spirit unto you; I will make known my words unto you" (Prov. 1:23, KJV). This is God's *guarantee* as we embark on this journey to understand, apply, and share these amazing Bible prophecies in preparation for Christ's soon return!

# Introduction

*"Do not seal the words of the prophecy
of this book, for the time is at hand."*

Rev. 22:10, NKJV

The following parable, inspired by the story of Jonah, depicts the urgency for studying and sharing Bible prophecy today:

Now the word of the Lord came to Joe, a Christian living in the last days of Earth's history, saying, "Arise, and go to Babylon, that great city, and cry against it, for their wickedness has come up before Me."

The last thing young Joe wanted to do was preach an unpopular message that was politically incorrect, so he decided to jump on the bandwagon with the crowd, crying, "Peace! Peace! When there was no peace."

However, the Lord was displeased with His unfaithful servant and allowed troublesome times to come upon Joe, his church, and his country. Although Joe and his friends all agreed that time was short and the signs of Christ's coming were taking place right before their eyes, they continued in their Laodicean state, asleep in the wealth of their religious knowledge and the Lord's many material blessings that had been lavishly bestowed upon them.

But some of the lost were afraid of the times in which they

lived, and they cried out to God, begging Him for the understanding of His Word. And since they had heard that the Bible had amazing, true prophecies, they went to Joe and shook him awake, crying, "Why are you sleeping in such a time as this? Arise, and call out to your God! Perhaps the Lord will have mercy upon us so that we might not perish at His return! We have gone from one source to another, trying to find out about Christ's second coming, but all we know is what we have learned from watching the "Left Behind" movies. Please tell us why all these judgments are coming upon our families and the entire world! Aren't you a Christian who has been taught Bible prophecy? Why are you not sharing its messages so that we can be saved?"

So, Joe idly replied, "Yes, I suppose I should share my biblical knowledge, but I am kind of rusty on the prophecies of Daniel and Revelation. It's been a long time since I have studied them. But I can tell you all about grace! I just don't want to scare people with all those wild beasts of Daniel and Revelation or their meanings for us today. I certainly don't want to be accused of judging others if they want to continue in their modern secular lifestyles."

Then those who had admitted their hopeless condition were exceedingly dismayed at Joe's lackadaisical attitude, for they realized that their only chance of understanding God's prophetic truth was being dismissed as unimportant and unnecessary. So, they prayed to the Lord in their distress that they would not be held responsible for the light that Joe didn't care to share with them.

Now God heard these searching souls' desperate cries and allowed double trouble to fall upon Joe and those like him because of their unfaithfulness to the Lord's special calling. And Joe cried out from the belly of despair, begging God to forgive his disobedience in keeping biblical truth all to himself! So, the Lord had mercy upon Joe and His Laodicean people and gave them another opportunity to warn the world of its final judgment and Christ's soon return.

And God said to Joe and His remnant church, "Arise, go to Babylon, that great city, and preach the prophecies found in the books of Daniel and Revelation. Explain them clearly so that all can understand."

So, this time, Joe obeyed, although he was still reluctant to share a message of the world's soon destruction when all his friends were going "green" to save the earth. However, feelings of guilt and fear of further trouble impelled him to cry out, "The Lord says that Babylon the great is fallen, is fallen, and has become a dwelling place of demons… For all the nations have drunk of the wine of the wrath of her fornications… Come out of her, my people, lest you share in her sins, and lest you receive of her plagues!" (Rev. 18:2-4).

And the people listened—and many repented—which dismayed and dumbfounded poor Joe! He had never expected such a turn of events because his theology professors in college had told him that preaching the unadulterated truth of God's Word to the masses didn't work. What should he do now? Having fulfilled his religious duty, Joe quickly left and went back home where he could escape the tedious task of answering a bombardment of questions from the crowds.

Feeling like a giant weight was still pressing down on his shoulders, Joe had time to ponder his perplexing success. What would all his church friends think when they heard what he had done? His message of judgment and the imminent return of Christ certainly didn't fit the popular model of mingling among the people and meeting their needs. This could really hurt his reputation! Who would want to hang out with Doomsday Preacher Joe? He just wished that God would free him of this special calling and allow him to go back to his easy lifestyle of watching TV, checking his social media, and playing video games.

However, the Lord did not give up! He continued to plead with Joe and His church to share the truths of Bible prophecy with the world before it was too late....

With whom in this parable can you relate most? Are you like Joe, who had much biblical knowledge but was afraid to share it with others? Or do you relate more to the crowd, who was trying to make sense of what was happening in the world and longing for answers that could only be found in the Bible? Either way, the Holy Spirit promises understanding and the ability to distinguish truth from error: "... when He, the Spirit of truth has come, He will guide you into all truth ... and He will tell you things to come" (John 16:13). You don't need to be a scholar! If you have the faith of a child, the Lord will explain how His Word applies to YOUR life today!

# DANIEL 2:31-45 (KJV)

³¹ *Thou, O king, sawest, and behold a great image. This great image, whose brightness was excellent, stood before thee; and the form thereof was terrible.* ³² *This image's head was of fine gold, his breast and his arms of silver, his belly and his thighs of brass,* ³³ *His legs of iron, his feet part of iron and part of clay.* ³⁴ *Thou sawest till that a stone was cut out without hands, which smote the image upon his feet that were of iron and clay, and brake them to pieces.* ³⁵ *Then was the iron, the clay, the brass, the silver, and the gold, broken to pieces together, and became like the chaff of the summer threshing floors; and the wind carried them away, that no place was found for them: and the stone that smote the image became a great mountain, and filled the whole earth.* ³⁶ *This is the dream; and we will tell the interpretation thereof before the king.* ³⁷ *Thou, O king, art a king of kings: for the God of heaven hath given thee a kingdom, power, and strength, and glory.* ³⁸ *And wheresoever the children of men dwell, the beasts of the field and the fowls of the heaven hath he given into thine hand, and hath made thee ruler over them all. Thou art this head of gold.* ³⁹ *And after thee shall arise another kingdom inferior to thee, and another third kingdom of brass, which shall bear rule over all the earth.* ⁴⁰ *And the fourth kingdom shall be strong as iron: forasmuch as iron breaketh in pieces and subdueth all things: and as iron that breaketh all these, shall it break in pieces and bruise.* ⁴¹ *And whereas thou sawest the feet and toes, part of potters' clay, and part of iron, the kingdom shall be divided; but there shall be in it of the strength of the*

iron, forasmuch as thou sawest the iron mixed with miry clay. [42] And as the toes of the feet were part of iron, and part of clay, so the kingdom shall be partly strong, and partly broken. [43] And whereas thou sawest iron mixed with miry clay, they shall mingle themselves with the seed of men: but they shall not cleave one to another, even as iron is not mixed with clay. [44] And in the days of these kings shall the God of heaven set up a kingdom, which shall never be destroyed: and the kingdom shall not be left to other people, but it shall break in pieces and consume all these kingdoms, and it shall stand for ever. [45] Forasmuch as thou sawest that the stone was cut out of the mountain without hands, and that it brake in pieces the iron, the brass, the clay, the silver, and the gold; the great God hath made known to the king what shall come to pass hereafter: and the dream is certain, and the interpretation thereof sure.

# A Statue of the Future

Have you ever wondered what the future holds? Some people try to find out by following their horoscopes or asking crystals. Others pay to have their future revealed by palm readers. Still others contact the spirits of the dead. However, the only true way to know what will occur in the future is to read the Bible's prophecies. They alone can give accurate and meaningful insights about what is to come! One of the most important reasons for studying the prophecies of Daniel and Revelation is the evidence they provide, proving the validity of God's Word and the Lord's faithful guidance of His followers throughout time (Is.14:24). His hand is constantly leading humanity's footsteps toward the culmination of His soon return and the fulfillment of His plan of salvation. But as crazy as it sounds, the Bible uses history to teach about the future, so one must begin the quest for what lies ahead by looking at what has happened in the past (Eccl. 3:15).

## Seeing the Future

Similar to most now, King Nebuchadnezzar, who ruled ancient Babylon during the time of Daniel, wanted to know his destiny. One night, God granted his desire in a dream, outlining important events that would occur during his day until the end of time. There was only one problem—Nebuchadnezzar could not understand the Lord's symbolism, so the message didn't make any sense! Many people today are a lot like this king. God's

3

prophecies in the books of Daniel and Revelation seem too difficult to understand! But the Lord has promised wisdom if one asks (James 1:5; Prov. 1:23). Christ's followers must simply claim His promises in faith, and in turn, He will be faithful to give them understanding of His Word.

## The Metal Man

How many of us have ever been haunted by a nightmare? Probably most! That was exactly what happened to King Nebuchadnezzar. In his sleep, he saw a statue of a man composed of different materials, mainly metal (Dan. 2:32-45). The head was made of gold, the chest and arms of silver, the belly and thighs of bronze, the lower legs of iron, and the feet and toes of iron and clay (Dan. 2:32-33). Then a stone, "cut out without hands," struck the image on its feet and broke the idol into pieces (Dan. 2:34, KJV). The iron, clay, bronze, silver, and gold were crushed together, and the wind carried them away so that no trace of them could be found. Then the stone became a great mountain and filled the entire earth (Dan. 2:35). King Nebuchadnezzar knew that the dream had to be important. But he had no idea what it meant! Fortunately, God did not leave him to figure it out all by himself! The Lord sent His prophet, Daniel, to interpret the dream. Likewise, God promises today to send His Holy Spirit to explain the prophecies of His Word (Jn. 16:13). By prayerfully comparing scripture with scripture, anyone can discover the secrets of God's Word!

## The Head of Gold—King Nebuchadnezzar of Babylon

Nebuchadnezzar's dream portrayed a panoramic view of the world's kingdoms associated with God's people and their downward spiritual spiral throughout Earth's history (2 Tim. 3:13). In Daniel's day, God's nation of Israel had been taken captive by the Babylonians and were under King Nebuchadnezzar's rule.

That is why God, through the prophet, Daniel, told Nebuchad-nezzar that he was the "head of gold" (Dan. 2:38, KJV). As king, he understood that he was the "head" or ruler, but who or what was represented by the gold? The Lord did not give details about the meaning of the gold. Instead, Daniel simply said that after King Nebuchadnezzar, there would arise another kingdom (Dan. 2:39), so the gold must have had something to do with the kingdom of Babylon. However, Lamentations 4:1-2 states, "How the gold has become dim! How changed the fine gold!... *The precious sons of Zion, valuable as fine gold,* how they are regarded as *clay pots,* the work... of the potter!" (NKJV; Italics added). This text compares the "sons of Zion" to gold deteriorating into clay pots. Therefore, gold could also symbolize God's people living in Babylon and their characters.

## The Chest and Arms of Silver—Medo-Persia

Just as the dream predicted, the next world kingdom, repre-sented as silver, arose in 539 BC.[1] After Babylon fell to the Medes and Persians (Jer. 51:11; Dan. 8:20), intermarriage and idolatry continued to chip away at Israel's spiritual foundation. Through-out history, the Lord patiently worked with His people during their captivity to their eastern relatives who were also Shem's de-scendants,[2] the lineage of Abraham (Isaac—Israelites/Ishmael—Arabs). In Malachi 3:3, God proclaims, "as a refiner and purifier of silver," He shall "purify the sons of Levi and purge them as gold and silver" (KJV). In this text, the Bible refers to God's people as refined "gold and silver" (Zech. 13:9; Hag. 2:8). Despite being encompassed by pagan practices, the Lord's true followers would continue to obey God, allowing Him to purify their hearts from sin.

---

[1] https://en.wikipedia.org/wiki/Fall_of_Babylon
[2] *Josephus* (Antiquities 1.6.4.)

However, some would succumb to the culture of the day and worship false idols of gold and silver. This idolatry eventually resulted in God's people, the "silver and gold," being captured by the Gentiles, and in 331 BC, Medo-Persia was conquered by the kingdom of Greece.[3]

## Belly and Thighs of Bronze – Greece

With a whirlwind of victories, Alexander the Great defeated Medo-Persia, and the nation of Israel fell into the hands of the bronze kingdom, Greece, represented by the belly and thighs of the statue in Nebuchadnezzar's dream (Dan. 2:32; Jer. 6:28-30; compare Dan. 8:21). In this defeat, world leadership was seized by the West, and the lineage of Abraham lost their rulership, largely because of their spiritual apostasy (Joel 3:5-6). Famous Greek philosophers, such as Plato and Aristotle, introduced pagan Greek philosophies and mingled them with the biblical truths of God's Word. These pagan ideas only compounded the malignant corruption that already existed among the Lord's people and resulted in religious confusion and the eventual evolution of humanistic, postmodern philosophies that are so prevalent today.

The bronze upper thighs of the statue in Nebuchadnezzar's dream indicate that the Greek culture would continue even after its defeat by Rome, symbolized by the iron lower legs. The Bible often combines bronze and iron (Is. 48:4; Jer. 6:28), using it to figuratively portray the result of God's people in Gentile captivity (Lev. 26:19; Deut. 28:23). For example, in Dan. 4, the tree stump of Nebuchadnezzar's second dream was bound by chains of iron and bronze (Dan. 4:15). Also, in Daniel's vision of the beasts, the fourth world kingdom ruling God's people (Rome) is described

---

[3] http://www.eyewitnesstohistory.com/alexander.htm

as having "iron teeth" and "nails of bronze" (Dan. 7:19). However, despite the pagan influences of the Greeks and Romans, God promises spiritual freedom for His people by saying, "For He has broken the gates of bronze and cut the bars of iron in two" (Ps. 107:16, NKJV; compare Is. 45:2 & Jer. 15:12).

## Legs of Iron Becoming Foot/Toes of Iron Mixed with Clay – Rome/Divided Europe

Defeating Greece in 168 BC,[4] the fourth world kingdom of Rome, represented by the legs of iron, would continue its powerful rule over the Jewish nation throughout the time of Christ and beyond. During this period of history, the Pharisees and Sadducees fought against paganism by making the Jewish religion so ritualistic and rigid that most Israelites lost their passion to search the Scriptures. As a result of this lack of prophetic knowledge, Israel did not recognize Jesus as the Messiah when He came to Earth. Tragically, such legalism, paired with the paganism of Rome, nearly extinguished the spiritual and moral excellence in the Jewish nation. This sad state would continue in God's people throughout Rome's iron rule, spanning the majority of Christian history during the time of the New Testament church.

In the fourth century, the Roman Empire grew so vast that it became necessary to divide the rulership of its territory. Under Emperor Diocletian, the eastern part of Rome became the Byzantine Empire, mainly retaining its pagan Greek heritage, predicted in the combination of the brass thighs (Greece) and iron lower legs (Rome).[5] The western part of Rome, although influenced by Greek culture, stayed loyal to the pope and Roman Catholicism.[6]

---

[4] https://en.wikipedia.org/wiki/Battle_of_Pydna

[5] https://en.wikipedia.org/wiki/Diocletian

[6] https://worldhistory.us/ancient-history/eastern-vs-western-roman-empire-compared.php

This papal leg of Rome grew continually in political power, especially after 330 AD when Constantine decided to move his capital to Constantinople.[7] Such governmental change gave the papacy additional political power, and in 538 AD, Justinian's declaration of the pope's religious and civil authority over the entire Roman Empire went undisputed.[8]

Sadly, despite many godly members seeking reform within the Catholic Church system, spiritual corruption multiplied. Influenced by culture and paganism, the church developed its own rituals, which became so prominent that traditions were exalted above the Scriptures. Worse yet, God's common people did not have public access to His Word. The pope's combination of political and religious power continued to thrive in the divided kingdom of Europe, even after 1054 AD when the Great Schism between Western Roman Catholicism and Eastern Greek Orthodoxy occurred. This Roman grip of control would persist throughout the entire Dark Ages.

However, in the 1500s, the Protestant Reformation arose, bringing persecution which resulted in the spread of Christianity across Europe (foot/toes) and eventually to America (foot/toes). This religious persecution spanned the history of divided Europe. But finally, in 1798, Rome lost its political power when the pope was taken captive by Napoleon's general, Berthier.[9] At last, persecution ended! Protestant Christians were given a reprieve. However, the iron will of the papacy would persevere until the end of time, even though its political power would be temporarily restrained until the last world kingdom would propel its prominence once again.

---

[7] https://en.wikipedia.org/wiki/Constantinople
[8] https://ijhssnet.com/journals/Vol_7_No_1_January_2017/7.pdf
[9] https://en.wikipedia.org/wiki/Pope_Pius_VI

The final world kingdom, represented as clay in Nebuchad-nezzar's dream (Dan. 2:41-43), would arise after Rome's loss of power in the late 1700s. Daniel 2:42 (KJV) states, "… part of iron, and part of clay, so the *kingdom*" (not just God's people every-where) would be molded by God like a potter molds clay (Is. 64:8; 43:21; Jer. 18:6; italics added).

## Foot/Toes of Clay Mixed with Iron – United States of America

Only one prominent Christian nation arose in the late 1700s after the loss of papal rule in divided Europe (Dan. 2:41). It was the nation of the United States of America, the Protestant refuge containing both Christians and Jews, represented as clay (Jer. 18:4, 6; Gal. 3:28-29; Is. 64:8). Unfortunately, in accordance with the Bible, the "gold" of both spiritual and physical Israel has con-tinued to deteriorate into inferior "clay" (Lam. 4:1-2; Ps. 2:8-9). Moreover, the prophecy of Rome's iron being mixed with clay and mingling with "the seed of men" is even more prominent today (Dan. 2:43). In 2017, the Lutherans, along with several other mainline Protestant denominations, signed an ecumenical state-ment with the papacy concerning the doctrine of justification by faith.[10] This same doctrine was the cornerstone of Luther's protest against the Catholic Church, originally catapulting the beginning of the Protestant Reformation. Because of the current ecumenical unity of Protestants and Catholics, many have claimed that the Protestant Reformation has ended. In fact, most Americans say Catholics and Protestants today are more religiously similar than they are different.[11] Prophecy predicts that this attempt of min-gling iron with clay will result in the combination of church and

---

[10] http://www.romereports.com/en/2017/07/15/reformed-churches-join-catholics-and-lutherans-on-the-doctrine-of-justification/
[11] http://www.pewforum.org/2017/08/31/u-s-protestants-are-not-defined-by-refor-mation-era-controversies-500-years-later/

state, destroying the United State's civil and religious freedom (Rev. 13:15). However, the governments of Rome and the U.S. will not be integrated, just as iron doesn't mix with clay.

Tragically, this great haven of religious freedom that Christ formed Himself, like a potter forms clay, will be shattered, just like the statue was shattered by a stone cut from a mountain without human hands in Nebuchadnezzar's dream (Dan. 2:43, 45; Jer. 18:6-7, 10; Lam. 4:1, 6; Is. 14:4-5). Likewise, the Bible teaches that all will be judged by God's law that was cut from a mountain without human hands and written with the Lord's own finger (Exodus 24:12; 31:18). Moreover, the stone in the king's dream represents Jesus (Eph. 2:20; Rom. 9:33), as well as His law (the foundation of His kingdom [Is. 28:16; Rom. 9:31-32]). This stone will break the covenant formed by Protestant America and the papacy and crush the wicked, enabling God's "mountain" kingdom to fill the earth at Christ's second coming (Dan. 2:35, 44-45; Zech. 8:3; Rev. 21:10; Joel 3:17; Micah 4:1-2).

Today we have the tremendous privilege of looking back at the fulfillment of the biblical prophecy found in Nebuchadnezzar's dream. Just as predicted, spiritual/moral values have continued to lessen with the rise and fall of each world kingdom, and we are now living in the toenails of the statue's feet! Since the prophecy of Daniel 2 has proven its accuracy throughout history, Christ's return must be very near! The question is—how will this truth affect us today? Will Jesus find our hearts hard as iron or soft as clay when He returns to take us home?

# Discussion Questions for Daniel 2

*(Please refer to the appendix at the back of this book
to answer the questions following each chapter)*

1.  *How can one encourage someone hesitant to study prophecy?*

2.  *What Bible promises can be claimed? (Prov. 1:23; James 1:5)*

3.  *Why is studying prophecy so important for us today?
    (Is. 14:24)*

4.  *Why did the metals become worth less and less as history
    progressed throughout each world kingdom? (Dan. 2:39)*

5.  *Who is represented by the "head of gold," and what kingdom
    did he rule? (Dan. 1:1; 2:37-38)*

6.  *Whom might the gold symbolize in the kingdom of Babylon?
    (Lam. 4:1-2)*

7.  *What kingdom does the silver represent? (Dan. 2:39; Dan.
    8:20; Jer. 51:11) How was the silver kingdom related to Israel?
    (Hag. 2:8)*

8.  *What Gentile kingdom does the bronze belly and thighs sybol-
    ize? How did this pagan shift in world leadership affect God's
    people's understanding of biblical prophecy? (Dan. 2:32, 39;
    8:21; Joel 3:5-6)*

9.  *According to history, what Gentile kingdom defeated Greece
    and was symbolized by iron legs? (Dan. 2:40)*

10. *How are brass and iron often referenced together in the Bible
    in a negative light? (Jer. 6:28; Is. 48:4; Deut. 28:23; Lev. 26:19;
    Jer. 15:12; Is. 45:2)*

11. *Some have purported that the clay mixed with iron represents all of God's people in the world. Where does one find proof that the Bible is speaking of a certain kingdom/nation? (Dan. 2:41-42)*

12. *Why is the United States the only nation that seems to fit the description of the clay kingdom mixed with iron, and how does the timing of its rise give a clue? (Dan. 2:42)How are the iron (papal Rome) and clay (Protestant America) being mingled today? (Dan. 2:41-42)*

13. *What does the stone symbolize? (Dan. 2:45; Ex. 24:12; Rom. 9:31-33; Is. 8:13-16)*

14. *What does the mountain represent? (Dan. 2:35, 44-45; Joel 3:17; Rev. 21:10; Zech. 8:3)*

# Daniel 7:2-14, 23-27 (KJV)

*2 Daniel spake and said, I saw in my vision by night, and, behold, the four winds of the heaven strove upon the great sea. 3 And four great beasts came up from the sea, diverse one from another. 4 The first was like a lion, and had eagle's wings: I beheld till the wings thereof were plucked, and it was lifted up from the earth, and made stand upon the feet as a man, and a man's heart was given to it. 5 And behold another beast, a second, like to a bear, and it raised up itself on one side, and it had three ribs in the mouth of it between the teeth of it: and they said thus unto it, Arise, devour much flesh. 6 After this I beheld, and lo another, like a leopard, which had upon the back of it four wings of a fowl; the beast had also four heads; and dominion was given to it. 7 After this I saw in the night visions, and behold a fourth beast, dreadful and terrible, and strong exceedingly; and it had great iron teeth: it devoured and brake in pieces, and stamped the residue with the feet of it: and it was diverse from all the beasts that were before it; and it had ten horns. 8 I considered the horns, and, behold, there came up among them another little horn, before whom there were three of the first horns plucked up by the roots: and, behold, in this horn were eyes like the eyes of man, and a mouth speaking great things. 9 I beheld till the thrones were cast down, and the Ancient of days did sit, whose garment was white as snow, and the hair of his head like the pure wool: his throne was like the fiery flame, and his wheels as burning fire. 10 A fiery stream issued and came forth from before him: thousand thousands ministered unto him,* and ten thousand times ten thousand stood before him: the judgment was set, and the books were opened. [11] I beheld then because of the voice of the great words which the horn spake: I beheld even till the beast was slain, and his body destroyed, and given to the burning flame. [12] As concerning the rest of the beasts, they had their dominion taken away: yet their lives were prolonged for a season and time. [13] I saw in the night visions, and, behold, one like the Son of man came with the clouds of heaven, and came to the Ancient of days, and they brought him near before him. [14] And there was given him dominion, and glory, and a kingdom, that all people, nations, and languages, should serve him: his dominion is an everlasting dominion, which shall not pass away, and his kingdom that which shall not be destroyed...

[23] Thus he said, The fourth beast shall be the fourth kingdom upon earth, which shall be diverse from all kingdoms, and shall devour the whole earth, and shall tread it down, and break it in pieces. [24] And the ten horns out of this kingdom are ten kings that shall arise: and another shall rise after them; and he shall be diverse from the first, and he shall subdue three kings. [25] And he shall speak great words against the most High, and shall wear out the saints of the most High, and think to change times and laws: and they shall be given into his hand until a time and times and the dividing of time. [26] But the judgment shall sit, and they shall take away his dominion, to consume and to destroy it unto the end. [27] And the kingdom and dominion, and the greatness of the kingdom under the whole heaven, shall be given to the people of the saints of the most High, whose kingdom is an everlasting kingdom, and all dominions shall serve and obey him.

# Four Beasts and the Judgment

Have you ever watched a child place a penny into a spiral? The penny whirls faster and faster as it reaches the middle, and then suddenly, PLOP! It falls through the hole. One important principle in studying prophecy is that history repeats itself and then continues as a giant chain of events. The Bible states, "That which has been is what will be, that which is done is what will be done…. It has already been done in ancient times" (Eccl. 1:9-10, NKJV). However, instead of the links being all the same size, each link seems to be getting smaller with time, resulting in history repeating faster and faster, like a penny spinning in a spiral. Christ also taught that the same Bible prophecy could relate to different periods in history when He predicted the signs of both the destruction of Jerusalem in 70 AD and His second coming simultaneously (Matt. 24:2-3). This principle of repetition in different time periods is vital for an accurate understanding of prophecy today.

Another important prophetic principle is that only the world kingdoms affecting God's people are represented in Bible prophecy. That is why pagan nations, such as India, are not directly referenced in God's Word. Yet, Jesus longs for His people to spread the gospel to all nations, sharing the good news of salvation and His soon return! As the Lord's direction of human history is displayed in the fulfillment of Bible prophecy, faith in His Word will

15

increase. Indeed, Christ is the "Alpha and Omega, the Beginning and the End" (Rev. 1:8). His Word proves its accuracy throughout the past, the present, and the future (Rev. 1:19; Is. 46:10).

## Daniel's Vision

The first great link in God's chain of history is found in Daniel's vision in chapter seven. The Lord repeats and expands His predictions concerning the four major world kingdoms that would rule His people and then focuses on His warnings about the "little horn" power playing a prominent role in the persecution of His saints throughout Earth's history (Dan. 7:24-25, NKJV). In this vision, Daniel beheld a lion, a bear, a leopard, and a "terrible" beast that trampled the remnant of God's people under its feet (Dan. 7:7, 19, KJV) and had a "little horn" (Dan. 7:8, KJV). Each of these beasts represented kingdoms (Dan. 7:23) and arose from the "Great Sea" (Dan. 7:2, KJV), meaning a densely populated area (Is. 17:12-13; Rev. 17:15). The Aramaic word for "sea" is "yam," meaning "a large body of water." When it is used with an article (the), it refers to the "Mediterranean Sea." These wild beasts, rising from the winds of conquest (Dan. 7:2; Jer. 4:11-13; 49:36-37), symbolize earthly world kingdoms located around the Mediterranean Sea that would conquer and rule God's people, beginning during Daniel's time and extending throughout history (Dan. 7:23). The four beasts that Daniel saw in vision coincide with the metals in the statue of Nebuchadnezzar's dream; only this time, God gives more details about each kingdom, focusing specifically on the "little horn" ascending from the Roman empire as a religious and political power combined.

As Daniel watched each kingdom rise and fall, his heart was broken by the spiritual and moral deterioration of God's people. It seemed that the Gentile nations consumed the Lord's followers as they assimilated into paganism. Yet, God did not leave His faithful ones hopeless! This desolation by pagan and papal rulership would finally be deferred when a latter nation, founded upon religious freedom, would become a haven for God's church.

## Lion with Eagle's Wings – King Nebuchadnezzar/Babylon

The first beast that Daniel saw rising from the sea was like a lion with an eagle's wings that were plucked off, and it was lifted up from the earth (Dan. 7:4; Jer. 4:7,13). The lion stood up like a man, and a man's heart was given to it (Dan. 7:4). This symbolic lion referred to Judah's defeat by King Nebuchadnezzar of Babylon (Gen. 49:9; Eze. 21:25-27; Jer. 50:43-45; Num. 23:23-24). However, its eagle's wings (extremities [Is. 8:8; 18:1, KJV]) that became *"plucked,"* ("mrat," from the root word, *"marat,"* meaning *bald-headed)* would span throughout history to the rulership of "Mystery Babylon the Great" (Rev. 17:5, KJV; Is. 21:8-9; Rev. 18:2). The combination of these two latter kingdoms was symbolized by the eagle—Rome and the United States. The two different locations of this beast, one rising from the sea and one lifting from the earth, may also refer to the dual application of these kingdoms (Dan. 7:4, 17). The Lord predicts His people's spiritual downfall by saying, "I have forsaken mine house, I have left my heritage… Mine heritage is unto me as a lion in the forest; it crieth out against Me… *like a speckled bird* (Jer. 12:7-8, KJV; meaning "bird of prey"- vulture/eagle). Because most of God's people would forsake His Law, they would lose their world leadership until Christ, the "Lion of Judah," (Rev. 5:5), would ultimately restore God's kingdom by His second coming.

In fulfillment of Bible prophecy, history proves the kingdom of Babylon fell in 539 BC when Persian soldiers diverted the river that ran through the capital city, entering the unlocked gates and taking the kingdom by surprise (Jer. 51:37-38; Is. 45:1). Babylon was conquered because the king praised the idols of *"gold, and of silver, of brass, of iron, of wood, and of stone"* (Dan. 5:4, KJV). Interestingly, a similar list of idols is found in Revelation 9:20 (KJV): "And the rest of the men, which were not killed by these plagues, yet repented not of the works of their hands, that they should not worship devils, and idols of *gold, and silver, and brass, and stone, and of wood,* which neither can see, nor hear, nor walk." The Bible prophesies that idolatry would repeat itself in the last days with "Mystery Babylon, the Mother of harlots and abomination of the earth" (Rev. 17:4-5, KJV). Just as the Bible predicted, the worship of statues has reappeared within the Christian church, venerated in Catholic cathedrals. Sadly, Belshazzar's legacy of idolatry continues today, not only with the worship of literal statues, but with idols of celebrities, wealth, or anything else that is valued above God.

### Bear with Three Ribs in its Mouth and Raised on One Side–Medo-Persia

After Belshazzar's defeat, Daniel saw the rise of the kingdom of Medo-Persia, symbolized by a ferocious bear (Dan. 7:5; compare Lam. 3:10-11). Cyrus, the Persian king, crushed Babylon, Lydia, and Egypt which were signified by the three ribs in the bear's mouth (Dan. 7:5; compare Zech. 9:7). Then he united the kingdom of Medo-Persia (represented by the two arms of silver in Dan. 2:32 and the ram in Dan. 8:20). Persian dominance was also predicted by the bear being raised on one side (Dan. 7:5). However, the Lord used this Persian king, Cyrus, called his *"anointed"* (Is. 45:1, KJV), to grant permission for Jerusalem to be rebuilt (Ezra 1:2-3). Similarly, centuries later, God would use an Ottoman ruler to order Jerusalem's walls to be rebuilt during the Protestant Reformation (explained further in the chapters to come).

## Leopard With Four Heads and Four Wings – Greece

The rulership of God's people switched from the East to the West when Greece defeated Medo-Persia. The Lord may have implied this transfer of rulership from Shem's descendants of the East to the Gentiles of the West by stating, "For from the rising of the sun (east), even to its going down (west), My name shall be great among the Gentiles…" (Mal. 1:11, NKJV). This third-world kingdom was symbolized by a leopard-like beast with four heads and four wings (Dan. 7:6; compare Dan. 8:21; Jer. 5:6; 13:23). The swiftness of its leader, Alexander the Great, is likened to four bird wings (Deut. 28:49). Conquering most of the then-known world, Alexander fulfilled the prediction that the "wings" of his western kingdom would encompass all four corners of the earth (directions [Dan. 7:6, KJV; Matt. 24:31; Eze. 7:2; Jer. 9:26]), including Egypt to the South, Assyria to the North, and Persia to the East. The four heads of the leopard represent the fact that the kingdom of Greece would later be divided into the four cardinal directions by Alexander's generals after his death: Cassander, Lysimachus, Seleucus, and Ptolemy.[12] Throughout history, the Greek culture would continue its influence on Western society in philosophy, science, education, and art. Characteristics of this leopard-like beast, as well as the former beasts, would later reappear in the sea beast who is "like unto a leopard, his feet as the feet of a bear, and his mouth as the mouth of a lion" (Rev. 13:2, KJV). Therefore, this end-time nation would legislate religious and moral confusion like Babylon (lion), spread its influence through violence (bear), and manifest pagan Greek philosophies and culture (leopard).

---

[12] https://www.worldhistory.org/article/94/the-hellenistic-world-the-world-of-alexander-the-g/

## Terrible Beast – Rome

Lastly, the fourth beast that Daniel saw was different from the rest, possibly because it was a composite beast, having huge iron teeth, ten horns, and feet with nails of bronze that trampled God's remnant (Dan. 7:7; compare Rev. 13:1-2). History shows that this powerful beast could only be referring to Rome, the fourth-world kingdom rising after the fall of Greece; however, the Roman Empire would absorb the Greek culture, predicted in its bronze nails (Dan. 7:19). This combined pagan kingdom would relentlessly persecute Christians, spanning before and after the time of Christ and continuing with fervor, especially during the third century. Years later, the iron teeth of Rome would temporarily be broken, but its Greek nails would continually claw Christianity, becoming the foundation of today's postmodern society.

## The Little Horn of Rome

Next, Daniel's attention was drawn to this terrible beast's ten horns, specifically, the "little horn" that uprooted three others (Dan. 7:8; *Note: the number ten can be symbolic of a larger or total amount* [Dan. 1:20; Matt. 25:1-13; Lk.15:8-10, Rev. 2:10]). In the Bible, a "horn" symbolizes a political, and sometimes religious, power (Dan. 7:24; 8:21-22; Zech. 1:18-19; Rev. 5:5-6; 17:12; Lam. 2:3). This little horn arose from the terrible beast, the Roman empire, after it was divided into several European nations. History proves there was only one political power that came from the Roman Empire and conquered the following three nations: the Heruli, Vandals, and Ostrogoths.[13] In fact, it was the same political /religious entity that ruled the Roman Empire after Justinian's decree in 533 AD[14] and the Ostrogoths' defeat in 538 AD.[15]

---

[13] https://www.ccel.org/g/gibbon/decline/volume2/chap41.htm

[14] http://www.moellerhaus.com/studies/JUS533.HTM

Yet, the Bible is even more specific! It predicts this civil power would also be religious because it would blasphemy God, persecute His saints, and "think to change times and law" (Dan. 7:8, 25, NKJV). Moreover, it had the eyes of a man (religious leader [Is. 29:10]), a mouth speaking pompous words (Dan. 7:8), and its appearance and influence were greater than the others (Dan. 7:20). Likewise, in the New Testament, the apostle, Paul, likely describes this false religious leader by calling him the *"man of sin,"* the *"son of perdition who opposeth and exalteth himself above all that is called God, or that is worshipped; so that he as God sitteth in the temple of God, shewing himself that he is God"* (2 Thess. 2:3-4; KJV; italics added). Likewise, the disciple, John, refers to him as the antichrist (I Jn. 2:18, 22; 4:3; 2 Jn. 1:7).

These prophets point to the arrogance of this little horn power which would culminate in its claim of infallibility as *"the emblem of Jesus Christ,"*[16] fulfilling the prophecy that the little horn would "speak pompous words against the Most High" (Dan. 7:25, NKJV; italics added). Furthermore, many faithful servants of God would sacrifice their lives and be burned at the stake because of the mandates of this little horn, fulfilling the prediction that it would "war with the saints" and prevail against them (Dan. 7:21, KJV). Finally, through its own ecclesiastical authority, the little horn would attempt to change God's day of worship and delete the second commandment to allow homage to saints,[17] fulfilling the biblical prophecy that it would "think to change times and

---

[15] https://en.wikipedia.org/wiki/Siege_of_Rome_(537%E2%80%93538)
[16] https://www.nytimes.com/2013/02/18/world/europe/what-do-you-call-a-retired-pope-and-is-he-still-infallible.html; https://www.britannica.com/topic/papal-infallibility
[17] https://www.beginningcatholic.com/catholic-ten-commandments; https://grace-thrufaith.com/ask-a-bible-teacher/why-are-thecatholic-10-commandments-different/; https://www.vatican.va/archive/ENG0015/_INDEX.HTM

law" (the Ten Commandments [Ex. 20:4-6, 8-11]; Dan. 7:25, NKJV). History proves that only one political/religious power fits this description of this little horn—*the Roman Catholic papal system!* Fortunately, the Lord knew many of His faithful people were still within the Catholic Church, so Daniel was not given this dismal picture of the future without a ray of hope!

## The Investigative Judgment Begins

The power of the little horn would be interrupted after a "time, times, and half a time" (Dan. 7:25), when "judgment was made in favor of the saints" (Dan. 7:22, NKJV). Using the biblical day-for-a-year principle found in Numbers 14:34 and Ezekiel 4:6, three and a half times 360 days in a Jewish year equals 1,260 prophetic days or years. After the Ostrogoths' defeat in 538 AD, imperial Rome had transformed into papal Rome, allowing Justinian's decree declaring the supremacy of the papacy to be implemented.[18] The papacy's political power continued throughout the Middle Ages. At last, it was struck a devastating wound foretold in Revelation 13:3. Napoleon's French general, Berthier, captured Pope Pius VI in 1798 AD,[19] ending the papacy's political reign of 1,260 years, the exact time that the Bible had predicted! (Dan. 7:25).

During this same period of history, a new nation was forming, a nation based upon the Christian principle of religious freedom. This last world-renowned kingdom, likely represented in Daniel 2:34 as clay, would rule along with the iron of the papacy until Christ's second coming (Dan. 7:22). It would continue throughout troublous times until Jesus's return when "… the greatness of the kingdoms under the whole heaven" would be "given to

---

[18] https://www.ijhssnet.com/journals/Vol_7_No_1_January_2017/7.pdf
[19] https://en.wikipedia.org/wiki/Pope_Pius_VI

the people of the saints of the Most High" (Dan. 7:27, KJV).

After Daniel saw the representations of Babylon, Medo-Persia, Greece, and Rome, his attention was drawn to a beautiful scene taking place in Heaven. He watched as Jesus, the "Son of Man" (Matt. 18:11), came to the "Ancient of Days," a fitting description of God, the Father (Is. 44:6-7; Rev. 1:4-5), to begin judgment in the heavenly courts by opening and reviewing the books (Dan. 7:9-10, 13, 26; NKJV). When did this event occur? This investigative judgment would begin after the rise and fall of these four world nations and the little horn power sometime after 1798 AD (Dan. 7:11-12). Daniel was not given the exact starting date until a later vision. However, following the temporary loss of political papal rule, the investigative judgment would begin for God's people (Dan. 7:9-12).

Today, we are living in the final days of this heavenly judgment for all who claim to be Christians (Rev. 14:7). How quickly Earth's history is closing! The Bible says judgment begins in the *"house of God"* (I Peter 4:17, KJV; compare Eze. 9:6), and it is now in process for God's people (Dan. 7:9-14). However, we have nothing to fear! (Jude 24). The good news is that anyone can receive Christ's white robe of righteousness! (Zech. 3:3-5; Rev. 3:5). We just have to ask the Lord to cleanse our hearts from sin and allow Him to change us into His image through His power working in our lives (Ps. 51:2, 7-13). In fact, Christians should be happy the judgment is taking place because it means that soon Jesus will come, and sin will be destroyed forever!

Just like a penny in a spiral, Daniel 7's vision reviews the same world kingdoms found in the vision of Daniel 2, but its primary focus is upon the rule of the "little horn" which would span 1,260 years throughout the Dark Ages (Dan. 7:25).[20] Then, the Lord would begin the judgment of His church and give His people religious freedom in a nation founded upon biblical principles (Dan. 2:27). Because God's Word accurately foretells the rise and fall of each of these world nations with amazing detail, its prophecies prove their validity. No human being could have predicted the world's future hundreds of years before it occurred! Therefore, we must study and apply the Bible's prophecies to our lives today. Praise the Lord that we can trust the faithfulness of God's Word and the ever present watchcare of our Lord who knows the future!

---

[20] In Dan. 7:25, the Aramaic meaning of the word for "time" ("iddan") means "a set period of time" or a "year." Using the meaning of a "year," "a time, times, and half a time" is 3.5 times or 3.5 years. Additionally, the Jewish year during Daniel's time contained 360 days, and Bible prophecy historically uses the principle of a day for a year (Numbers 14:34; Ezekiel 4:6). Therefore, if one multiplies 3.5 by 360 years, the product equals 1,260 years. If 1,260 years are added to 538 AD, the sum ends in 1798 AD, which is the very year that the pope was taken captive, and the papacy's political rule ended.

| Daniel 2's Statue/Idol | Daniel 7's Beasts/Kingdoms (Dan. 7:23) |
|---|---|
| **Rise/Fall Nations Ruling God's People Throughout History** (Dan. 2:21; 7:12, 14, 27; Eccl. 3:11, 14) | **The Great Sea** ("yam"-"Mediterranean") **Sea- populated** (Dan. 7:2; Rev. 17:15; Is. 17:12) |
| **Babylon–Gold Head** [Dan. 2:37-38]<br><br>Head- King Nebuchadnezzar (Dan. 2:37-38)<br><br>Gold- Israel/God's People (Lam. 4:1-2; Hag. 2:5, 8; Joel 3:5-6)<br><br>Kings of East- God's followers (Dan. 11:44; Matt. 2:1) | **Lion–Babylon** [Dan. 7:4; Jer. 5:6, 15; 50:43-44]<br><br>Lion–Judah (Gen. 49:9; Jer. 12:7-8, KJV)<br><br>Wings-extremity (Dan. 7:4; Is. 8:8; Jer. 49:22)<br><br>Eagle–swift devourer (Jer. 4:13; Deut. 28:49; Dan. 4:33; Hab. 1:8; Lam. 4:19;Hosea 8:1) Plucked- ("bald"-"marat") (Dan. 7:4; Micah 1:16)<br><br>Stood/two feet–rulership (Dan. 7:4; Ps. 47:3)<br><br>Man's heart–character (Dan. 7:4; Eze. 36:26-27)<br><br>Last-day nation–like mouth of a lion (Rev. 13:2) |

| Medo-Persia–Silver Chest/Arms (Dan. 2:32) | Bear–Medo-Persia (Dan. 7:5; Lam. 3:10-11) |
|---|---|
| 2 Arms–Medes/Persians (Dan. 2:32; 8:20; Jer. 51:11) | 3 Ribs in teeth- Babylon, Lydia, Egypt (Dan. 7:5) |
| Silver–God's people (Mal. 3:3; Zech. 13:9; Hag. 2:9; Eze. 22:18-22; Jer. 6:30; Joel 3:5-6) | Raised on one side– Persian dominant (Dan. 7:5) |
| Kings of the East– God/followers (Matt. 2:1-2) | Told to devour flesh–violent (Dan. 7:5) |
| Cyrus–God's anointed (Is. 45:1) | Persecutes Israel (Gen. 16:11-12, 20; 2 Chron. 7:16-17; Amos 5:18-19; Prov. 28:15) |
| Abraham's descendants– Ishmael/Esau (Gen. 25:12-16; 27:40; 28:9) | Last-day nation– like feet of a bear (Rev. 13:2) |

| Greece–Bronze/Belly/Thighs (Dan. 2:32) | Leopard–Greece (Dan. 7:6; 8:21; Jer. 5:6; 13:23) |
|---|---|
| **Greek** (Joel 3:5-6; Dan. 8:21) | **4 bird wings–worldwide** (Is. 8:8; Jer. 49:22) |
| **Bronze/Iron united** (Lev. 26:19; Dan. 4:15; Jer. 15:12; 6: 28; Deut. 28:23; Ps. 107:16; Is. 45:2; 48:4; Micah 4:13) | **Spotted–symbol of sin** (Jer. 13:23; Eph. 5:27) |
| **Evolves into Byzantine/ Roman Empire** (Dan. 7:19) | **4 heads–4 generals** (Dan. 7:6; Deut. 1:15) |
| **Change of leadership to Gentile West** | **Rulership of N, S, E, W** (Dan. 7:6; Luke 13:29) |
| | **Last-day nation–like a leopard** (Rev. 13:2) |

| Rome–Iron Legs (Dan. 2:33) | Terrible Strong Beast–Rome (Dan. 7:7) |
|---|---|
| Bronze/Iron–Greek influence in Rome (Dan. 7:19) | Huge iron teeth/nails of bronze (Dan. 7:19) |
| Conquerors of God's people (Ps. 2:8-9) | Devours & breaks (Dan. 7:19, 23) |
| God's people–transfers from East to West Gentiles (Mal. 1:11; Is. 60:17) | Tramples God's remnant (Dan. 7:19) |
| | Different–composite (Dan. 7:7, 19) |
| | 10 horns–ruling powers (Dan. 7:20, 24; 13:1) |
| | Terrible nation (Jer. 15:20-21; Is. 25:3; 29:5, 20) |

| Europe/USA–Iron/Clay /Feet/Toes (Dan. 2:33) | Little Horn–Papacy (Dan. 7:7-8, 20; Zech. 1:19) |
|---|---|
| Divided—partly strong /partly fragile (Dan. 2:41-43) | Rises from terrible beast with iron teeth (Rome) |
| Clay- Spiritual Israel/USA (Lam. 4:1-2; Is. 41:25; 45:9; Is. 64:8; Jer. 18:4, 6; Micah 5:8; Rom. 9:20-28) | Uproots 3 other horns (Heruli, Vandals, Ostrogoths wiped out by papacy [Dan. 7:7-8]) |
| Divided kingdom/ conquers nations (Dan. 2:42; Ps. 2:8-9) | Eyes like a man-Pope (Dan. 7:8; Is. 29:10)

Speaks pompous words (Dan. 7:8, 25; 2 Thess. 2:3-4; Rev. 13:5-7) |

| Christ/Law—Stone/Mountain Kingdom (Dan. 2:34-35, 45; Rom. 9:32-33; I Peter 2:4-10) | Investigative Judgment Starts (Dan. 7:10, 26; Mal. 3:1-3 Mal. 3:1-3]; |
|---|---|
| Jesus's kingdom based on His law (Zech, 12:3; Ex 24:12; 31:18) | Books opened (Rev. 22:19) |
| Crushes metal idol (world kingdoms [Dan. 2:35]) | Ancient of Days- God the Father (Dan. 7:9-10; Is. 44:6-8) |
| Mountain fills the earth (New Jerusalem [Dan. 2:35; Dan. 9:16; Rev. 21:10]) | Son of Man- Jesus (Matt. 18:11) |
| | Christ receives His kingdom (Dan. 7:14,27) |

# Discussion Questions for Daniel 7

1. What principles are vital for understanding when studying prophecy? (Eccl 1:9; Matt. 24:2-3)

2. What do "beasts" in Bible prophecy represent? (Dan. 7:17, 23)

3. How is the description of Nebuchadnezzar/Babylon similar to the description of the lion? (Dan. 7:4; Dan. 4:33; Jer. 50:43-44)

4. Who else is compared to a lion? (Num. 23:23-24; Jer. 12:7-9)

5. What modern religious/political power will repeat Babylon's idolatry in the last days? (Dan. 5:1-4; Rev. 9:20; 17:4-5)

6. What kingdom is symbolized by the ferocious bear with three ribs in its mouth and raised on one side? (Dan. 7:5; compare Dan. 8:20; Lam. 3:10-11)

7. Why would Cyrus, King of Persia, be called God's "anointed?" What was he anointed to do? (Is. 45:1; Ezra 1:2-3)

8. What kingdom is represented by the leopard? What is represented by the leopard's four heads and four wings? (Dan. 7:6; compare Dan. 8:21-22).

9. Why did God allow world rulership to switch from Seth's descendants in the East (Abraham's lineage) to the Gentiles of the West? (Deut. 28:45-47; Mal. 1:11)

10. Describe the terrible beast kingdom. How was it different from the rest? (Dan. 7:7, 19; compare Rev. 13:1-2)

11. Describe the "little horn" on the terrible beast. (Dan. 7:8, 24-25; 8:20-26)

12. *How do we know that the "little horn" symbolizes a political and/or religious power? (Zech. 1:18-19; Lam. 2:3; Rev. 5:6; 13:1; 17:12-14)*

13. *How do the New Testament writers likely describe this "little horn" power? (2 Thess. 2:3-4; I Jn. 2:18, 22; 4:3; 2 Jn. 1:7)*

14. *Why is it important for all to know that the investigative judgment is occurring right now? (I Peter 4:17; Eze. 9:4-6; Rev. 14:7)*

15. *Why shouldn't Christians be fearful of this judgment that is taking place currently? What has Christ provided for us? (Zech. 3:3-5; Jude 24; Rev. 3:5)*

# Daniel 8:13-14, 19-25 (KJV)

*¹³ Then I heard one saint speaking, and another saint said unto that certain saint which spake, How long shall be the vision concerning the daily sacrifice, and the transgression of desolation, to give both the sanctuary and the host to be trodden under foot? ¹⁴ And he said unto me, Unto two thousand and three hundred days; then shall the sanctuary be cleansed...*

*¹⁹ And he said, Behold, I will make thee know what shall be in the last end of the indignation: for at the time appointed the end shall be. ²⁰ The ram which thou sawest having two horns are the kings of Media and Persia. ²¹ And the rough goat is the king of Grecia: and the great horn that is between his eyes is the first king. ²² Now that being broken, whereas four stood up for it, four kingdoms shall stand up out of the nation, but not in his power. ²³ And in the latter time of their kingdom, when the transgressors are come to the full, a king of fierce countenance, and understanding dark sentences, shall stand up. ²⁴ And his power shall be mighty, but not by his own power: and he shall destroy wonderfully, and shall prosper, and practise, and shall destroy the mighty and the holy people. ²⁵ And through his policy also he shall cause craft to prosper in his hand; and he shall magnify himself in his heart, and by peace shall destroy many: he shall also stand up against the Prince of princes; but he shall be broken without hand.*

# The Investigative Judgment

Sitting in a courtroom can be a little overwhelming. Everyone rises solemnly when the judge, in his long black robe, enters the room. The gavel strikes and the courtroom is called into session. Witnesses testify. Lawyers make their defenses. Such proceedings can bring trepidation to the bravest heart! However, if the judge is a friend, how differently one might feel waiting for the court's verdict! Praise God for His assurance that when we choose Jesus as our Savior and live to honor Him, He not only becomes our Judge (Jn. 5:22), but He is also our Witness (Rev. 3:14) and our Defense Attorney (Heb. 7:25; I Jn. 2:1), who grants us the victory through His sacrifice (I Cor. 15:57). The courtroom, then, is simply the venue for our vindication.

Perhaps Daniel may have also felt a bit overwhelmed as he saw the history of God's people unfold before his eyes. He even switches languages from Aramaic to Hebrew in chapter eight, most likely because the rest of the book of Daniel pertains specifically to the Lord's followers. His second vision picks up from his previous one and uses symbolism associated with the sanctuary service. In this vision, Daniel saw two animals—a ram and a goat. Because of his Jewish background, he would have immediately associated these animals with the Day of Atonement, the judgment day, when God's temple and people were cleansed from sin.

## The Historical Ram and Goat

In his vision, Daniel saw a ram that pushed "westward, northward, and southward" (Dan. 8:4, KJV), meaning that it originally came from the East, the land of Abraham's descendants (Acts 7:2-4). The ram had two horns, one higher than the other, and the higher one came up last (Dan. 8:3). This description is similar to the bear that was raised on one side (Dan. 7:5) and the statue that had two silver arms (Dan. 2:32). The angel, Gabriel, interpreted the meaning of the ram as the "kings of Media and Persia" (Dan. 8:20, KJV). Historically, the Persians arose last and were more powerful than the Medes, so the two horn powers could accurately represent these two kings, and the ram, their combined kingdom of Medo-Persia.

Then Daniel beheld a goat that came from the West and had a "notable horn" between its eyes (Dan. 8:5, KJV). When Alexander the Great conquered Medo-Persia, power over God's people transferred from the East to the Western Gentile rulership of Greece. This defeat is likely portrayed in Daniel 8:7 when the goat attacked the ram and trampled him. As a result, the goat kingdom became great, despite its pagan horn being broken and "four notable ones" coming up "toward the four winds of heaven" (Dan. 8:8, KJV). Again, history confirms that when Alexander the Great died, his four generals divided the kingdom of Greece: to the North, Lysimachus took Thrace and much of Asia Minor; to the South, Ptolemy I ruled Egypt; to the East, Seleucus governed Mesopotamia; and to the West, Cassander controlled Macedonia and Greece.[21] God's people were spread out into each of these four directions (Dan. 7:2; Jer. 49:32, 36; Zech. 2:6; Mark 13:27).

---

[21] http://www.fsmitha.com/h1/ch12dis.htm

## The Little Horn

Daniel then saw one last symbol in his vision that displayed the same pagan characteristics as the goat. It originated from one of the "four winds of heaven," the four directions of conquest in which the Greek kingdom was divided (Dan. 8:8, KJV). From one of these "winds," a "little horn," or political power, would arise (Dan. 8:9). As previously stated, this little horn stemmed from the terrible beast kingdom following Greece — the Roman empire, which assimilated the pagan Greek culture and evolved into papal Rome (Dan. 7:6-8, 19-20). This horn, according to Daniel 8:9 (KJV), grew great "toward the south, and toward the east, and toward the pleasant land" (where God rules in the North [Is. 14:13; Jer. 3:17-19]). Therefore, the little horn originated from the West, the same direction as the goat (Dan. 8:5). Likewise, Daniel 7:7-8 affirms that the little horn grew from the fourth world kingdom which history proves is Rome, so it is logical to conclude that this civil/religious horn power is Roman Catholicism, *not Catholic church members themselves*, but the papal system which continued to rule Europe even after the demise of the pagan Roman Empire.

Emerging out of the western kingdom of the goat, the pope would "exalt himself as high as the Prince of the host" (Christ [Acts 5:31; Rev. 1:5]; Dan. 8:11, KJV]) by claiming the sovereignty of Jesus Christ on Earth (Dan. 8:11). He would exalt his "throne above the stars of God" (Dan. 8:10, NKJV; "stars"- angels/God's people [Rev. 1:20; Dan. 12:3; Gen. 15:5]) and claim to sit where God sits, "in the sides of the north" (Is. 14:13, KJV). Also, he would "cast down some of the stars to the ground" (like Lucifer in Heaven [Rev. 12:4]), "trample them" (Dan. 8:10, NKJV), and "destroy the mighty, and the holy people" (Dan. 8:24, KJV). The papacy would persecute God's remnant just like the terrible beast of pagan Rome from which it arose (Dan. 7:19-21); especially during the Dark Ages when millions were martyred for their faith. An army (the Swiss guard) would also be given to the pope, and he would "cast truth down to the ground" and do "all this and prosper" (Dan. 8:12, NKJV). "Through his cunning" he would "cause deceit to prosper under his rule," and he would exalt himself in his heart," and "destroy many in their prosperity" (Dan. 8:25, NKJV). Finally, he would "even rise against the Prince of princes," but at Christ's coming, he would be "broken without human means" (Dan. 8:25, NKJV). Only the papacy has fulfilled each of these descriptions throughout history by claiming to be God on Earth and changing the Ten Commandments by its own assertion of divine authority and tradition.

Moreover, Daniel was given the 2300-day/year prophecy that would cover from the days of these ancient kingdoms to the second coming of Christ, specifically pointing to the time when God's sanctuary would be cleansed (Dan. 8:14; Num. 14:34; Eze. 4:6). Unfortunately, the angel left, and Daniel was perplexed until Gabriel appeared years later and told him when this prophecy would begin.

## The Symbolism of the Ram and the Goat Today

Although one can see God's hand in the rise and fall of these ancient kingdoms of Medo-Persia and Greece, could this sanctuary imagery of a ram and a goat have a broader application for God's people living now, just before Christ's return? The fact that Gabriel states that Daniel's vision refers to "the time of the end" (Dan. 8:17, KJV), "the last end of the indignation" (Dan. 8:19, KJV), and at a "time appointed the end shall be" (Dan. 8:19, KJV) would indicate that it does. Therefore, the history of these ancient kingdoms must apply to God's people today!

The Bible often uses kingdoms and kings interchangeably. In Daniel 7:17 (KJV), God's Word states, "those great beasts, which are four, are four kings," and in Daniel 7:23 (KJV), "the fourth beast shall be the fourth kingdom." Also, the Bible uses ancient kingdoms and their characteristics to represent modern kingdoms. For example, in Revelation 11:8, the ancient fallen kingdoms of Sodom, Egypt, and Jerusalem describe a modern kingdom that would come to power in the last days of Earth's history. The defining moral and spiritual characteristics of these ancient nations would be seen in this modern nation—the immorality of Sodom, the paganism of Egypt, and the spiritual corruption of Jerusalem. So, the Bible uses past literal kings/kingdoms and their characteristics as symbols to represent modern kings/kingdoms today.

## King of God's People

Interestingly, Gabriel identifies the ram with two horns as the *kings* of the Medes and Persians *("Parac," meaning "pure")*. As stated previously, God called Cyrus, the ancient king of Persia, His "anointed" because the Bible prophesies that he would issue the decree that would allow the Jews to rebuild the temple in Jerusalem (Is. 45:1). However, ultimately, God is the true Builder and King of His people (1 Sam. 12:12). As a result of Christ's life, death, and resurrection, the Lord is presently constructing His temple in His people's hearts today through the power of the Holy Spirit (1 Cor. 3:16), and very soon, Jesus will defeat Satan and his hosts and rule forever upon the new earth (Rev. 21:1-5). So, the Father, the Son, and the Holy Spirit are the true Kings of God's people!

## The Ram—Christ Our Sacrifice

Moreover, the ram or lamb is a common symbol of Christ and His death on behalf of mankind. In the book of Genesis, God substitutes a ram for Isaac as a burnt offering, signifying that man's sin would be transferred to Jesus (Gen. 22:8, 13). Christ is the true sacrificial Ram/Lamb, not only for Isaac but for all of God's people (Jn. 1:29). This symbolism is also portrayed in the sanctuary service, especially on the Day of Atonement, when a ram was offered as a sin offering (Lev. 16:3, 5; 1 Pet. 1:18-19). However, at the cross, Christ gave His life to fulfill the requirements of the law, and since then, no more sacrifices have been required (Matt. 27:51; Heb. 10:19-20). Today, Jesus is in the heavenly sanctuary making atonement for sin as our High Priest (Heb. 10:19, 21). His mediation is explained in Hebrews 9:22-24 (KJV):

> And almost all things are by the law *purged with blood,* and without shedding of blood is no remission. It was therefore necessary that the patterns of the things in the heavens should be purified with these; but the heavenly things themselves with better sacrifices than these. For *Christ is not entered into the holy places made with hands, which are the figures of the true, but into heaven itself, now to appear in the presence of God for us.* (italics added)

Christ's mediation and sacrifice for our sin are further illustrated in the book of Revelation when all of Heaven and Earth sing: "Worthy is the Lamb that was slain to receive power, and riches, and wisdom, and strength, and honour, and glory, and blessing" (Rev. 5:12, KJV). In Revelation, the word, "lamb," is used twenty-seven times to describe Jesus (Rev. 5:6).[22] Therefore, a ram or a lamb may represent Christ and His mediatory work and sacrifice on our behalf.

---

[22] https://biblehub.com/topical/l/lamb.htm

40

## Horns of the Ram

Furthermore, the Old Testament refers to God's people as rams/lambs (Jer. 50:8, 17; Is. 40:11). John applies the same word for lamb, *"arnion,"* to describe Christ's followers in John 21:15. Additionally, Revelation also refers to a beast (kingdom [Dan. 7:23]) coming out of the earth, having "two horns like a lamb," which represents a nation founded on the principles of Christianity (Rev. 13:11, KJV). But what about the horns, the powers of Christ's kingdom? The Lord warns Israel's leaders, "Behold, I shall judge between sheep and sheep, between rams and goats... Because you have... butted all the weak ones with your *horns...* therefore, I will save my flock..." (Eze. 34:17, 21-22, NKJV; italics added). The two horns of the Ram's kingdom, then, could refer to the power of the leaders that claim to be shepherds over God's people. Horns, then, could very well symbolize the corrupt civil and religious leadership in both ancient Israel and the United States, the nation founded upon Protestant Christianity, rising last and politically more prominent than the Jewish nation in Earth's final days.

## The Goat–Satan and His Followers

In contrast to the Ram (Christ and His kingdom), the *Complete Jewish Bible* refers to the "shaggy male goat" as symbolizing the "king of Greece" (Dan. 8:21, NKJV). Who might a Greek symbolize in the Bible? The New Testament uses the term, "Greeks," to represent Gentiles (Col 3:11; Gal. 3:28; I Cor. 10:32). So, the king of Greece could also refer to the king of the Gentiles. Then what exactly is the *"shaggy, male goat?"* This Hebrew phrase refers to the goat used for the sin offering in the temple service (2 Chron. 29:23), but the word, *"sa iyr,"* used in Daniel 8:21 and 2 Chronicles 29:23 for a male goat(s), can also be translated as *"devil"* or *"demons,"* as it is in Lev. 17:7. Even today, a goat's head is one of the main symbols of the occult.[23]

Likewise, this same symbolism of Satan and his kingdom was acted out in the sanctuary service on the Jewish Day of Atonement. The high priest would lay his hands upon the head of the scapegoat and confess over its head the sins of God's people. Then it would be released alive to wander in the desert, representing the Devil's responsibility for sin and his destiny of wandering the desolate earth for a thousand years after Christ's second coming (Lev. 16:8-10, 21-22; Rev. 20:1-3). Jesus also used goats as a symbol of the wicked who are cursed and thrown into the eternal fire prepared for Satan and his angels (Matt. 25:41). So, this goat symbol in Daniel 8 could very well be a representation of Satan and his Gentile kingdom (the goat), warring against Christ and His followers (the Ram).

## The Great Controversy Between Christ and Satan

Daniel's vision in chapter eight, then, is likely a figurative picture of the great controversy between Christ's followers and Satan's. Just as predicted, the Lord's people sacrificed their world leadership to the western Gentile Greek and Roman kingdoms, and God's church (the Ram's kingdom) was left under the goat's political rulership. Daniel 8 specifically focuses on the goat's papal "little horn" and its persecution of God's people throughout the Dark Ages (Dan. 7:8, 25; 8:9-12). Furthermore, the prophecy predicts that the Lord's sanctuary would be cleansed after 2,300 days, and the persecution of God's people would then end for a time (Dan. 8:13-14). Although Daniel was not shown when the 2,300 days would occur until later, Gabriel did assure him that the little horn's power would finally be broken (Dan. 8:25).

---

[23] https://www.spiritualsatanist.com/essays/satanism/baphomet-why-goats-are-satanic.html

Christ's "ram" kingdom would be given a reprieve from the "goat's" rule. However, prophecy warns that the political influence of the papacy would rise again (Rev. 13:1-7). Today, one can see this return of the pope's civil and religious power, even within the United States. However, God's Word states that the little horn will finally be destroyed at Christ's second coming, and after a thousand years, Satan and his hosts will be forever annihilated (Matt. 25:33, 41; Rev. 20:2-3, 7-10; Mal. 4:1, 3; Eze. 28:14, 18-19). The Lord pledges salvation for His people from the Devil and his followers in Zechariah 9:13, 16 (NKJV):

> For I have… raised up your sons, O Zion (ram), against your sons, O Greece (goat), and made you like the sword of a mighty man…. The Lord their God will save them in that day as the flock of His people. For they shall be like the jewels of a crown, lifted like a banner over His land. (parentheses supplied)

Although many might see the signs of the papacy's comeback and the continual loss of countless religious freedoms in the world today, God's Word confirms that the Devil and his kingdom will, at last, be defeated. Praise God that Christ (the Ram) and His people are promised to win in the end!

# Discussion Questions for Daniel 8

1. Why might Daniel switch from using Aramaic to Hebrew in this chapter?

2. What is the historical interpretation of the ram and its two horns? (Dan. 8:3-4; 20)

3. What is the historical interpretation of the goat and its notable horn? (Dan. 8:5, 21)

4. What direction does the little horn originate, but, like Lucifer, what direction does it spiritually claim to be from? (Dan. 8:5, 9; Is.14:13)

5. How does Bible prophecy describe the '"little horn?" (Dan. 7:8, 20-21; 8:9-12, 23-25)

6. How has the papacy fulfilled the description of the "little horn," both historically and currently?

7. Why do the symbols of the ram and goat most likely have more than one meaning? (Dan. 8:17, 19; Rev. 11:8)

8. Who does the Bible symbolically refer to as the Ram/Lamb? (Rev. 5:6, 12; Jn. 1:29; Gen.22:8,13; 1 Pet. 1:18-19)

9. Who else could the ram/lamb and its horns symbolize? (Matt. 25:31-33; John 21:15; Jer. 50:6-8; Is. 40:11; Eze. 34:17, 21-22)

10. Who does the symbol of the goat represent? (Matt. 25:32-33, 41)

11. Who can "Greeks" refer to in the Bible? (Col 3:11; Gal. 3:28; I Cor. 10:32)

12. How does the sanctuary service on the Day of Atonement symbolize the goat's (Satan/the wicked's) eventual destruction? (Lev. 16:22; Rev. 20:1-3, 7, 10)

13. What time prophecy was given to Daniel in this chapter that left him perplexed until he was given the starting event for it in Daniel 9:25? (Dan. 8:14)

14. What assurance is given to us today as part of God's "Ram/ Lamb" kingdom concerning the outcome of the great controversy between Christ and His people and Satan and his followers (the goat)? (Zech. 9:13, 16)

# Daniel 9:3-5; 13-19 (KJV)

*3 And I set my face unto the Lord God, to seek by prayer and supplications, with fasting, and sackcloth, and ashes: 4 And I prayed unto the Lord my God, and made my confession, and said, O Lord, the great and dreadful God, keeping the covenant and mercy to them that love him, and to them that keep his commandments; 5 We have sinned, and have committed iniquity, and have done wickedly, and have rebelled, even by departing from thy precepts and from thy judgments*

*13 As it is written in the law of Moses, all this evil is come upon us: yet made we not our prayer before the Lord our God, that we might turn from our iniquities, and understand thy truth. 14 Therefore hath the Lord watched upon the evil, and brought it upon us: for the Lord our God is righteous in all his works which he doeth: for we obeyed not his voice. 15 And now, O Lord our God, that hast brought thy people forth out of the land of Egypt with a mighty hand, and hast gotten thee renown, as at this day; we have sinned, we have done wickedly. 16 O Lord, according to all thy righteousness, I beseech thee, let thine anger and thy fury be turned away from thy city Jerusalem, thy holy mountain: because for our sins, and for the iniquities of our fathers, Jerusalem and thy people are become a reproach to all that are about us. 17 Now therefore, O our God, hear the prayer of thy servant, and his supplications, and cause thy face to shine upon thy sanctuary that is desolate, for the Lord's sake.*

*18 O my God, incline thine ear, and hear; open thine eyes, and behold our desolations, and the city which is called by thy name: for we do not present our supplications before thee for our righteousnesses, but for thy great mercies. 19 O Lord, hear; O Lord, forgive; O Lord, hearken and do; defer not, for thine own sake, O my God: for thy city and thy people are called by thy name.*

# Daniel 8:13-14 (KJV)

*13 Then I heard one saint speaking, and another saint said unto that certain saint which spake, How long shall be the vision concerning the daily sacrifice, and the transgression of desolation, to give both the sanctuary and the host to be trodden under foot? 14 And he said unto me, Unto two thousand and three hundred days; then shall the sanctuary be cleansed.*

# Daniel 9:24-27 (KJV)

*24 Seventy weeks are determined upon thy people and upon thy holy city, to finish the transgression, and to make an end of sins, and to make reconciliation for iniquity, and to bring in everlasting righteousness, and to seal up the vision and prophecy, and to anoint the most Holy. 25 Know therefore and understand, that from the going forth of the commandment to restore and to build Jerusalem unto the Messiah the Prince shall be seven weeks, and threescore and two weeks: the street shall be built again, and the wall, even in troublous times. 26 And after threescore and two weeks shall Messiah be cut off, but not for himself: and the people of the prince that shall come shall destroy the city and the sanctuary; and the end thereof shall be with a flood, and unto the end of the war desolations are determined.* [27] *And he shall confirm the covenant with many for one week: and in the midst of the week he shall cause the sacrifice and the oblation to cease, and for the overspreading of abominations he shall make it desolate, even until the consummation, and that determined shall be poured upon the desolate.*

# Understanding the Future

Have you ever read a book or watched a movie that left you hanging in suspense at the end? Likely, your immediate response was to get the sequel as soon as possible so you could find out what happens! Perhaps this is how Daniel felt after his vision in chapter 8. He had been left hanging following his last vision, and he knew that he needed help understanding the time period of the 2,300-day prophecy. So, he did what we still need to do now—he fasted and prayed! (Dan. 9:3). He not only prayed for himself, but Daniel also interceded on behalf of his nation. He asked God for both personal and national forgiveness, and the Lord heard his prayer! God sent Gabriel to give Daniel the "sequel" of his vision (Dan. 9:22-23), just as He will answer our request for wisdom to understand His prophecies today (James 1:5). Lovingly, Jesus promises to give us His Holy Spirit who will show us "things to come" (John 16:13, KJV).

## The Beginning and the End of the Historical 2,300-Day Prophecy

Daniel needed to know when to start the 2,300-day prophecy to figure the closing date for the cleansing of the sanctuary and the beginning of the judgment (Dan. 8:13-14; compare 7:10). He knew that 2,300 days could represent 2,300 years in Bible prophecy by using the day-for-a-year principle found in Numbers 14:34 and Ezekiel 4:6. Because he stated in Daniel 10:1 (NKJV), "… the message was true, *but the appointed time was long*," he understood that the vision of the 2,300 days would span a lengthy period of time, but he had to know its starting date. In answer to his prayer, Daniel was given the event that would signal its beginning: "the *going forth of the commandment* to restore and build Jerusalem" (Dan. 9:25 [KJV]; italics added). Although the Bible records three such decrees (Ezra 1:1-4; 6:3-12; 7:11-25), the first two focused on rebuilding the temple, whereas the third decree of 457 BC included building Jerusalem's actual city structure in fulfillment of Daniel 9:25 (KJV): "… the *streets shall be built again and the wall*, even in troublesome times" (compare Ezra 6:14, 7:11-26, 9:9; Neh. 2:17; 6:15-16; italics added).[24] Once Daniel knew the starting date, he could figure out the length of time God's truth would be trampled before the temple would be cleansed. This prophecy would end in 1844 AD,[25] approximately the same time the United States would rise as a world nation.

A few years before the close of the 2,300-day/year prophecy (Dan. 8:14), William Miller, an American Baptist preacher, along with others, discovered its significance.[26] As a result of Miller preaching that Christ would return in 1844, the Advent Movement spread rapidly during the Second Great Awakening. Unfortunately, the Millerites did not clearly understand what would happen at the end of the 2,300 years. They thought that Jesus would return and cleanse the earth (the commonly

---

[24] https://biblearcheology.org /abr-projects-main/the-daniel-9-24-27- project-2/4589 -the-going-forth-of-artaxerxes-decree-part1; and https://www.whitehorsemedia.com /docs/The-Commandment-to-Re-build-Jerusalem-JN-Andrews.pdf

[25] *To figure the historical 2,300-day/year prophecy, one must begin at 457 BC and proceed 2,300 years. However, because the years before Christ's birth count backward, 457 years must be subtracted from 2,300 years, which ends in 1843 AD. Then another year must be added because there is no year 0 when changing from BC to AD. Therefore, one arrives in 1844 AD.*

[26] https://en.wikipedia.org/wiki/William_Miller_(preacher)

accepted definition of the sanctuary at that time). However, they later discovered that on the Day of Atonement, falling that year on October 22, 1844, Jesus moved from the Holy Place to the Most Holy Place in the *heavenly sanctuary*, beginning His work of judgment (Dan. 7:9-14; Ps. 9:7-8; Heb. 8:1-6; 9-10). Christ's mediatory work as the High Priest in the heavenly temple would cleanse the hearts of God's people from sin during the investigative judgment (Is. 53:11-12; Heb. 10:19-21, 29-30), sealing them by His Spirit for the day of His return (2 Cor. 1:21-22).

## Jesus and His Followers Given a Kingdom

The overt persecution of God's people by the papacy ceased towards the end of the French Revolution in 1798 when Pope Pius VI was taken captive by the French general, Berthier, and the papacy lost its political rule in Europe (Dan. 7:25). About this same time, the United States of America was being formed, which would become the haven of religious freedom for the world. The prophet, Daniel, predicted that God the Father would give Jesus "dominion, glory, and a kingdom" (Dan. 7:14). This kingdom may also be inferred in Revelation 1:5-6 (KJV) when the text states that Jesus is the "prince of the kings of the earth… and hath made us kings and priests unto God and his Father." Although Christ's kingdom will ultimately be fulfilled at His second coming, God's followers would first prosper on Earth through the religious freedom provided in the United States, allowing a repetition of Deuteronomy 30:16 (NKJV): "The Lord your God will bless you in the land which you go to possess." God has blessed the United States and made this country *"kings" of the earth*—politically, financially, and most of all, spiritually. However, with these privileges come equally as great responsibilities!

## Christ's Warning to His Nation

Sadly, as America's commitment to God continues to diminish, change is coming quickly! Instead of heeding the Lord's voice through obeying His law, this country's leadership has largely turned its back on the spiritual heritage of its founding fathers. Jesus warns:

> But if thine heart turn away, so that thou will not hear; but shall be drawn away, and worship other gods, and serve them; I denounce unto you this day, that ye shall surely perish, and that ye shall not prolong your days upon the land...." (Deut. 30:17-18, KJV)

Repeating the same sad cycle as Israel of old, the United States, God's blessed and chosen nation for spreading Protestant Christianity to the world, is apostatizing, just as prophecy has predicted (Rev. 13:11-16), but a faithful remnant will remain until Christ's coming (Rev. 12:17). They will obey "the commandments of God and the faith of Jesus" (Rev. 14:12, KJV). How kind and gracious is the Lord who keeps His "covenant and mercy to them that love Him, and to them that keep His commandments!" (Dan. 9:4, KJV).

## Our Response

Today, more than ever, we need to pray the prayer of Daniel for our nation and apply his words to our life:

> O Lord, great and awesome God, who keeps His covenant and mercy with those who love Him, and with those who keep His commandments, we have sinned... we have done wickedly and rebelled, even departing from Your precepts and Your judgments. Neither have we heeded Your servants the prophets, who have spoken in Your name to our kings, and our princes, to our fathers, and all

the people of the land.... O my God, incline your ear and hear, and open Your eyes and see our desolations and the city which is *called by your name*, for we do not present our supplications before You because of our righteous deeds, but because of Your great mercies. O Lord, hear! O Lord, forgive! O Lord, listen and act! Do not delay for Your own sake, my God, for Your city and *Your people are called by Your name*." (Dan. 9:4-6, 18-19, NKJV; italics added)

We are God's people *"called by His name"* (compare Acts 15:14, 17; 11:26; Rom. 9:24-26)—Christians—after Christ, Himself. Many live in a country that claims Christianity (United States)—the city *"called by His name"* (Is. 62:11-12). Therefore, we must "turn from our iniquities," pay attention to God's truth (Dan. 9:13), and be prepared when "the Son of Man will send out His angels and... gather out of His kingdom all things that offend, and those who practice lawlessness" (Matt. 13:41, NKJV). He promises to keep His covenant with those who keep His commandments!

## The Seventy-Week Prophecy–Then and Now

After Daniel finished his heartfelt prayer of intercession on behalf of his nation, God sent the angel, Gabriel, to reveal the specific amount of probationary time "cut off" from the 2,300-day/year prophecy for the Jews: "Seventy weeks are determined ("cha-thak"- "cut off," "divided," "decreed") for your people and for your holy city" (Dan. 9:24, NKJV; compare Matt. 18:21-22). Gabriel then gave Daniel the starting point of the prophecy: "from the going forth of the commandment to restore and to build Jerusalem," which occurred in 457 BC (Dan. 9:25, KJV; Ezra 7:6-13). Again, Daniel understood that the vision of the 2,300 days must span a long period of time (Dan. 10:1); therefore, the seventy-week prophecy could not just refer to seventy literal weeks. The Hebrew word for "weeks" in Daniel 9:24 is *"shabuwa,"* which can mean *"a period of seven days or seven years."* The 70 weeks (70 x 7), then, could equal 490 years. This historical seventy-week prophecy would begin in 457 BC at the rebuilding of Jerusalem and its walls and continue 490 years to 34 AD (Dan. 9:25; Ezra 6:14; 7:7-9; 9:9; Neh. 2:17; 6:15-16). Both the historical 2,300-day/year prophecy and the seventy-week prophecy would begin on this same starting date because it is the only event given to signal the onset of both prophecies. Moreover, Daniel refers to Gabriel as the one "whom I had seen in the vision *at the beginning,"* who had come to help him understand his former vision of Daniel 8 and to explain the seventy-week portion that had been "cut off" from the 2,300 years (Dan. 9:21-23; italics added).

Gabriel continued by giving Daniel even more details. He stated after "sixty-two weeks, the Messiah shall be cut off" (Dan. 9:26, NKJV), and "until Messiah the Prince there shall be seven weeks and sixty-two weeks" (Dan. 9:25, NKJV). If seven weeks are added to sixty-two weeks, the sum totals sixty-nine weeks of years. Then if this total is multiplied by seven, it equals 483 years. If 483 years are added to 457 BC (the date of the decree to rebuild ancient Jerusalem and its walls [Ezra 7:7-9, 11-25; 9:9]), one arrives in 27 AD. What happened in this very year? Jesus Christ, the Messiah, was anointed at His baptism and began His ministry on Earth in the *exact year* that the seventy-week prophecy predicted! Shortly afterward, the Messiah would die or be "cut off, but not for himself" (Dan. 9:26, KJV; Lk. 3:22; 4:18).

Furthermore, Gabriel told Daniel that Christ "shall confirm a covenant with many for one week: but in the middle of the week He shall bring an end to sacrifice and offering" (Dan. 9:27, NKJV). Jesus confirmed his covenant with His people at His baptism in 27 AD (Matt. 3:11, 15; Rom. 11:27). Then in the middle of the seven-year "week," or three-and-a-half years later in 31 AD,

Christ died on the cross, ending the need for the sacrificial system in the sanctuary (Heb. 9:8-14). The four-inch-thick curtain separating the Holy from the Most Holy Place was miraculously torn from top to bottom by an unseen hand, creating an "open door" for Gentiles, as well as Jews, to enter into God's presence through the gift of salvation obtained by the death of Jesus (Mt. 27:51; Rev. 3:20; 4:1). In giving His life, Christ was truly "cut off but not for himself" (Dan. 9:26, KJV). Sadly, three-and-a-half years later, in 34 AD, the Jewish leadership formally rejected Christianity at the stoning of Stephen, and the gospel commission switched primarily to the Gentiles (Matt. 21:43; Acts 7). God called Saul, who became Paul, to preach to the Gentiles, declaring in Galatians 3:28 (KJV), "There is neither Jew nor Greek, there is neither bond nor free, there is neither male nor female: for ye are all one in Christ Jesus."

Amazingly, Gabriel gave Daniel the *exact years* of Christ's baptism in 27 AD, His death on the cross in 31 AD, and the ending of the probationary time for the Jewish nation as a whole in 34 AD. Yet, when Jesus was born, according to Jewish tradition, the leaders of Israel had put a curse upon anyone studying the time prophecies found in the book of Daniel.[27] The Jewish people were forbidden to research when the Messiah would come and when their "appointed time" of being God's chosen nation would end. Perhaps if they had been encouraged to study these time prophecies, the Jews as a whole would have recognized Jesus as the Messiah and not crucified their own King! (Mark 15:2). Amazingly, this sad fate was predicted hundreds of years before it occurred in the historical seventy-week prophecy of Daniel 9.

---

[27] http://www.come-and-hear.com/sanhedrin/sanhedrin_97.html; https://amazingdiscoveries.org/AD-Header-Downloads-References-Rabbin-icCurse

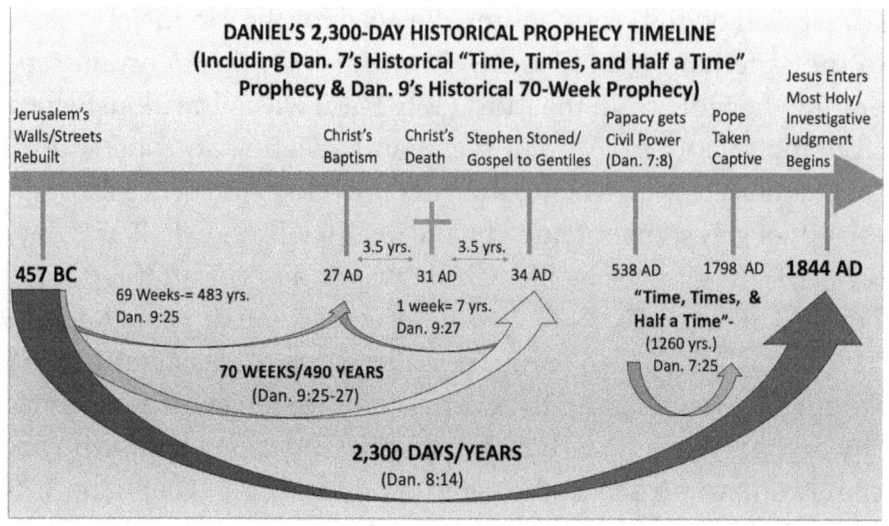

DANIEL'S 2,300-DAY HISTORICAL PROPHECY TIMELINE
(Including Dan. 7's Historical "Time, Times, and Half a Time"
Prophecy & Dan. 9's Historical 70-Week Prophecy)

## Protestant America Repeating the Prophecies of Daniel 9?

Could the same thing be happening to Protestant Christianity today? God's Word states, "that which has been is what will be done... it has already been in ancient times before us" (Eccl. 1:9-10, NKJV). Christ applies the prophecy of the destruction of Jerusalem to the end of the world. Moreover, Revelation 11:8 (KJV) predicts that Jesus would again be figuratively "crucified" by a modern nation in the last days which "spiritually is called Sodom and Egypt, where also our Lord was crucified." Jeremiah 5:24 (KJV) may imply that the seventy-week prophecy could happen more than once: "... Neither say they in their heart, 'Let us now fear the Lord our God, that giveth *rain*, both the *former and the latter, in his season.* He reserveth unto us the *appointed weeks* of the *harvest*'" (italics added). The word for "reserve" *(shamar)* can mean *"mark."* Could God be marking down our *"appointed weeks"* today in His spiritual *"harvest"* judgment, leading to the *"season"* of the *"latter rain,"* just before the closing of the allotted time for national repentance, specifically in Protestant America?[28] (Rev. 14:15).

---

[28] See Appendix for EGW's support of repeated prophecy

Once again, Daniel 9:25 states that at the rebuilding of Jeru-salem, the seventy-week prophecy would begin (Ezra 7; Neh. 2:17; 6:15-16). Has this ever occurred in modern times? Yes! Sol-yman (Soliman) the Magnificent, an Ottoman Turk, commanded that Jerusalem's walls be rebuilt as early as 1534 AD (even though the walls were not completed until 1541).[29] Interestingly, in 1534, Martin Luther published the Old and the New Testament in the common German language of the people, enabling the spread of God's truth which would spiritually rebuild the Lord's church during the Protestant Reformation.[30] Also, Henry VIII separated from the Catholic Church to form the Church of England (the first Protestant Church), striking a decisive blow to the papacy.[31] To counter the Protestant Reformation, the Jesuit order of the Cath-olic Church was also established, which would result in the death of countless Protestant martyrs.[32] All of these events occurred at the same time that Solyman decreed the rebuilding of Jerusalem's walls, possibly referred to in Isaiah 60:10 (KJV), "the sons of strangers shall *build up thy walls*, and their kings shall minister unto thee" (italics added). Could this event signal the repetition of Daniel 9's seventy-week prophecy for Protestantism?

Moreover, Solyman, this Ottoman ruler, was named after King Solomon, the builder of the original Jewish temple. Some historians have argued that Protestantism would have never suc-ceeded in Europe without the financial aid of Solyman and the Ottoman Empire during this time in history.[33] So, the influence

---

[29] *Dictionary of the Holy Bible* by Charles Taylor - "…Solyman built the present walls in 1534." (See additional references at the end of the chapter)

[30] Carl C. Christensen, "Luther and the Woodcuts to the 1534 Bible,"*Lutheran Quarterly*, Winter 2005, Vol. 19 Issue, pp. 392–413.

[31] https://www.parliament.uk/about/living-heritage/transformingsociety/private-lives/religion/collections/common-prayer/act-of-supremacy/

[32] https://www.history.com/this-day-in-history/jesuit-order-established; http://www.alphanewsdaily.com/Number-of-Protestants-Killed-By-Popes.html

[33] https://www.jewishvirtuallibrary.org/suleyman

of this Turkish Sultan seems far more than just coincidental! If Daniel 9's prophecies were to repeat, and for example, one begins figuring them at 1534 AD, the earliest date for Solyman's decree of the rebuilding of Jerusalem's walls (Micah 7:11), some amazing discoveries follow!

First, however, one must review the 2,300-day prophecy found in Daniel 8:14 (KJV) that predicts, *"Unto two thousand three hundred days, then the sanctuary shall be cleansed."* Using the timing of a day-equals-a-year found in Numbers 14:34 and Ezekiel 4:6, one can conclude that the historical 2,300-day prophecy began in 457 BC with Artaxerxes's edict to rebuild Jerusalem and ended in 1844 when Christ moved from the Holy Place to the Most Holy Place to begin the investigative judgment process (Ezra 6:14; Dan. 7:9-14, 22; Heb. 9). Since Christ cleansed the Jewish temple *twice* during His earthly ministry, both at the beginning and the end, it is logical that the 2,300-day prophecy of the cleansing of the sanctuary could repeat (Jn. 2:15; Lk. 19:45; Dan. 8:14). Moreover, the 2,300-day prophecy in Daniel 8:14 uses two Hebrew words for the word translated as "day" — *"boqer,"* meaning "morning," and *"ereb,"* meaning "evenings." The text literally means, "Unto two thousand and three hundred *mornings and evenings*, then shall the sanctuary be cleansed" (italics added). If one compares Daniel 8:14 to verse 26, this prophecy seems to indicate that it may have more than one fulfillment: possibly in the "morning" for the Jews (the historical 2,300-day prophecy) and later in the "evening" for Protestants.

If this prophecy were to repeat a second time, it must correspond to the seventy-week prophecy of Daniel 9. However, this time, instead of using a day-equals-a-year to calculate its duration, God's method of time calculation found in Leviticus 25:8 and Deuteronomy 16:9 will be utilized. In Leviticus 25:8 (NKJV), the Lord instructs His people to count time in cycles of forty-nine years: "And you shall count seven sabbaths of years for yourself, *seven times seven years*; and the time of the seven sabbaths of years shall be to you *forty-nine years*" (italics added). This method of counting time in cycles of forty-nine years was a common practice for the Jews during the Second Temple era. Josephus, the Book of Jubilees, and the Dead Sea Scrolls all speak of the priests using cycles of forty-nine years.[34] Likewise, in Deuteronomy 16:9, God instructs, "You shall count seven weeks (*"shebuwa"* = *"sevens"*) for yourself…" (parenthesis added). The Hebrew word for "weeks" in this text can mean *"seven days or years."* This is the same Hebrew word found in Daniel 9:24-27 for the word, *"weeks,"* which could refer to either *weeks of days or years*. Therefore, if one multiplies 2,300 days by seven sevens (forty-nine), the total is 112,700 days. Then if the 112,700 days are divided by 365 days in a year,[35] the quotient comes to 308 years. If this total is added to the year of 1534 AD, one arrives at the "Midnight Cry" of the Millerite Movement, heralding the beginning of the investigative judgment in 1844 and the publication of its significance. This method of calculation of the 2,300-day prophecy simply reaffirms the former day-year method, largely repeating the latter part of the historical 2,300-day/year prophecy. It seems to serve as a second witness, signaling the beginning of the investigative judgment and the urgent message of its importance for God's people! (Mat. 18:16).

Concerning the seventy-week prophecy, then, the Bible states in Daniel 9:25 (NKJV): "Know therefore and understand that

---

[34] https://design-of-time.com/jubilee.htm
[35] *360 days of a Jewish year are used in historical time prophecies & 365 (365.25) days are used in a modern year for the repetition of prophecies applying specifically to the Protestant era. The Bible does not specify either but likely uses both, depending on the time period and the audience.*

from the going forth of the command to restore and build Jerusalem… there shall be *seven weeks* and sixty-two weeks…" (italics added). This verse gives further evidence that this time prophecy is likely being counted in "seven-week" (7 X 7) or forty-nine-year increments. Unlike the 2300-day prophecy, however, the seventy-week prophecy is figured in *weeks of years* instead of mere days. Therefore, one should not multiply by forty-nine because the seventy weeks are already in forty-nine-year cycles. Additionally, the prophecy states that there will be a total of sixty-nine weeks (or 483 years) until "the street shall be built again, and the wall, even in *troublesome times*" (Dan. 9:25). After this time, the *"Messiah shall be cut off…"* (Dan. 9:26, KJV; italics added). Astoundingly, if sixty-nine weeks or 483 years are added to 1534 AD, for example, one arrives precisely in 2017, the year that Protestants and Catholics compromised on the doctrine of justification, purportedly ending the Protestant Reformation.

Most Christians would agree that up to 2017, even in "troublous times" (Dan. 9:25, KJV), God's truth, specifically the primary Protestant doctrine of justification by faith in Christ alone, marched steadily forward. But in 2017, everything changed! In that very year, the Lutherans and many other mainline Protestant denominations officially united back with the Catholic Church upon the doctrine of justification, the very same doctrine which had previously begun the Protestant Reformation.[36] This shocking confederacy resulted in the combination of the doctrine of justification by faith and the doctrine of salvation through works, purported by the pope who "opposes and exalts himself above all that is called God" (2 Thess. 2:4, NKJV). Moreover, Daniel 9:26 (KJV) may further emphasize this atrocity between the Protes-

---

[36] http://www.romereports.com/en/2017/07/15/reformed-churches-join-catholics-and-lutherans-on-the-doctrine-of-justification/

tants and the "man of sin" by predicting that "the people of the prince that shall come shall destroy the city and the sanctuary." The end of it shall be with a flood (of spiritual deception [Rev. 12:9, 15-16]) and unto the end of the war (Christ's second coming), desolations are determined" (Dan. 9:26, KJV; parentheses supplied). These "desolations" in this prophecy may very well include this attack upon biblical justification by faith that decimated Protestantism in 2017.

Daniel 9:27 (NKJV) further expounds, "But in the middle of the week He shall bring an end to sacrifice and offering…" In the historical application of the seventy-week prophecy, the close of "sacrifice and offering" referred to the tearing of the temple curtain at Christ's death, ending the sacrificial system. Similarly, in its modern repetition, in the middle of its last seven years (2020), could Protestant America have "cut off" or "crucified" Jesus afresh by nationally departing from His Word as a result of denying Christ's death on the cross as the only means of salvation? (Rev. 11:8). The prophet, Habakkuk, may have referred to this repetition of desolation when he cried out, "… revive Your work *in the midst of the years! In the midst of the years* make it known; In wrath remember mercy" (Hab. 3:2, NKJV; italics added). Could Daniel's prophecy now warn that Protestant America as a whole has broken her covenant with God, and judgments have begun to fall to awaken His people? (Dan. 9:13-14, 18-19). Habakkuk also declares: "… before him went the pestilence (sickness)" (Hab. 3:5, KJV). Could the outbreak of Covid at this very time in history have been a wake-up call, warning the world of Christ's soon coming? One thing is certain, because of the global physical and economic devastation of Covid, plus the fires, storms, and violent protests, 2020 has gone down in history as unprecedented! Never before has the entire world been so engulfed by tragedy! (Hab. 3:6).

Also, in 2020, the Roman pontiff summoned the world's political, spiritual, social, and sports leaders to come together to, in the pope's own words, "reinvent the global education alliance" in order "to form mature individuals capable of overcoming division and antagonism, and to restore the fabric of relationships for the sake of a more fraternal humanity… to nurture the dream of a humanism rooted in solidarity…."[37] This astounding act of calling for the unity of all these leaders under the pope's authority is likely a striking fulfillment of Habakkuk's prophecy: "… He is a proud man … and he is like death, and cannot be satisfied. He gathers to himself all nations and heaps up for himself all peoples" (Hab. 2:5, NKJV). Tragically, instead of Jesus, the pope has largely become the world's religious leader and his political power continues to grow in the United States, especially since Catholics now hold primary national offices, including the majority of the Supreme Court.[38] Could this transfer of spiritual leadership result in Christ's refusal of the polluted offerings from the apostate Protestant/Catholic Church, ending God's protection and favor of the United States? (Jer. 14:12-13).

Daniel 9:27 (NKJV) continues by saying, "And on the 'wing' ("*kanaph*"= "*extremity*") of the abominations (Rev. 17:4-5; 21:27) shall be one who makes desolate ("man of sin" [2 Thess. 2:3-4]), even until the consummation (earth's closing events), which is determined is poured out on the desolate" (God's cup of indignation [Rev. 14:10]; parentheses supplied). Could the "wing" or ending date of the proposed repeated seventy-week prophecy (2024) predict national devastations? Persecution of God's people? Even the conclusion of Protestant America as God's chosen nation similar to what occurred to the Jewish nation in 34 AD? Christ may have hinted at such a set time for national

---

[37] https://cruxnow.com/vatican/2019/09/pope-to-launch-global-educational-pact-next-year/

[38] https://news.gallup.com/opinion/polling-matters/391649/religion-supreme-court-justices.aspx

repentance when He told his disciples that they must forgive up to "seventy times seven," or 490 times, eerily similar to Daniel 9's 490-year prophecy (Matt.18:22; Dan. 9:24).

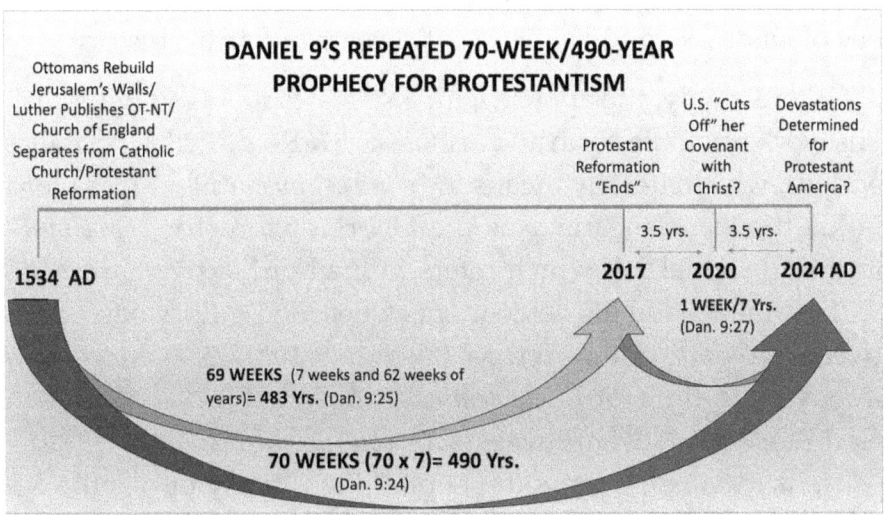

## An Alternative Application of the Repetition of Daniel's Seventy-week Prophecy

Another particularly fascinating way of figuring the repetition of Daniel's seventy-week prophecy is by using the starting date of 1541 AD when the walls of Jerusalem were completed. Daniel 9:25 (KJV) states that the seventy-week prophecy would begin "from the going forth of the commandment ("debar" meaning "a word" or "oracle" [prophecy]) to restore ("shuwb" meaning "repetition") and to build Jerusalem." If one examines the meanings of the words closely, this text could be saying that from the time that the *prophecy* concerning the building of Jerusalem is *repeated*, the seventy-week prophecy would begin. Therefore, if one begins the seventy-week prophecy in 1541 when the walls of Jerusalem were finished, sixty-nine weeks (483 years) end in 2024, and seventy weeks end in 2031. The middle of the week (three and a half years added to 2024) would end in 2027, exactly 2000 years after the baptism of Jesus. Also, the ending date of 2031 is exactly 2000 years after the Messiah's death on the cross. Both of these dates were predicted in the historical seventy-week prophecy of Daniel 9 and likely end 6,000 years of Earth's history.

Interestingly, the apostle Paul also states that God will finish His work upon the earth and *"cut it short"* (Rom. 9:28, KJV; italics added), which literally means to *"contract by cutting."* This word holds the same meaning as the Hebrew word for *"covenant"* found in Daniel 9:4, which refers to the Lord's covenant made with Abraham and his descendants when God's glory passed between two parts of the sacrifice (Gen. 15:9-10; 17:2, 7). Moreover, it may tie to the word, *"determined"* in Daniel 9:24 (KJV) when God says that "seventy weeks are *determined* (*"chathak"*- *"cut,"* *"divided,"* *"decreed"*) for your people." Plus, it may mirror the description of the Messiah being *"cut off* (*"karath"*- *to covenant*), but not for Himself,"* (Dan. 9:26, NKJV) which is further explained in the same verse as God's people breaking their covenant relationship with Him. Such parallels may indicate that the seventy-week prophecy is part of God's covenant with His people, applied to the Jewish nation, and repeated for Protestants today, just as Abraham's sacrifice was divided into two parts. This prophecy, then, should be a vital wake-up call for God's people living now!

Regardless of the dates used to figure the repetition of the seventy-week prophecy, God's people must be cognizant of the times in which they are living, confess their sins, and live righteously *today* so that they will be prepared when Christ returns (Matt. 4:17). Since the Bible does not give any prophecies predicting the date of Christ's second coming ("but of that day and hour, knows no man…" [Matt. 24:36, KJV]), God's faithful followers must pray for the Holy Spirit to help them understand and apply prophecy to their lives NOW while there is still time!

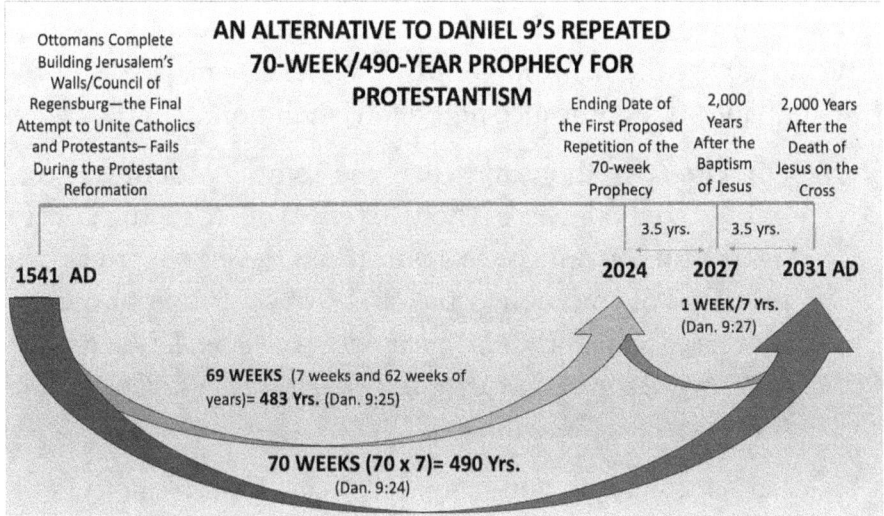

**AN ALTERNATIVE TO DANIEL 9'S REPEATED 70-WEEK/490-YEAR PROPHECY FOR PROTESTANTISM**

Ottomans Complete Building Jerusalem's Walls/Council of Regensburg—the Final Attempt to Unite Catholics and Protestants– Fails During the Protestant Reformation

Ending Date of the First Proposed Repetition of the 70-week Prophecy

2,000 Years After the Baptism of Jesus

2,000 Years After the Death of Jesus on the Cross

1541 AD    2024    2027    2031 AD

3.5 yrs.    3.5 yrs.

1 WEEK/7 Yrs. (Dan. 9:27)

69 WEEKS (7 weeks and 62 weeks of years)= 483 Yrs. (Dan. 9:25)

70 WEEKS (70 x 7)= 490 Yrs. (Dan. 9:24)

## Signs of Christ's Coming

As the end of time draws nearer, God's prophecies seem to be spiraling faster and faster! Recently, an additional application of the seventy-week prophecy has likely occurred. The Bible predicts the re-establishment of the Jewish nation as a sign for God's people: "This shall be a sign unto thee… the remnant that is escaped of the house of Judah shall again take root downward, and bear fruit upward: For out of Jerusalem shall go forth a remnant…." (Is. 37:30-32, KJV; compare Jer. 23:3, 7-8; Zech. 10:6-9). Likewise, Daniel 9:25 may outline the timing of this prophecy by stating that the seventy weeks would begin with the rebuilding of Jerusalem. The Hebrew word for "build" is *"banah"* which can also mean to *"repair," "to establish"* or *"to cause to continue."* Has this occurred since the 1500s in Jerusalem? Again, the answer is "Yes!"

## Beginning Again

On June 7, 1967, in the Six-Day War, Israeli troops captured Jerusalem and the Western Wailing Wall (the remnant of the original Jewish temple), winning Israeli control of Jerusalem for the first time in 2,000 years. Testimonies from witnesses affirm this historic event and its significance to the Jewish nation:

> For some two thousand years the Temple Mount was forbidden to the Jews…. The Western Wall, for which every heart beats, is ours once again…You have given the great privilege of completing the circle, of returning to the nation its capital and its holy center" (*Commander Motta Our to his brigade upon their recapture of Jerusalem's Old City and holy sites*).

> I am speaking to you from the plaza of the Western Wall, the remnant of our Holy Temple… This year in Jerusalem—*rebuilt!* (General Shlomo Goren, Chaplain of the Israeli Defense Forces).[39] (parentheses added)

On this date of June 7, 1967, the city of Jerusalem and its Wailing Wall was finally recovered for the Jewish nation as God had promised, "… I will bring back the captivity of Jacob's tents and have mercy on his dwelling places; the city shall be built upon its own mound…" (Jer. 30:18, NKJV). Could this historic event once again begin a repetition of Daniel 9's prophecy?

In review, the Lord outlines His method of figuring time in Leviticus 25:8 (NKJV), "And you shall count seven sabbaths of years for yourself, *seven times seven years*" or "*forty-nine years*" (italics added). Furthermore, as previously mentioned, Daniel 9:25 hints at counting in multiples of forty-nine years by referring to

---

[39] http://www.sixdaywar.org/content/ReunificationJerusalem.asp

sixty-nine weeks of years as "*seven weeks* and sixty-two weeks" (italics & parenthesis added). Applying this method to Daniel 9's seventy-week (490-year) prophecy and counting by forty-nine-year cycles like the Jewish priests of old (Lev. 25:8; Is. 29:1), one discovers that there are ten forty-nine-year cycles. If one of these forty-nine-year cycles is "cut off" (similar to the seventy-week prophecy cut from the 2300-day prophecy) and the Hebrew root words for the timing found in the seventy-week prophecy are applied, some amazing results follow!

For example, Daniel 9:24 (KJV) states, "Seventy (*"shib'iym"-multiple of 7*) weeks are determined (*"chathak"- "cut off"*) upon thy people and upon thy holy city...." (parenthesis added). If the root word, *"sheba,"* meaning *"seven,"* is used instead of *"seventy,"* this text would read, "*Seven* weeks (or *forty-nine years*) are determined (*"cut off"* from the seventy-week prophecy) for your people and your holy city" (italics & parenthesis added). This method of figuring time, using a tenth of 490 years, or a forty-nine-year rotation based on the Hebrew root words, could then be applied to the sixty-nine weeks portion of the same prophecy. Daniel 9:25 states, "There shall be seven weeks and sixty weeks (equaling sixty-nine weeks) and after this, the "Messiah" would be "cut off, but not for Himself" (Dan. 9:26, NKJV). As stated previously, Christ is the head of His nation, and when this prophecy is talking about the Messiah being "cut off," it could likely be talking about God's people in the Protestant nation of the United States being "cut off" from His spiritual leadership. If a tenth of sixty-nine weeks (Dan. 9:25), 6.9 weeks, is multiplied by seven, it totals 48.3 years. Then, if forty-eight years are added to the date that Jerusalem was "restored" to the Jews in 1967, the sum ends in the year, 2015.

Did something significant happen in 2015 that would cause Christ's leadership of His Protestant church in the United States to be "cut off"? It was in this very year that the pope addressed the U.S. Congress for the first time in history. But Daniel's prophecy is even more precise! If the remaining .3 years are multiplied by 365 days, they equal 109.5 days. Then, if forty-eight years and 109 days are added to June 7, 1967 (the date that Jerusalem and the Western Wall were regained), one arrives on *September 24, 2015*. This is the *exact date* that Pope Francis spoke to Congress, advising the United States to join the Paris Agreement concerning climate change![40] Never before had a pope addressed the U.S. Congress in a formal session! The ancient prophecies found in Daniel 9, therefore, could give God's people today astounding insight into the timing of when the pope would begin his rise to civil power, specifically in the United States. But why would Pope Francis unabatedly urge U.S. leadership to unite with the world's nations in saving the planet through legislated climate control? This political consensus headed by the pope could give him powerful world leadership, which inadvertently might usher in compliance with his encyclical, *Laudato Si*, which promotes Sunday as a "day of rest."[41]

Heeding papal urgings, in December of 2015 (during the "middle of the week" [Dan. 9:27]), world leaders met in Paris to form a global pact on climate change.[42] A few months later, the U.S. Secretary of State, John Kerry, executed Pope Francis's counsel by signing this climate covenant, along with 171 other world nations on April 2016.[43] Could this year also be predicted in

---

[40] https://www.theguardian.com/world/ng-interactive/2015/sep/24/pope-francis-addresses-congress-annotated

[41] https://www.huffpost.com/entry/popefrancisworldleader_n_56041e79e4b003l0ed fa4d0f ; https://catholicecology.net/blog/laudato-si-day-praise-which-heals-our-relationships

[42] https://unfccc.int/process-and-meetings/the-paris-agreement/the-paris-agreement

Daniel 9's prophecies? If the root-word meaning of "seventy weeks" in Daniel 9:24 is used (seven sevens), forty-nine years may be added to 1967 which ends precisely in 2016, *the same time that the Paris Agreement was signed in alignment with Pope Francis' counsel!* This amazing application of prophecy is likely further explained in Daniel 9:27 (NKJV): "… and on the wing of abominations, shall be *one who makes desolate*" (italics added). Moreover, in 2016, the Heritage Foundation in Washington D. C. predicted a *devastating* impact on the U.S. economy as a result of the Paris Agreement.[44] Could it be that God's incredible prophecies, introduced in Daniel's visions and explained in more detail by John in the book of Revelation, are occurring now and are still in progress? Like the penny in the spiral, these predictions seem to be repeating faster and faster with more and more precision!

Realizing that the prophecies of Daniel 9 are likely repeating in modern times compels us to pray more earnestly to "teach us to *number our days,* that we may apply our hearts unto wisdom" (Ps. 90:12, KJV; italics added). Applying these Bible prophecies now is vital for our salvation so that none will be deceived! (Matt. 24:3-5). Will we turn from our iniquities and pay attention to His truth? (Dan. 9:13). Or will Protestant Christians living today repeat the same sad history of the Jewish nation and reject the prophetic warnings found in God's Word, making Jesus weep because His people "did not know the *time*" of their "*visitation*"? (judgment [Lk. 19:41-44; Jer. 50:27-28]). Instead, may we fast and pray, like Daniel, asking for the Holy Spirit to help us heed the Lord's timely warnings through His prophets to prepare for His soon return!

---

[43] https://www.usatoday.com/story/news/world/2016/04/22/paris-climate-agreement-signing-united-nations-new-york/83381218/

[44] https://www.heritage.org/environment/report/consequences-paris-protocol-devastating-economic-costs-essentially-zero

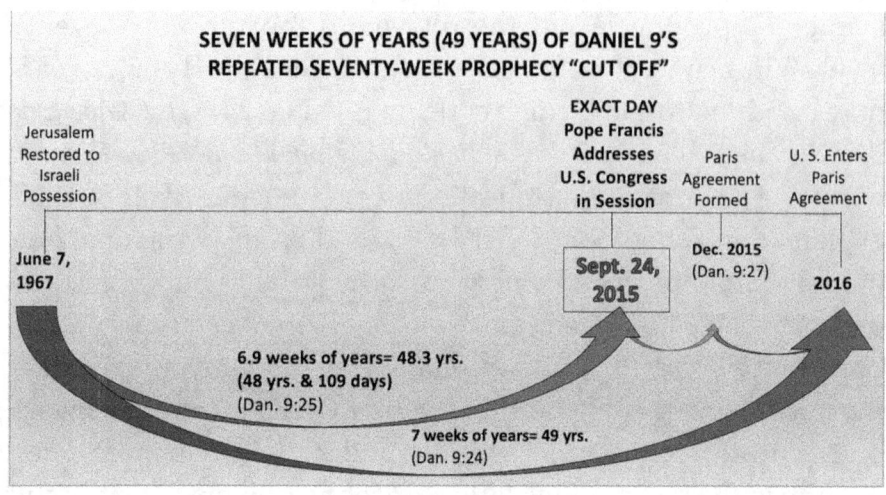

SEVEN WEEKS OF YEARS (49 YEARS) OF DANIEL 9'S
REPEATED SEVENTY-WEEK PROPHECY "CUT OFF"

Jerusalem
Restored to
Israeli
Possession

June 7,
1967

EXACT DAY
Pope Francis
Addresses
U.S. Congress
in Session

Paris
Agreement
Formed

U. S. Enters
Paris
Agreement

Sept. 24,
2015

Dec. 2015
(Dan. 9:27)

2016

6.9 weeks of years= 48.3 yrs.
(48 yrs. & 109 days)
(Dan. 9:25)

7 weeks of years= 49 yrs.
(Dan. 9:24)

## Additional Sources for the Decree to Rebuild Jerusalem's Walls by Solyman in 1534 AD:

The present walls were built by the Sultan Solyman in 1534.

*A Geography of the Bible: Compiled by the American Sunday School Union* by Alexander, Addison

"The fortified wall around Jerusalem was built by the Sultan Soliman, in 1534, and seems nearly to correspond to the walls which protected the city in the times of the Crusaders."

*The Pilgrim's Handbook to Jerusalem and its Neighborhood* by Liévin (de Hamme)

"The walls which form the present inclosure of Jerusalem, if we may believe various accounts,* were built about the year 1534, by Sultan Soliman, only son of Selim I."

*d'Anville's Dissertation on the Extent of ancient Jerusalem.

"Selim, the Turkish sultan, reduced Egypt and Syria, including Jerusalem, in 1517, and his son Solyman built the present walls in 1534."

*Ruins of Ancient Cities; with General and Particular Accounts of their Rise, Fall, and Present Condition* by Charles Bucke

"Selim, the Turkish sultan, reduced Egypt and Syria, including Jerusalem, in 1517, and his son Solyman built or reconstructed the present walls in 1534."

*ATS Bible Dictionary* http://biblehub.com/topical/j/jerusalem.htm

# Discussion Questions for Daniel 9

1. What event signaled the beginning of Daniel's 2,300-day and seventy-week prophecies? (Dan. 9:25; Micah 7:11)

2. When Christ moved into the Most Holy Place of the heavenly temple in 1844 at the end of the historical 2,300-day/year prophecy, what work did He begin? (Dan. 7:9-10; Heb. 9:24, 27; 10:30)

3. What responsibilities do Christians have as God's people "called by His name?" How should this title affect our daily lives? (Dan. 9:18-19; Acts 15:17)

4. How many years did God give the Jews as His chosen nation? (Dan. 9:24; Matt. 18:21-22)

5. In the historic seventy-week prophecy, what important event happened in 27 AD? (Dan. 9:25; Matt. 3:16) In 31 AD? (Dan. 9:26; John 19:30) What happened in 34 AD, and what did it signify? (Dan. 9:24; Acts 7:59; 13:46)

6. How might Eccl. 1:9-10 support that Bible prophecies can apply to more than one event and time period in history? How did Christ likely teach this? (Matt. 24:1-3)

7. Why might the rebuilding of Jerusalem's walls restart Daniel 9's seventy-week prophecy? (Dan. 9:25)

8. How did the unity of Catholics and Protestants "corrupt" true Protestantism in 2017? (Dan. 9:26)

9. Why is it important to realize that prophetic dates refer to important **signs** of Christ's coming, NOT the **date** of His coming? (Matt. 24:36, 44)

10. *Why is it important for our salvation to understand Bible prophecy and how it applies to our lives right now? (Ps. 90:12; II Tim. 3:13-17)*

# Daniel 10:1-6, 12-14, 20-21 (KJV)

*[1] In the third year of Cyrus king of Persia a thing was revealed unto Daniel, whose name was called Belteshazzar; and the thing was true, but the time appointed was long: and he understood the thing, and had understanding of the vision. [2] In those days I Daniel was mourning three full weeks. [3] I ate no pleasant bread, neither came flesh nor wine in my mouth, neither did I anoint myself at all, till three whole weeks were fulfilled. [4] And in the four and twentieth day of the first month, as I was by the side of the great river, which is Hiddekel; [5] Then I lifted up mine eyes, and looked, and behold a certain man clothed in linen, whose loins were girded with fine gold of Uphaz: [6] His body also was like the beryl, and his face as the appearance of lightning, and his eyes as lamps of fire, and his arms and his feet like in colour to polished brass, and the voice of his words like the voice of a multitude…*

*[12] Then said he unto me, Fear not, Daniel: for from the first day that thou didst set thine heart to understand, and to chasten thyself before thy God, thy words were heard, and I am come for thy words. [13] But the prince of the kingdom of Persia withstood me one and twenty days: but, lo, Michael, one of the chief princes, came to help me; and I remained there with the kings of Persia. [14] Now I am come to make thee understand what shall befall thy people in the latter days: for yet the vision is for many days…*

[20] *Then said he, Knowest thou wherefore I come unto thee? and now will I return to fight with the prince of Persia: and when I am gone forth, lo, the prince of Grecia shall come.* [21] *But I will shew thee that which is noted in the scripture of truth: and there is none that holdeth with me in these things, but Michael your prince.*

# The Cosmic Conflict

Have you ever wanted to travel through time faster than the speed of light with no one able to stop you? Daniel must have had a similar feeling when he realized the vision was true but "the time appointed was long" (Dan. 10:1, KJV). Interestingly, the Hebrew word for "time appointed" in this text is "tsaba," which has the connotations of a great war (Dan.10:1). What long war had Daniel seen in his previous visions? It was the great controversy between Christ/His followers and Satan/his dark kingdom. This conflict is vital for God's people to understand because it is the backset of biblical prophecy. All must choose a side in this war, and no one wants to be deceived! (Eph. 6:12; Matt. 24:24; 2 John 1:7)

The Bible predicts that the Devil will use an antichrist religious/political power that will speak "pompous words against the Most High," "persecute the saints," and try to "change times and law" (Dan. 7:25, NKJV; I Jn. 2:18, 22; 4:3; 2 Thess. 2:3-4). Moreover, this leader will "destroy the mighty, and also the holy people, through his cunning," "cause deceit to prosper under his rule," and "exalt himself in his heart." Plus, he will "destroy many in their prosperity" and "even rise against the Prince of princes..." (Dan. 8:24-25, NKJV). As stated previously, only one power in history, arising from the Roman Empire, fits this description! It is the papacy, the "little horn" power of the pope that "exalts himself as high as the Prince of the host" (Dan. 8:11, NKJV). History has proven that the papacy has persecuted and killed countless faithful Protestants and even today claims God's divine authority. No wonder Daniel was distressed by the length of the papacy's terrible war against God's faithful remnant!

In fact, Daniel was so upset that he mourned and fasted for three full weeks (Dan. 10:2). The Bible emphasizes Daniel's fast in verse 3, "I ate no pleasant food, nor meat or wine came into my mouth, nor did I anoint myself at all, till three whole weeks were fulfilled" (Dan. 10:3, NKJV; italics added). Previously, Daniel had described this type of fasting by stating, "And I set my face unto the Lord God to seek by prayer and supplications, with fasting, and sackcloth, and ashes" (Dan. 9:3, KJV). These fasts were not some special diet plan that would merely benefit physical health. Instead, the purpose of Daniel's fast was to humbly confess his sins and the sins of his people and ask God to not "delay" in hearing his cry (Dan. 9:19). The fact that Daniel prayed and fasted is a powerful example for us today! The Lord, Himself, directly pleads with His people living before His second coming:

> Consecrate a fast, call a sacred assembly; gather the elders and all the inhabitants of the land into the house of the Lord your God, and cry out to the Lord. Alas for the day! For the day of the Lord is at hand! (Joel 1:14-15, NKJV; italics added)

This urgent call for prayer and fasting is desperately needed to obtain victory in the great controversy between good and evil because Jesus, Himself, declares that the Devil and his hosts sometimes cannot be overcome except "by prayer and fasting" (Matt. 17:21, KJV). Therefore, Christians living today, in preparation for Christ's second coming, need to set aside specific times for this type of supplication, both corporately and individually.

Moreover, Daniel and his three friends practiced this fervent intercession because it had given them exponential wisdom over their peers when they had originally been taken to Babylon. At that time, Daniel "purposed in his heart that he would not defile himself with the portion of the king's delicacies, nor with the wine…" (Dan. 1:8, KJV; compare I Cor. 3:16-17). Instead of complying with the king's mandate of what must be put into his body, Daniel and his three friends asked for a simple diet of vegetables ("pulse" [Dan. 1:12, KJV]- likely containing fruits and whole grains) and water for ten days. As a result, "God gave them knowledge and skill in all learning and wisdom; and Daniel had understanding in all visions and dreams" (Dan. 1:17, KJV). God honored their desire to keep their bodies as a "temple of the Holy Ghost" (I Cor. 6:19, KJV). Amazingly, when the king tested Daniel and his three friends, they were "ten times better than all the magicians and astrologers that were in all his realm" (Dan. 1:20, KJV; italics added). Interestingly, Daniel and his friends faced this health test first before they faced the decrees of forced worship found a few chapters later in Daniel 3 and 6.

Likewise, today, the Lord will give wisdom to all who ask Him, concerning the choices that they make regarding their health and worship. He promises:

> … If you receive my words, and treasure my commands within you, so that you incline your ear to wisdom, and apply your heart to understanding; yes, if you cry out for discernment, and lift up your voice for understanding… then you will understand the fear of the Lord, and find the knowledge of God. For the Lord gives wisdom; from His mouth comes knowledge and understanding. (Prov. 2:1-6, NKJV)

Like Daniel, if God's people humble themselves by confessing their sins and the sins of their nation, then He will give them wisdom "liberally and without reproach" (James 1:5, NKJV). Prayer and fasting, then, helps sincere Christians understand what should be put into their bodies and how such choices may affect their ability to worship the Lord.

As a result of Daniel's earnest supplication, he was given a vision of the Son of Man similar to John's vision in Revelation 1. Both Daniel and John describe Jesus as being clothed in the priestly attire of a robe with a golden belt (Dan. 10:5; Rev. 1:13). They also both describe Christ's eyes like torches of fire, his feet like fine brass, and his face shining with light (Dan. 10:6; Rev. 1:14-16; 2:18). These similar descriptions of Jesus seem to link the books of Daniel and Revelation together, expounding upon each other's prophecies throughout history, with specific relevance to the end of time. This description of Jesus, mediating in the heavenly sanctuary as our High Priest, gives us a tiny glimpse of the Lord's work for those who claim His blood as payment for the forgiveness of sin (Rom. 8:33-34).

After Daniel saw Jesus ministering in the heavenly temple, the angel reminded him of the spiritual warfare that was taking place with the earthly rulers of Persia and Greece. In Daniel's day, the conflict between good and evil was particularly strong throughout the twenty-one days that Daniel fasted and prayed for wisdom (Dan. 10:12-13). Currently, with evil multiplying at unprecedented speed, God's people are called to pray and fast as Christ's coming nears. The Lord promises to empower His followers just as He did when He touched Daniel and said, "… greatly beloved, fear not! peace be unto thee; be strong, yea, be strong!" (Dan. 10:19, KJV). He reiterates this same promise today and adds: "Fear thou not, for I am with thee; be not dismayed, for I am thy God. I will strengthen thee; yea, I will help thee; yea, I will uphold thee with the right hand of my righteousness" (Is. 41:10, KJV). Praise the Lord that although the battle rages, God's people have nothing to fear with Christ on their side! (Rom 8:31).

The details of this spiritual war between good and evil would be further outlined to Daniel in the future, but not before the angel assured him that Michael, his Prince, would win this fight against God's enemies. Jude 1:9 explains that Michael is the "archangel," meaning the "Chief over all the angels" in Heaven, which is a reference to Jesus, Himself, called the "Angel of God" and the "Angel of the Lord" in the Old Testament (Ex. 14:19 compare 13:21; Judges 6:22-24).

Therefore, Christ, the Prince, will empower God's people to overcome Satan and his hosts by providing His church with spiritual armor (Eph. 6:10-18; Dan. 12:1). God's followers will prevail in the end because Jesus has already won man's salvation at the cross (I Cor. 15:56-57; Dan. 10:21). The Bible promises that by submitting to the Lord, one may "resist the devil, and he will flee" (James 4:7, KJV). Moreover, "… greater is he that is in you, than he that is in the world" (1 John 4:4, KJV). Satan, therefore, is a defeated foe, and soon, Christ will come and set up His kingdom on the recreated earth. Then, at last, the cosmic conflict will be ended, and the devil and sin will be no more!

# Discussion Questions for Daniel 10

1. *Why is it vital that we study prophecy in the context of the great controversy between Christ and Satan? How does awareness of this controversy protect us? (Eph. 6:12; Matt. 24:24; 2 John 1:7)*

2. *What specific political and spiritual power in history has Satan used to persecute God's people? How is it regaining its prominence today? (Dan. 7:25; 8:11, 24-25; I Jn. 2:18, 22; 2 Thess. 2:3-4)*

3. *How did fasting and prayer help Daniel and his three friends? Why is it vital that we heed their example of praying and fasting today? (Dan. 10:1-2; 9:3, 19; Joel 2:12-13, 28-29)*

4. *Why was it so important for Daniel and his friends to keep their bodies as the temple of the Holy Spirit and not defile themselves? Why is it just as important for us to do the same today? (Dan. 1:8, 17, 20; I Cor. 3:16-17; 6:19-20; Matt. 17:18-21)*

5. *Compare Daniel's vision of the Son of Man to John's (Dan. 10:5-6; Rev. 1:14-16). How is Christ portrayed in both visions? Why is this description of Jesus significant in describing his work in the heavenly sanctuary today? (Heb. 9:15, 24; Rom 8:34)*

6. *What evidence did God show Daniel in his vision of the great controversy between good and evil? How has God promised to protect us in this spiritual battle between Christ and Satan? (Dan. 10:13, 19-20; Is. 41:10; Rom. 8:31)*

7. *Who is Michael, and what does He do for God's people? (Dan. 10:21; 12:1; Ex. 14:19 compare 13:21; Judges 6:22-24; Jude 1:9)*

8. *How can we be prepared daily for the battle against the demonic influences of sin in our lives? What promises are we given that we can overcome Satan through Christ's power? (Eph. 6:10-18; James 4:7; 1 John 4:4)*

# Daniel 11 (KJV)

*¹ Also I in the first year of Darius the Mede, even I, stood to confirm and to strengthen him. ² And now will I shew thee the truth. Behold, there shall stand up yet three kings in Persia; and the fourth shall be far richer than they all: and by his strength through his riches he shall stir up all against the realm of Grecia. ³ And a mighty king shall stand up, that shall rule with great dominion, and do according to his will. ⁴ And when he shall stand up, his kingdom shall be broken, and shall be divided toward the four winds of heaven; and not to his posterity, nor according to his dominion which he ruled: for his kingdom shall be plucked up, even for others beside those. ⁵ And the king of the south shall be strong, and one of his princes; and he shall be strong above him, and have dominion; his dominion shall be a great dominion. ⁶ And in the end of years they shall join themselves together; for the king's daughter of the south shall come to the king of the north to make an agreement: but she shall not retain the power of the arm; neither shall he stand, nor his arm: but she shall be given up, and they that brought her, and he that begat her, and he that strengthened her in these times. ⁷ But out of a branch of her roots shall one stand up in his estate, which shall come with an army, and shall enter into the fortress of the king of the north, and shall deal against them, and shall prevail: ⁸ And shall also carry captives into Egypt their gods, with their princes, and with their precious vessels of silver and of gold; and he shall continue more years than the king of the north. ⁹ So the king of the south shall come into his kingdom, and shall* return into his own land. <sup>10</sup> *But his sons shall be stirred up, and shall assemble a multitude of great forces: and one shall certainly come, and overflow, and pass through: then shall he return, and be stirred up, even to his fortress.* <sup>11</sup> *And the king of the south shall be moved with choler, and shall come forth and fight with him, even with the king of the north: and he shall set forth a great multitude; but the multitude shall be given into his hand.* <sup>12</sup> *And when he hath taken away the multitude, his heart shall be lifted up; and he shall cast down many ten thousands: but he shall not be strengthened by it.* <sup>13</sup> *For the king of the north shall return, and shall set forth a multitude greater than the former, and shall certainly come after certain years with a great army and with much riches.* <sup>14</sup> *And in those times there shall many stand up against the king of the south: also the robbers of thy people shall exalt themselves to establish the vision; but they shall fall.* <sup>15</sup> *So the king of the north shall come, and cast up a mount, and take the most fenced cities: and the arms of the south shall not withstand, neither his chosen people, neither shall there be any strength to withstand.* <sup>16</sup> *But he that cometh against him shall do according to his own will, and none shall stand before him: and he shall stand in the glorious land, which by his hand shall be consumed.* <sup>17</sup> *He shall also set his face to enter with the strength of his whole kingdom, and upright ones with him; thus shall he do: and he shall give him the daughter of women, corrupting her: but she shall not stand on his side, neither be for him.* <sup>18</sup> *After this shall he turn his face unto the isles, and shall take many: but a prince for his own behalf shall cause the reproach offered by him to cease; without his own reproach he shall cause it to turn upon him.* <sup>19</sup> *Then he shall turn his face toward the fort of his own land: but he shall stumble and fall, and not be found.* <sup>20</sup> *Then shall stand up in his estate a raiser of taxes in the glory of the kingdom: but within few days he shall be destroyed, neither in anger, nor in battle.* <sup>21</sup> *And in his estate shall stand up a vile person, to whom they shall not give the honour of the kingdom: but he shall come in peaceably, and* obtain the kingdom by flatteries. <sup>22</sup> And with the arms of a flood shall they be overflown from before him, and shall be broken; yea, also the prince of the covenant. <sup>23</sup> And after the league made with him he shall work deceitfully: for he shall come up, and shall become strong with a small people. <sup>24</sup> He shall enter peaceably even upon the fattest places of the province; and he shall do that which his fathers have not done, nor his fathers' fathers; he shall scatter among them the prey, and spoil, and riches: yea, and he shall forecast his devices against the strong holds, even for a time. <sup>25</sup> And he shall stir up his power and his courage against the king of the south with a great army; and the king of the south shall be stirred up to battle with a very great and mighty army; but he shall not stand: for they shall forecast devices against him. <sup>26</sup> Yea, they that feed of the portion of his meat shall destroy him, and his army shall overflow: and many shall fall down slain. <sup>27</sup> And both of these kings' hearts shall be to do mischief, and they shall speak lies at one table; but it shall not prosper: for yet the end shall be at the time appointed. <sup>28</sup> Then shall he return into his land with great riches; and his heart shall be against the holy covenant; and he shall do exploits, and return to his own land. <sup>29</sup> At the time appointed he shall return, and come toward the south; but it shall not be as the former, or as the latter. <sup>30</sup> For the ships of Chittim shall come against him: therefore he shall be grieved, and return, and have indignation against the holy covenant: so shall he do; he shall even return, and have intelligence with them that forsake the holy covenant. <sup>31</sup> And arms shall stand on his part, and they shall pollute the sanctuary of strength, and shall take away the daily sacrifice, and they shall place the abomination that maketh desolate. <sup>32</sup> And such as do wickedly against the covenant shall he corrupt by flatteries: but the people that do know their God shall be strong, and do exploits. <sup>33</sup> And they that understand among the people shall instruct many: yet they shall fall by the sword, and by flame, by captivity, and by spoil, many days. <sup>34</sup> Now when they shall fall, they shall be holpen with a little help: but many *shall cleave to them with flatteries.* [35] *And some of them of understanding shall fall, to try them, and to purge, and to make them white, even to the time of the end: because it is yet for a time appointed.* [36] *And the king shall do according to his will; and he shall exalt himself, and magnify himself above every god, and shall speak marvellous things against the God of gods, and shall prosper till the indignation be accomplished: for that that is determined shall be done.* [37] *Neither shall he regard the God of his fathers, nor the desire of women, nor regard any god: for he shall magnify himself above all.* [38] *But in his estate shall he honour the God of forces: and a god whom his fathers knew not shall he honour with gold, and silver, and with precious stones, and pleasant things.* [39] *Thus shall he do in the most strong holds with a strange god, whom he shall acknowledge and increase with glory: and he shall cause them to rule over many, and shall divide the land for gain.* [40] *And at the time of the end shall the king of the south push at him: and the king of the north shall come against him like a whirlwind, with chariots, and with horsemen, and with many ships; and he shall enter into the countries, and shall overflow and pass over.* [41] *He shall enter also into the glorious land, and many countries shall be overthrown: but these shall escape out of his hand, even Edom, and Moab, and the chief of the children of Ammon.* [42] *He shall stretch forth his hand also upon the countries: and the land of Egypt shall not escape.* [43] *But he shall have power over the treasures of gold and of silver, and over all the precious things of Egypt: and the Libyans and the Ethiopians shall be at his steps.* [44] *But tidings out of the east and out of the north shall trouble him: therefore he shall go forth with great fury to destroy, and utterly to make away many.* [45] *And he shall plant the tabernacles of his palace between the seas in the glorious holy mountain; yet he shall come to his end, and none shall help him.*

# The Great Controversy Today

Historically, the Middle East has had a turbulent reputation, often erupting in war. The United States and the United Nations are politically entangled in the violent instability of this part of the world. However, as war threatens, God's faithful are not to fear! The Lord knows the "beginning and the end" (Rev. 22:13, KJV). He is in control of the present, just as He has been in the past and will be in the future (Rev. 1:8).

In Daniel's last vision (recorded in chapters 10-12), the Bible traces the history of God's people to the end of time. Daniel 11:2 (KJV) states, "Behold there shall stand up yet three kings (kingdoms- Dan. 7:17, 23) in Persia; and the fourth shall be far richer."

After the Achaemenid Empire (550–330 BC) which was in power when Daniel had his last vision, three more prominent, *strictly Persian*, dynasties arose—Sasanian Empire (224–651 AD), the Safavid dynasty (1501–1736 AD), and the Afsharid/Zand dynasty (ruling simultaneously- Afsharid: 1736–1796 AD/Zand dynasty: 1751–1794 AD). The fourth Persian kingdom was the Qajar dynasty[45] (1796–1925 AD), which was the richest, likely because

---

[45] The Pahlavi dynasty ruled after the Qajar kingdom, but it is considered to be an Iranian kingdom because Persia became Iran in 1935. Then in 1979, Iran became a republic. Other ruling kingdoms throughout history were not considered strictly Persian.
(https://en.wikipedia.org/wiki/History_of_Iran;https://www.britannica.com/place/ancient-Iran/Persian-dynasties;https://aspirantum.com/blog/persian-empire)

of the discovery of oil in 1908 and the tremendous income it would produce. As a result, the West, namely the United States and Europe (including Greece, a member state of the European Union), have today become dependent on Iran (Persia) for much of their oil. The resulting energy crisis "stirred up" considerable political unrest in accordance with Daniel 11:2 "… and the fourth shall be far richer than them all; by his strength, through his riches, he shall stir up all against the realm of Greece" (Dan. 11:2, NKJV), meaning that he shall provoke the realm of Greece or the Gentile nations (Gal. 3:28-29; Col. 3:11).

Next, the Bible recaps the Gentile history of Greece and Rome that was previously covered during the Persian Empires (similar to how Daniel 7 recaps Daniel 2's prophecy) by stating, "And a mighty king shall stand up that shall rule with great dominion, and do according to his will"; this kingdom would be "divided toward the four winds of heaven," and it would be *"plucked up, even for others beside those"* (Dan. 11:3-4, KJV; 8:8, 21; italics added). History proves that Greece conquered Persia in 331 BC and was divided between Alexander's four generals. Then the Greek culture was absorbed into the Roman Empire and continued in the Catholic Church, illustrated in the conversion of the Greek gods into Catholic saints.[46] Daniel 8:23-24 (NKJV) expounds on the pope's rule in the Dark Ages by saying, "And in the latter time… a king shall arise, having fierce features, who understands sinister schemes…. He shall destroy the mighty, and also the holy people." This papal persecution occurred from the 14th to the 17th centuries during the Protestant Reformation.

During this time, faithful martyrs objected to the pope's usurped authority of God who claimed to be "the Vicar of

---

[46] Calvin, John. (1854). *A Treatise on Relics*. Edinburgh, Johnstone, and Hunter. p. 2.

Christ,"[47] robbing the Lord of His kingdom in the rightful location of the North. This northern location was originally where God resided in the Holy Place of the sanctuary (Ex. 40:22; 25:30; John 6:35, 51). Moreover, the Bible states that the "city of our God," "the great King," is located in the North (Ps. 48:1-2, KJV). However, like Lucifer, himself, the papacy has exalted its "throne above the stars of God," claiming to sit "in the sides of the north" and be "like the Most High" (Is. 14:13-14, KJV). Also, the Bible describes the antichrist by stating, "he shall also stand up against the Prince of princes" (Dan. 8:25, KJV; I Jn. 4:3); and ascend from the iron and bronze kingdoms of Rome and Greece (Dan. 2:39-40), called "the northern iron and bronze" (Jer. 15:12, NKJV). Therefore, in Daniel 11, the papacy is referred to as the self-proclaimed "king of the North."

The pope's political rulership over God's people would prevail until 1798 AD when the papacy would lose its civil power during the French Revolution. At that time, the papal authority would be "plucked up," in harmony with Dan. 11:4, and the king of the south would "be strong, and one of his princes," and he would become stronger than the king of the North and have great dominion (Dan. 11:5, KJV). However, the papacy would continue to fight for civil authority over God's people by spiritually attacking the king of the South.

Who is this king of the South that likely arose to world power after the papacy's fall in 1798? In Daniel 11, the king of the South is a symbol of a great nation containing God's people (such as Egypt and Sodom [Dan. 9:15; Is. 1:8-11]), symbolically located in

---

[47] https://www.papalencyclicals.net/leo13/l13praec.htm;
https://www.nbcbayarea.com/news/national-international/Pope-Titles--196518461.html?amp=y

the South (Dan. 11:8; Is. 30:1-6, 15; Eze. 16:46). This modern country is further described in Revelation 11:8 (KJV) as being spiritually called "Sodom and Egypt, where also our Lord was crucified." Similar to these ancient nations, this modern country is defiant against God like Egypt (Dan. 11:5, 8, 42-43; Ex. 5:2), known for its immorality like Sodom (Jude 1:7; Lam. 4:6; Eze. 16:46-48; Jer. 23:14; Is. 1:9-10; Lk. 17:29-30), and unfaithful to its spiritual vows like ancient Israel (Eze. 16:2, 26-30), crucifying Christ through its national apostasy (Heb. 6:4-6). It is a country that claims to be Christian but has rebelled against God, legislated national promiscuity, and idolized the lies of its apostate political/religious leaders. According to history, there is only one prominent Christian nation that arose to world power after 1798 that is fulfilling these specific characteristics today—the United States of America. The *king* of the South, then, would logically represent the United States' primary national leader(s).

However, the prophecy does not end there! It continues in Daniel 11:6 (KJV) by speaking of the king of the South's daughter that joins "together" and makes an "agreement" with the usurper king of the North (the papacy). What does this daughter symbolize? Ezekiel 23:2-3 (NKJV) states that God's people are *"daughters of one mother*—they committed harlotry in Egypt," *in the South* (Is. 30:3-7). Additionally, Ezekiel 16:46 (NKJV) declares, "to the *south* of you, is *Sodom and her daughters."* So, when these texts speak of harlot "daughters" coming from "one mother," it appears to be occurring in the symbolic location of the South (Eze. 16:44, 46). As proposed previously, the "South" may prophetically refer to the United States. Moreover, because a woman symbolizes a church in Bible prophecy (Jer. 6:2; Hosea 3:1; Eph. 5:23-32), these texts could be speaking of God's people residing in "daughter" churches, specifically in the United States, that have become corrupted by "Mystery, Babylon the Great, the *mother* of harlots and of the abominations of the earth" (Rev. 17:5-6, KJV; italics added). Only one modern entity asserts that it is the *mother church* of Christianity — the Roman Catholic Church! Who, then, would be its daughters? History has proven that the "daughters" coming from this "one mother" are the Protestant churches. So, the daughter of the king of the South would logically refer to the apostate Protestant churches specifically located in the United States. Tragically, many American Protestant churches have united back with their harlot mother, the papacy, who allegedly claims to be the king of the North (Dan. 11:6; Eze. 16:43-44; Zech. 2:6-8; Rev. 17:4-6).

After understanding who is symbolized by the king of the North (the papacy asserting the authority of God) and the king of the South (the national leader of the United States) and its spiritual daughter (the apostate American Protestant churches), one is prepared to study the rest of Daniel 11.[48] This prophecy seems to outline the history of God's people after the fall of the papacy in 1798 by introducing the king of the South: "And the king of the South shall be strong, and one of his princes, and he shall be strong above him, and have dominion; his dominion shall be a great dominion" (Dan. 11:5, KJV). Again, this text is likely referring to only one primary world-renowned nation during this period of history — the United States. After the fourth Persian kingdom ended in 1925, the United States of America rose to "unprecedented global power" following the World Wars.[49] However, the papacy was not to be left behind without a fight! The pope immediately began to rebuild his authority over God's

---

[48] *Previous historic applications of the prophecies of Daniel 11 may also apply; however, the main thrust of this prophecy is "in the end of years" (Dan. 11:6, KJV).*
[49] https://world101.cfr.org/historical-context/world-war/how-did-united-states-become-global-power

people, this time specifically targeting his efforts in Protestant America.

In 1979, for the first time in history, Pope John Paul II met with U.S. President Jimmy Carter in the White House.[50] The pope also toured six American cities and was greeted by huge enthusiastic crowds; *Time* magazine, called him, "John Paul Superstar." This pope's popularity was a huge comeback to the political/religious power of the papacy in the United States. Later Pope John Paul II would work with U.S. President Ronald Reagan to bring down the Iron Curtain of Communism.[51] Since then, this pope has been proclaimed to be one of the "most charismatic and influential religious leaders of the 20th Century."[52]

Moreover, his 1995 encyclical, *"Ut Unum Sint,"* strongly encourages interfaith dialogue united under papal leadership,[53] which is just what Daniel 11:6 predicts:

> ... At the end (*"qets"* - end of time) of years (*"shaneh"* - year, revolution of time [Ps. 102:24]), they shall join forces, for the daughter of the king of the South (Protestant churches of the USA) shall go to the king of the North (the papacy) and make an agreement; but she shall not retain power of her authority, and neither he nor his authority shall stand, but she shall be given up, with those who brought her... ." (Dan. 11:6, NKJV; parentheses added)

If the daughter of the king of the South represents the Protestant churches of America and the king of the North symbolizes

---

[50] https://time.com/4044254/pope-white-house-1979/

[51] https://www.usnews.com/opinion/articles/2015/09/24/ronald-reagan-pope-john-paul-ii-and-the-alliance-that-won-the-cold-war

[52] https://www.sfgate.com/news/article/POPE-JOHN-PAUL-II-1920-2005-Beloved-2718398.php

[53] http://www.usccb.org/beliefs-and-teachings/ecumenical-and-interreligious/resources/quotes-from-church-teaching-on-ecumenism-and-interfaith-dialogue.cfm

the Roman Catholic papacy, then did American Protestants form an agreement with the Catholic Church during this time? Yes! In 1994, a group of American evangelical leaders went to prominent Catholic scholars with the first major ecumenical document based on common points of doctrine called, *Evangelicals and Catholics Together*.[54] This agreement, signed by both evangelicals and Catholics, was a result of the interfaith dialogue that had begun in 1967, after the Second Vatican Council. Its principles would later become a benchmark of the Moral Majority in the 1970s.[55]

The Bible then states that a religious leader would arise from "a branch of *her* roots" (Protestantism), who would "enter the fortress of the king of the north (the Vatican), and deal against them and prevail" (Dan. 11:7, KJV; parentheses supplied). The spiritual warfare mentioned in this verse is likely symbolic of the conversion of many Catholics to Protestantism; moreover, this religious leader would "continue more years than the king of the north" (Dan. 11:8, KJV). Did a prominent American evangelist convert a large number of people, visit the Vatican, and end up living longer than Pope John Paul II during this time? Yes! Billy Graham converted a tremendous amount of people during his crusades—an estimated 2.2 million.[56] He also visited the Vatican in 1981 and 1990[57] and outlived Pope John Paul II by thirteen years.[58] His powerful influence on the evangelical ecumenical movement continues today.

---

[54] https://www.latimes.com/archives/la-xpm-1993-06-22-mn-5726-story.html https://www.firstthings.com/article/1994/05/evangelicals-catholics-together-the-christian-mission-in-the-third-millennium

[55] https://oxfordre.com/religion/display/10.1093/acrefore/9780199340378.001.0001/acrefore-9780199340378-e-97;jsessionid=74B5C65BA06ECE3299F1A5D68F60-A757

[56] https://factsandtrends.net/2018/02/21/billy-grahams-life-ministry-by-the-numbers/

[57] https://www.latimes.com/archives/la-xpm-1990-01-20-ca-221-story.html

[58] https://www.history.com/this-day-in-history/pope-john-paul-ii-dies; https://memorial.billygraham.org/official-obituary/

Additionally, the visit by Pope John Paul II to the United States in 1993 resulted in stirring up strife (Dan. 11:10-12) between the U.S. president and the papacy over the issue of abortion,[59] as well as sexual molestation by the Catholic clergy in the United States.[60] This political conflict with the pope would grow until Bill Clinton was impeached in 1998.[61] Then, Pope John Paul II would return to the United States for his last time, possibly corresponding to Daniel 11:13 (NKJV), "For the king of the North will return and muster a multitude greater than the former, and shall certainly come at the end of some years...." His public appearance in the United States in 1999 drew a crowd of over 100,000 people at the St. Louis Trans World Dome for the January 27th mass—what is believed to be the largest indoor gathering in the United States.[62] This popular pope's historic visit had an astounding impact on Protestant America and paved the way for future ecumenical relations between Catholics and Protestants.

Daniel 11 continues its description of the false king of the North in verses 15-19 by stating that the armies "of the south" nor his "chosen people," shall have any "strength to withstand" him (Dan. 11:15, KJV). He will do "according to his own will and none shall stand before him: he shall stand in the glorious land, which by his hand shall be consumed" (Dan. 11:16, KJV). How did Pope John Paul II gain authority over spiritual Israel (Micah 5:8; Eph. 2:11-19) in God's modern "glorious land," "a goodly heritage of the hosts of nations" (Jer. 3:17-19), the United States of America? The following verse states that the king of the North would be given "the daughter of women (the Protes-

---

[59] https://www.nytimes.com/1993/08/13/us/pope-challenges-president-s-stance-on-abortion.html
[60] https://www.bbc.com/news/world-44209971
[61] https://www.congress.gov/congressional-report/105th-congress/house-report/830/
[62] https://web.archive.org/web/20130616165933
http://www.ewtn.com/jp99/update.htm

tant churches) corrupting her…" (Dan. 11:17, KJV; parenthesis supplied). Did something significant happen in 1999 between the Protestant churches of America and the Roman Catholic papacy? Yes! This is the same exact year that the historic *"Joint Declaration on the Doctrine of Justification"* by the Lutheran World Federation and the Catholic Church occurred.[63] This proclamation between the Catholics and the Lutherans would later climax in 2017 when many of the mainline Protestant churches would declare unity with the papacy on the doctrine of justification, purportedly ending the Protestant Reformation.[64]

Daniel 11:18 (NKJV) continues, "After this he shall turn his face to the coastlands." Pope John Paul II returned to Italy's Mediterranean coast, and two years later, the United States would suffer one of the most devastating Islamic terrorist attacks in its history. On September 11, 2001, during the fall of the Twin Towers in New York City, "more than 2,600 people died at the World Trade Center; 125 died at the Pentagon; 256 died on the four planes…. This immeasurable pain was inflicted by 19 young Arabs acting at the behest of Islamist extremists headquartered in distant Afghanistan."[65] It would take ten years for U. S. forces to catch the mastermind behind this terrorist attack, but Osama bin Laden was eventually killed in a military raid on his compound hideout in Pakistan.[66] This terrible tragedy possibly correlates with Daniel 11:14 (NKJV): "Now in those times many shall rise up against the king of the South (USA). Also, violent men (i.e. Islamic terrorists) of your people shall exalt themselves

---

[63] https://www.lutheranworld.org/what-we-do/unity-church/joint-declaration-doc-trine-justification-jddj;
http://www.vatican.va/roman_curia/pontifical_councils/chrstuni/documents/rc_pc_c hrstuni_doc_31101999_cath-luth-joint-declaration_en.html
[64] https://www.ncronline.org/news/world/reformed-churches-endorse-catholic-lu-theran-accord-key-reformation-dispute
[65] https://govinfo.library.unt.edu/911/report/911Report_Exec.htm
[66] https://www.history.com/this-day-in-history/osama-bin-laden-killed-by-u-s-forces

in fulfillment of the vision, but they shall fall." As a result of this attack, the U.S. Patriot Act was passed, and many American constitutional rights were lost.[67]

Following the aftermath of this national tragedy, in 2005, Pope John Paul II died or would "stumble and fall, and not be found" (Dan. 11:19, KJV). His funeral would leave the world mourning and become one of the largest gatherings of world dignitaries in history up to that time.[68] Incredulously, the United States was represented at this pope's funeral by three American presidents — George W. Bush, George H. W. Bush, and Bill Clinton — along with the secretary of state, Condoleezza Rice, and the New York mayor, Michael Bloomberg.[69]

Even after multiple court cases proving the guilt of child molestation by numerous Catholic priests in the United States under Pope John Paul II's papal rulership, this pope's "reproach" would "cease" (Dan. 11:18, KJV). In 2004, the American government passed a resolution that "commended the life and achievements of His Holiness, Pope John Paul II" after President Bush, with House and Senate support, gave him the Medal of Freedom.[70] However, the ample evidence of pedophilia by the United States Catholic clergy would continue to haunt the papacy even after Pope John Paul II's death. Daniel 11:18 (NKJV) states, "… but a ruler shall bring the reproach against them (the Catholic Church) to an end, and with the reproach removed, he shall turn back on him" (parentheses supplied). Astonishingly, American

---

[67] https://www.aclu.org/other/aclu-testimony-hearing-america-after-911-freedom-preserved-or-freedom-lost-senate-judiciary

[68] https://www.nytimes.com/2013/12/10/world/africa/nelson-mandela-south-africa.html?_r=0

[69] https://www.washingtonpost.com/wp-srv/photo/pope/dignitaries/day.html

[70] https://www.congress.gov/congressional-record/2005/04/18/extensions-of-remarks-section/article/E678-2

government officials chose to honor this pope despite the mountain of evidence concerning sexual abuse of minors found against Catholic clergy during his leadership.

After the death of Pope John Paul II, Pope Benedict XVI became the pope for eight short years. He criticized the United States tax havens for robbing the poor,[71] which is similar to the prediction found in Daniel 11:20 (NKJV), "Then shall arise in his place one who imposes (*"abar,"* can mean *"meddle"*) taxes on the glorious kingdom...." Moreover, in 2013, for no apparent reason, Pope Benedict XVI resigned—something that had not occurred in the Catholic Church for almost six hundred years;[72] likewise, Daniel 11:20 states, "but within a few days, he shall be destroyed, but not in anger or in battle."

Daniel 11:21(KJV) continues: "And in his place shall arise a vile person to whom they will not give the honor of royalty; but he shall come in peaceably, and seize the kingdom with intrigue." On March 13, 2013, Jorge Bergoglio became Pope Francis, replacing Pope Benedict in a peaceful transition. He is the first pope from the Americas and a Jesuit, an order of the Catholic Church formed in 1534 AD to oppose the Protestant Reformation. This Jesuit order was notorious for its cruel martyrdom of Protestants throughout Europe. According to John Wesley, by forty years after the beginning of the Protestant Reformation, more than *forty-five million* martyrs had been slain by the Jesuit Inquisition and other methods of Roman cruelty (italics added).[73]

---

[71] https://www.theguardian.com/world/2008/dec/07/pope-benedict-vatican-tax-havens-credit-crunch

[72] https://www.washingtonpost.com/local/pope-benedict-to-resign-citing-age-and-waning-energy/2013/02/11/f9e90aa6-743b-11e2-8f84-3e4b513b1a13_stor "Doctrine of Original Sin", Part I, section II.8, 1757, Wesley's Works, edited by Thomas Jackson, vol. 9, pp. 17-192

[73] http://www.alphanewsdaily.com/Number-of-Protestants-Killed-By-Popes.html

Ironically, in direct contrast to his Jesuit vows, Pope Francis is known for his merciful teachings of helping the poor, the marginalized, and the neglected. Unlike his predecessors, he has purported a humble lifestyle by traveling in a Ford Focus, living in a Vatican guest house instead of the Vatican palace, and cooking his own meals. Furthermore, he is quoted as saying, "Call me Francis," and has been named the common "people's pope."[74] His reputation has gained him the title of "Person of the Year" by the *"Times,"* and a nomination for the Nobel Peace Prize in 2014.[75] Notably, Daniel 11:21 (NKJV) predicts a religious leader whom "they will not give the honor of royalty, but he shall come in peaceably and seize the kingdom by intrigue."

Riding on a wave of unprecedented popularity, Pope Francis has pushed global political leaders, including those from the United States, to come into agreement on his socialistic agenda. He has vigorously opposed capitalism and economic inequality and urged governments to redistribute wealth.[76] In fact, Pope Francis has called capitalism the "dung of the devil" and blames it as "the underlying cause of global injustice and a prime cause of climate change."[77] Moreover, the pope urged former U. N. Secretary-General Ban Ki-moon "the world body must do more…" and encouraged the "legitimate redistribution of wealth,"[78] which parallels Daniel 11:39 (KJV), "he shall cause them to… divide the land for gain." Furthermore, Francis declared "a just distribution of the fruits of the earth and human

---

[74] https://poy.time.com/2013/12/11/person-of-the-year-pope-francis-the-peoples-pope/

[75] https://www.reuters.com/article/us-usa-pope-personoftheyear/pope-francis-named-times-person-of-the-year-idUSBRE9BA0JF20131211

[76] https://www.washingtonpost.com/news/acts-of-faith/wp/2017/07/13/confidant-of-pope-francis-offers-scathing-critique-of-trumps-religious-supporters/

[77] https://www.nytimes.com/2015/07/12/world/americas/in-fiery-speeches-francis-excoriates-global-capitalism.html

[78] https://www.reuters.com/article/us-pope-un/u-n-should-encourage-redistribution-of-wealth-pope-says-idUSKBN0DP0WU20140509

labor is not mere philanthropy. It is a *moral obligation*" (italics added).[79] The pope's insistence aligns with Daniel 11:24 (NKJV):

> He shall enter peaceably even into the richest places of the province, and he shall do what his fathers have not done, nor his forefathers: he shall disperse among them the plunder, spoil, and riches; and he shall devise plans against the strongholds, but only for a time.

On September 24, 2015, Francis made history by being the first pope to address the United States Congress in a formal session. In this meeting, he urged U.S. national leaders to take immediate governmental action against pollution, climate change, and irresponsible consumerism. *The Guardian* summarized Pope Francis's appeal to Congress by saying that he had "laid out a bold vision of a more compassionate America which could use its might and ingenuity to heal the 'open wounds' of a planet ravaged by hatred, pollution, and inequality."[80] Interestingly, Bible prophecy predicts that a "wound" would be "healed," and "all the world" would follow the beast (the papacy) (Rev. 13:3, KJV). Evidence of the pope's worldwide influence became prominent just a few months later when over a hundred and eighty nations (including the U.S.) came together and signed the Paris Agreement concerning climate change.[81] This historic global pact was compliant with Pope Francis's second encyclical, entitled, *"Laudato Si, On Care of our Common Home,"* declared by the *New York Times* to be "one of the shrewdest documents issued by the Vatican during the past century" that "reveals Francis as a wily and sophisticated politician of the first order."[82]

When Pope Francis returned to the Vatican in 2015, after

[79] https://fortune.com/2015/09/14/pope-francis-capitalism-inequality/
[80] https://www.theguardian.com/world/2015/sep/24/pope-francis-congress-speech
[81] https://unfccc.int/process/the-paris-agreement/status-of-ratification
[82] https://www.nytimes.com/2015/06/29/opinion/the-popes-ecological-vow.html

his historic speech to the United States Congress in formal session, he pushed Protestant, Islamic, Jewish, Orthodox, and a variety of other religious world leaders to unite on common points of faith. Pope Francis told 700 representatives of Islam, Judaism, and other faiths, "Religions, in particular, cannot renounce the urgent task of building bridges between peoples and cultures."[83] Moreover, he invited all to enter the "ark of fraternity," or, he warned, "there will not be a future."[84]

Tragically, in 2017, most mainline Protestant churches joined the pope's "ark of fraternity" by signing, *From Conflict to Communion,* a declaration of unity between the Lutherans and Catholics on the doctrine of justification, which some have claimed, ended the Protestant Reformation.[85] Daniel 11:22 (NKJV) expounds, "With the force of a flood they shall be swept away from before him and be broken and also the prince of the covenant." This flood imagery is used in Revelation 12:15 (KJV), "So the serpent (Satan [Rev. 12:9]) cast out of his mouth water as a flood, after the woman (church [Jer. 6:2]), that he might cause her to be carried away of the flood" (parenthesis added; compare Jer. 46:7). This "flood" of ecumenicalism, supported by Protestant leaders, was the result of the papal scheming that occurred in the 2016-2017 meetings of the Council of Cardinal Advisors, a small handful of influential leaders that Pope Francis appointed to guide him, likely aligning with Daniel 11:23 (NKJV): "And after the league is made with him he shall act deceitfully, for he shall come up and become strong with a small number of people." This "flood" of deception would sweep away the biblical doctrines of Christ's church through ecumenical compromise.

---

[83] https://www.americamagazine.org/faith/2019/02/04/pope-francis-worlds-religious-leaders-we-build-future-together-or-there-will-be-no
[84] ibid
[85] https://www.ncronline.org/news/world/reformed-churches-endorse-catholic-lutheran-accord-key-reformation-dispute

Not all, though, have been supportive of Pope Francis's ecumenical initiative. Because of the wide differences still existing between Catholic and Protestant doctrines, some conservative religious leaders have accused Pope Francis of deceptive teachings by stating:

> ... the Roman Catholic Church's basic view of salvation, which is dependent on the mediation of the Church, the distribution of grace by means of its sacraments, the intercession of the saints, and purgatory, is still firmly in place, even after the Joint Declaration.[86]

They claim that neither side is correct in stating that the theological differences in their respective denominations have been reconciled, and this ecumenical unity does not represent the truth of God's Word.[87]

However, the vast majority of Catholic and Protestant leaders have applauded this interdenominational alliance, ignoring the doctrinal differences and only highlighting the similarities. Pope Francis, himself, made a sweeping summary of this ecumenical event by stating, "Today, Lutherans and Catholics, Protestants, all of us agree on the doctrine of justification."[88] Similarly, the Lutheran World Federation's assistant general secretary, Dr. Kaisamari Hintikka, concurred, "The fact that all the historical churches of the west have now a shared understanding of justification is a wonderful way to mark the Reformation anniversary.... *What used to divide us, now actually unites us"*[89] (italics & bold type added). In stark contrast to this ecumenicalism,

---

[86] https://www.thegospelcoalition.org/article/is-the-reformation-over-a-statement-of-evangelical-convictions/

[87] ibid

[88] https://www.catholicnewsagency.com/news/full-text-pope-francis-inflight-press-conference-from-armenia-45222

[89] http://www.anglicannews.org/news/2017/10/lutherans,-catholics-methodists-reformed-and-anglicans-drawn-into-deeper-communion.aspx

Daniel 11:27 (NKJV) warns, "Both these kings' hearts shall be bent on evil, and they shall speak lies at the same table…. For the end will still be at the *appointed time*" (*"mow'ed"* [compare Dan. 11:29, 35).

Although the purported purpose of this Protestant/Catholic declaration is to bring peace and stability to all Christians, Pope Francis has openly declared his disdain for those who keep Christ's covenant (God's law [Jer. 31:31-33]). In fact, during a homily delivered on January 27, 2017, in Casa Santa Marta, Pope Francis criticized "Christians who avoid taking risks out of concern for the Ten Commandments."[90] He claimed that these fundamentalists suffer from "cowardliness," warning that such people become "paralyzed," and are unable to "go forward."[91] Piggybacking on these statements, he also declared "Christians, who do not have the will to continue… who do not struggle for a change of things, for new things to come," fight against those changes which "would be a good for everybody."[92] He even went further by stating "religious fundamentalism must be combated. It is not religious, God is lacking, it is *idolatrous*"[93] (italics added). These claims align with Daniel 11:28 (NKJV):

> While returning to his land with great riches (supporters), his heart shall be moved against the holy covenant (the Ten Commandments); so he shall do damage and return to his own land (Italy). (parentheses added)

Moreover, Pope Francis accused religious fundamentalists of having the mental structure of "violence in the name of God."[94]

---

[90] https://www.lifesitenews.com/news/watch-pope-accuses-his-critics-of-coward-liness-for-overfocus-on-following-1

[91] ibid

[92] ibid

[93] https://www.ncronline.org/blogs/ncr-today/pope-francis-continues-his-critique-re-ligious-fundamentalism

[94] https://www.catholicworldreport.com/2016/08/09/francis-and-fundamentalism/

While stressing that commandment-keeping Christians must abandon this brutal mindset, he declared "Muslim terrorism does not exist."[95] Likewise, Daniel 11 states that the king of the North would "corrupt by flatteries" those who "do wickedly against the covenant (the Ten Commandments [Dan. 11:30, 32; parentheses added]).

In contrast to his accusations against commandment-keeping Christians, Pope Francis has championed a dramatic positive change of attitude towards practicing homosexuals. When meeting Juan Carlos Cruz, the pope excused his gay lifestyle by stating, "It doesn't matter. God made you like this," echoing his former question concerning homosexuality, "Who am I to judge?"[96] Recently, Pope Francis has publicly supported same-sex marriages,[97] which, along with the papacy's mandate of priestly celibacy, likely aligns with Daniel 11:37 (KJV): "He shall regard neither the God of his fathers nor the desire of women, nor regard any god: for he shall magnify himself above all."

What gives Pope Francis the right to make such astonishing unfounded statements? Perhaps one of the reasons for the world's rapt attention to his declarations is the fact that he claims to be the "Vicar of Jesus Christ" on Earth with the divine authority of Heaven itself.[98] Interestingly, Daniel 11:36 (KJV) says:

> And the king shall do according to his will; and he shall exalt himself, and magnify himself above every god, and shall speak marvelous things against the God of gods, and

---

[95] https://www.dailymail.co.uk/news/article-4237706/Muslim-terrorism-does-not-exist.html; https://cruxnow.com/vatican/2019/01/08/popes-outreach-to-islamic-world-in-2019-has-deep-roots/

[96] https://www.cnn.com/2018/05/25/world/pope-lgbt/index.html

[97] https://www.nytimes.com/2020/10/21/world/europe/pope-francis-same-sex-civil-unions.html

[98] https://www.nbcnewyork.com/news/national-international/Pope-Titles--196518461.html

shall prosper till the indignation be accomplished: for that is determined shall be done (compare Dan. 8:19, 23-25; 9:26-27).

The pope continues to "prosper," and his claim as Heaven's voice on Earth today goes largely undisputed. A plethora of voices now asserts that "among all the world's political and social leaders, Pope Francis stands increasingly alone as the most powerful force for global peace and stability."[99]

However, the Bible declares that the papacy will "honor the God of forces" (Dan. 11:38, KJV) and destroy the 'inherent, natural, and unalienable rights" of freedom of religion, such as found in the American Bill of Rights (Rev. 13:7, 15). In direct contrast to these efforts, the Word of God never supports forcing anyone against his or her conscience!

Also, Bible prophecy predicts that the papacy will gain political power over the king of the South and its riches (the U.S. symbolized as Egypt [Dan. 11:42-43; Jer. 46:7-12]), even though Daniel 11:40 (KJV) warns, "And at the time of the end shall the king of the South (the U.S.) push at him." The Hebrew word for "push" in this text is *"nagach,"* which means to *"butt with horns."* This symbolism likely refers back to the larger conflict between the ram and the goat found in Daniel 8, which represents the great controversy between Christ's people (the ram) and Satan's (the goat). In the end, however, the papacy will not prevail, and Jesus and His remnant people will be victorious! (Dan. 8:25). Daniel 11:44-45 (KJV) promises:

> But tidings out of the east (where Christ returns [Matt. 24:27]) and out of the north (God's rightful kingdom location [Is. 41:25]) shall trouble him (the false king of the

---

[99] https://international.la-croix.com/news/the-radical-theological-vision-of-pope-francis/10477

North [the papacy])… And he shall plant the tabernacles of his palace between the seas (people [Rev. 17:15]) and the glorious holy mountain (God's kingdom—spiritual Israel, specifically Protestant America [Dan. 9:15-20; Eze. 20:40; Micah 5:8]), *yet he shall come to his end, and none shall help him.* (parentheses, italics, and bold print added)

Praise God that the historical accuracy of the Bible's prophecies can be verified, which gives the Lord's people trust in His predictions that still lie in the future! One day soon, the papacy will be destroyed at Christ's second coming, and Jesus, the rightful King of the North, will win the final victory! (Ps. 48:1-2).

Daniel 11 gives many warnings against the deceptions of the papacy and its insatiable desire for control over Protestant America and the whole world. The question is, *will we pay attention?*

| DANIEL 2 | DANIEL 7 | DANIEL 8 | DANIEL 11 |
|---|---|---|---|
| **Head- Gold** Nebuchadnezzar (**Babylon**/Jews) (605-539 B.C.) | **Lion** Eagle's Wings Plucked Stood/Man's Heart | | |
| **Shoulders/Arms** Silver **Medo-Persia** (539-331 B.C.) | **Bear** Side Raised 3 Ribs in Mouth Told to Devour | **Ram** Medo-Persia Abraham's Seed God's Kingdom | 3 More Kingdoms of Persia; Then 4rth Richer & Stronger |
| **Belly & Thighs** Brass- **Greece** (331-168 B.C.) | **Leopard** 4 Heads/4 Bird Wings Given Dominion | **Goat** Greece/Gentiles Satan's Kingdom | Mighty King Great Dominion Kingdom Divided into 4 & Uprooted (Greece) |
| **Two Lower Legs** Iron- Rome (168 B.C. – 476 A.D.) | **Terrible Beast** Iron Teeth/Brass Nails Ten Horns Tramples Remnant | From 1 of 4 Divided Kingdoms of Greece (Rome) | From 1 of 4 Divided Kingdoms of Greece (Rome) |
| **Feet** Iron & Clay **Papacy & USA** (476 A.D. - 2nd Coming) | **Little Horn** Defeats 3 Other Horns Wars Against Saints | **Little Horn** Sly, Proud King Destroys Saints (Roman Papacy) | **King of North** (Roman Papacy) **King of South** (USA) |

# Discussion Questions over Daniel 11

1. *How does the summary of Persian history give us a clue to the timing of the events Daniel saw in chapter 11? (Dan. 11:2)*

2. *How is the history of Greece and Rome likely summarized in Daniel 11:3-4? (Compare Dan. 8:8)*

3. *How do we know that Rome combined with Greece is symbolically located in the north? (Dan. 2:39-40; Jer. 15:12)*

4. *Why does the papacy desire to be the "king of the North"? Who is the true "King of the North?" (Is. 14:13; Ps. 48:1-2)*

5. *Who is likely symbolized by the "king of the South" and further described in Revelation 11:8 as being* **spiritually** *called "Egypt, Sodom, and where our Lord was crucified?" (Dan. 11:5, 8; 42-43; Is. 30:1-2, 6-7 [Egypt]; Eze. 16:46; Lam. 4:6 [Sodom]; Lk. 23:28, 33; Heb. 6:3-6 [Jerusalem- where Christ was crucified])*

6. *Who may be represented by the "daughter" of the "king of the South?" (Dan. 11:6; Jer. 6:2 [woman- Zion/God's people]; Rev. 17:5 [mother - Mystery Babylon]; Eze. 23:2-3 [daughters])*

7. *What happened between the "daughter of the king of the South" and the "king of the North" that likely occurred in 1994? (Dan. 11:6)*

8. *What happened again in 1999 and 2017 that propelled the unity of Catholics and Protestants, and what doctrine did they unite upon? (Dan. 11:17)*

9. *What historic event in the USA likely corresponds to Daniel 11:14, and what was its effect on the rights of American citizens?*

10. *Why does Daniel 11:20 possibly parallel Pope Benedict XVI's resignation?*

11. *What specific disturbing characteristics has Pope Francis displayed that seem to parallel Daniel 11, verses 21? 23? 24? 28? 30? 32a? 36? 37? 38? 39?*

12. *What comfort are we promised concerning the final outcome of the **false** king of the North? (Dan. 11:44-45) What will the true King of the North (Christ) do when He returns in the East? (Is. 41:25; Dan. 2:44-45)*

# Daniel 12 (KJV)

*¹ And at that time shall Michael stand up, the great prince which standeth for the children of thy people: and there shall be a time of trouble, such as never was since there was a nation even to that same time: and at that time thy people shall be delivered, every one that shall be found written in the book. ² And many of them that sleep in the dust of the earth shall awake, some to everlasting life, and some to shame and everlasting contempt. ³ And they that be wise shall shine as the brightness of the firmament; and they that turn many to righteousness as the stars for ever and ever. ⁴ But thou, O Daniel, shut up the words, and seal the book, even to the time of the end: many shall run to and fro, and knowledge shall be increased. ⁵ Then I Daniel looked, and, behold, there stood other two, the one on this side of the bank of the river, and the other on that side of the bank of the river. ⁶ And one said to the man clothed in linen, which was upon the waters of the river, How long shall it be to the end of these wonders? ⁷ And I heard the man clothed in linen, which was upon the waters of the river, when he held up his right hand and his left hand unto heaven, and sware by him that liveth for ever that it shall be for a time, times, and an half; and when he shall have accomplished to scatter the power of the holy people, all these things shall be finished. ⁸ And I heard, but I understood not: then said I, O my Lord, what shall be the end of these things? ⁹ And he said, Go thy way, Daniel: for the words are closed up and sealed till the time of the end. ¹⁰ Many shall be purified, and made white, and tried; but the wicked shall do wickedly: and none of the wicked shall understand; but the wise shall understand.* [11] *And from the time that the daily sacrifice shall be taken away, and the abomination that maketh desolate set up, there shall be a thousand two hundred and ninety days.* [12] *Blessed is he that waiteth, and cometh to the thousand three hundred and five and thirty days.* [13] *But go thou thy way till the end be: for thou shalt rest, and stand in thy lot at the end of the days.*

# The Time is Now

"What time is it?" All of us have probably asked this question. Time is an intricate part of human life because our days are numbered—our time is running out! As Daniel watched the closing scenes of his last vision (Dan. 10-12), he saw Michael (Christ), the "great prince who stands watch over the sons of your people..." arise to administer justice (Dan. 12:1, NKJV). When Jesus went back to Heaven after His resurrection, He was *seated* at the right hand of His Father (Acts 2:34-36). However, when Daniel saw Christ *stand*, this posture signals the close of probation and the execution of judgment (Is. 3:13). Then, the Bible warns, there will be a "time of trouble such as never was since there was a nation" (Dan. 12:1, KJV).

This great time of trouble occurs when Jesus declares, "He that is unjust, let him be unjust still; he that is filthy, let him be filthy still; and he that is righteous, let him be righteous still; and he that is holy, let him be holy still" (Rev. 22:11, KJV). All of the earth's inhabitants will have made their final decision—either to obey God and the everlasting law of His kingdom (The Ten Commandments [Ex. 20:1-17]) or Satan and his law of "Do what thou wilt."[100] Desolation of the earth from the seven last plagues will quickly follow after this final pronouncement of judgment as

---

[100] https://www.learnreligions.com/thelema-95700

Christ leaves His mediatory work in the heavenly sanctuary. However, Daniel is promised, "And at that time, thy people shall be delivered, every one that shall be found written in the book" (Dan. 12:1, KJV [Book of Life- compare Rev. 13:8; 20:15; 21:27]).

These words must have brought Daniel a measure of comfort, but he still longed to know more about the timing of these events. Then he heard a voice ask in Daniel 12:6 (KJV), "… How long shall it be to the end of these wonders?" In answer to this question, Daniel saw "a man clothed in linen" (priestly attire [Eze. 44:16-18]) standing "upon the waters of the river," who held up "his right hand and his left hand unto heaven" and swore "by him that liveth for ever…" (Dan. 12:5-7, KJV). This is clearly a reference to the pre-incarnate Christ, who had previously appeared between the banks of the river and instructed Gabriel to make Daniel understand the vision (Dan. 8:16). Moreover, Daniel describes this "man clothed in linen" in nearly the same manner as John describes Jesus in the book of Revelation: "… One like the Son of Man, clothed with a garment down to the feet and girded about the chest with a golden band" (Rev. 1:13). John also records a similar location and actions in Revelation 10:5-6 (KJV) when he writes of one standing upon the sea and the earth," who "lifted up his hand to heaven and sware by Him who liveth for ever…." This same body posture is found in Deuteronomy 32:40-43 when the Lord promises "vengeance to mine adversaries" and "atonement for His land and His people" (Deut. 32:43, NKJV). Only One of the Godhead could covenant with mankind by raising His hand in an oath (Deut. 32:39-40; Eze. 20:42; 36:7; Is. 49:22; 62:8), and Christ had been granted this right by giving His life for humanity at the cross (Is. 49:16; Heb. 7:20-28).

The prophecies in Daniel 12 are some of the most mysterious

in the entire Bible. Therefore, one must examine carefully Christ's answer to Daniel's question when the Lord held up His hands and swore by Him that "liveth for ever that it shall be for a time, times, and an half; and when he shall have *accomplished* to scatter the power of the holy people, all these things shall be finished" (Dan. 12:7; italics added). The Hebrew word for "accomplished," in this verse is *"kalah,"* the same word used in Daniel 9:27 for *"consummation."* "...and on the wings of abominations shall be one who makes desolate, even until the *consummation ("kalah")...*" This parallel may be a clue that Daniel 9's seventy-week prophecy ties to Daniel 12's time prophecies. This comparison will be further explored as one discovers that Daniel 12's 1,290-day and 1,335-day prophecies likely end in the same years as the repeated sixty-nine and seventy-week prophecies found in Daniel 9. Additionally, the seven weeks cut from Daniel 9's proposed repeated seventy-week prophecy appears to finish in the same year as Daniel 12:7's "time, times, and a half" prophecy.

So, what does Christ mean when He stated "the power of the holy people" would be shattered after a *"time, times, and a half"*? (Dan. 12:7). This timing **seems** to repeat the period mentioned in Daniel 7:25 (NKJV) that has been shown to predict the papacy's reign and its persecution of God's people:

> He shall speak pompous words against the Most High, shall persecute the saints of the Most High and shall intend to change times and law. Then the saints shall be given into his hand for a *time, times, and half a time.* (italics added)

In this text, the Aramaic word for *"time"* is *"iddan,"* meaning a *"year."* If one uses the historic day-for-a-year prophetic timing, 3.5 could be multiplied by 360 days in a Jewish year to get 1,260 days/years, which then could span from 538 AD to 1798 AD, the years that the papacy ruled politically in Europe.

However, the Hebrew word for "time" in Daniel 12:7 is *"mow'ed."* It is **not** the same word for "time" (*"iddan"*) used in Daniel 7. It is instead the same word used in Daniel 8:19, 10:1, and 11:27, 29, and 35 translated as the **"time appointed."** It means a *"fixed time or season,"* an *"appointed meeting for a definite purpose,"* and *"a signal or sign appointed beforehand."* Because it does not mean a "year" like the word for "time" in Daniel 7:25, perhaps Daniel 12's prophecy could refer to a different time period and events than those found in Daniel 7. It seems to better fit the meaning of the "time, times, and half a time" prophecy in Revelation 12:14 (KJV):

> And to the woman (the church [Jer. 6:2]) were given two wings of a great eagle, that she might fly into the wilderness, into her place, where she is *nourished* (compare Eze. 34:25-28) for *a time, and times, and a half of time* (*"kairos"* meaning *"a season or period of time"* [compare Gal. 4:10, KJV/NKJV]) from the face of the serpent." (Satan [Rev. 12:9]; parentheses & italics added*)

The Greek word for "time" in this passage in Revelation is *"kairos,"* meaning a *"set time,"* *"a fixed time,"* and *"the decisive epoch waited for."* This meaning of the word for "time" is nearly identical to the meaning of the Hebrew word in Daniel 12:7. Therefore, could this time prophecy refer to the same time period as Revelation and coincide with a period of history when the church would be *"nourished,"* and the "power of the holy people" would be "completely shattered," and "all these things" would "be finished"? (Dan. 12:7, NKJV).

Back in Daniel 12:7, the word, *"mow'ed"* refers to an *"appointed time"* (compare Dan. 11:27, 29, 35; Hab. 2:3). Similarly, in Daniel 8:19 (KJV), the Lord told Daniel, "Behold, I will make thee know what shall be *in the last end of the indignation; for at the **time appointed** the end shall be"* (italics & boldface added). The word for *"time appointed"* is none other than the word, ***"mow'ed,"*** the same Hebrew word for *"time, times, and a half"* in Daniel 12:7. According- ing to Daniel 8:19, the *"last end of the indignation"* would occur at the close of this time prophecy. The Hebrew word for indignation is *"za' am,"* meaning *"fury,"* especially of the Lord's displeasure with sin. By comparing Daniel 12:7, one can conclude that some- thing would happen among God's people ("Zion, city of... so- lemnities," [*"mow'ed"* - Is. 33:20, KJV]) after a "time, times, and a half" that would make Him angry and propel the final events of Earth's history. Interestingly, in Jeremiah 8:7 (KJV), the Lord mourns that His people do not recognize their *"appointed times"* for judgment. He cries: "Yea, the stork in the heaven knoweth her *appointed times ("mow'ed")* ... but my people do not know the *judgment* of the Lord." This text seems to associate the "appointed time" *("mow'ed")* with God's judgment, which began at the "cleansing *("tsadaq"= "to do or bring justice")* of the sanctuary" predicted in Daniel 8:13-14. The time prophecies, then, in Daniel 12, would likely start at the close of the 2300-day prophecy in 1844, the beginning date of the investigative judgment (Dan. 7:10; Heb. 10:19-21, 29-30; Deut. 32:34-36; 40-43). If one calculates these prophecies using God's method of timing found in Leviticus 25:8 and figures rotations of forty-nine years like the Jewish priests of old, a "time" (forty-nine-years) would be added with "times" (two forty-nine-year periods equaling ninety-eight years) "and an half" (24.5 years), totaling 171.5 years (Dan. 12:7; compare Is. 29:1). Then, if 171 and a half years is added to 1844, one arrives in 2015. This is the same year that Pope Francis made his unprece- dented speech to the U.S. Congress in formal session (something that no other pope has ever done before), and the papacy's political power significantly rose in the United States!

In his address to Congress, the pope urged the U.S. to join the world in taking immediate action on climate change and other social problems. Pope Francis stated:

> In Laudato Si', I call for a courageous and responsible effort to "redirect our steps," and to avert the most serious effects of the environmental deterioration caused by human activity. I am convinced that we can make a difference and I have no doubt that the United States – and this Congress – have an important role to play. Now is the time for courageous actions and strategies, aimed at implementing a "culture of care" and "an integrated approach to combating poverty, restoring dignity to the excluded, and at the same time protecting nature.[101]

The United States Secretary of State, John Kerry, followed the pope's counsel just seven months later on April 22, 2016, when he signed the Paris Agreement, along with over 171 other world leaders at that time.[102] Later, it was signed by President Obama before he left office.[103]

This historic event, urged by Pope Francis, bound the United States in an official global pact with most of the world's leading nations concerning climate change. Not surprisingly, this alliance has been reconfirmed by an executive order from President Biden,[104] who is Catholic.

---

[101] https://www.washingtonpost.com/local/social-issues/transcript-pope-franciss-speech-to-congress/2015/09/24/6d7d7ac8-62bf-11e5-8e9edce8a2a2a679_story.html
[102] https://www.cbsnews.com/news/us-climate-pact-un-signing-ceremony-paris-agreement-cop21/
[103] https://obamawhitehouse.archives.gov/blog/2016/09/03/president-obama-united-states-formally-enters-paris-agreement
[104] https://www.whitehouse.gov/briefing-room/presidential-actions/2021/01/27/executive-order-on-tackling-the-climate-crisis-at-home-and-abroad/

Amazingly, Daniel 12's "time, times, and an half" prophecy can be figured even more precisely if one begins the 171 and a half years on the date of October 22, 1844, the actual ending date of the 2,300-day prophecy. If 171 years are added to October 22, 1844, this prophecy ends on October 22, 2015. Then if an additional six months are added, one arrives on April 22, 2016, the *exact day of the signing of the Paris Agreement!* This is also the same year that ends the seven weeks cut from Daniel 9's proposed repeated seventy-week prophecy. Moreover, this type of world unity happening on this specific date in history has never occurred previously! One CNN commentator declared, "... the (Paris) agreement shows something that never has been apparent before: *The world is united on this issue.*"[105] More importantly, the world's alliance on climate change may have a far more reaching political and religious impact in the near future, and all of this may be happening in accordance with the timing of Daniel 12's prophecy!

Some might ask why the pope of Rome would be so interested in an agreement on climate change. Perhaps Pope Francis's own words in *"Laudato Si"* holds the key:

> Sunday, like the Jewish Sabbath, is meant to be a day which heals our relationships with God, with ourselves, with others and with the world. Sunday is the day of the Resurrection, the "first day" of the new creation, whose first fruits are the Lord's risen humanity, the pledge of the final transfiguration of all created reality. It also proclaims "man's eternal rest in God"... The law of weekly rest forbade work on the seventh day (cites Ex. 23:12)... And so the day of rest, centered on the Eucharist, sheds its light on the whole week, and motivates us to greater concern for nature and the poor.[106]

---

[105] http://www.cnn.com/2016/04/21/opinions/sutter-paris-agreement-whats-next/
[106] http://w2.vatican.va/content/francesco/en/encyclicals/documents/papa-fran-

By encouraging Sunday-keeping as a "day of rest" that "motivates us to greater concern" for nature and the environment, Pope Francis has second-handedly encouraged the world to unite under his leadership in worshipping on Sunday, the first day of the week, instead of on Saturday, the seventh day, in direct opposition to God's fourth commandment that states: *"Remember the Sabbath day to keep it holy. Six days shall thou labor and do all thy work. But the seventh day is the Sabbath of the Lord thy God"* (Ex. 20:8-10, KJV; italics supplied).

The Lord, Himself, sanctified the *seventh-day Sabbath* as a memorial of creation and commanded us to **remember** it! (Gen. 2:2-3). Jesus and the apostle, Paul, also kept it holy (Lk. 4:16; Acts 18:1, 4). Moreover, not one verse in the entire Bible says that Christ changed the Sabbath to Sunday, the first day of the week! Instead, God's Word says that the Sabbath is the Lord's covenant (Is. 56:6), and He will not alter a word from His lips (Ps. 89:34) nor should one word be added or taken away from His commandments (Deut. 4:2). He outlines His covenant in Ezekiel 20, which refers to keeping His Sabbath day holy. Also, the Lord states, "It is easier for heaven and earth to pass away" than for the smallest letter of His "law to fail" (Lk. 16:17, NKJV). Furthermore, He declares, "I am the Lord, I change not" (Mal. 3:6, KJV), and "If ye love me, keep my commandments (Jn. 14:15, KJV).

However, Daniel 7:25 (NKJV) warns God's people about one who would *"intend to change **times** (the Sabbath) **and law** (the Ten Commandments)"* (boldface & parentheses added). Daniel 8:19 gives a clue to God's reaction to the change of His "times and law" by stating that His anger would occur at the "time appointed" in the "last end of the *indignation*." Based on these texts, God is likely not pleased with what happened in 2015-2016 when the United States signed the Paris Agreement promoted by the

cesco_20150524_enciclica-laudato-si.html

Roman pontiff who unabashedly claims to have changed God's holy Sabbath and His Law (the Ten Commandments [Ex. 20:1-17]).

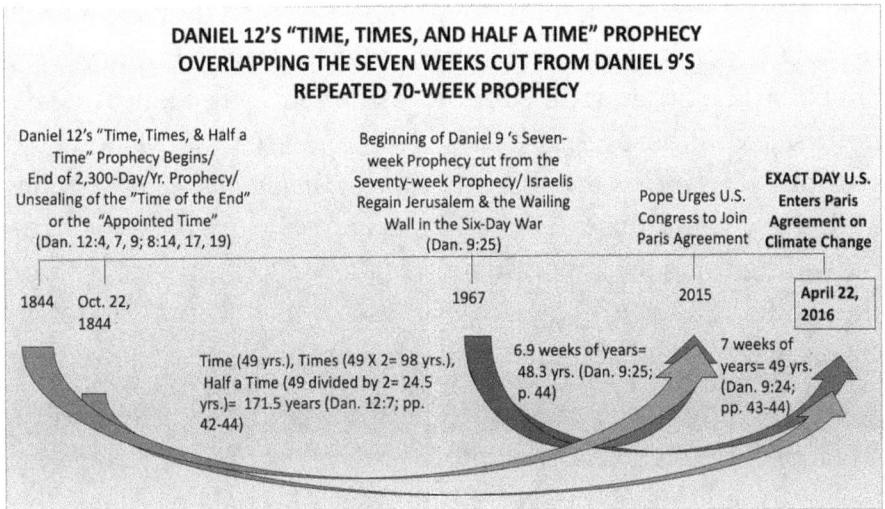

**DANIEL 12'S "TIME, TIMES, AND HALF A TIME" PROPHECY OVERLAPPING THE SEVEN WEEKS CUT FROM DANIEL 9'S REPEATED 70-WEEK PROPHECY**

Daniel 12's "Time, Times, & Half a Time" Prophecy Begins/ End of 2,300-Day/Yr. Prophecy/ Unsealing of the "Time of the End" or the "Appointed Time" (Dan. 12:4, 7, 9; 8:14, 17, 19)

Beginning of Daniel 9 's Seven-week Prophecy cut from the Seventy-week Prophecy/ Israelis Regain Jerusalem & the Wailing Wall in the Six-Day War (Dan. 9:25)

Pope Urges U.S. Congress to Join Paris Agreement

**EXACT DAY U.S. Enters Paris Agreement on Climate Change**

1844    Oct. 22, 1844    1967    2015    **April 22, 2016**

Time (49 yrs.), Times (49 X 2= 98 yrs.), Half a Time (49 divided by 2= 24.5 yrs.)= 171.5 years (Dan. 12:7; pp. 42-44)

6.9 weeks of years= 48.3 yrs. (Dan. 9:25; p. 44)

7 weeks of years= 49 yrs. (Dan. 9:24; pp. 43-44)

But Christ does not end His warning in Daniel 12 with the "time, times, and a half" prophecy. He also states in verse 11, "And from the time that the *daily* sacrifice shall be taken away, and the abomination that maketh desolate set up, there shall be a thousand two hundred and ninety days" (KJV; italics added). This prophecy is said to have begun when the "daily" sanctuary offerings of the Holy Place were "taken away" (Dan. 12:11; 8:13; 11:31). When did this likely occur? As previously stated, at the close of the historic 2,300-day prophecy, Christ moved into the Most Holy Place in 1844, ending the *"daily"* ministration in the Holy Place of the heavenly sanctuary (Dan. 7:9-14; Heb. 9:11-12; 24-25). Therefore, the 1290-day prophecy most likely began in 1844, again giving further evidence of this starting date for the other time prophecies found in Daniel 12. Moreover, if seven weeks (49 days) are multiplied by 1,290 days (God's timing found in Deut. 16:9; compare Lev. 25:8), they total 63,210 days. Then if this total is divided by 365 days in a year, it comes to 173 years. If 173 years are added to 1844, one arrives in the infamous year of 2017, the *very year* that most of the mainline Protestant Churches united back with the Catholic Church on the doctrine of justification by faith. This doctrine, according to Luther, is the "head and cornerstone" of Protestantism: "It alone begets, nourishes, builds, preserves, and defends the church of God, and without it, *the church of God cannot exist for one hour*" (italics added).[107] Could this 2017 ecumenical atrocity, then, have begun the setting up of the "abomination of desolation" and woes upon the United States of America because of its spiritual harlotry? (Eze. 16:22-23; Hab. 2:7, 9, 12, 15, 19; Rev. 18:10).

Interestingly, the modern repetition of Daniel 9's seventy-week prophecy could predict the same year of 2017 by referring to it as the ending of the sixty-ninth week of years. In review, this date is figured by adding 483 years (69 X 7) to 1534 AD (when the Ottomans commanded Jerusalem's walls be rebuilt [Dan. 9:25]), which ends in 2017. Daniel 9 also speaks of "one who will make desolate" rising to power at the end of the "abominations" (Daniel 9:27, NKJV; compare Dan. 11:30-31). Both Daniel 9 and 12 seem to predict this same year using two different time prophecies that refer to similar events which Jesus declares would happen at the end of time (Matt. 24:15; compare Eze. 7-8).

How did the Christian world begin setting up this "abomination of desolation" in 2017? As stated previously, Protestant leaders united themselves with the papacy which has blatantly tried to change God's holy law and promotes that salvation is a combination of faith and works, specified by the traditions of the Roman Catholic Church. This stark difference from the original Protestant doctrine of justification by faith alone cannot be over-emphasized! It was on this belief that Protestants originally

---

[107] https://www.issuesetcarchive.org/issues_site/resource/archives/preus.htm

separated themselves from the "mother" church and its "abominations" because they proclaimed that Christ gained man's redemption at the cross and good works could not earn salvation (Rev. 17:5, KJV; Rom. 3:24-28). Therefore, this controversial union on the doctrine of justification in 2017 has prompted many to declare that mainline Protestants have united under the authority of the papacy and its unbiblical teachings, thus ending the protest of the Reformation.

The ecumenical movement between Protestant America and the Catholic Church is further mapped out in the book of Revelation, which picks up where Daniel's last vision ends. As previously stated, Daniel's description of the Son of Man in Daniel 10:5-6 parallels the description of John's vision of the Son of Man in Revelation 1:13-15, likely tying the two books together. The rest of the book of Revelation fills in missing details that describe the process of Protestantism joining Catholicism, which, in turn, ushers in the closing events of Earth's history. Therefore, God, in His compassion for His people, has given a roadmap that outlines the signs, specifically occurring at certain times, that would take place just before Christ's second coming. It is the duty of God's watchmen today to read and understand these prophecies found in the books of Daniel and Revelation so that none will be deceived during these last days!

Unfortunately, like Daniel, some may be overwhelmed by God's timing and cry, "'Although I heard, I did not understand.' Then I said, 'My lord, what shall be the end of these things?'" (Dan. 12:8, NKJV). The promise of wisdom for this dilemma is found in Daniel 12:10 (KJV): "Many shall be purified, and made white, and tried; but the wicked shall do wickedly, and none of the wicked shall understand, but the wise shall understand." If God's people pray for wisdom, they are promised that they *will* comprehend these prophecies (James 1:5). He will make them clear to His followers (Jn. 16:13).

In fact, Daniel is told that a blessing is given to those who *wait* and come "to the one thousand three hundred and thirty-five days" (Dan. 12:12, NKJV). Interestingly, Habakkuk was also told to wait: "for the vision is yet for an *appointed time ("mow'ed")*, but *at the end*, it will speak, and it will not lie; though it tarry, *wait for it*; because it will surely come, it will not tarry" (Hab. 2:3, KJV; italics added). The same Hebrew word for "wait" used in both passages is *"chakah,"* meaning *"to wait for or long for."* What were Habakkuk and Daniel supposed to wait for? It was for the *"appointed time"* or *"mow'ed,"* that would occur *"at the end."* As previously shown, this same "appointed time" is referred to in Daniel 8:19, "… for at the *time appointed (mow'ed), the end shall be"* (KJV; italics added) and Daniel 12:7's (KJV), "time *("mow'ed)*, times, and a half." Likely these texts, then, point to a specific time in the end.

Since both Daniel 12:7's "time, times, and a half" prophecy and Daniel 12:11's 1290-day prophecy likely began in 1844 when the daily sacrifice ended at the close of the 2300-day prophecy, it is logical to use this same starting date for Daniel 12:12's prophecy of the 1,335-day prophecy. Therefore, if 1,335 days are multiplied by forty-nine (Deut. 16:9; compare Lev. 25:8), they total 65,415 days. Then if this product is divided by 365 days in a year, it totals 179 years. If this time period is added to October 22, 1844 (the ending date of the 2,300-day prophecy), it ends in October of 2023. Amazingly, this is just before the close of the repeated seventy-week prophecy beginning in 1534 AD, the earliest command to rebuild Jerusalem's walls by the Ottomans, and ending 490 years later in 2024.

According to this 1335-day prophecy of Daniel 12, God's people are promised that if they wait and stay committed to Him throughout this time, they will receive a blessing (Dan. 12:12; compare Is. 30:18; 40:31). The apostle, Paul, states in the New Testament:

> Cast not away therefore your confidence, which hath great recompense of reward. For ye have need of patience, so that after ye have done the will of God, ye might receive the promise: *"For yet a little while and he that shall come will come and will not tarry.* Now the just shall live by faith...." (Heb. 10:35-38, KJV; italics added)

This prophecy does not specify just what all this blessing entails, but God will soon reward His faithful followers and end the desolation of His church. (Ps. 58:10-11; Is. 30:18; Eze. 22:25-31; Is. 29:13). Furthermore, He will bring His people back into an obedient covenant relationship with Him (Eze. 20:38). Moreover, the Lord will pour out the Latter Rain so that His people will have abundant power to proclaim His soon return! (Jer. 5:24).

Our prayer today should echo the Psalmist's: "Lead me in thy truth, and teach me: for thou art the God of my salvation: On thee do I wait all the day" (Ps. 25:5, KJV). May we stay ever faithful as we wait for the fulfillment of God's Word, knowing that the time for His return is near, even at the very door!

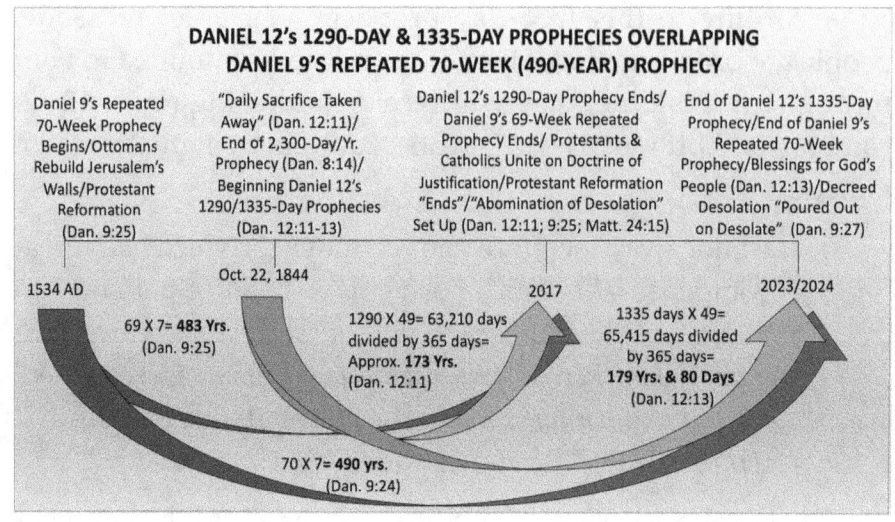

**DANIEL 12's 1290-DAY & 1335-DAY PROPHECIES OVERLAPPING DANIEL 9'S REPEATED 70-WEEK (490-YEAR) PROPHECY**

| Daniel 9's Repeated 70-Week Prophecy Begins/Ottomans Rebuild Jerusalem's Walls/Protestant Reformation (Dan. 9:25) | "Daily Sacrifice Taken Away" (Dan. 12:11)/ End of 2,300-Day/Yr. Prophecy (Dan. 8:14)/ Beginning Daniel 12's 1290/1335-Day Prophecies (Dan. 12:11-13) | Daniel 12's 1290-Day Prophecy Ends/ Daniel 9's 69-Week Repeated Prophecy Ends/ Protestants & Catholics Unite on Doctrine of Justification/Protestant Reformation "Ends"/"Abomination of Desolation" Set Up (Dan. 12:11; 9:25; Matt. 24:15) | End of Daniel 12's 1335-Day Prophecy/End of Daniel 9's Repeated 70-Week Prophecy/Blessings for God's People (Dan. 12:13)/Decreed Desolation "Poured Out on Desolate" (Dan. 9:27) |

1534 AD

Oct. 22, 1844

2017

2023/2024

69 X 7= **483 Yrs.** (Dan. 9:25)

1290 X 49= 63,210 days divided by 365 days= Approx. **173 Yrs.** (Dan. 12:11)

1335 days X 49= 65,415 days divided by 365 days= **179 Yrs. & 80 Days** (Dan. 12:13)

70 X 7= **490 yrs.** (Dan. 9:24)

# Discussion Questions for Daniel 12

1. *How can we deduce that the "man clothed in linen" that swore an oath is Jesus, not a common man or angel, and why would this be important? (Dan. 12:6-7; 8:15-16; Rev. 1:13; Deut. 32:39-40)*

2. *What promise does Christ make to the wise who study these prophecies? What should we do if we don't understand? What did Daniel do? (Dan. 12:3, 10; 9:3, 20-23)*

3. *When did the historical "time, times, and half" prophecy of Daniel 7:25 occur, corresponding to the time that the papacy ruled politically in Europe?*

4. *How does the meaning of the words, "time, times, and half" in Daniel 12:7 differ from Daniel 7:25 and is nearly identical to Rev. 12:14?*

5. What happened at the end of the proposed repetition of the "time, times, and half" prophecy found in Daniel 12:7?

6. Why is the pope's urgency to fight climate change by resting on Sunday instead of God's seventh-day Sabbath in direct conflict with the Ten Commandments? What example did Christ and His apostles leave concerning the sacredness of the seventh-day Sabbath? (Ex. 20:8-11; Deut. 4:2; Lk. 16:17; 4:16; Acts 18:4; Jn. 14:15)

7. What happened at the end of the repeated 1,290-day prophecy, likely concluding in 2017? Why is this year so significant to Protestantism? How does it correspond to Daniel 9's proposed repeated sixty-ninth-week prophecy? (Dan. 12:11; 9:25)

8. Although the Protestant nation of America may be in danger, what are we to individually wait for? (Dan. 12:12; Hab. 2:3; Ps. 25:5; 27:14)

9. What promises does the Lord make to all who wait on Him? (Is. 30:18; 40:31)

# Revelation 1 (KJV)

*¹ The Revelation of Jesus Christ, which God gave unto him, to shew unto his servants things which must shortly come to pass; and he sent and signified it by his angel unto his servant John: ² Who bare record of the word of God, and of the testimony of Jesus Christ, and of all things that he saw. ³ Blessed is he that readeth, and they that hear the words of this prophecy, and keep those things which are written therein: for the time is at hand. ⁴ John to the seven churches which are in Asia: Grace be unto you, and peace, from him which is, and which was, and which is to come; and from the seven Spirits which are before his throne; ⁵ And from Jesus Christ, who is the faithful witness, and the first begotten of the dead, and the prince of the kings of the earth. Unto him that loved us, and washed us from our sins in his own blood, ⁶ And hath made us kings and priests unto God and his Father; to him be glory and dominion for ever and ever. Amen. ⁷ Behold, he cometh with clouds; and every eye shall see him, and they also which pierced him: and all kindreds of the earth shall wail because of him. Even so, Amen. ⁸ I am Alpha and Omega, the beginning and the ending, saith the Lord, which is, and which was, and which is to come, the Almighty. ⁹ I John, who also am your brother, and companion in tribulation, and in the kingdom and patience of Jesus Christ, was in the isle that is called Patmos, for the word of God, and for the testimony of Jesus Christ. ¹⁰ I was in the Spirit on the Lord's day, and heard behind me a great voice, as of a trumpet, ¹¹ Saying, I am Alpha and Omega, the first and the last: and, What thou* seest, write in a book, and send it unto the seven churches which are in Asia; unto Ephesus, and unto Smyrna, and unto Pergamos, and unto Thyatira, and unto Sardis, and unto Philadelphia, and unto Laodicea. [12] And I turned to see the voice that spake with me. And being turned, I saw seven golden candlesticks; [13] And in the midst of the seven candlesticks one like unto the Son of man, clothed with a garment down to the foot, and girt about the paps with a golden girdle. [14] His head and his hairs were white like wool, as white as snow; and his eyes were as a flame of fire; [15] And his feet like unto fine brass, as if they burned in a furnace; and his voice as the sound of many waters. [16] And he had in his right hand seven stars: and out of his mouth went a sharp twoedged sword: and his countenance was as the sun shineth in his strength. [17] And when I saw him, I fell at his feet as dead. And he laid his right hand upon me, saying unto me, Fear not; I am the first and the last: [18] I am he that liveth, and was dead; and, behold, I am alive for evermore, Amen; and have the keys of hell and of death. [19] Write the things which thou hast seen, and the things which are, and the things which shall be hereafter; [20] The mystery of the seven stars which thou sawest in my right hand, and the seven golden candlesticks. The seven stars are the angels of the seven churches: and the seven candlesticks which thou sawest are the seven churches.

# A Snapshot of Jesus

Have you ever made a photo album of your favorite pictures? Maybe it contained snapshots of you and your sweetheart or perhaps pictures of you and your child. No matter who is in the photos, those pictures hold a special place in your heart. You treasure the album because it reminds you of the people you love! Did you realize that the book of Revelation is a photo album of Christ's "snapshots" of Himself and His bride? The Lord invites His children to see glimpses of His eternal love through the pages of the book of Revelation, which in its very name means *"a revelation of Jesus Christ"* (Rev. 1:1, KJV). Studying the prophecies of Daniel and Revelation without gazing in admiration of the Savior is like buying a camera but never taking a picture of your loved one!

The book of Revelation begins with a beautiful snapshot of the Trinity (1 Jn. 5:7). John starts his letter by stating in Revelation 1:4-5: "Grace be unto you and peace from him which is, and which was and which is to come (God, the Father [Rev. 1:6]), and from the seven Spirits which are before His throne (the Holy Spirit working through the seven churches [Rev. 3:1; 4:5; 5:6; Is. 11:2]), and from Jesus Christ"... who "loved us, and washed us from our sins in his own blood" (Rev. 1:5, KJV; compare Heb. 12:23-24). Each member of the Godhead has a specific role in man's redemption. Moreover, God, the Father, sent His Son to die so that Christ's followers could become "kings and priests" and live in truth through the power of the Holy Spirit, who reveals "things to come" (Rev. 1:6, KJV; Jn. 16:13, KJV). Additionally, Jesus promises a blessing to those that read and obey the "words of this prophecy and keep those things which are written therein…" (Rev. 1:3, KJV; 22:7). So all of the Godhead play active parts in man's salvation, preparing the Lord's people for Christ's return when every eye will behold His coming in the clouds (Rev. 1:7; Matt. 24:30).

It is no surprise, then, that the first chapter of Revelation describes Jesus as the Son of Man, resurrected in all His glory, located in the midst of the seven golden lampstands (churches [Rev. 1:12, 20]). John heard a voice as loud as a trumpet on the "Lord's Day," which Christ states is His seventh-day Sabbath (Rev. 1:10; Mk. 2:27-28; Matt.12:8; Is. 58:13; Ex. 20:8-11). This voice called John's attention to the vision of Jesus, clothed in priestly garments, which represents His current work of intercession in Heaven, mediating for His earthly followers (Rev. 1:13; compare Dan. 10:5; Is. 53:12; Heb. 4:14-15; 8:1-6). Christ is pictured as walking among the lampstands (His churches [Rev. 1:20]), demonstrating His constant care and leadership of His work on Earth.

John further describes Jesus as the "faithful witness, the first-born from the dead, and the ruler over the kings of the earth" (Rev. 1:5, NKJV; compare 3:14; Col. 1:18; Rom. 8:29). His head and hair were white as wool (Rev. 1:14; compare Is. 1:18; Prov. 16:31); His eyes were like fire (Rev. 1:14; Dan. 10:6; 2:22); and His feet shone like fine brass, refined in a furnace (Rev. 1:15; 2:18; Dan. 10:6). John saw a two-edged sword (God's powerful Word [Heb. 4:12]), coming from the Lord's mouth, and Christ's countenance gleamed like the "sun shineth in its strength" (Rev. 1:16; Dan. 10:6; Mal. 4:2). His voice echoed throughout the earth, powerful "as many waters" (Rev. 1:15, KJV; Jn. 4:13-14), and in His right hand of favor (Is. 41:10), He held "seven stars" (compare Dan. 12:3) or "seven angels of the seven churches" (Rev. 1:16, 20, KJV). Interestingly, in Revelation 21:17, a man is called an "angel." The Greek word for *"angel"* is *"angelos,"* which simply means, *"messenger."* So, the resurrected Lord is pictured as holding His people, the messengers of His Word, safely in His hands (Ps. 139:10). What a beautiful portrait of the Savior!

Moreover, Jesus states, "Fear not; I am the first and the last. I am he that liveth... and have the keys of hell and of death" (Rev. 1:17-18, KJV; Hosea 13:14). Christ's followers can trust His plan for their lives, and they don't have to worry about what lies ahead! This lack of fearfulness is one of the main reasons He sent His love letter of Revelation. He longs for all His children to have faith and assurance in facing the future (Rev. 1:4), so He tells them about "the things which are, and the things which shall be hereafter" (Rev. 1:19, KJV; compare Is. 42:9).

The Lord wants everyone to know the end of the story of the great controversy between good and evil—**Christ wins!** He is the one who wears the victor's crown! Jesus is the "King of Kings and Lord of Lords!" Revelation 19:11-13, 15-16 (KJV) states:

> And I saw heaven opened, and behold, a white horse, and he that sat upon him was called Faithful and True, and in righteousness he doth judge and makes war. His eyes were as a flame of fire, and on his head were many crowns, and he had a name written that no man knew but he himself. And he was clothed with a vestiture dipped in blood: and his name is called The Word of God. And the armies which were in heaven followed him on white horses, clothed in fine linen, white and clean. And out of

His mouth goeth a sharp sword, that with it he should smite the nations: And he shall rule them with a rod of iron… And he hath on His vesture and on His thigh a name written: KING OF KINGS AND LORD OF LORDS.

Soon every eye will see Christ's literal coming in the clouds, just like He returned to Heaven (Acts 1:9-11; Rev. 1:7; Luke 17:23-24; Matt. 24:30-31; I Thess. 4:16-17). Then, no one will need to look at a "photo album" and long for Jesus anymore. Instead, we will see Him face to face! (1 Cor. 13:12). Therefore, we have nothing to fear as we hold fast to the promises of God's Word!

# Discussion Questions for Revelation 1

1. *What photographs of family or friends are your favorites and why? How does Revelation 1 give us a snapshot of Jesus that portrays His great love for us? (Rev. 1:5)*

2. *What does the title of the book, "Revelation," mean? Who and what is it revealing? (Rev. 1:1-2)*

3. *How is the Trinity displayed in Revelation 1? What roles do each play in man's salvation? (Rev. 1:4-6; I Jn. 5:7; Jn. 1:1-5, 14, 18; 1 Jn. 3:1; Jn. 16:7-15)*

4. *How do we know what day is the "Lord's Day?" (Rev. 1:10; Mk. 2:27-28; Ex. 20:8-11)*

5. *Compare the description of Jesus in Daniel 10:5-6 with Revelation 1:14-16. What are the similarities and differences?*

6. *What is Christ's current work for His people in the heavenly sanctuary? (Rev. 1:5; Is. 53:12; Heb. 4:14-16; 8:1-2, 6)*

7. *How does Jesus "walking among the seven golden lampstands" give us a picture of Christ's love for His church? What do the lampstands represent? (Rev.1:12-13, 20)*

8. *How does the Lord, holding the seven stars in His hands, encourage His people today? What can the stars/angels figuratively represent? (Rev. 1:16, 20; 21:17; Dan. 12:3)*

9. *Why did Jesus send us the messages in Revelation? (Rev. 1:3, 19; Is. 42:9)*

10. *Who will see Christ's second coming? How does the Bible describe the Lord's return? (Rev. 1:7; 19:11-16; Acts 1:11; Luke 17:23-24; Matt. 24:30-31; I Thess. 4:16-17)*

# Revelation 2 (KJV)

*1 Unto the angel of the church of Ephesus write; These things saith he that holdeth the seven stars in his right hand, who walketh in the midst of the seven golden candlesticks; 2 I know thy works, and thy labour, and thy patience, and how thou canst not bear them which are evil: and thou hast tried them which say they are apostles, and are not, and hast found them liars: 3 And hast borne, and hast patience, and for my name's sake hast laboured, and hast not fainted. 4 Nevertheless I have somewhat against thee, because thou hast left thy first love. 5 Remember therefore from whence thou art fallen, and repent, and do the first works; or else I will come unto thee quickly, and will remove thy candlestick out of his place, except thou repent. 6 But this thou hast, that thou hatest the deeds of the Nicolaitanes, which I also hate. 7 He that hath an ear, let him hear what the Spirit saith unto the churches; To him that overcometh will I give to eat of the tree of life, which is in the midst of the paradise of God. 8 And unto the angel of the church in Smyrna write; These things saith the first and the last, which was dead, and is alive; 9 I know thy works, and tribulation, and poverty, (but thou art rich) and I know the blasphemy of them which say they are Jews, and are not, but are the synagogue of Satan. 10 Fear none of those things which thou shalt suffer: behold, the devil shall cast some of you into prison, that ye may be tried; and ye shall have tribulation ten days: be thou faithful unto death, and I will give thee a crown of life. 11 He that hath an ear, let him hear what the Spirit saith unto the churches; He that overcometh shall not be hurt*

*of the second death.* <sup>12</sup> *And to the angel of the church in Pergamos write;
These things saith he which hath the sharp sword with two edges;* <sup>13</sup> *I
know thy works, and where thou dwellest, even where Satan's seat is:
and thou holdest fast my name, and hast not denied my faith, even in
those days wherein Antipas was my faithful martyr, who was slain
among you, where Satan dwelleth.* <sup>14</sup> *But I have a few things against
thee, because thou hast there them that hold the doctrine of Balaam, who
taught Balac to cast a stumblingblock before the children of Israel, to
eat things sacrificed unto idols, and to commit fornication.* <sup>15</sup> *So hast
thou also them that hold the doctrine of the Nicolaitanes, which thing I
hate.* <sup>16</sup> *Repent; or else I will come unto thee quickly, and will fight
against them with the sword of my mouth.* <sup>17</sup> *He that hath an ear, let
him hear what the Spirit saith unto the churches; To him that overcometh will I give to eat of the hidden manna, and will give him a white
stone, and in the stone a new name written, which no man knoweth saving he that receiveth it.* <sup>18</sup> *And unto the angel of the church in Thyatira
write; These things saith the Son of God, who hath his eyes like unto a
flame of fire, and his feet are like fine brass;* <sup>19</sup> *I know thy works, and
charity, and service, and faith, and thy patience, and thy works; and the
last to be more than the first.* <sup>20</sup> *Notwithstanding I have a few things
against thee, because thou sufferest that woman Jezebel, which calleth
herself a prophetess, to teach and to seduce my servants to commit fornication, and to eat things sacrificed unto idols.* <sup>21</sup> *And I gave her space
to repent of her fornication; and she repented not.* <sup>22</sup> *Behold, I will cast
her into a bed, and them that commit adultery with her into great tribulation, except they repent of their deeds.* <sup>23</sup> *And I will kill her children
with death; and all the churches shall know that I am he which searcheth
the reins and hearts: and I will give unto every one of you according to
your works.* <sup>24</sup> *But unto you I say, and unto the rest in Thyatira, as
many as have not this doctrine, and which have not known the depths
of Satan, as they speak; I will put upon you none other burden.* <sup>25</sup> *But*

*that which ye have already hold fast till I come. 26 And he that over-cometh, and keepeth my works unto the end, to him will I give power over the nations: 27 And he shall rule them with a rod of iron; as the vessels of a potter shall they be broken to shivers: even as I received of my Father. 28 And I will give him the morning star. 29 He that hath an ear, let him hear what the Spirit saith unto the churches.*

# Crucial Counsel for Christ's Church Today

# Part 1

Many have heard of the parable of the foolish man who was stranded on his rooftop in the middle of a flood. Desperately, the man prays that God will rescue him; however, when given the opportunity, he repeatedly refuses to leave his roof. As the man is drowning, he asks God why he was not saved. The Lord simply replies, "I sent you a boat and a helicopter. What more did you want?" Similarly, Jesus has sent seven specific messages found in the book of Revelation, chapters two and three, that apply to His church throughout history and extend to the end of time. The question is, are we willing to heed Christ's urgent warnings and be saved?

### The Ephesian Message

Today Christianity is facing many of the same challenges as the church in Ephesus and its symbolic time period during the first century following Christ's resurrection. Sadly, these Christians were rebuked for forgetting their "first love" (Rev. 2:4-5). Many Gnostic teachings, resulting from the mixture of Christianity and paganism, attacked the early church. One such false teacher who promoted the beliefs of the Nicolaitans was Cerinthus, a contemporary of the apostle, John, who taught against the biblical view of creation.[108] Perhaps from John's influence, the Ephesians were not deceived by the Nicolaitans and hated their deeds just as

---

[108] https://www.cogwriter.com/cerinthus.htm

Christ did (Rev. 2:6). However, in this present age, these same false teachings have saturated God's church. Evolution is so prominent in today's culture that many Christians purport this theory's philosophy in place of a literal six-day creation. In fact, a Pew Research survey found that sixty-six percent of Catholics and sixty-five percent of mainline Protestant church members believe in Darwin's theory of evolution.[109] Additionally, Pope Francis has embraced this philosophy by saying it goes "hand in hand with religious doctrine."[110] He also claims that the Big Bang theory, widely accepted as the origin of the world, "does not contradict the creative intervention of God—on the contrary, it requires it," and "evolution in nature is not in contrast with the notion of creation."[111] Amazingly, most Protestant churches agree! Although today scientific philosophies are attacking the Bible, Revelation 14:7 (KJV) says, "Fear God and give glory to him… worship him who made heaven, and earth, and the sea, and fountains of water."

Mercifully, Jesus, our Creator, promises His people that He walks in the midst of the seven candlesticks (churches [Rev. 1:20]) and holds the seven stars in His right hand (Rev. 2:1). His people are the apple of His eye! (Zech. 2:8). He commends the Ephesians for their hard work and their patience; they have persevered and labored for His name's sake, not becoming weary (Rev. 2:2-3). Also, they have tested those who claimed to be apostles (but are liars), and have not tolerated evil (Rev. 2:2). Yet, Christ warned that they needed to repent and do their first works (Rev. 2:5), promising that if they would overcome through His power, they would eat from the tree of life in the Paradise of God (Rev. 2:7).

---

[109] https://www.pewforum.org/2019/02/06/the-evolution-of-pew-research-centers-survey-questions-about-the-origins-and-development-of-life-on-earth/
[110] http://www.usnews.com/news/articles/2014/10/28/pope-francis-backs-the-big-bang-theory-evolution)
[111] ibid

Jesus repeats this assurance for those of us living today. He lovingly implores:

> If my people which are called by my name (Christians) shall humble themselves, and pray and seek my face, and turn from their wicked ways; then I will hear from heaven, and will forgive their sin, and will heal their land." (2 Chron. 7:14, KJV; parenthesis added)

If we will repent and obey God's commandments through Christ's power, then we may "have the right to the tree of life" on the day when Christ returns to take us home" (Rev. 22:14, KJV).

## The Smyrnean Message

Just as Satan attacked the Ephesians, he also warred against the church of Smyrna through overt persecution, just as he does today (Rev. 2:9-10; Matt. 5:11-12). According to *Easton's Bible Dictionary*, the name *"Smyrna"* means *"myrrh,"* the incense used to anoint the dead, which is symbolic of the Christian persecution throughout history. Like in Smyrna during the first through the third centuries after Christ's death, persecution around the world is rampant currently. According to a recent article, more people have been martyred for their faith during the twentieth century than in "all the previous centuries combined."[112] In fact, "during this century," there are "documented cases in excess of twenty-six million martyrs. From AD 33 to 1900," only "fourteen million martyrs" have been documented.[113] This is almost twice as many Christians dying for their faith recently than the total of all the martyrs since Christianity first began!

---

[112] https://www.christianity.com/church/church-history/timeline/1901-2000/modern-persecution-11630665.html
[113] ibid

However, the physical assault on God's people pales in comparison to the spiritual battle within both the ancient church of Smyrna and the church today. Satan often uses so-called Christians to cause confusion and disruption (Rev. 2:9). Unfortunately, the Devil's subtle, yet devastating attack has resulted in internal conflicts within the modern church. Controversial issues such as women's ordination, homosexuality, transgenderism, woke philosophies, mandated vaccination, etc. are damaging the church's effectiveness in spreading the gospel.

Although physical and spiritual persecution has taken a toll upon God's people, Christ admonishes, "Do not fear any of those things that you are about to suffer..." (Rev. 2:10, NKJV). Instead, He promises, "Be faithful until death, and I will give you a "crown of life" (Rev. 2:10).

### The Pergamon Message

Similar to the believers in Smyrna, the church of Pergamon (Pergamos) also suffered affliction from pagan, and later, papal Rome during the fourth to the sixth centuries. According to tradition, the faithful martyr, "Antipas," referred to in Revelation 2:13, was the martyred bishop of Pergamon.[114] However, the name "Antipas" is derived from two Greek words: *"anti,"* meaning *"against,"* and *"pater,"* meaning *"father,"*[115] the same meaning as the Latin word for *"pope."*[116] Antipas, therefore, could be a symbolic name for the countless martyrs who stood against the pope throughout the ages.

Sadly, as overt persecution lessened, Satan found a more effective means of assailing God's people through the "stumbling

---

[114] https://oca.org/saints/lives/2013/04/11/101052-hieromartyr-antipas-the-bishop-of-pergamum-and-disciple-of-st-jo

[115] http://www.name-doctor.com/about-us.html

[116] https://www.dictionary.com/e/pope-benedict-name/

block" of compromise (Rev. 2:14-15). This spiritual cancer climaxed in the eventual infiltration of the beliefs of the Nicolaitans, who proposed a lifestyle of "sexual misconduct,"[117] "unrestrained indulgence," and "indifference in how a man lived."[118] Unfortunately, this carnal Christianity is still prevalent within the church currently, despite Jesus, Himself, stating twice that He hates this teaching of cheap grace (Rev. 2:6, 15). Unfortunately, when the Lord's law of love is not manifested in the life of a believer, worldly compromise is the sad result! Such was the case in the church of Pergamon—God's mercy was turned into lasciviousness. Sexual immorality, physically and spiritually, prevailed (Rev. 2:14). Likewise, within Christianity today, promiscuity is largely accepted. One report found that "sixty-one percent of Christians said they would have sex before marriage," and "fifty-six percent said that it's appropriate to move in with someone after dating for a time."[119] These findings are the sad result of God's people conforming to cultural norms. Weak morals are simply a symptom of a deeper spiritual malady among God's church throughout the ages.

Christ pleads with His people to repent or else He will "fight against them with the sword" of His mouth (Rev. 2:16, KJV; His Word [Heb. 4:12;]). But to all who overcome, Jesus promises that He will give them manna to eat (Christ [Jn. 6:50-51]) and a white stone with a new name (forgiveness/pure character [Is. 1:18; 62:1-2; Rev. 2:17]).

## The Thyatiran Message
In addition to the Pergamon church, the church of Thyatira was

---

[117] https://journals.sagepub.com/doi/pdf/10.1177/000842989402300407

[118] https://www.biblegateway.com/resources/encyclopedia-of-the-bible/Nicolaitans

[119] http://www.christianpost.com/news/christians-are-following-secular-trends-in-premarital-sex-cohabitation-outside-of-marriage-says-dating-site-survey-113373

also warned against sexual immorality, but this time Christ included the harlot, Jezebel, who called herself a prophetess and seduced God's servants (Rev. 2:20). Because the Bible often uses a harlot to symbolize a corrupt spiritual power (Jer. 3:1, 6; Eze. 16:14-15; Rev. 17:4-5), this "woman" likely represents the apostate church system rising to civil rule during the Dark Ages and claiming to be the "mother" of Christianity. Just as Jezebel mixed paganism with Judaism, the papacy has mixed paganism with Christianity, committing spiritual adultery. Like Thyatira, this church was given time during the Protestant Reformation to repent, but it did not (Rev. 2:21).

Today, one cannot only see religious corruption but physical abuse within the Catholic Church. In fact, "over 300 predator priests" in the United States alone have been prosecuted for multiple credible accounts of child molestation.[120] CNN reported that more than a thousand children have been molested over the past seven decades.[121] Yet initially, the Vatican prevented Catholic priests in the United States from taking action to confront this sexual abuse and only recently announced new in-house measures which rely "on the very same church structures that have been receiving and routing abuse allegations for years."[122]

In addition to this blatant immorality, Pope Francis has repeatedly excused homosexuality. For example, he told Stephan K. Amos, referring to his gay lifestyle, that "*it doesn't matter who you are or how you live your life,* you do not lose your dignity" (italics added).[123] However, this statement contradicts Leviticus 20:13

---

[120] https://www.cnn.com/2018/08/24/us/catholic-clergy-sex-abuse-state-investigations/

[121] ibid

[122] https://www.washingtonpost.com/world/vatican-establishes-new-rule-for-sexual-abuse-complaints-and-coverups-involving-bishops/2019/05/09/4571e0b0-71b5-11e9-9331-30bc5836f48e _story.html? noredirect=on&utm_term =.c6ff26916dde

[123] https://cruxnow.com/church-in-uk-and-ireland/2019/04/pope-francis-tells-gay-

(NKJV), "If a man lies with a male as he lies with a woman, both of them have committed an abomination." This contradiction of the Bible by the pope, as well as the multiple accounts of sexual abuse by Catholic clergy, are prime evidence that both spiritual and physical corruption continue to exist within the Catholic Church system.

Unfortunately, the pope's changing view of homosexuality has had a far-reaching effect. "In 2003, all major religious groups opposed same-sex marriage, with the exception of the religiously unaffiliated."[124] But according to a recent study, most religious groups now favor the legalization of same-sex marriage, including two-thirds of Catholics, Orthodox, and white mainline Protestants.[125] Therefore, the Bible's teaching against homosexuality is no longer accepted as the standard of many Christians' lifestyle practices.

This acceptance of papal falsehood has become prominent in the Protestant churches today, despite the firm commitment to biblical truth handed down from the Reformation, the symbolic time period of Thyatira. Throughout the Dark Ages, countless reformers sealed their testimonies with their blood in their effort to purify God's church from the papacy's unbiblical teachings. However, presently, the Lutherans and the World Communion of Reformed Churches (including 80 million members of Congregational, Presbyterian, Reformed, United, Uniting, and Waldensian churches) have joined with the Catholic Church on common beliefs. In 2017, both of these groups declared, "We rejoice together that the historical doctrinal differences on the doctrine of

man-you-do-not-lose-your-dignity-on-bbc-show
[124] http://publicreligion.org/research/2014/02/2014-lgbt-survey
[125] https://religionnews.com/2018/05/01/same-sex-marriage-has-support-among-most-american-religious-groups-study-shows/

justification no longer divide us."[126] Sadly, such ecumenical alliances between Catholics and Protestants continue to multiply today.

Like the church of Thyatira, many Protestant churches now are no longer protesting religious and physical immorality. They instead are committing spiritual adultery by uniting under the pope's leadership and adopting his liberal, cultural norms (Rev. 2:22; compare Eze. 23:37-39). However, God's people must not be seduced by this current ecumenical deception! Just as their forefathers did during the Protestant Reformation, true Christians must determine to faithfully adhere to the teachings of the Bible and the Bible only. Jesus promises:

> And he who overcomes, and keeps My works until the end, to him I will give power over the nations—'He shall rule them with a rod of iron; They shall be dashed to pieces like the potter's vessels'—and He will give him the morning star (Christ [Rev. 22:16]). (Rev. 2:26-28, NKJV)

In summary, all four of the messages found in the second chapter of the book of Revelation have pertinent and vital information for Christians living right now. Jesus pleads urgently, "He who hath an ear, let him hear what the Spirit saith to the churches" (Rev. 2:29, KJV). May we not resist God's Word, the means of our salvation, and drown in Satan's flood of deception! (Rev. 12:15-16). Instead, let us heed Christ's crucial warnings for His church today!

---

[126] https://religionnews.com/2017/07/06/reformed-churches-endorse-catholic-lutheran-accord-on-key-reformation-dispute/

# Discussion Questions for Revelation 2

1. What specific lesson can we learn from the message and history of Ephesus, specifically regarding the doctrine of creation versus evolution? (Rev. 2:2, 4-6; compare Rev. 14:7)

2. What does the name, "Smyrna," mean, and why is it a fitting description of God's people throughout the ages? (Rev. 2:8-10; Matt. 5:11-12) What surprising source does persecution sometimes come from? (Rev. 2:9)

3. What could the name, "Antipas," symbolize? (Rev. 2:13)

4. Why is compromise so dangerous for the church? (Rev. 2:14) What lifestyle was purported by the Nicolaitans, and how does Christ view this lifestyle? (Rev. 2:6, 14-15)

5. Who or what might "Jezebel" represent? Why might she be used as a symbol of this entity? (Rev. 2:20; 17:4-5; Jer. 3:1, 6; Eze. 16:14-15)

6. How is sexual immorality still prevalent in our society today? Why does God use immorality as a symbol of spiritual idolatry and corruption? (Eze. 23:37-39)

7. How might the Protestant churches today be committing spiritual adultery through their unity with the Catholic Church?

# Revelation 3 (KJV)

*¹ And unto the angel of the church in Sardis write; These things saith he that hath the seven Spirits of God, and the seven stars; I know thy works, that thou hast a name that thou livest, and art dead. ² Be watchful, and strengthen the things which remain, that are ready to die: for I have not found thy works perfect before God. ³ Remember therefore how thou hast received and heard, and hold fast, and repent. If therefore thou shalt not watch, I will come on thee as a thief, and thou shalt not know what hour I will come upon thee. ⁴ Thou hast a few names even in Sardis which have not defiled their garments; and they shall walk with me in white: for they are worthy. ⁵ He that overcometh, the same shall be clothed in white raiment; and I will not blot out his name out of the book of life, but I will confess his name before my Father, and before his angels. ⁶ He that hath an ear, let him hear what the Spirit saith unto the churches. ⁷ And to the angel of the church in Philadelphia write; These things saith he that is holy, he that is true, he that hath the key of David, he that openeth, and no man shutteth; and shutteth, and no man openeth; ⁸ I know thy works: behold, I have set before thee an open door, and no man can shut it: for thou hast a little strength, and hast kept my word, and hast not denied my name. ⁹ Behold, I will make them of the synagogue of Satan, which say they are Jews, and are not, but do lie; behold, I will make them to come and worship before thy feet, and to know that I have loved thee. ¹⁰ Because thou hast kept the word of my patience, I also will keep thee from the hour of temptation, which shall come upon all the world, to try them that dwell upon the earth. [11] Behold, I come quickly: hold that fast which thou hast, that no man take thy crown. [12] Him that overcometh will I make a pillar in the temple of my God, and he shall go no more out: and I will write upon him the name of my God, and the name of the city of my God, which is new Jerusalem, which cometh down out of heaven from my God: and I will write upon him my new name. [13] He that hath an ear, let him hear what the Spirit saith unto the churches. [14] And unto the angel of the church of the Laodiceans write; These things saith the Amen, the faithful and true witness, the beginning of the creation of God; [15] I know thy works, that thou art neither cold nor hot: I would thou wert cold or hot. [16] So then because thou art lukewarm, and neither cold nor hot, I will spue thee out of my mouth. [17] Because thou sayest, I am rich, and increased with goods, and have need of nothing; and knowest not that thou art wretched, and miserable, and poor, and blind, and naked: [18] I counsel thee to buy of me gold tried in the fire, that thou mayest be rich; and white raiment, that thou mayest be clothed, and that the shame of thy nakedness do not appear; and anoint thine eyes with eyesalve, that thou mayest see. [19] As many as I love, I rebuke and chasten: be zealous therefore, and repent. [20] Behold, I stand at the door, and knock: if any man hear my voice, and open the door, I will come in to him, and will sup with him, and he with me. [20] To him that overcometh will I grant to sit with me in my throne, even as I also overcame, and am set down with my Father in his throne. [22] He that hath an ear, let him hear what the Spirit saith unto the churches.*

# Crucial Counsel for Christ's Church Today
# Part 2

In May of 1980, Harry Randall Truman, an eighty-three-year-old man, received an urgent request from authorities to evacuate the premises of the Mount Saint Helens Lodge at Spirit Lake. Unfortunately, Truman refused to heed their admonition, and both he and the lodge were buried under 150 feet of mud and rubble when the volcano erupted.[127] Likewise, Christ has given His church three additional warnings in the third chapter of Revelation in the messages of Sardis, Philadelphia, and Laodicea that are especially urgent for the salvation of His people today.

## The Sardian Message
Currently, Christian spirituality is dying in the United States, much like it did in the church of Sardis and its symbolic time period following the Protestant Reformation. During this period of history, disputes arose within Christianity, resulting in the unwarranted number of Protestant denominations still in existence today. Just as the Sardis church had the reputation of being alive but was spiritually dead (Rev. 3:1), God's church today must remember the biblical truths that they have received and repent. Christ warns, "If therefore thou shalt not watch, I will come upon thee as a thief, and thou will not know what hour I will come upon thee" (Rev. 3:3, KJV).

---

[127] https://www.usatoday.com/story/news/nation-now/2015/05/17/mount-st-helens-people-stayed/27311467/

Yet, even in this dismal condition, Jesus promises that He holds the seven stars in His hands (Rev. 1:20; 3:1). Like the stars in Heaven (Dan. 12:3), God's leaders are directed by Christ; otherwise, they would become "fallen stars," and the church would diminish and eventually perish. The Lord promises, however, to preserve a faithful remnant who will not defile their garments (Rev. 3:4; character [Zech. 3:3-4]). Moreover, He clothes them in white and does not blot out their names from the Book of Life, but confesses their names before His Father and His angels (Rev. 3:5). How wonderful it is that Jesus is the Head of His work, and it is under His control! Although conflict rages, Christ will not allow controversies to destroy His church. However, just as Jesus rebuked the church of Sardis for their hypocrisy (Rev. 3:1), Christ counsels us today to be watchful (Rev. 3:2). Otherwise, Christ may come as a thief, and we might be unprepared for His soon return! (Rev. 3:3; compare I Thess. 5:2-6).

### The Philadelphian Message

In contrast to Sardis, the church of Philadelphia receives no rebuke, only encouragement to persevere even if it has little strength (Rev. 3:8). This description of God's church seems to point to a time when it is faithful to the Lord, but it is physically very small (compare Zech. 4:9-10). Jesus introduces Himself to this remnant by saying that He holds the "key of David" and "openeth, and no man shutteth and shutteth and no man openeth" (Rev. 3:7, KJV). Of what door is He speaking? In Revelation 3:7-8, Christ passes through the heavenly door of the Holy Place and moves into the Most Holy Place where the Ark of the Covenant holds the Ten Commandments (Rev. 4:1, 2, 5; Rev. 11:19). This change of location signals the beginning of the investigative judgment for God's people, based upon the imperative standards of God's Law (Dan. 7:10, 26). It is no coincidence, then, that during the Great Awakenings of the 19th century (the likely symbolic time period of Philadelphia), the importance of keeping the fourth commandment, the seventh-day Sabbath, was rediscovered. However, Sabbath-keeping, today, continues to be challenged, especially by the papacy that has tried to "change times and law" (Daniel 7:25, NKV).

For example, recently, Pope Francis referred to the "commandment to keep Sunday" (not found in the Bible) and stated that Sunday, the first day of the week, is the "day of rest."[128] Throughout history, the Catholic Church has claimed to have changed the Ten Commandments, not only the fourth commandment that says to rest on Saturday, the seventh-day Sabbath but also the second that says not to bow down to idols, which has been deleted entirely.[129] Moreover, in 2018, the Salt and Light Catholic Media Foundation published an article that possibly explains why the pope claims to have the authority to alter God's Law:

> Pope Francis breaks Catholic traditions whenever he wants because he is "free from disordered attachments." Our Church has indeed entered a new phase: with the advent of this first Jesuit pope, *it is openly ruled by an individual rather than by the authority of Scripture alone or even its own dictates of tradition plus Scripture.* (italic supplied)[130]

According to this Catholic source, the pope has the power to supersede God's Word. Christ knew that this kind of deception would happen in the closing days of Earth's history, and He, in

---

128 https://www.catholicnewsagency.com/news/true-rest-is-found-in-christ---not-escapism-pope-says-46719
129 http://www.the-ten-commandments.org/romancatholic-tencommandments.html
130 https://web.archive.org/web/20180814070212/http://saltandlighttv.org/blog-feed/getpost.php?id=72516

contrast, grants a special blessing to all who keep His command-ments (Rev. 3:10; 22:14).

However, presently, some Christians are stressing a "Jesus only" philosophy that downplays the practical application of God's law manifested in righteous living. Christ warns His faith-ful followers of the "synagogue of Satan" (Rev. 3:9) who claim to be a part of God's remnant church but have crucified Christ and caused reproach upon His teachings (Heb. 6:6; Is. 5:20-21). These deceived brethren work to make void the law of God and cause confusion among His people (Rom. 3:31). However, like the church of Philadelphia, Jesus *commends* those who have kept His commandments and have not denied His name (Rev. 3:8-10).

In fact, He states, "Because thou hast kept the word of my pa-tience, I also will keep thee from the hour of temptation, which shall come upon all the world, to try them that dwell upon the earth" (Rev. 3:10, KJV). This hour of trial may have referred to the Great Disappointment that occurred in 1844 when Christ's followers thought Jesus would return. Although God's people were tested severely during this time, the Lord promised them, "Behold, I come quickly: hold thou fast which thou hast, that no man take thy crown" (Rev. 3:11, KJV). He continues by assuring them that if they overcome, they will become a foundational "pil-lar" of God's remnant church (grounded in truth [1 Tim. 3:15]) and have a new name (Rev. 3:12; compare Is. 62:1-2).

## The Laodicean Message

In direct contrast to Philadelphia, the Laodicean church receives no commendations by Christ; instead, its rebuke is a decisive warning for Christians today (Rev. 3:15-17). The tepid water piped into the city of Laodicea was a fitting symbol of its church's lukewarm spiritual condition.[131] Unfortunately, this lukewarm state is still evident in God's people presently. In a recent survey, Americans were asked, "If Jesus suddenly came back to earth, would He approve or disapprove of modern Christianity?" A mere seventeen percent said He would approve, and *eighty-three percent* said He would disapprove (italics added).[132] These statistics are evidence that lukewarm Christians, who are a part of the symbolic "synagogue of Satan," war against the purity of God's church today (Rev. 2:9, 3:9). Unfortunately, these imposters attack the church from within and tarnish its witness to the world.

Tragically, God's people often display this lukewarm condition in their lack of biblical knowledge. Although most Americans claim to be Christians, according to a Barna study, the majority don't believe that Satan or the Holy Spirit exists. And even though the Bible is very clear about the sinless nature of Christ, twenty-two percent believe that Jesus sinned while He was on the earth.[133] The Lord looks down upon His people's pitiful condition and calls them "poor, blind, and naked" (Rev. 3:17). He lovingly bids them to buy from Him gold refined in the fire, white garments, and eye salve (Rev. 3:18).

Gold, for the ancient Laodiceans, was abundant, and many were likely shocked at Christ's reference to their poverty, just as most Americans would be today. In contrast, the Laodiceans lived in a prosperous commercial center, located on a main trade

---

[131] https://archive.org/stream/citiesandbishop01ramsgoog/citiesandbishop01ramsgoog_djvu.txt (accessed 4-17-2022);https://theopolisinstitute.com/leithart_post/laodicean-water/

[132] https://themuslimtimes.info/2013/09/20/would-jesus-approve-or-disapprove-of-modern-christianity-poll-results/

[133] https://www.barna.com/research/most-american-christians-do-not-believe-that-satan-or-the-holy-spirit-exist/

route, so most citizens lived a luxurious life.[134] Likewise, in the United States, wealthy lifestyles are common. For example, NBA superstar, Michael Jordan, was paid more money than the 30,000 Indonesian workers *combined* who made shoes for Nike.[135] So when Jesus counsels both the Laodiceans and His church today to buy gold, what does He mean? First Peter 1:7 (NKJV) states that "the genuineness of your faith" is "more precious than gold." Therefore, the gold that the Lord longs to give His people is the gold of faith, tried by trials, and displayed in godly lives.

In addition to faith, Jesus invites His church, in both ancient and modern times, to buy from Him the eye salve of the Holy Spirit (Rev. 3:18). Interestingly, the Laodiceans were known for their purported knowledge of medicine, exemplified in their eye salve.[136] Doctors in the military of the United States still wear the symbol of a staff with a serpent(s) entwined around it, which likely originated from the cult of Aesculapius found in Laodicea.[137] When Christ appeals to His people throughout the ages to buy eye salve, He is offering them spiritual discernment to recognize their desperate need. Moreover, the message to the Laodiceans is especially applicable to those of us living today who boast that we know the truths of God's Word but do not allow its sanctifying power to change our lives. Jesus calls all of us to spend time with Him daily in His Word and prayer, allowing Him to change us into His image so that we might be prepared for His second coming (Matt. 13:15-16).

---

[134] https://turkisharchaeonews.net/site/laodicea-lycus

[135] https://www.american.edu/sis/faculty/upload/Global-reach-Workers-fight-MNCs-Nation-March-96.pdf

[136] https://turkisharchaeonews.net/site/laodicea-lycus

[137] https://www.ncbi.nlm.nih.gov/pmc/articles/PMC4439707/;
https://archive.org/stream/citiesandbishop01ramsgoog/citiesandbishop01ramsgoog_djvu.txt

Both now and in the past, Christ longs to give His followers white garments, which is purity of character (Is. 1:18). The ancient Laodiceans largely gained their prosperity by selling exquisite clothing made of black wool.[138] Perhaps this is the reason why Jesus offers them *His* white garments, referred to as the "righteousness of the saints" (Rev. 19:8, KJV). However, currently, when one talks about good works, it is often looked upon as legalism. Many Christian churches inadvertently teach this falsehood when they declare that the Ten Commandments were nailed to the cross, and love is all that matters. Instead of turning God's grace into a license to sin, Jesus pronounces a blessing on all who obey the commandments of the Lord out of their love for Him. He identifies His remnant people as those who "keep the commandments of God and have the testimony of Jesus Christ" (Rev. 12:17, KJV; 22:14; compare Jn. 14:15). Today, we are promised that if we persevere, we will sit with the Lord who is on His throne, just as Christ sat down with His Father who is on His throne (Rev. 3:21).

Finally, the Lord offers a snapshot of His tender mercy and patience in His closing words to the Laodiceans: "Behold, I stand at the door and knock. If any man hear my voice, and open the door, I will come in to him and sup with him and he with me" (Rev. 3:20, KJV). Christians are admonished not to wait but to open the door of their hearts to the Savior. Jesus pleads with both the Laodiceans and His modern church by declaring, "As many as I love, I rebuke and chasten: be zealous therefore, and repent" (Rev. 3:19, KJV; compare Job 36:9-10). Especially in these last days, we must accept His correction, repent of our sins, display a godly character, and unite in the mission of proclaiming Jesus's second coming to the world.

---

[138] https://turkisharchaeonews.net/site/laodicea-lycus

In summary, the letters to the seven churches found in the second and third chapters of Revelation present Christ's counsel to His church, not only throughout history but specifically to those of us living right now. Each of these messages contains harbingers that a spiritual "volcano" is about to explode, ending probation for all of mankind. Persistently, the Lord is knocking on every heart, urging us to accept His admonition and be saved. Will we open the door and choose to heed His warnings today?

## MESSAGES TO THE 7 CHURCHES (Rev. 2-3)

| Ephesus | Smyrna | Pergamos | Thyatira | Sardis | Philadelphia | Laodicea |
|---|---|---|---|---|---|---|
| Apostolic Church | Persecuted Church | Compromised Church | Apostate Church | Dead Church | Faithful Church | Lukewarm Church |
| **Description of Christ:** Holds 7 stars/walks among 7 lampstands | **Description of Christ:** First & Last/ dead & resurrected | **Description of Christ:** Holds a sharp, 2-Edged sword (Word of God [Heb. 4:12]) | **Description of Christ:** Eyes of fire/feet of brass | **Description of Christ:** Has 7 Spirits of God/ holds 7 stars | **Description of Christ:** Holy; true/holds the key of David/opens- no one shuts; shuts- no one opens | **Description of Christ:** Amen/Faithful/True Witness/Beginning of Creation |
| **Praises for Church:** Resisted evil/ persevered/labored/ hated deeds of the Nicolaitans (cheap grace) | **Praises for Church:** Rich in faith & good works, even though suffering poverty & tribulation | **Praises for Church:** Held fast to Christ's name/faithful unto death | **Praises for Church :** Love, service, faith, patience/last works exceed first | **Praises for Church:** Few have not defiled garments/worthy | **Praises for Church:** Did not deny God's word or name/ persevered | **Praises for Church:** None |
| **Warnings to Church:** Lost first love/ lampstand may be removed | **Warnings to Church:** Some are in the Synagogue of Satan/ will be tested & imprisoned | **Warnings to Church:** Some hold to the doctrine of Balaam (idolatry & immorality) & the Nicolaitans (cheap grace) | **Warnings to Church:** Commits sexual immorality & idolatry | **Warnings to Church:** Reputation of being alive, but dead/repent or be unprepared for Christ's coming | **Warnings to Church:** None (except little strength) | **Warnings to Church:** Lukewarm/wretched, miserable, poor, blind, & naked |
| **Commands to Church:** Told to be faithful/repent/ do first works | **Commands to Church:** Told to not fear persecution | **Commands to Church:** Told to repent or Christ will fight against them with the sword of His mouth | **Commands to Church:** Told to hold fast to what they have | **Commands to Church:** Told to watch/ strengthen what remains/ remember heritage | **Commands to Church:** Told to hold fast to what they have/don't lose their crown | **Commands to Church:** Told to buy gold (faith), white raiment (purity), eye salve (discernment) |
| **Promises to Church:** Will eat from the Tree of Life | **Promises to Church:** Will receive a crown of life/ not hurt in the second death | **Promises to Church:** Will give the hidden manna, a white stone, & a new name (pardoned & given a pure character) | **Promises to Church:** Will rule over the nations/given the Morning Star (Christ) | **Promises to Church:** Will be clothed in white raiment/name not blotted out from the Book of Life | **Promises to Church:** Will be kept from the hour of trial/will be a pillar in the temple/ given a new name | **Promises to Church:** Will chasten/dine together/sit on a throne with Christ |

# Discussion Questions for Revelation 3

1. What time period does the church of Sardis represent, and how does the message to Sardis specifically apply to us living in the last days? (Rev. 3:1-3; I Thess. 5:2-6)

2. When is the symbolic time period of Philadelphia, and how does judgment correspond to this timing? (Rev. 3:7-8; 11:19; Dan. 7:10, 26)

3. Who often consists of the "synagogue of Satan," and why are these members so dangerous for God's people? (Rev. 3:9; 2:9; Heb. 6:6; Is. 5:20-21)

4. How is the church of Laodicea different from the others? Why does this church receive no commendations? (Rev. 3:15-17) How do we see this spiritual "lukewarmness" in the church today?

5. Why does Christ say that the church of Laodicea is poor when it had an abundance of gold? How is this true for us today? What type of gold does Jesus want His church to buy from Him? (Rev. 3:17-18; I Peter 1:7)

6. What eye salve does Christ offer, and who especially needs this eye salve? (Rev. 3:18-19; Matt. 13:15-16)

7. What does "white raiment" symbolize? (Rev. 3:18; 19:8; Zech. 3:3-4) How do we know that keeping God's commandments is not legalism? (Rev. 12:17; 22:14; Jn. 14:15)

8. How should we view God's discipline and correction in our lives today? Why does God discipline us? (Rev. 3:19-20; Job 36:9-10, KJV)

# Revelation 4 (KJV)

*¹ After this I looked, and, behold, a door was opened in heaven: and the first voice which I heard was as it were of a trumpet talking with me; which said, Come up hither, and I will shew thee things which must be hereafter. ² And immediately I was in the spirit: and, behold, a throne was set in heaven, and one sat on the throne. ³ And he that sat was to look upon like a jasper and a sardine stone: and there was a rainbow round about the throne, in sight like unto an emerald. ⁴ And round about the throne were four and twenty seats: and upon the seats I saw four and twenty elders sitting, clothed in white raiment; and they had on their heads crowns of gold. ⁵ And out of the throne proceeded lightnings and thunderings and voices: and there were seven lamps of fire burning before the throne, which are the seven Spirits of God. ⁶ And before the throne there was a sea of glass like unto crystal: and in the midst of the throne, and round about the throne, were four beasts full of eyes before and behind. ⁷ And the first beast was like a lion, and the second beast like a calf, and the third beast had a face as a man, and the fourth beast was like a flying eagle. ⁸ And the four beasts had each of them six wings about him; and they were full of eyes within: and they rest not day and night, saying, Holy, holy, holy, Lord God Almighty, which was, and is, and is to come. ⁹ And when those beasts give glory and honour and thanks to him that sat on the throne, who liveth for ever and ever, ¹⁰ The four and twenty elders fall down before him that sat on the throne, and worship him that liveth for ever and ever, and cast their crowns before* the throne, saying, [11] Thou art worthy, O Lord, to receive glory and honour and power: for thou hast created all things, and for thy pleasure they are and were created.

# God's Throne Room in the Sanctuary

As children, many of us have dressed up as a prince or princess and pretended to sit on a throne and wear a golden crown. But what would it be like to peek into the heavenly sanctuary where God, Himself, sits on His throne, crowned in His majesty? John must have been at a loss for words as he gazed in vision through the sanctuary's open door revealing God's throne in the Holy Place (Rev. 4:1, 5; compare Eze. 1:26-28). Unfortunately, John's human mind could not fully comprehend what he beheld in the heavenly sanctuary where Christ ministered following His resurrection (I Pet. 3:21-22; Heb. 8:1-2). Therefore, the Lord instructed John to write down what he saw using symbols to describe the heavenly realities he beheld to help his readers comprehend the glories of Heaven (Rev. 1:1-2). This figurative language is found throughout the book of Revelation, and it is important that God's Word alone, not private interpretations, explain the symbols' meanings and how they portray literal realities (Is. 28:9-10; 2 Tim. 3:16; 2 Peter 1:20-21).

Amazingly, the Lord was willing to allow John, a mere human being, to behold His glorious presence in Heaven. Yet, sadly, as the King of the Universe, Christ, the Creator, is so often refused entrance into humanity's hearts and left, instead, standing outside knocking (Rev. 3:20). However, Jesus, in His great love and mercy, invited John to have a glimpse of His superhuman qualities, despite John's apparent struggle to describe God's majesty in the heavenly sanctuary and the glory he beheld (1 Cor. 2:9).

In the north of the Holy Place of the heavenly sanctuary (Ps. 48:2), John beheld the Lord's throne at the table of shewbread (Ex. 25:30- "before [*"paniym"*] Me always," meaning, *"before the face of God"*). The glory of His throne shone across from the seven lamps in the heavenly sanctuary as Christ ministered in the Holy Place following His resurrection (Rev. 4:5; Heb. 1:3; 9:2, 11-12, KJV). Interestingly, God's throne room is located in His temple, tying His royal Presence to the ministration of the sanctuary service modeled in the Old Testament (Ex. 40:34; Ps. 77:13). Additionally, the entire theme of Revelation 4 seems to center around the throne of God, repeating the word, "throne," again and again. This chapter also appears to expound upon Revelation 3:21 (KJV) when Christ declares: "To him that overcometh, will I grant to sit with me on my *throne*, even as I also overcame, and set down with my Father in His *throne*" (italics added). What an amazing promise!

John describes the glory of God in the throne room as One who is like "jasper and a sardius stone in appearance" (Rev. 4:3, NKJV). Interestingly, these same stones were located on the breastplate of the high priest and had the names of the tribes of Israel written on them (Ex. 28:17-21). Also, John saw a rainbow around God's throne that resembled an emerald, which was a jewel on the high priest's breastplate (Rev. 4:3; Ex. 28:17). Furthermore, these same stones will be found in the foundational walls of the New Jerusalem, having the names of Israel written on them (Rev. 21:12, 19). Perhaps John's description of the Lord being decked in these precious jewels helps Christ's followers today to realize that He is both the King and High Priest in the heavenly sanctuary, ministering in the Most Holy Place on our behalf (Heb. 8:1-2, 6; 9:24-25). Moreover, the names of God's people are located right next to His heart, like the high priest's breastplate, signifying His love and grace for His children. No wonder the Bible says that the Lord's people will be like jewels in His crown (Zech. 9:16) and will be "called by a new name, which the mouth of the Lord shall name!" (Is. 62:2-3, KJV).

Similar to John, the prophet, Ezekiel, saw a vision of God's throne and described it as having the appearance of a sapphire stone (Eze. 1:26). Moses and the seventy elders also saw a sapphire stone under the Lord's feet "like the very heavens in its clarity" (Ex. 24:10, NKJV). Afterward, God gave Moses the Ten Commandments written by His own finger upon tablets of stone (Ex. 24:12; 31:18), most likely composed of the same sapphire jewel mentioned previously in this passage (Ex. 24:10). This blue stone, then, could represent God's law as the foundation of His throne and the everlasting covenant of His kingdom. Interestingly, the term, "blue laws," still describes religious laws in the United States today. The sapphire foundation of the Lord's throne in the heavenly sanctuary, therefore, likely portrays the importance of God's law, still binding, that exemplifies His character of justice and mercy towards His people.

Then John heard a voice like a trumpet from the throne of God, mixed with lightning and thunder. He saw "seven lamps of fire burning before the throne" (Rev. 4:5, KJV). According to Revelation 1:20, the seven lamps of fire may represent the Holy Spirit's work through the seven churches. Moreover, the lightning from the Lord's throne is symbolic of God's Word shining forth from His messengers (Ps. 119:105). The Greek word for lightning, *"astrape,"* means the *"gleam of a lamp"* and is from the word, *"astrapto,"* defined as *"to lighten, shine, flash,"* and *"aster,"* meaning, *"a star"* (compare Dan. 12:3). Also, Revelation 1:20 states that the Son of Man holds the seven stars (*"angelos,"* meaning *"messengers"*) in His right hand and walks continually among the lampstands (churches). Therefore, the connection between Christ and His people is intimate, reminding them that He is their Immanuel—*"God with us!"* (Matt. 1:23; italics added).

Next, John saw a sea of glass with four beasts full of eyes in front and back in the midst of the throne and around the throne (Rev. 4:6, KJV). This description of four beasts is most likely using symbolic language to describe four specific groups, which include the redeemed (Rev. 5:8-9; 19:1-6). As previously learned from the study of the book of Daniel, "beasts" represent "kingdoms" (Dan. 7:23). Also, Revelation 17:15 (KJV) portrays "water" as "peoples, multitudes, nations, and tongues." Plus, Isaiah 29:10 (KJV) states that eyes can represent prophets or "seers." Jesus describes the eye as "the lamp of the body" (Matt. 6:22, NKJV), and Revelation 1:20 (NKJV) associates "lamps" with God's church. So, these four beasts possibly represent four groups or kingdoms that include spiritual leaders of Christ's followers (Rev. 5:6).

These same groups in God's kingdom are pictured as praising the Lord in song, singing: "Holy, holy, holy, Lord God Almighty, which was and is and is to come!" (Rev. 4:8, KJV). Furthermore, Revelation 19:1-6 describes the four beasts and the twenty-four elders, in connection with the great multitude, taken from every tribe and tongue and people and nation (Rev. 5:8-10; 19:1, 4). They are also His servants and those who fear Him, both small and great (Rev. 19:5). Moreover, the four "beast" kingdoms, including both saints and angels, praise God for being their Creator (Rev. 4:9-11, KJV). However, the saved and the twenty-four elders specifically praise Christ as their Redeemer and reign "on the earth" (Rev. 5:8-10, KJV).

Each of these beast kingdoms is figuratively represented by four specific animals that possibly portray God's angelic guidance throughout mankind's history (Eze. 1:10). For example, the first beast was like a lion and introduces the first seal—the white horse of Christianity (Rev. 4:7; 6:1-2). This lion is used in the Bible to represent the Jewish nation and can symbolize the rulership of Christ, the Lion of Judah (Gen. 49:9; Rev. 5:5; Hos. 11:10).

Sadly, the Jews, however, were conquered and scattered into pagan nations (Hos. 8:3-6). Many became martyrs, possibly represented by the second calf-like beast kingdom (Rev. 4:7), which was a sacrificial animal in God's sanctuary services (Lev. 9:3). Moreover, the Greek word for a calf is *"moschos,"* which means *"a young heifer,"* and is often associated with the color red and blood (Num. 19:2-5). Additionally, Esau's descendants, the Edomites (lineage of Ishmael [Gen. 36:9; Mal. 1:2-4]), were linked with the color, red, and a sword, representing violence (Gen. 25:30; Is. 63:1-2; Amos 1:11; Rev. 6:3-4). This calf-like beast introduced the red horseman with a sword, likely indicating that persecution of God's people would spread worldwide, originating in Jewish/Arab conflicts, and intensifying throughout Christian history.

The third beast or kingdom to dominate God's people in Earth's history had a "face as a man," which possibly represents Gentile rulership (Rev. 4:7, KJV; I Peter 4:1-3; Lk. 21:24). After the Western nations of Greece and Rome conquered God's people in the East, the mixture of popular culture and biblical principles became rampant. The governmental influence continued to grow throughout the centuries of Greek and Roman rule until finally, Constantine's combination of church and state ended the overt persecution of Christians through civil protection. However, worldly compromise devastated the church! This dark time

171

period in Christian history is illustrated when the third beast opens the third seal of the black horse, likely representing humanistic government (Rev. 6:5). However, even during the darkness of spiritual apostasy, God still preserved a faithful remnant among the Gentiles.

Eventually, the Roman pontiff seized civil and religious power, rising as swiftly as a "flying eagle" or *"aetos,"* (Rev. 4:7), figuratively symbolizing Rome in the Greek language. This flying eagle unleashes the fourth seal of the pale horse of papal rule (Rev. 6:7). From 538-1798 AD, Roman Catholicism touted governmental authority throughout the Dark Ages. However, the Lord would use the Protestant Reformation to break the civil grip of the papacy in Europe and spread true Christianity to the rising nation of the United States of America, symbolized nationally by the bald eagle (compare Deut. 32:8-12; Micah 1:16). Daniel 7 may have hinted at the United States' political rise and eventual unity with Roman papal power when Babylon is represented as having *eagle's wings,* meaning *extremities* (Dan. 7:4; Is. 8:8). Likewise, the book of Revelation refers to a modern civil/religious power associated with God's remnant in the last days of Earth's history called "Mystery Babylon," which refers to a corrupt church/state system (Rev. 17:1-6, 18; Hos. 8:1). So, this figure of a swift eagle may also include God's last-day followers living during the time of apostate Protestant America united with the papacy. Therefore, the lion (Jews), the calf (Christian martyrs), the man (Gentile converts), and the flying eagle (God's faithful last-day remnant) possibly represent the Lord's guidance of His followers by the hosts of Heaven throughout these four different time periods in Earth's history leading up to Christ's second coming.

Because the twenty-four elders are named in addition to the four living beasts, the elders may symbolize leaders in each of these four heavenly groups. The Greek word for elders is *"pres-byteros"* meaning *"senior," "forefather,"* or *"a term of respect for an office"* (i.e. members of the Jewish Sanhedrin). Also, the similarity of the chiefs of the twenty-four divisions of priests in the Old Testament may be a clue to the leadership role of these elders (1 Chron. 24:4-5, 7–19). Additionally, John saw the twenty-four elders clothed in white robes with crowns of gold on their heads, sitting around God's throne (Rev. 4:4). These elders, then, are likely from the earth because Revelation 5:8-10 pictures them as praising Christ for redeeming them by His blood; plus, they are taken from every tribe and tongue and people and nation. Also, the white robes and the number of elders are similar to the twenty-four divisions of Old Testament priests who took turns serving in the earthly temple services. Moreover, the thrones and crowns on the elders' heads are reminiscent of Christ's promise that His people would be clothed in white garments (Rev. 3:5), wear a crown (Rev. 3:11; James 1:12), and sit with Him upon His throne (Rev. 3:21). Plus, the twenty-four elders describe themselves as being rewarded as "kings and priests," ruling over the *earth* (Rev. 4:10-11; 5:9-10; Is. 24:23). Considering these descriptives, the twenty-four elders may be composed of some of those raised from the dead at Christ's resurrection which are heavenly representatives of God's people on Earth (Matt. 27:52-53; compare Heb. 12:22-23). However, they could also simply symbolize the leaders of God's church on earth under the guidance of the heavenly hosts (Eze. 1).

Finally, all of the Lord's followers are pictured as worshipping before His throne, located not only in Heaven but also on Earth—at God's "footstool" (Is. 66:1). Perhaps one of the most amazing lessons learned from John's vision is that Christians now worship at the bottom or "footstool" of God's throne, along with the twenty-four elders and the four living beasts who proclaim: "Thou art worthy, O Lord, to receive glory and honour and power" (Rev. 4:11, KJV). Especially as Jesus's coming nears, it is imperative that we gather together with fellow believers and lift our hearts in praise, harmonizing with the heavenly hosts (Heb. 10:25). May we look forward eagerly to the day when we will cast our crowns at Christ's feet in humble admiration of our Creator and worship Him forever face to face! (Rev. 4:10).

---

### PROPOSED CHRONOLOGICAL ORDER OF REVELATION'S 7s

KEY:

*7 Churches Led by the 7 Spirits of God*- Symbolized as **Lightning** *("astrape"- "gleam of lamp"- Rev. 1:20; 2-3)*- **Enlightening** *of God's Word/Spirit (Rev. 4:5; 5:6; Ps. 119:105); Latter Rain (Zech. 10:1- "flashing clouds"); Judgments (Hos. 6:5)*

*7 Seals/7 Thunders*- Symbolized as **Thundering**- *(Rev. 6:1; compare Job 39:19);* **7 Thunders**- *Repetition of 7 Seals*- *(Rev. 6; 8:1; 10:2-3);* **Execution of God's Word**- *Events at Specific Times (Job 36:29-33; 37:1-5; Is. 29:5-6)*

*7 Trumpets*- Symbolized as **Noises** *(KJV, "phone"- meaning a "sound," "tone," "voice" [Rev. 4:1; Rev. 8-9]);* **Warnings of God's Word** *(Ex. 19:19; KJV); Resulting in an* **Earthquake**- *"seismos"- meaning "shaking," from "seio"- "to agitate the mind," "cause to tremble" (Ex. 19:16-18; Rev. 11:13; 16:18-19)*

*7 Plagues*- Symbolized as **Hail**- *Power of God's Word in Judgment (Is. 28:17; Ps. 18:12-14);* **Plagues** *(Ex. 9:18-24; Rev. 16:21)*

---

**Rev. 4:5- (After Christ's Ascension to Heaven- Protestant Reformation)**- Lightnings- (Spirit of God working in the 7 churches to enlighten the earth with God's Word); Thunderings (7 Seals [1-4]- time periods); Noises (KJV) (7 Trumpets follow)

**Rev. 8:5- (Protestant Reformation- 1844)**- Noises (7 Trumpets continue & repeat [1-4]), Thunderings (Seals [5-6]; Thunder 1); Lightnings (God's Spirit/Word/Great Awakenings of God's people/Midnight Cry); Earthquake (Great Disappointment)

**Rev. 11:19- (1844- Present)**- Lightnings (Formation of God's remnant); Noises (Trumpets [5-6]- 3 Angels' Messages); Thunderings (7th Seal- Silence in Heaven/Seals repeat as Thunders [2-5]); Earthquake (Shaking); Great Hail (Judgments)

**Rev. 16:18- (Just Before Christ's 2nd Coming)**- Noises (7th Trumpet); Thunderings (7 Thunders [5th continues through 7th]); Lightnings (God's Spirit/Latter Rain); Great Earthquake (Close of Probation); Great Hail (7 Last Plagues)

# Discussion Questions for Revelation 4

1. What important principle should we follow when studying the symbolism in the book of Revelation? (Is. 28:9-10; 2 Tim. 3:16; 2 Peter 1:20-21)

2. When John looked through the "open door" in his vision, whom and what did he see? Where was God's throne located immediately after Christ's resurrection? (Rev. 4:1-2, 5; Heb. 1:3; 9:11-12, KJV; Ex. 25:30; Ps. 48:2)

3. What stones are used to describe God and His throne room? What is significant about the locations of these stones on the high priest's breastplate? How does their location give us a clue that Christ has a close connection with us today? (Rev. 4:3; Ex. 28:17-21; Rev. 21:12, 18-19)

4. What is particularly fascinating about the blue sapphire stone? What meaning does the sapphire stone likely contain when describing God's throne? (Eze. 1:26; Ex. 24:10, 12; Rev. 21:19)

5. What was Christ doing in the Holy Place of the heavenly sanctuary, just after His resurrection? What is He doing for us in the Most Holy Place today? (Heb. 8:1-2, 6)

6. What do the four "beasts," "sea of glass," and "eyes in front and back" likely represent? (Rev. 4:6-9, KJV; Dan. 7:23; Rev. 17:15; Is. 29:10)

7. What may the lion, the calf, the man, and the eagle possibly symbolize? (Rev. 4:7 compare Eze. 1:10; "lion" [Gen. 49:9]; "calf" [Lev. 9:3 compare Rom. 8:36]; "man" [I Pet. 4:1-3]; "eagle" [Hos. 8:1]

8. What does the description and number of elders likely represent? (Rev. 4:4; 1 Chron. 24:4-5, 7-18)

9. How are Christ's followers pictured in Revelation 4? What are they doing? What part of God's throne is His earthly kingdom? (Rev. 4:6, 9-11; Rev. 5:8-9; Is. 66:1)

10. Specifically, as we near Christ's second coming, why is it so important that we gather together with other believers to worship? What should we be doing, represented by the twenty-four elders and the four living beasts? (Heb. 10:25; Rev. 5:9-10, KJV)

# Revelation 5 (KJV)

*¹ And I saw in the right hand of him that sat on the throne a book written within and on the backside, sealed with seven seals. ² And I saw a strong angel proclaiming with a loud voice, Who is worthy to open the book, and to loose the seals thereof? ³ And no man in heaven, nor in earth, neither under the earth, was able to open the book, neither to look thereon. ⁴ And I wept much, because no man was found worthy to open and to read the book, neither to look thereon. ⁵ And one of the elders saith unto me, Weep not: behold, the Lion of the tribe of Judah, the Root of David, hath prevailed to open the book, and to loose the seven seals thereof. ⁶ And I beheld, and, lo, in the midst of the throne and of the four beasts, and in the midst of the elders, stood a Lamb as it had been slain, having seven horns and seven eyes, which are the seven Spirits of God sent forth into all the earth. ⁷ And he came and took the book out of the right hand of him that sat upon the throne. ⁸ And when he had taken the book, the four beasts and four and twenty elders fell down before the Lamb, having every one of them harps, and golden vials full of odours, which are the prayers of saints. ⁹ And they sung a new song, saying, Thou art worthy to take the book, and to open the seals thereof: for thou wast slain, and hast redeemed us to God by thy blood out of every kindred, and tongue, and people, and nation; ¹⁰ And hast made us unto our God kings and priests: and we shall reign on the earth. ¹¹ And I beheld, and I heard the voice of many angels round about the throne and the beasts and the elders: and the number of them was ten thousand times* ten thousand, and thousands of thousands; [12] *Saying with a loud voice, Worthy is the Lamb that was slain to receive power, and riches, and wisdom, and strength, and honour, and glory, and blessing.* [13] *And every creature which is in heaven, and on the earth, and under the earth, and such as are in the sea, and all that are in them, heard I saying, Blessing, and honour, and glory, and power, be unto him that sitteth upon the throne, and unto the Lamb for ever and ever.* [14] *And the four beasts said, Amen. And the four and twenty elders fell down and worshipped him that liveth for ever and ever.*

# Worthy is the Lamb

Many young girls love to write in their diaries and then lock them up with a key. They don't want anyone to read the secrets they have written inside! As John beheld the history of the Christian Church, he saw a similarly locked scroll in the right hand of Him who sat on the throne (Rev. 5:1). This scroll likely consisted of seven scrolls rolled up inside each other, sealed with seven seals (specific time periods [Rev. 20:3; Dan. 12:4, 9]). Moreover, the scroll had writing on the inside and on the back, the same way that the Ten Commandments were written (Rev. 5:1; Ex. 32:15). Likewise, Zechariah saw a scroll written on both sides that contained curses for hypocrites who claimed to be God's people, but lied, breaking the ninth commandment (Zech. 5:3-4; Ex. 20:16). Furthermore, the prophet Ezekiel had a vision of a scroll written inside and out that contained "lamentations, mourning, and woe" against a rebellious nation and its "fathers" or leaders (Eze. 2:3, 9-10, KJV). Therefore, John likely gazed at a comparable scroll that included curses against all who had broken God's law during specific time periods throughout the history of the earth.

As John watched the terrible fate of fallen humanity, he wept in fear that no one was worthy to open the scroll's seals and atone for the sin of mankind (Rev. 5:4). But then he was bidden to behold the "Lion of the tribe of Judah" (Rev. 5:5; Jesus as the head of the OT Jewish lionlike kingdom [Gen. 49:9-10]). Amazingly, this mighty "Lion" had chosen to become a lowly "Lamb" (Rev. 5:5-6; Christ as the head of the NT Christian lamblike kingdom [Jn. 1:29; Is. 53:7; Dan. 7:23]). This Lamb looked "as it had been slain," which was a constant reminder of the infinite price that God had paid for man's redemption (Rev. 5:6, KJV). All of Heaven hushed at the sight of the Son of Man, who had lived a perfect life on the earth, died the second death for mankind, and was resurrected to reign with His Father (Rev. 5:13).

As Christ drew near the Almighty's throne, He stood as man's Intermediary. The gulf between Heaven and Earth had been bridged through the blood of the Lamb! All of humanity now had the opportunity of gaining eternal life through the forgiveness of sin. Even as Jesus approached His Father, His followers were represented in His "seven horns and seven eyes, which are the seven Spirits of God sent forth into all the earth" (Rev. 5:6, KJV). These seven horns (powers [Ps. 75:10]) are likely symbolic of the seven churches (Rev. 2-3). Moreover, the seven eyes represent the spiritual leaders of God's people (Is. 29:10), inspired by the seven Spirits of God, which is the Holy Spirit working through the seven churches during seven specific historical eras (Rev. 4:5; 5:6; Is. 11:2; Eph. 1:13; Jn. 16:13).

While John watched in awe, Jesus, the Lamb of God, took the scroll out of the right hand of His Father, who sat upon His throne in judgment (Rev. 5:7; Ps. 9:7-8). Through this solemn act, Christ symbolically took upon Himself mankind's curses contained in the scrolls (Gal. 3:13). All of Heaven gasped in amazement at the thought of such a costly sacrifice! Such incomprehensible love brought the entire universe to its knees in adoration before the Lamb of God (Rev. 5:8). The four beast kingdoms and the twenty-four elders could contain themselves no longer! They immediately broke forth in praise to Jesus for being saved by His blood and elevated as priests and kings with Christ (Rev. 1:5-6; Is. 53:5). They sang:

> You are worthy to take the scroll and to open its seals; For You were slain, and have *redeemed us* to God by Your blood out of every tribe, tongue, and people, and nation, and have *made us priests and kings* unto our God, and *we shall reign on the earth.* (Rev. 5:9, NKJV; italics added)

No angel could make this joyful proclamation! Only the redeemed could sing this new song after Christ's resurrection when He had returned to Heaven with the firstfruits of His saints (Matt. 27:52-53; Heb. 12:22-23). From that time on, Jesus had gained the right to receive worship from mankind as their Creator, Judge, and Redeemer (Rev. 4:11; 15:3-4; Jn. 5:22; Rev. 5:9). Forever, the righteous will be reminded of Christ's unfathomable sacrifice by the nailprints in his hands and sing praises to Him in humble adoration! (Rev. 5:13; Is. 49:16). Also, astonished at such selfless love, John saw the angelic choir unite their voices with the redeemed in praise to the Son of Man (Rev. 5:11). The unsealing of the history of the world's nations throughout the ages would follow this praise service, but not before all of Heaven had exclaimed, "Worthy is the Lamb that was slain to receive power, and riches, and wisdom, and strength, and honour, and glory, and blessing!" (Rev. 5:12, KJV).

Today on Earth, may we join the heavenly hosts in praise to Jesus, the One who broke the seven seals and took the curse of sin upon Himself: "Christ hath redeemed us from the curse of the law, being made a curse for us..." (Gal. 3:13, KJV; compare Is. 53:4). May we reflect God's character in honor of His sacrifice for our salvation and proclaim with the angels, "Blessing and honour, and glory, and power, be unto him who sitteth upon the throne, and unto the Lamb, for ever and ever!" (Rev. 5:13-14, KJV; compare Eph. 2:4-10). Amen!

# Discussion Question for Revelation 5

1. What can "seals" refer to in Bible prophecy? (Rev. 20:2-3; Dan. 12:4, 9)

2. How is the description of the scroll that John saw similar to the Ten Commandments? What clue might this description give us as to the possible contents of the scroll? (Rev. 5:1; Ex. 32:15; Zech. 5:3-4)

3. Why is Christ pictured as both a Lion and a Lamb? How do these two titles represent His work during two specific time periods for God's people on Earth? (Rev. 5:5-6; Gen. 49:9-10; Jn. 1:29; Dan. 7:23)

4. What do the Lamb's (Christs) seven horns most likely represent? (Rev. 5:6; Ps. 75:10)

5. What do the seven eyes most likely symbolize? (Rev. 5:6; Is. 29:10)

6. What function does the Holy Spirit play in the history of God's church, following the resurrection of Christ? (Rev. 4:5; 5:6; Is. 11:2; Eph. 1:13; Jn. 16:13)

7. Why do the description of the living creatures (beasts- KJV) and the twenty-four elders indicate that they probably include God's people from the earth, not just angels? (Rev. 5:8-10; Dan. 7:23; Matt. 27:52-53)

8. What did Christ take upon Himself on our behalf? (Gal 3:13; Is. 53:4)

9. Why is the Lamb worthy of all our praise today? How should we live as a result? (Rev. 5:9, 12; Eph. 2:4-10)

# Revelation 6 (KJV)

¹ *And I saw when the Lamb opened one of the seals, and I heard, as it were the noise of thunder, one of the four beasts saying, Come and see. ² And I saw, and behold a white horse: and he that sat on him had a bow; and a crown was given unto him: and he went forth conquering, and to conquer. ³ And when he had opened the second seal, I heard the second beast say, Come and see. ⁴ And there went out another horse that was red: and power was given to him that sat thereon to take peace from the earth, and that they should kill one another: and there was given unto him a great sword. ⁵ And when he had opened the third seal, I heard the third beast say, Come and see. And I beheld, and lo a black horse; and he that sat on him had a pair of balances in his hand. ⁶ And I heard a voice in the midst of the four beasts say, A measure of wheat for a penny, and three measures of barley for a penny; and see thou hurt not the oil and the wine. ⁷ And when he had opened the fourth seal, I heard the voice of the fourth beast say, Come and see. ⁸ And I looked, and behold a pale horse: and his name that sat on him was Death, and Hell followed with him. And power was given unto them over the fourth part of the earth, to kill with sword, and with hunger, and with death, and with the beasts of the earth. ⁹ And when he had opened the fifth seal, I saw under the altar the souls of them that were slain for the word of God, and for the testimony which they held: ¹⁰ And they cried with a loud voice, saying, How long, O Lord, holy and true, dost thou not judge and avenge our blood on them that dwell on the earth? ¹¹ And white robes were given*

*unto every one of them; and it was said unto them, that they should rest yet for a little season, until their fellowservants also and their brethren, that should be killed as they were, should be fulfilled. <sup>12</sup> And I beheld when he had opened the sixth seal, and, lo, there was a great earthquake; and the sun became black as sackcloth of hair, and the moon became as blood; <sup>13</sup> And the stars of heaven fell unto the earth, even as a fig tree casteth her untimely figs, when she is shaken of a mighty wind. <sup>14</sup> And the heaven departed as a scroll when it is rolled together; and every mountain and island were moved out of their places. <sup>15</sup> And the kings of the earth, and the great men, and the rich men, and the chief captains, and the mighty men, and every bondman, and every free man, hid themselves in the dens and in the rocks of the mountains; <sup>16</sup> And said to the mountains and rocks, Fall on us, and hide us from the face of him that sitteth on the throne, and from the wrath of the Lamb: <sup>17</sup> For the great day of his wrath is come; and who shall be able to stand?*

# The Thunder of History Unsealed

Have you ever beheld the power of a severe thunderstorm during the night? Thunder booms! Lightning streaks across the black sky! John must have felt a similar awe as he saw the Lamb (Jesus [Jn. 1:29]) and heard the thunderous voice of the first beast (Rev. 6:1, KJV). Amazed, he beheld Christ's lionlike beast/kingdom (Dan. 7:23), the first time period of Christian history, breaking from its seal (Rev. 6:1; 4:7; 5:5; Micah 5:8). Rolled into one large scroll, these seven smaller sealed scrolls symbolize events affecting God's church during specific time periods, beginning at Christ's resurrection and corresponding to the messages of the seven churches (Rev. 6:1; 5:1; Dan. 12:4, 9). They give additional insights into God's work on Earth and Satan's attacks against it during each specific period of history.

In a flash, John saw a white horse with a victorious Rider holding a bow in his hand. A crown was given to this Rider, and He went forth "conquering and to conquer" (Rev. 6:2). This white horse, a beast used in war (Prov. 21:31), symbolizes a kingdom (Dan. 7:23). Also, the color white in the Bible represents purity (Is. 1:18; Rev. 7:14). Therefore, this first kingdom must represent a righteous kingdom. A similar beast and its Rider are further described in Revelation 19:11 (KJV): "… behold, a white horse; and he that sat upon him was called Faithful and True, and in righteousness, he doth judge and make war." By comparing this verse with Revelation 1:5, one can deduce that this is Jesus, Himself, the "Faithful Witness," leading His heavenly army and empowering His followers on Earth. Additionally, the Rider's bow and crown represent victory for God's church, specifically after Christ's resurrection, as it rides forth to conquer. Symbolizing the time period of the early church of Ephesus (Rev. 2:1-7), Christ's white horse kingdom is promised to be "more than conquerers through him who loved us" (Rom. 8:37, KJV). In Isaiah 63:13-14 (KJV), the Lord says that He leads His people *as an horse* in the wilderness, that they should not stumble," and in Jeremiah 51:20-22 (NKJV), He promises, "With you, I will break the nation in pieces; With you I will destroy kingdoms; with you I will break in pieces *the horse and its rider*" (italics added). Jesus gallops forth victoriously with His white horse kingdom, battling the satanic attacks of the wicked nations and false religions that war against Christianity (Prov. 21:31). Praise the Lord that final victory is sure through Christ! He promises, "… I will destroy the strength of the kingdoms of the heathen, and I will overthrow the chariots and those that ride in them; *The horses and their riders shall come down*" (Hag. 2:22, KJV; italics added; compare Micah 5:9-10). Nonetheless, Satan and his hosts put up a fierce battle, using the ungodly to fight against God's church, likely symbolized in the next three seals.

Competing with the breath-taking glory of Jesus on His white horse, the second seal unleashes another rider on a fiery red horse, introduced by the second calf-like beast, which had instructed John to "come and see" (Rev. 6:3; 4:7). This time the rider held a great sword "to take peace from the earth, and that they should kill one another" (Rev. 6:4, KJV). In contrast to white, red is often used as a biblical symbol of sin. Isaiah 1:18 (KJV) states, "… though your sins be as scarlet, they shall be as white as snow;

though they be red like crimson, they shall be as wool." In this text, sin is illustrated through the color scarlet red. Additionally, John's description of the second horse includes another hint that this red beast kingdom is of evil origin. The Greek word used to describe the second horse is *"pyrrhos,"* translated as *"fiery red"* in Revelation 6:4 (NKJV). It is the same word used later to describe the red dragon (the Devil and his kingdom [Rev. 12:3, 9; Dan. 7:23]) that makes war with God's remnant people who "keep the commandments of God and have the testimony of Jesus Christ" (Rev. 12:17, KJV). Also, the very fact that this horse's rider takes peace from the earth and sheds blood with a sword illustrates its wicked nature (Eze. 35:5-6). Considering these descriptives, what satanic force throughout Christian history has killed God's faithful followers, beginning during the time of the early church and continuing today? Historical records show that early Christians were persecuted by pagan rulers such as Nero, Domitian, and Diocletian. They put thousands of Christians to death during the symbolic time period of the church of Smyrna just because these martyrs refused to bow down to Roman gods. Ever since then, paganism has battled against Christianity with its great sword of persecution, threatening Jesus's followers to either give up their faith or lose their lives. Yet, despite these violent attacks, the Devil beheld the seed of the martyrs' blood producing a great harvest of souls for God's kingdom! So, out of genius born of necessity, Satan combined paganism with Christianity, enforced by civil law.

This diabolical mixture caused John to hear the voice of the third beast kingdom with a face like a man (Rev. 6:5; 4:7). Likely representing the time of the church of Pergamon, this dark horse kingdom was as black as midnight (black= spiritual darkness [2 Pet. 2:17-18; Jn. 3:19]). The Bible also associates the color black with famine (Lam. 5:10, KJV), which can symbolically describe a spiritual hunger for biblical instruction: "… not a famine of bread, nor a thirst for water, but of hearing (understanding) the words of the Lord" (Amos 8:11, KJV; parentheses added). This spiritual famine was likely produced by the mixture of biblical standards with worldly culture, resulting in a deprivation of the undefiled Word of God. Specifically, during Constantine's Roman rule, spiritual compromise and corruption within the church became so prominent that John heard a voice likely describing outrageous prices for the food of God's Word (Rev. 6:6). However, this scarcity of true biblical principles/morals, resulting in spiritual darkness, continues its deadly attack on the Lord's church even today.

Additionally, the rider of the black horse had a pair of scales in his hand, likely symbolizing civil rule (Rev. 6:5; Lev. 19:36; Eze. 45:9-10; Micah 6:10-12). These scales are similar to the description of the pagan Greek goddess, Themis, who originated during the early Roman empire.[139] Today she is known as "Lady Justice" and is sculptured into the United States Supreme Court building, holding scales in her hands.[140] She is also known for her "ability to foresee the future," and her "talent for prophecy."[141] Moreover, she stands as an "intermediary between divine justice and human justice," which is represented by the scales in her hand.[142] This mixture of man's secular civil power with "divine justice" may symbolize the amalgamation of church and state, which occurred when Constantine legalized Christianity throughout Rome, integrating it with paganism and civil law. This decree, however, temporarily ended the overt persecution of Christians,

---

[139] https://itsaboutjustice.com/symbol-justice/
[140] https://www.supremecourt.gov/about/figuresofjustice.pdf
[141] https://itsaboutjustice.com/symbol-justice/
[142] ibid

possibly referred to when John heard a voice commanding that no harm be done to the "oil" and "wine," a figure of speech symbolizing the blessings of God's people (Deut 11:14; Jer. 31:12).

John then heard the voice of the fourth beast, described as a flying eagle, a symbol of Rome (Rev. 6:7; 4:7; Hosea 8:1-3). In 538 AD, the Roman Catholic Church obtained civil power, ending Christianity's reprieve from persecution. Thousands of Christians died during the long years of the Dark Ages, which nearly extinguished biblical truth during the iron rule of the papacy in Europe. God's church languished without any strong biblical guidance. Unlike the living green grass and trees that the righteous are often compared to in the Bible (Jer. 17:7-8; Ps. 52:8), the "pale" horse kingdom of the fourth seal is described as being "*chloros,*" a "*greenish yellow*" of sickly, dying vegetation. Jeremiah 30:6 (KJV) associates this color with pain, a fitting symbol of the church's physical and spiritual suffering: "… I see every man with his hands on his loins, as a woman in travail; and all faces are turned into paleness" ("*yeraqown*" meaning both "*human fright*" and "*greenish yellow of dying plants*"). Also, paleness ties to the concept of shame, such as in Jeremiah 50:12 (NKJV), speaking of the fall of Babylon, "Your *mother* shall be deeply ashamed ("*buwsh*"= "*to pale*"; compare Is. 29:22). Similarly, Revelation 17:5 speaks of "Mystery Babylon, the *Mother* of Harlots," and describes the return of papal power mixed with apostate Protestantism. So, the paleness of this fourth beast likely describes the spiritual sickness of God's church during the Dark Ages, continuing throughout the last days when apostate Protestantism will unite with its "*mother,*" Roman Catholicism.

Furthermore, the rider of the pale beast kingdom is said to be "*Death,*" himself; plus, "*Hell,*" (meaning "*the grave*") follows him.

"And power was given unto them over the fourth part of the earth to kill with sword, and with hunger, and with death, and with the beasts of the earth" (Rev. 6:7-8, KJV). Although the Devil is the ultimate hellion of death, in Habakkuk 2:5, the Bible describes a man that "transgresseth by wine; he is a proud man... *as hell and is as death,* and cannot be satisfied, but gathereth unto him all nations..." (italics added). This verse likely refers to the antichrist, under Satan's control, who mixes God's truth with the wine of error and gathers nations under his leadership (I Jn. 2:18; 4:3; Rev. 13:5-7; Dan. 7:25; 8:23-25). What religious/political power did most Protestant reformers believe was the antichrist? It was the papacy, which had been given its authority by the kings of the earth to spearhead the martyrdom of thousands of Protestant Christians throughout history.[143] The New Testament further describes the antichrist as the "man of sin" and the "son of perdition" who "opposeth and exalteth himself above all that is called God or that is worshiped, so he is as God sitteth in the temple of God, shewing himself that he is God" (2 Thess. 2:3-4, KJV). Even now, the pope claims infallibility, yet many of today's Protestant leaders continue strengthening ecumenical ties with the Catholic Church and its papal leadership (Is. 28:15). Because of this deadly amalgamation, Protestantism, specifically in the United States, has deteriorated into its current sickly state, largely losing its once vibrant first love (Rev. 2:4).

As John beheld the breaking of the fifth seal, his vision switched from the four horsemen to the symbolic representation of God's people crying out from beneath the altar, "How long, O Lord, holy and true, dost thou not judge and avenge our blood on those that dwell on the earth?" (Rev. 6:10, KJV). This figurative depiction of the bloodshed of God's people during the Protestant

---

[143] http://www.the-bible-antichrist.com/what-did-reformers-believe.html

Reformation is similar to Genesis 4:10 (KJV) when the Lord tells Cain, "… the voice of thy brother's blood crieth unto Me from the ground." Clearly, both passages portray a symbolic picture of martyrs, specifically those following the Reformation, pleading for God's retribution for their deaths. The Psalmist also records a similar plea, "How long, Lord?" before the "revenging of the blood of thy servants which is shed?" (Ps. 79:5, 10, KJV). Through symbolic imagery, John beheld the martyrs' heartfelt longing for justice, ascending to Jesus in the heavenly sanctuary. In response to their prayers, they were given Christ's white robes of right-eousness and were told to rest "a little while longer" until the work of their fellow servants had been completed (Rev. 6:11). However, their question of "How long?" has continued to swell, becoming especially prominent during the 1800s.

In the 1840s, a man named William Miller discovered that the prophet, Daniel, had also asked the question, "How long?" Interestingly, God had answered Daniel with a specific time proph-ecy: "Unto two thousand and three hundred days; then the sanctuary be cleansed" (Dan. 8:13-14, KJV). Using the biblical principle of a day-for-a-year (Num. 14:34; Eze. 4:6), Miller and several others around the world added 2,300 years to 457 BC (the starting date of Daniel 9:25's historical prophecy that began with the rebuilding of Jerusalem [Ezra 7:13-26). Unfortunately, the Millerites thought that Jesus would return to the earth on October 22, 1844, which resulted in the Great Disappointment, likely pre-dicted in Revelation 10:8-10. However, many diligent Bible stu-dents later discovered that Christ had moved from the Holy to the Most Holy Place in the *heavenly* sanctuary on this date to start the judgment in favor of the saints and complete His priestly me-diation for His people (Ps. 102:13; Heb. 9:11-12, 23-25, 28). Daniel 7:10 states: "the judgment was set and the books were opened" (compare Rev. 3:5; Mal. 3:16; Eccl.12:14). As an answer to prayer, the investigative judgment had begun that would culminate in the vindication of God's people at the second coming (I Pet. 4:17; Eze. 9:6; Rev. 6:10,16-17).

In addition to the discovery of the fulfillment of the 2,300-day/year prophecy, near the close of this same time period, signs in the sun, moon, and stars appeared as recorded in the sixth seal of Revelation. As this seal broke open, John saw a great earthquake, the sun became dark, and the moon turned to blood; then, the stars of heaven fell (Rev. 6:12-13). Jesus referred to these same signs "immediately after the tribulation of those days," likely citing what would occur after the persecution that the Protestants would suffer during the time of the Reformation (Matt. 24:29). The prophet, Joel, also predicted, "wonders in the heavens... the sun shall be turned into darkness and the moon into blood" (Joel 2:31, KJV).

These same signs were seen in New England during the mysterious "Dark Day" of May 19, 1780, that followed the great Lisbon Earthquake in 1755. The cause of this unprecedented darkness is still in debate today. No eclipses were recorded during this time, yet at noon, the sky turned as black as midnight, and both the sun and moon glowed red in the days following.[144] Many believed that the end of the world was near and tied these signs back to Bible prophecy. Adding even more excitement, the historic Leonid Meteor shower of 1833 was seen across the Eastern United States with reports of a firestorm of an estimated 240,000 meteors.[145] Again, the falling of the stars called attention to the nearness of Christ's second coming and the beginning of

---

[144] https://www.bbc.com/news/magazine-18097177
[145] https://www.space.com/9517-leonid-meteor-shower-revealed-shooting-star-show-brilliant-history.html

the investigative judgment, leaving many to wonder who would be able to stand in the day of God's wrath (Rev. 6:17).

This heart-wrenching question sparked a spiritual revival and ignited the Second Great Awakening in the 1800s when William Miller preached the Advent message based upon the close of the 2,300-day/year prophecy (Daniel 8:14). Just as Revelation 6:14 (KJV) refers symbolically to the "heavens departing as a scroll" when it is rolled up (finished), the work in the Holy Place of the heavenly sanctuary had ended and judgment had begun (Is. 34:4-5).

From the resurrection of Jesus to 1844, each of these seals has transpired just as the Bible has predicted. The next chapters of Revelation outline the events that span from the breaking of the seventh seal in 1844 to Christ's second coming. These six seals reveal how God has led His church down through history and warned of future challenges. Today, we can take comfort in knowing that the Lord does "nothing but he revealeth his secret unto his servants the prophets" (Amos 3:7, KJV). God's Word continues to prove Christ's faithfulness throughout time—He is truly the "Alpha and Omega," "the First and the Last!" (Rev. 1:11).

# Discussion Questions for Revelation 6

1. What is the proposed meaning of the white horse and its conquering Rider? (Rev. 6:2; Dan. 7:23; Is. 63:13-14; Prov. 21:31; Jer. 51:20-21; Rom. 8:37)

2. What is the proposed meaning of the red horse and its rider, and how do we see this same attack on God's people today? (Rev. 6:4; 12:3, 9, 17; Dan. 7:23; Eze. 35:5-6)

3. What is the proposed meaning of the black horse and its rider, and how does the combination of secular culture and Christianity result in spiritual corruption? (Rev. 6:5-6; Dan. 7:23; Lam. 5:9-10, KJV; Amos 8:11-12; Prov. 14:12)

4. What is the proposed meaning of the pale horse and its rider, and how is this rider regaining a stronghold in America today? (Rev. 6:7-8; Dan. 7:23; Hab. 2:5; II Thess. 2:3-4; I Jn. 2:18; 4:3)

5. What does the fifth seal, containing the cry of the martyrs, probably represent? What clue does Genesis 4:10 give that this depiction is symbolic? When and how did God most likely begin answering the martyrs' cry for justice? Why is this cry continuing even now? (Rev. 6:10-11; Ps. 79:5, 10; 1 Pet. 4:17-19)

6. Why is Christ's priestly work as our mediator important for us living today? (Rev. 7:1-4; Heb. 9:11-15, 23-25, 28)

7. What signs of the nearness of Christ's coming were predicted in the sixth seal? How were these signs observed in the 18th and 19th centuries? Why did God give these signs at this time in history? (Rev. 6:12-13; Joel 2:31; Dan. 8:13-14; Dan. 7:10)

8. What is God likely revealing to His people during each sealed time period and its events, beginning in John's day and spanning throughout history? Why does fulfilled prophecy strengthen our faith in God's prophecies that are still in the future? (Amos 3:7)

# Revelation 7 (KJV)

*¹ And after these things I saw four angels standing on the four corners of the earth, holding the four winds of the earth, that the wind should not blow on the earth, nor on the sea, nor on any tree. ² And I saw another angel ascending from the east, having the seal of the living God: and he cried with a loud voice to the four angels, to whom it was given to hurt the earth and the sea, ³ Saying, Hurt not the earth, neither the sea, nor the trees, till we have sealed the servants of our God in their foreheads. ⁴ And I heard the number of them which were sealed: and there were sealed an hundred and forty and four thousand of all the tribes of the children of Israel. ⁵ Of the tribe of Juda were sealed twelve thousand. Of the tribe of Reuben were sealed twelve thousand. Of the tribe of Gad were sealed twelve thousand. ⁶ Of the tribe of Aser were sealed twelve thousand. Of the tribe of Nephthalim were sealed twelve thousand. Of the tribe of Manasses were sealed twelve thousand. ⁷ Of the tribe of Simeon were sealed twelve thousand. Of the tribe of Levi were sealed twelve thousand. Of the tribe of Issachar were sealed twelve thousand. ⁸ Of the tribe of Zabulon were sealed twelve thousand. Of the tribe of Joseph were sealed twelve thousand. Of the tribe of Benjamin were sealed twelve thousand. ⁹ After this I beheld, and, lo, a great multitude, which no man could number, of all nations, and kindreds, and people, and tongues, stood before the throne, and before the Lamb, clothed with white robes, and palms in their hands; ¹⁰ And cried with a* *loud voice, saying, Salvation to our God which sitteth upon the throne, and unto the Lamb. <sup>11</sup> And all the angels stood round about the throne, and about the elders and the four beasts, and fell before the throne on their faces, and worshipped God, <sup>12</sup> Saying, Amen: Blessing, and glory, and wisdom, and thanksgiving, and honour, and power, and might, be unto our God for ever and ever. Amen. <sup>13</sup> And one of the elders answered, saying unto me, What are these which are arrayed in white robes? and whence came they? <sup>14</sup> And I said unto him, Sir, thou knowest. And he said to me, These are they which came out of great tribulation, and have washed their robes, and made them white in the blood of the Lamb. <sup>15</sup> Therefore are they before the throne of God, and serve him day and night in his temple: and he that sitteth on the throne shall dwell among them. <sup>16</sup> They shall hunger no more, neither thirst any more; neither shall the sun light on them, nor any heat. <sup>17</sup> For the Lamb which is in the midst of the throne shall feed them, and shall lead them unto living fountains of waters: and God shall wipe away all tears from their eyes.*

# Sealing of God's Remnant People

Have you ever traveled outside of your country and received a stamp in your passport? That stamp is your official governmental seal, valid for a specific amount of time. Likewise, God's people receive the "seal of the living God," which identifies them with Christ's kingdom and protects them during the time of the end (Rev. 7:2-3; 2 Tim. 2:19; Dan. 12:1).

In Revelation 7:1 (KJV), John saw four angels, standing at the "four corners of the earth" (directions [Matt. 24:31; Jer. 9:26]), holding back the physical and spiritual "winds" of strife until God's servants were sealed in their foreheads (Jer. 4:11-13; Rev. 7:1-3; 22:4). This time of sealing likely began in 1844 at the close of the 2,300-day prophecy and the breaking of the seventh seal (Dan. 8:14; Rev. 8:1). Moreover, this sealing continues today during the investigative judgment as Jesus ministers in the heavenly sanctuary (Acts 10:42; Heb. 9:15).

John heard the number of those sealed — 144,000 — 12,000 from each tribe of Israel (Rev. 7:4-8). The Bible makes it clear that those who are sealed are not made up of the *physical* tribes of Israel because the tribes listed in Revelation are different than those listed in the Old Testament (Gen. 49:3-28; Num. 1:5-15; 34:18-29; Deut. 27:12-13; 1 Chron. 2:1-2). Instead, the 144,000 are the remnant of *spiritual* Israel who has been saved by the blood of Christ (Eph. 2:11-13; Rev. 7:14). They are most likely the remnant of the "great multitude" ("*ochlos*" meaning *common people as opposed to leaders* [Rev. 7:9]) who have "come out of great tribulation," specifically the Protestant Reformation [Rev. 7:14; Matt. 24:29, KJV]).

This great multitude is pictured "before the throne of God" (which includes the earth- God's "footstool" [Is. 66:1]). They have served "Him day and night in His temple" (similar to the over-comers of the church of Philadelphia who are called "pillars" in the temple of God- Rev. 7:15; 3:12, KJV). Moreover, they have held fast to the truths of the living fountains of water (God's Word [Jn. 4:10; 7:38; compare Is. 49:10]) and have been promised that their tears will be wiped away from their eyes (because they have gone through great tribulation- Rev. 7:14, 17, KJV). The 144,000, then, are the remnant of this great multitude who are living in the last days of earth's history and have been sealed by the Holy Spirit for the day of redemption (2 Cor. 1:21-22).

But what is this mysterious seal on the foreheads of the 144,000? The Greek word for "sealed" that describes this special group is "*sphragizo*," meaning "*to set a mark on for preservation or security, to confirm authenticity.*" The Bible teaches that Christ's seal is His "Father's name," His character, exemplified in His holy law. Isaiah 8:16 (KJV) states, "Bind up the testimony, *seal the law* among my disciples." The Lord's covenant seal is symbolically written *only in the forehead*, meaning that a conscious decision must be made by God's followers to portray Christ's name (character) through His power manifested in their life of obedience to His law (Rev. 7:3, KJV; 14:1; Heb. 10:16). God's sealed people, then, are the answer to the question asked in Revelation 6:17 (KJV) "Who shall be able to stand?"

Unlike those who will receive the "mark of the beast" [Rev. 13:16-17]), God's remnant people "keep the commandments of

God" and have the "testimony of Jesus Christ," which is the "spirit of prophecy" (Rev. 12:17; 19:10, KJV). They understand Bible prophecy and obey the Ten Commandments, which is the transcript of God's character and the foundation of His kingdom. Through the new covenant, Christ's followers allow Him to write His "laws into their hearts" and "in their minds" and are promised that during the investigative judgment, "their sins and iniquities ("lawless deeds" [NKJV]) will be remembered no more" (Heb. 10:16-17).

Moreover, the Lord seals His followers with His seventh-day Sabbath, *God's seal of time* that commemorates Christ as the Creator (Is. 8:16; Ex. 20:8-11). Since quality time is the foundation of all meaningful relationships, the Sabbath is vital in fostering a close relationship with Jesus! The Lord instructs His people, "… walk in my statutes, and keep my judgments, and do them: And hallow my sabbaths; and they will be a sign between me and you, that ye may know that I am the Lord your God" (Eze. 20:19-20, KJV). The Hebrew word for *"sign"* in this text is *"owth," meaning "mark."* Therefore, Christ seals His followers with His law, marking their commitment to worship their Creator on the Sabbath, God's seal of loyalty (2 Cor. 1:21-22; Rev. 14:7, 12).

Revelation 7:9 (KJV) further describes God's people as being "clothed with white robes." These white robes of character are "garments of salvation" and "robes of righteousness" (Is. 61:10; Rev. 19:8; Job 29:14, KJV). They are given to Christ's followers who ask for their characters to be washed in the blood of the Lamb (Zech. 3:1-5; Is. 64:6; 61:10; Is. 1:18; Rev. 7:9-10, 14). Therefore, those who allow the Holy Spirit to cleanse their hearts from sin and purify their characters will daily live in Christ's righteousness, looking forward to His soon return! (Rev. 7:14, KJV; 1 Jn. 1:9).

Today, Christ's remnant people must wake up and declare, "Fear God and give glory to Him, for the hour of his judgment is come" (the investigative judgment that began in 1844) "and worship Him that made heaven, and earth, and the sea and fountains of water," (an allusion to the fourth commandment, Sabbath [Rev. 14:7; Ex. 20:11, KJV; parentheses added]). The 144,000, through the Holy Spirit, will lead God's people in the loud cry of the Three Angels' Messages (Rev. 14:6-12). As a result, many from "all nations, kindreds, peoples, and tongues" will be prepared to meet Christ at His second coming (Rev. 7:9). May we pray that we will be a part of God's remnant, spreading His truth and sealed for the day of redemption! (Eph. 4:30).

# Discussion Questions for Revelation 7

1. What is a seal used for? What does having God's seal do for His people? (2 Tim. 2:19; Rev. 7:2-3; Dan. 12:1)

2. What are the four angels "holding back" and why? (Rev. 7:2-3; Jer. 4:11-13)

3. How do we know that the tribes of Israel that compose the 144,000 are not representative of literal Israel? (Rev. 7:4-8; Eph. 2:11-13)

4. Where did the great multitude come from? What promises are given to them? (Rev. 7:13-17; Is. 49:10)

5. What is Christ's seal, where is it located, and why? (Is. 8:16; Rev. 7:2-3; 14:1; Heb. 10:16; Josh. 24:15)

6. What characteristics do those with God's seal portray? (Rev. 12:17; 19:10)

7. What, specifically, does the sealed of God have in their minds, and how does it benefit them? (Heb. 10:16-17; Is. 8:16)

8. Why is the Sabbath a "sign" or "mark" of identification for God's people? (Eze. 20:19-20; Rev. 14:7, 12; Ex. 20:8-11)

9. What does having a "white robe" represent, and why is it "white"? (Rev. 7:9, 14; 19:8, KJV; Is. 61:10; Job 29:14, KJV)

10. How are God's people described in Revelation 7:14, and how can we become "washed in the blood of the Lamb" today? (Zech. 3:1-7; I John 1:9)

11. What are God's people sealed for? (Eph. 4:30; 2 Cor. 1:21-22; Rev. 14:7, 12)

12. How are the 144,000 empowered, and what are they chosen to do? (Joel 2:23, 28-29; Rev. 14:6-12)

# Revelation 8 (KJV)

[1] *And when he had opened the seventh seal, there was silence in heaven about the space of half an hour. [2] And I saw the seven angels which stood before God; and to them were given seven trumpets. [3] And another angel came and stood at the altar, having a golden censer; and there was given unto him much incense, that he should offer it with the prayers of all saints upon the golden altar which was before the throne. [4] And the smoke of the incense, which came with the prayers of the saints, ascended up before God out of the angel's hand. [5] And the angel took the censer, and filled it with fire of the altar, and cast it into the earth: and there were voices, and thunderings, and lightnings, and an earthquake. [6] And the seven angels which had the seven trumpets prepared themselves to sound. [7] The first angel sounded, and there followed hail and fire mingled with blood, and they were cast upon the earth: and the third part of trees was burnt up, and all green grass was burnt up. [8] And the second angel sounded, and as it were a great mountain burning with fire was cast into the sea: and the third part of the sea became blood; [9] And the third part of the creatures which were in the sea, and had life, died; and the third part of the ships were destroyed. [10] And the third angel sounded, and there fell a great star from heaven, burning as it were a lamp, and it fell upon the third part of the rivers, and upon the fountains of waters; [11] And the name of the star is called Wormwood: and the third part of the waters became wormwood; and many men died of the waters, because they were made bitter. [12] And the fourth angel sounded, and the*

*third part of the sun was smitten, and the third part of the moon, and the third part of the stars; so as the third part of them was darkened, and the day shone not for a third part of it, and the night likewise.* [13] *And I beheld, and heard an angel flying through the midst of heaven, saying with a loud voice, Woe, woe, woe, to the inhabiters of the earth by reason of the other voices of the trumpet of the three angels, which are yet to sound!*

# The Trumpets Sound

Have you ever tried to call a loved one, and just as you hear the phone start to connect, the line goes dead? John might have felt a similar frustration as he watched the seventh seal burst open. He had just seen the familiar heavenly signs of Christ's second coming predicted in the Old Testament—the sun being darkened and the moon turning to blood (Joel 2:31) — and then suddenly he experiences… SILENCE… in heaven for about half an hour (Rev. 8:1).

This silence is exactly what happened in 1844 when God's faithful followers expected Jesus to return. The signs of Christ's coming—the great Lisbon earthquake, the unexplainable Dark Day, the spectacular 1833 meteor shower, as well as the ending of the 2,300-day/year prophecy—all seemed to point to Earth's final climax. However, as God's people stared expectantly into the sky on October 22, 1844, the heavens met their eager anticipation with … SILENCE … and disappointment, too great to describe, descended upon them as black as midnight!

This tragic misfortune of Christ's people was likely predicted in Revelation 10:8-10 when John was instructed to eat the seventh unsealed scroll that made his "belly bitter," but was "sweet as honey" in his mouth (Rev. 8:1; 10:9, KJV). Likewise, the early Advent believers joyfully "ate up" the message of Jesus's imminent return, just to have it turn bitter when silence followed in 1844, and Christ did not appear on the expected date. The ridicule that the Lord's followers endured after this great disappointment proved extremely trying, and many gave up their faith; however, a few decided to go back to God's Word and see where they had made their error.

Soon diligent Bible students discovered an explanation of why Jesus had not returned on October 22, 1844. Instead of coming to the earth, Christ had moved from the Holy Place into the Most Holy Place in the *heavenly* sanctuary to begin the investigative judgment of God's people (Rev. 8:1-5; Dan. 7:9-14; Heb. 8:1-2; 9:23-25; 10:19-21, 29-31). The end of the 2,300-day/year prophecy predicted this "cleansing" of the heavenly sanctuary from sin (Dan. 8:14), similar to what occurred on the Jewish Day of Atonement, instead of the final judgment of the earth being cleansed by fire (which was the commonly held belief at that time). These faithful few sent out the word of their discovery to others. As time passed, Adventists from different Protestant denominations joined together, united by their common beliefs of the soon return of Jesus and the understanding of the beginning of the investigative judgment in 1844.

As more and more of God's people searched the Scriptures, the seventh-day Sabbath that had largely been lost during the papacy's reign of the Dark Ages was also rediscovered. This truth of the seventh-day Sabbath, combined with the Advent hope and the sanctuary judgment message, inspired a small remnant of Christ's believers to form a new Protestant denomination which officially became the Seventh-day Adventist Church in 1863.

Such careful Bible searching took place during the seventh seal's silence, spanning "about a half an hour" (Rev. 8:1). Why silence at this time? Habakkuk 2:20 admonishes, "The Lord is *in His holy temple:* let all the earth keep *silence* before Him" (KJV; italics added). Zechariah 2:13 also declares, "Be *silent,* O all flesh, before the Lord: for he is *raised up out of His holy habitation"* (KJV; italics added). These two verses indicate that silence is associated with Christ moving out of the Holy Place and into the Most Holy Place in the heavenly sanctuary. Isaiah 41:1 (KJV) further states, "Keep *silence* before Me… let us come near together to *judgment"* (italics added). This verse likely refers to silence at the beginning of the investigative judgment that occurred in 1844, the close of the 2,300-day/year prophecy (Dan. 7:9-14; 8:14; Ps. 76:7-9). Therefore, during the seventh seal, about half an hour of silence likely transpired after Christ moved from the Holy Place to the Most Holy Place to begin His work of judgment.

But how long is *"about* a half an hour" in heavenly timing? As previously discovered, the timing of Bible prophecy can be calculated in more than one way (compare Is. 29:1). Second Peter 3:8 (NKJV) states, "Beloved, do not forget this one thing, that with the Lord, one day is as a thousand years, and a thousand years as one day." This heavenly timing is also spoken of in Psalm 90:4 (KJV), "For a thousand years in thy sight are but as yesterday…" If 1,000 years are divided by a twenty-four-hour day, one hour is approximately forty-one years. If forty-one years are divided in half, the total equals about twenty years for half an hour. So about half of an hour in Heaven's time is approximately twenty years of Earth's time according to the Bible. Amazingly, this is about the same time period that passed between 1844 and 1863, when the Seventh-day Adventist Church was being established. After the silence in Heaven ended, the newly organized Seventh-day Adventist church loudly proclaimed the Three Angels' Messages that included the truth of the investigative judgment.

After the breaking of the seventh sealed time period, John's attention was turned to seven angels who were given seven trumpets. Revelation 8:3-5 (NKJV) states:

> Then another angel, having a golden censor... stood at the altar. He was given much incense that he should offer it with the prayers of all the saints upon the golden altar.... And the smoke of the incense, with the prayers of the saints, ascended before God.... Then the angel took the censer, filled it with fire from the altar, and threw it to the earth. And there were noises, thunderings, lightnings, and an earthquake.

After John saw this angel (Christ, Himself, the Angel of God [Judges 6:22-24]) throw down the censer, signaling the end of probation for the established church system of the Dark Ages, he beheld the sounding of the seven angels (Rev. 8:4-6; Ps. 141:2).

The first four trumpets seem to link back to the timing of the fifth and sixth seals and be Christ's response to the martyrs' question, "How long?" (Rev. 6:10). As a result of the martyrs' pleas, fire from the altar of incense was thrown down upon the earth (Rev. 8:5). Fire, according to Acts 2:3-4, is a manifestation of the Holy Spirit (compare Heb. 12:29). So, God's Spirit was poured out at the sounding of the first trumpet, specifically during the Protestant Reformation (although previous historical soundings probably occurred). Moreover, the power of the Living Water of God's Word can be symbolized as hail (Jn. 1:14; 4:14; Jer. 17:13; Eph. 5:26; Ps. 18:13). Additionally, fire, "mingled with blood," could represent the fire of the Holy Spirit mingled with Christ's blood shed for sin (Jer. 23:29; Rev. 8:7; I John 5:6-8; Joel 2:28-30; Acts 2:19). God's Word declares in Isaiah 28:17 that "the hail will sweep away the refuge of lies" (compare Is. 30:30). So as a result of this "hailstorm" of biblical truth being "thrown to the earth," revivals broke out among a third of the Lord's people (symbolized as green grass/trees [Rev. 8:7; Is. 40:7; Jer. 17:7-8]). Zechariah 13:8-9 (NKJV) states:

> "And it shall come to pass in all the land," says the Lord. "That two-thirds in it shall be cut off and die. But one-third shall be left in it; I will bring the one-third through the fire, will refine them as silver is refined, and test them as gold is tested. They will call on My name, And I will answer them." I will say, "this is My people...."

The Advent Movement, sparked by the power of God's Word, could be the spiritual result of the "voices" (*"phone"* meaning *"sound of a musical instrument"* signaling the beginning of the repetition of the seven trumpets [Rev. 4:1]), "thunderings" (the beginning of the repetition of the seven seals as thunders [Rev. 6:1; 10:3-4]), "lightnings (the light of the Bible [Ps. 119:105]), "and an earthquake" (Rev. 8:5; compare Ex. 20:18). The Lisbon earthquake in 1755, was possibly a physical sign of the spiritual revival of the Holy Spirit that shook the world and triggered the next trumpet (compare the sixth seal [Rev. 6:12; Rev. 8:5; Joel 2:29-31]).

In 1798, the second trumpet likely sounded, heralding the political fall of the papacy. This collapse of civil power when the pope was taken captive was represented by a great mountain (kingdom [Rev. 8:8; Jer. 51:24-25; Rev. 17:4-5, 18]) being consumed by fire (the Holy Spirit [Acts 2:3-4]) and thrown into the sea (people [Rev. 17:15]). Additionally, a third of its creatures figuratively died and the sea became blood (one-third of Catholics converted to Protestantism and claimed Christ's blood for the atonement of their sin [Zech. 13:8-9; Matt. 26:28]). Also, the papacy's symbolic "ships" (weapons of spiritual warfare [Rev. 8:9, KJV; Is. 43:14-17]) were destroyed.

Next, the third trumpet sounded, and John saw a "great star" (angel [Rev. 1:20]) fall from Heaven (Lucifer [Is. 14:12]) "burning as it were a lamp" (Rev. 8:10, KJV). Christ predicted the fall of the Devil when he warned his disciples in Luke 10:18 (KJV), "I beheld Satan as lightning (*"astrape"- "lamp"*) fall from heaven." So, Satan figuratively fell from the revival of God's Word; however, the Devil caused the Bible's living waters [Jer. 17:13; John 4:10; Eph. 5:26]) to become bitter like wormwood (Amos 6:12; Is. 5:20), and a third spiritually died (Rev. 8:10-11; 17:15; Eze. 5:12). This figurative massacre was the tragic result of God's Word being corrupted by Satan's false teachings. Beginning during the time of the third trumpet, humanistic theories embittered the world, propelling the so-called "Age of *Reason*," or, ironically, the "Enlightenment," which would develop into modernism.[146] Interestingly, Revelation 9:2 (KJV) states that the air was "darkened by *reason* of the smoke...." This philosophy that manifested itself during the French Revolution was brought to the United States through the writings of authors such as Thomas Paine. These lies poisoned biblical truth and resulted figuratively in the spiritual death of a third of God's people. Humanistic reasoning, therefore, was Satan's counterattack against the revivals caused by the Great Awakenings.

Then the fourth trumpet sounded, and John beheld signs in the heavens—the sun, moon, and stars were darkened (Rev. 8:12). These heavenly occurrences, manifested in the Dark Day of 1780 and the falling of the stars in 1833, paralleled what John had seen in the sixth seal, indicating a similar time period leading up to the investigative judgment in 1844 (Rev. 6:12). Moreover, the darkening of a third of the sun, moon, and stars could represent a falling away of God's people, such as occurred during the Great

---

[146] https://www.philosophybasics.com/historical_reason.html

Disappointment when Jesus did not return to the earth as expected (Ps. 89:35-37; Gen. 15:5; Dan. 12:3).

After John saw these signs of Christ's coming, a loud cry went forth, "Woe, woe, woe to the inhabiters of the earth by reason of the other voices of the trumpets of the three angels which are yet to sound" (Rev. 8:13, KJV). Most likely, these woes of the last three trumpets correspond to the proclamation of the Three Angels' Messages (Rev. 14:6-12) and follow the seventh seal (Rev. 8:1; discussed in the next chapter).

In summary, the first four trumpets began their proposed repetition during the Protestant Reformation and extended throughout the first and second Great Awakenings, leading up to 1844, the close of the 2,300-day prophecy and the breaking of the seventh seal (Dan. 8:14; Rev. 8:1). They served as wake-up calls for God's children, emphasizing that the investigative judgment had begun in Heaven (Eze. 33:5, Amos 3:6-7; Dan. 7:10). Moreover, just as Daniel's visions repeat and expand in detail, so the first four trumpets in John's vision repeat the timing of the fifth and sixth seals. By faithfully studying these prophecies, we can sound His truth today to the world!

# Discussion Questions for Revelation 8

1. How might the silence of the seventh seal tie to Revelation 10:8-10? (Rev. 8:1; Zech. 2:13; Hab. 2:20)

2. Instead of returning to the earth, where did Christ go in 1844 at the end of the 2,300-day/year prophecy, and why? (Dan. 7:10, 22; 8:14; Ps. 76:7-9; Is. 41:1)

3. Why was Heaven "silent" during approximately half an hour of heavenly time between 1844 and 1863? (Rev. 8:1; 14:6-12)

4. How might God have answered the prayers of the martyrs in the fifth seal, ascending from the golden altar in Revelation 8:3-5? (Rev. 6:10; Ps. 141:2; Joel 2:28-30)

5. What could the symbol of hail mixed with fire and blood which burned up a third of the green grass and trees represent? (Rev. 8:7; Is. 28:17; Ps. 18:13; Acts 2:3-4; Jer. 23:29; I John 5:6-8; Is. 40:7; Jer. 17:7-8; Eze. 5:2)

6. What could the symbol of the great mountain burning with fire and the destruction of a third of the sea, the living creatures, and the ships represent? (Rev. 8:8; Jer. 51:24-25, 27; Rev. 17:4-5, 18; Is. 43:14)

7. Who is referred to as a "great star" falling to Earth, and how did he make God's Living Water bitter as wormwood? (Rev. 8:10; 1:20; Luke 10:18; Is. 14:12; Amos 6:12; Is. 5:20)

8. How does the fourth trumpet compare to the sixth seal? (Rev. 8:12; 6:12; Joel 2:10, 31)

9. What is the purpose of the first four trumpets? (Rev. 4:1; Eze. 33:5; Amos 3:6-7)

# Revelation 9 (KJV)

*¹And the fifth angel sounded, and I saw a star fall from heaven unto the earth: and to him was given the key of the bottomless pit. ²And he opened the bottomless pit; and there arose a smoke out of the pit, as the smoke of a great furnace; and the sun and the air were darkened by reason of the smoke of the pit. ³And there came out of the smoke locusts upon the earth: and unto them was given power, as the scorpions of the earth have power. ⁴And it was commanded them that they should not hurt the grass of the earth, neither any green thing, neither any tree; but only those men which have not the seal of God in their foreheads. ⁵And to them it was given that they should not kill them, but that they should be tormented five months: and their torment was as the torment of a scorpion, when he striketh a man. ⁶And in those days shall men seek death, and shall not find it; and shall desire to die, and death shall flee from them. ⁷And the shapes of the locusts were like unto horses prepared unto battle; and on their heads were as it were crowns like gold, and their faces were as the faces of men. ⁸And they had hair as the hair of women, and their teeth were as the teeth of lions. ⁹And they had breastplates, as it were breastplates of iron; and the sound of their wings was as the sound of chariots of many horses running to battle. ¹⁰And they had tails like unto scorpions, and there were stings in their tails: and their power was to hurt men five months. ¹¹And they had a king over them, which is the angel of the bottomless pit, whose name in the Hebrew tongue is Abaddon, but in the Greek tongue hath his name Apollyon. ¹²*

*One woe is past; and, behold, there come two woes more hereafter.* [13] *And the sixth angel sounded, and I heard a voice from the four horns of the golden altar which is before God,* [14] *Saying to the sixth angel which had the trumpet, Loose the four angels which are bound in the great river Euphrates.* [15] *And the four angels were loosed, which were prepared for an hour, and a day, and a month, and a year, for to slay the third part of men.* [16] *And the number of the army of the horsemen were two hundred thousand thousand: and I heard the number of them.* [17] *And thus I saw the horses in the vision, and them that sat on them, having breastplates of fire, and of jacinth, and brimstone: and the heads of the horses were as the heads of lions; and out of their mouths issued fire and smoke and brimstone.* [18] *By these three was the third part of men killed, by the fire, and by the smoke, and by the brimstone, which issued out of their mouths.* [19] *For their power is in their mouth, and in their tails: for their tails were like unto serpents, and had heads, and with them they do hurt.* [20] *And the rest of the men which were not killed by these plagues yet repented not of the works of their hands, that they should not worship devils, and idols of gold, and silver, and brass, and stone, and of wood: which neither can see, nor hear, nor walk:* [21] *Neither repented they of their murders, nor of their sorceries, nor of their fornication, nor of their thefts.*

# The Woes of the Last Three Trumpets

Have you ever looked into the darkness outside and suddenly a flash of light streaks across the sky from a falling star and disappears into blackness? This might have been how John felt as he stared into the dark gloom that had descended upon the world during the fifth trumpet. This spiritual darkness was caused by the deceptions of the Devil, the fallen angel, represented as the "star" fallen "from heaven unto the earth" (Rev. 9:1, KJV; Rev. 1:20).

## The Fifth Trumpet Sounds

As the apostle, John, watched, Satan, the fallen star of the third trumpet, was given authority over the earth, symbolized as the "key of the bottomless pit" (Rev. 8:10-11; 9:1-2, KJV). "Keys" in the Bible represent authority (Rev. 1:18; 3:7; 20:1; Matt. 16:19), and the "bottomless pit" (*"abyssos"*- *"abyss"*) most likely symbolizes the earth (Rev. 9:11; 11:7; 17:8; 20:1-3; Is. 24:1-3, 21-22). As a result, the "sun and the air were darkened by reason…" of the Devil's deceptions (Rev. 9:2, KJV). Then from the depths of this satanic "smoke," false teachers went forth as "locusts," like "many horses running to battle," reminiscent of the horsemen's spiritual warfare outlined in the seals (Rev. 9:7, 9 compare Rev. 6:1-8 [KJV}; "locusts" [Nahum 3:15-17; Jer. 51:14, 27]). These false teachers were compared to "scorpions" with stingers of deception in their tails (Rev. 9:3, 5, 10, 19; Luke 10:19; Eze. 2:6; Is. 9:15). On their heads were crowns of something like gold (first seal of

Christianity [Rev. 9:7; 6:2]) with "faces of men" (humanism [Rev. 9:7]). Furthermore, they were disguised with women's hair, symbolizing the covering of a church (Rev. 9:8; I Cor. 11:15; Jer. 3:20; 7:28-29), yet their teeth were destructive as lions' teeth (Babylon's teachings [Rev. 9:8; Jer. 50:17, Micah 3:5]). These false teachers destroyed men with their mouths, speaking blasphemies (Rev. 13:2, 5; Eze. 22:25-26; 2 Thess. 2:4). They also had "breastplates of iron," (Rome [Rev. 9:9; Dan. 2:40]). Moreover, they had a "king," the "angel of the bottomless pit," over them (Satan [Rev. 9:11; 20:2-3]), who is named *"Abaddon" or "Apollyon" ("destroyer"* [Rev. 9:11; Rev. 6:8]).

However, the Devil's deceptions were not allowed to sway those sealed in their foreheads who had made a conscious decision to obey God's law, including the Sabbath (Rev. 9:4; 12:17; Is. 8:16; Eze. 20:20). Luke 10:19 (KJV) states, "Behold, I give you power to tread on *serpents and scorpions,* and over *all the power of the enemy:* and nothing shall by any means hurt you" (italics added; compare Rev. 9:3, 5, 10; 12:9; Eze. 2:6).

Yet, the false teachers were not prevented from tormenting the *apostate* Christians for "five months" (Rev. 9:10, KJV). Although the time prophecies of the fifth and sixth trumpet, using a day-for-a-year method, ended in the 1840s (the close of the historical 2,300-day prophecy), the context of the fifth trumpet indicates that they would repeat after October 22, 1844, the proposed ending date of the fourth trumpet and the beginning of the seventh seal (Rev. 8:1). If one uses the principle of timing found in Lev. 25:8 and Deut. 16:9, five months can be multiplied by forty-nine, equaling 245 months. Then if these months are divided into years, the total is twenty years and five months, which, added to 1844, ends in 1864/1865. Specifically, during 1844-1865, spiritualism spread its demonic smoke across America (Rev. 9:2), beginning with Spear's visions, Davis's mesmerism,[147] and the mysterious "knockings" of the Fox sisters.[148] Although the belief of contacting the dead is strictly forbidden in God's Word (Lev. 20:6, 27), spiritualism reared its ugly head, even in the United State's White House! President Lincoln, through his wife, Mary, was involved with a spiritist, Nettie Colburn, who counseled the president concerning the Civil War and held seances in the White House during 1863-1865 (end of "five months" [Rev. 9:10])[149] Amazingly, spiritualism continued its growth in America until, by the end of the Civil War, a third of the U.S. population — 11 million[150] out of 31 million[151] — subscribed to this religion. Prophecy likely refers to these demonic manifestations and their proponents as "scorpions" with "stings in their tails" that would spiritually "torment" men and kill a third of them in the sixth trumpet (Rev. 9:3, 5, 10, 18-19; Lk. 10:18-19, KJV).

Additionally, Edwin Irving, the founder of the Catholic Apostolic Church, became the precursor of modern Pentecostalism during this time, emphasizing the spiritualistic gift of tongues. This tongue-speaking was not used to spread the gospel in foreign languages as was described in Acts 2:1-11 but was instead called "supernatural stirrings."[152] Irving promoted these "stirrings" as "Spirit Baptism and tongues," which "would become the primary teaching of Classic Pentecostalism."[153] He was given

---

[147] https://www.mentalfloss.com/article/571569/spiritualist-god-machine; https://www.mentalfloss.com/article/507314/how-shoemaker-became-americas-most-controversial-mystic-and-inspired-edgar-allan-poe

[148] https://www.historynet.com/the-fox-sisters-spiritualisms-unlikely-founders.htm

[149] https://archive.org/details/wasabrahamlin2031mayn/page/n239/mode/2up; http://troytaylorbooks.blogspot.com/2014/02/do-you-ever-find-yourself-talking-to.html; http://www.mrlincolnswhitehouse.org/residents-visitors/marys-charlatans/marys-charlatans-nettie-colburn-1841-1892/

[150] http://austintexas.gov/sites/default/files/files/Parks/OHenry/spiritualism.pdf

[151] https://www.history.com/news/civil-war-deadlier-than-previously-thought

[152] https://core.ac.uk/download/pdf/58820129.pdf

[153] ibid

the title, "angel" of the Catholic Apostolic Church (compare "angel" [Rev. 9:11] and covering of "woman's hair" [church— Rev. 9:8])[154] Also, he taught that Christ had a sinful human nature ("face of a man" [Rev. 9:7]) and would return in 1864, twenty years after the Great Disappointment of 1844 ("five months" [Rev. 9:10])[155] He believed in a "universal church" (ecumenicalism ["teeth like lions"- Rev. 9:8; Eze. 22:25-26])[156] and his followers formed the Catholic Apostolic Church of New York in 1851.[157] This church continued promoting tongue-speaking, which may be described as the "sound of their wings was as the sound of chariots of many horses running into battle" (Rev. 9:9, KJV). The Greek word for "sound" in this text is *"phone,"* which means *"language, noise (of an instrument), voice, speech,"* and is similar to the sound of the babbling noise of glossolalia when a congregation is speaking in tongues (Is. 29:4). This phenomenon would become the cornerstone of modern Pentecostalism in the United States, growing from the Holiness Movement and the Wesleyan Methodist Connection in 1843,[158] and masquerading as a Protestant Christian belief ("crowns like gold" [Rev. 9:7; 6:2]).

Then John heard the angel proclaim that the first woe was passed, and there were two more woes to come (Rev. 9:12). Next, the sixth trumpet sounded with "a voice from the four horns of the golden altar which is before God" (Rev. 9:13, KJV). This voice is likely from Christ, Himself, ministering in the Most Holy Place of the heavenly temple in front of the altar of incense where the saints' prayers are continually rising (Rev. 8:3-4; Heb. 9:24-25). Also, the four horns of the altar may be symbolically tied to the four winds of the four corners of the earth that were restrained

---

[154] ibid
[155] https://www.britannica.com/biography/Edward-Irving
[156] ibid
[157] http://s-media.nyc.gov/agencies/lpc/lp/2077.pdf
[158] https://christianhistoryinstitute.org/magazine/article/holiness-movement-timeline

from blowing earlier and causing worldwide harm (Rev. 7:1-3; compare Dan. 8:8). This time the four angels who had been "bound" at the Euphrates River were released (Rev. 9:13-14; Jude 1:6; Jer. 46:6-10; Rev. 12:15; 16:12). This symbolic 200-million army of false religious teachers wore breastplates of "fiery red," (spiritualism/second seal (Rev. 9:17; 6:4; 12:3, 9 [NKJV]); hyacinth blue/black (humanistic civil government/third seal [Rev. 6:5, NKJV]); and pale/sulfur yellow (Roman Catholicism/fourth seal [Rev. 6:8, NKJV]). They rode on horses with heads like lions (Babylon/apostate Christianity [Rev. 9:17; 13:2; 17:5; Jer. 50:17; Eze. 22:25-26, KJV]) and out of their mouths came fire, smoke, and brimstone (wickedness [Rev. 9:17-21; Is. 9:18-19, KJV]). These false teachers led by demons spiritually kill a third of mankind (compare the fall of a third of the angels [Rev. 9:15; 12:4, 7-9; 1:20; Nahum 3:1-4; Eze. 5:2, 12]).

Later in the vision, John was shown that the Devil is symbolized as "that old serpent" (Rev. 12:9, KJV), and Isaiah 9:15 (KJV) further explains, "the prophet that teacheth lies, he is the tail." Describing such attacks, the Bible states: "for their power is in their mouth and in their tails: for their tails were like unto serpents, and had heads, and with them they do hurt" (Rev. 9:19, KJV). So, this scheme by Satan (serpent) and his false teachers (tail) wars against God's people through the deceptive teachings of spiritualism, humanism, and Roman Catholicism, specifically in the United States, the most prominent Protestant nation in the world.

Moreover, the Bible predicts that this war was prepared for "an hour, and a day, and a month, and a year" (Rev. 9:15, KJV). Using a day for a year, Josiah Litch figured this timing and added it to the five months in the fifth trumpet to predict the fall of the

Ottoman Empire in the 1840s.[159] However, if one uses the same previous timing as the fifth trumpet and each period is multiplied by forty-nine, the total of the sixth trumpet comes to fifty-three years. Then if this product is added to 1864 (the proposed ending date of the repeated fifth trumpet), it comes to the year, 1917, the same year that the U.S. entered WWI[160] and the Ottoman occupation of Jerusalem was defeated,[161] heralding the end of the Ottoman Empire.

Could this proposed repeated trumpet at this very time in history also be a warning that Satan would launch an all-out spiritual battle against Protestant America by uniting the earth's nations as a result of this first worldwide physical war? (Rev. 12:17). If the precise total of the fifth and sixth trumpets (73 years, 6 months, and 21 days) is added to Oct. 22, 1844, (the day Christ began the investigative judgment in Heaven), the total ends in the year, 1918, the same year that U.S. President Wilson was forming the League of Nations, the precursor to the United Nations.[162] Moreover, the very next year, the League of Nations encouraged international cooperation with the Catholic Holy See.[163] Presently, the Roman Catholic Church and the World Council of Churches work together through the ecumenical office of the United Nations to demonstrate their long-standing commitment to the UN and the ideals embodied in the UN Charter and "to give voice to the ethical, moral and spiritual values which must undergird international relations."[164] The Bible predicts that this

[159] https://www.diggingfortruth.org/digging-deeper/prophecies-in-5th-and-6th-trumpet/revelation-9---the-391-year-prophecy
[160] https://www.history.com/this-day-in-history/america-enters-world-war-i
[161] https://www.history.com/topics/middle-east/history-of-israel
[162] https://www.woodrowwilsonhouse.org/league-of-nations/
[163] https://en.wikipedia.org/wiki/Holy_See_and_the_United_Nations
[164] https://www.ncregister.com/news/are-the-holy-see-and-the-united-nations-too-close-for-comfort

ecumenical unity of the world's nations in cooperation with the papacy will eventually lead to the persecution of God's people (Rev. 13:15).

Moreover, at the same time that the League of Nations was being formed in 1918, spiritualism rose to its height in the United States, partly as a result of so many lives that were lost in WWI and the outbreak of the Spanish flu epidemic.[165] This climax of spiritualism that began in the early 1800s during the repetition of the fifth trumpet is likely referred to in the sixth trumpet when the Bible states that men would be killed; however, they would not repent of demon worship and sorceries (Rev. 9:15, 21).

Also coinciding with this peak of spiritualism, classical Pentecostalism was founded in the early 1900s, uniting interracially in the same year of 1918[166] and growing currently to over 200 million adherents worldwide (Rev. 9:16)[167] This phenomenon may be represented as "fire and smoke and brimstone" that comes out of the mouths of false teachers (Rev. 9:17, KJV). Since fire is a symbol of the Holy Spirit (Act. 2:3-4), this false "fire" may be referring to a false manifestation of the Holy Spirit, such as speaking in tongues by Pentecostals/Charismatics. The Pentecostal Movement has become a third "strand" of Christianity, following Catholicism and Protestantism, because of its tremendous growth in just over a hundred years.[168] Moreover, its astounding ecumenical influence between Protestants and Catholics is described in the following quote:

> The Charismatic movement had a tremendous potential to create trust and destroy suspicion between conflicting

---

[165] https://www.history.com/news/flu-pandemic-wwi-ouija-boards-spiritualism
[166] https://www.liquisearch.com/united_pentecostal_church_international/history
[167] https://www.liquisearch.com/pentecostalism/statistics_and_denominations
[168] https://bryanhodge.net/2021/11/10/denominations-pentecostals/

groups to provide a platform on which people could talk honestly and openly without being polarized.... *Already by bringing together Roman Catholics and Protestants, the Charismatic movement has worked miracles.* (Italics added)[169]

Furthermore, this ecumenism is currently growing between Catholics, mainline Protestants, Jews, and secular humanists who have recently united on several current political issues. For example, many humanists and Protestants have come together on social doctrines under Harvard's Values in Action initiative, a "centerpiece of humanistic thought and social action," that builds "alliances between religious and nonreligious individuals and communities" and unites them on common ground.[170] Other shared political views among these groups are immigration[171] and same-sex marriages, which became a U.S. nationwide law on June 26, 2015.[172] Also, mainline Protestant denominations united with the Roman Catholic Church by supporting global climate action with non-Christians.[173] Such efforts simply illustrate the current mixing of church and state in political activism, although the Bible specifically warns against mixing the secular with the spiritual:

> "... for what fellowship hath righteousness with unrighteousness? And what communion hath light with darkness? And what concord hath Christ with Belial (Satan

[169] Tim Dowley, *Introduction to the History of Christianity* (Fortress Press, 2006)
[170] https://americanhumanist.org/paths/christianity/
[171] https://neworleans.adl.org/news/catholics-protestants-jews-and-humanists-speak-up-for-obamas-immigration-order/
[172] https://www.hrc.org/resources/stances-of-faiths-on-lgbt-issues-humanism; https://www.theatlantic.com/politics/archive/2015/04/religious-americans-support-gay-marriage/391646/; https://www.npr.org/sections/thetwo-way/2015/06/26/417717613/supreme-court-rules-all-states-must-allow-same-sex-marriage
[173] https://journals.sagepub.com/doi/pdf/10.1177/0096340215599789

and his followers)? Or what part hath he that believeth with an infidel?" (2 Cor. 6:14-15; KJV; parenthesis added).

Sadly, the Bible states that this unity between the church and world governments will ultimately result in the loss of both civil and religious freedom (Rev. 13:15-17).

Revelation 9 prophesies that the earth's inhabitants will ignore God's trumpet warnings (Is. 66:16, KJV) and "worship demons, and idols of gold, silver, brass, stone, and wood... And they did not repent of their murders or their sorceries or their sexual immorality or their thefts" (Rev. 9:20-21, NKJV; compare Dan. 5:4, 23). However, with tender mercy, the Lord continues to send fervent wake-up calls to arouse His people from their deathly spiritual stupor, as He did during the Great Awakenings of the past. Even more desperately needed now, these warnings trumpet the urgency for repentance and reformation, pleading with God's people to declare to all of the earth's inhabitants: "Prepare ye the way of the Lord. Make His paths straight!" (Matt. 3:3, KJV; compare Amos 3:6). May we diligently sound this warning cry today in eager expectation of Christ's soon return!

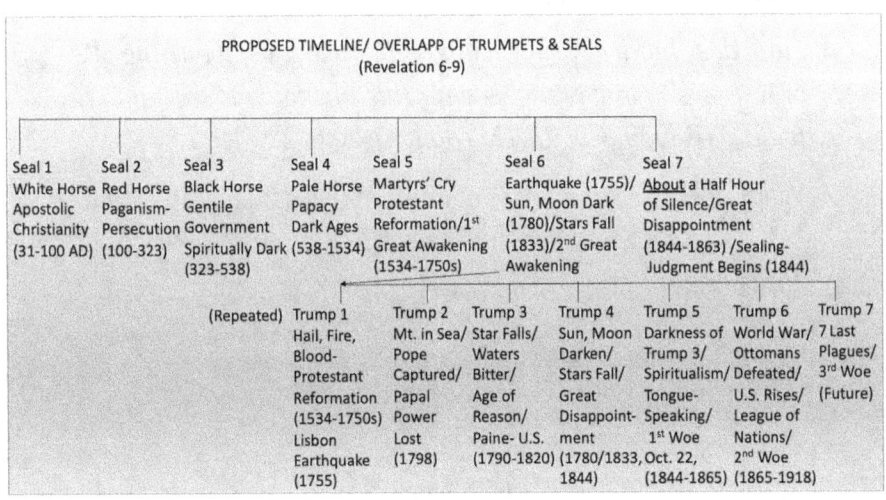

PROPOSED TIMELINE/ OVERLAPP OF TRUMPETS & SEALS
(Revelation 6-9)

| Seal 1 | Seal 2 | Seal 3 | Seal 4 | Seal 5 | | Seal 6 | | Seal 7 | |
|---|---|---|---|---|---|---|---|---|---|
| White Horse | Red Horse | Black Horse | Pale Horse | Martyrs' Cry | | Earthquake (1755)/ | | About a Half Hour | |
| Apostolic | Paganism- | Gentile | Papacy | Protestant | | Sun, Moon Dark | | of Silence/Great | |
| Christianity | Persecution | Government | Dark Ages | Reformation/1st | | (1780)/Stars Fall | | Disappointment | |
| (31-100 AD) | (100-323) | Spiritually Dark | (538-1534) | Great Awakening | | (1833)/2nd Great | | (1844-1863) /Sealing- | |
| | | (323-538) | | (1534-1750s) | | Awakening | | Judgment Begins (1844) | |

| | | (Repeated) | Trump 1 | Trump 2 | Trump 3 | Trump 4 | Trump 5 | Trump 6 | Trump 7 |
|---|---|---|---|---|---|---|---|---|---|
| | | | Hail, Fire, | Mt. in Sea/ | Star Falls/ | Sun, Moon | Darkness of | World War/ | 7 Last |
| | | | Blood- | Pope | Waters | Darken/ | Trump 3/ | Ottomans | Plagues/ |
| | | | Protestant | Captured/ | Bitter/ | Stars Fall/ | Spiritualism/ | Defeated/ | 3rd Woe |
| | | | Reformation | Papal | Age of | Great | Tongue- | U.S. Rises/ | (Future) |
| | | | (1534-1750s) | Power | Reason/ | Disappoint- | Speaking/ | League of | |
| | | | Lisbon | Lost | Paine- U.S. | ment | 1st Woe | Nations/ | |
| | | | Earthquake | (1798) | (1790-1820) | (1780/1833, | Oct. 22, | 2nd Woe | |
| | | | (1755) | | | 1844 | 1844) | (1865-1918) | |
| | | | | | | | (1844-1865) | | |

# Discussion Questions for Revelation 9

1. Who does a "star fallen from Heaven to the earth" represent? How did this event affect God's people, especially in the United States? (Rev. 9:1-3; Rev. 1:20; 12:3, 9, 17)

2. Who is represented by "locusts," "horses in battle," and "scorpions," with stingers in their tails? What promises are God's people given concerning them? (Rev. 9:3, 7, 9-10, 19; compare Rev. 6:4-8; Jer. 51:14, 27; Nahum 3:15-17; Eze. 2:6; Lk. 10:19)

3. What might "lions' teeth" represent? How do these false teachings destroy the church like lions destroy their prey? (Rev. 9:8; Eze. 22:25-26)

4. Who may be symbolized as "the angel of the bottomless pit," and how are Christ's people spiritually protected from his deceptions? (Rev. 9:11; 20:2-3; Rev. 9:4; Is. 8:16; Eze. 20:20)

5. How do the "breastplates of iron" refer back to Daniel's vision and give us a clue from where these false teachers originate? (Rev. 9:9; Dan. 2:40)

6. How does biblical prophecy possibly warn us about the false gift of tongues? How are we seeing this phenomenon demonstrated today? (Rev. 9:8-9; 13:13; compare Acts 2:3-4)

7. What does the symbolism of having "heads like lions" and "tails like serpents" possibly mean? (Rev. 9:17-19; Eze. 22:25-26; Is. 9:15; Rev. 12:3-4, 9)

8. What is the purpose of the trumpet calls? (Amos 3:6-7; Is. 66:16, KJV)

# Revelation 10 (KJV)

*¹ And I saw another mighty angel come down from heaven, clothed with a cloud: and a rainbow was upon his head, and his face was as it were the sun, and his feet as pillars of fire: ² And he had in his hand a little book open: and he set his right foot upon the sea, and his left foot on the earth, ³ And cried with a loud voice, as when a lion roareth: and when he had cried, seven thunders uttered their voices. ⁴ And when the seven thunders had uttered their voices, I was about to write: and I heard a voice from heaven saying unto me, Seal up those things which the seven thunders uttered, and write them not. ⁵ And the angel which I saw stand upon the sea and upon the earth lifted up his hand to heaven, ⁶ And sware by him that liveth for ever and ever, who created heaven, and the things that therein are, and the earth, and the things that therein are, and the sea, and the things which are therein, that there should be time no longer: ⁷ But in the days of the voice of the seventh angel, when he shall begin to sound, the mystery of God should be finished, as he hath declared to his servants the prophets. ⁸ And the voice which I heard from heaven spake unto me again, and said, Go and take the little book which is open in the hand of the angel which standeth upon the sea and upon the earth. ⁹ And I went unto the angel, and said unto him, Give me the little book. And he said unto me, Take it, and eat it up; and it shall make thy belly bitter, but it shall be in thy mouth sweet as honey. ¹⁰ And I took the little book out of the angel's hand, and ate it up; and it was in my mouth sweet as honey: and as soon as I had eaten it, my belly was bitter.* [11] *And he said unto me, Thou must prophesy again before many peoples, and nations, and tongues, and kings.*

# No More Delay

Have you ever received a gift, but you were told that you had to wait to open it? The delay probably seemed like an eternity until the allotted time finally arrived, and you could rip off the wrapping paper and discover what was inside! Perhaps John felt a similar excitement as he saw a mighty angel coming down from Heaven. This glorious event must have seemed like a long-awaited present after seeing the degeneration of Christ's church that would occur in the future.

Suddenly, he beheld a "mighty angel" who was "clothed with a *cloud*" (Rev. 10:1, KJV; Ex. 19:9), a "*rainbow* was upon his head" (Gen. 9:12-13), "his face was as it were the sun" (Mal. 4:2; Rev. 1:16), and "his feet as *pillars of fire*" (Ex. 13:21). Immediately, John must have realized that this was no common angel! Undoubtedly, he was reminded of God's covenant to never again destroy the earth with water when he saw the *rainbow* over the Angel's head (Gen. 9:16-17). Moreover, this description fits the "angel of God," the Lord, Himself, who led Israel with a *pillar of fire* by night and a *cloud* by day (Ex. 14:19; Is. 4:5).

Additionally, John saw a "little book" open in the Angel's hand (Rev. 10:2, KJV). The Greek word for "little book" in this text stems from the word, "*biblion*," meaning a "*small book, scroll.*" John noted that this scroll was "opened" or unsealed, which would logically refer back to the scroll with the seven broken seals, and likely contained the prophecies of Daniel (Rev. 5:1, 5; Dan. 12:9). Moreover, the scroll was "written inside and on the back" like the Ten Commandments (Rev. 5:1, NKJV; compare Zech. 5:1-4; Ex. 32:15). Woes and "mourning" (*"hegeh"*- *"rumbling"* as *"thunder"* [Eze. 2:9-10; Rev. 10:4]) against those who disobey God's law were likely included in this scroll, leaving John in distress until he was shown that Christ had taken these curses upon Himself for His people (Rev. 5:4-7; Dan. 9:11; Gal. 3:13).

Then, John saw this mighty Messenger "set his right foot upon the sea and his left foot on the earth" (possession [Josh 1:3]) "lifted up his hand to heaven" and swear by "him who liveth forever and ever, who created heaven and the things that therein are, the earth, and the things that therein are, and the sea, and the things which are therein… " (Rev. 10:2, 5-6, KJV). The fact that this promise is sworn by the everlasting Creator of Heaven, Earth, and the sea gives it authority and utmost importance! The title of Creator God found in this covenant is also referred to in Revelation 14:7 (KJV), "… and worship him that made heaven, and earth, and the sea, and the fountains of water." As previously shown, this command in Revelation echos Exodus 20:11 (KJV), "For in six days the Lord made *heaven and earth, the sea, and all that in them is*, and rested the seventh day: wherefore, the Lord blessed the sabbath day, and hallowed it" (italics added). From these texts, God's law is the foundation of His government and His covenant with His people, both in the Old Testament and in the New (Deut. 4:13; Heb. 10:16). Therefore, Christ's seal of the Sabbath includes His *title*, Creator, and His *territory* (Heaven, the earth, the sea and all things in each of them), similar to national seals today (Rev. 10:6).

Because a covenant relationship with Christ results in obedience to the Ten Commandments, Satan viciously attacks those keeping God's law, specifically in the last days of Earth's history (Rev. 12:12, 17; I Jn. 2:3-6). If the Devil can tempt the righteous to intentionally disobey God's commandments, *even in one point,* then the covenant is no longer in effect, and the Lord's protection is withdrawn (James 2:10; Jer. 11:3-8). However, Satan knows that if God's people confess their sins and return to keeping His law, the covenant is restored (II Chron. 7:14; Lev. 26:40-45). Moreover, Jesus is performing priestly mediation right now in Heaven for His people, presenting His blood sacrifice to cover their sin (Heb. 8:1-2, 6; 9:15). But Christ does not stop there! In fulfillment of His promise, He declares, "This is the covenant I will make with them after those days, saith the Lord, I will put My laws into their hearts, and in their minds will I write them" (Heb. 10:16, KJV). These laws are "written not with ink, but with the Spirit of the living God, not on tables of stone, but in fleshy tables of the heart" (2 Cor. 3:3, KJV). The Lord's followers are promised power to "keep the commandments of God" as the result of their "faith in Jesus" (Rev. 14:12, KJV). Furthermore, God's people can do "all things through Christ" (Phil. 4:13, KJV), and "with God, nothing shall be impossible" (Lk. 1:37, KJV). Therefore, Jesus, Himself, bestows upon His followers the forgiveness and cleansing of sin, *plus* the power to obey His Law just as He promises (I Jn. 1:9; 5:3-4). In fact, Christ swears to keep His covenant with His people by raising His hands in a solemn oath! (Rev. 10:5-6; Lk. 1:72-75).

Like in John's vision (Rev. 10:2, 5-6), Daniel also saw the Lord's covenant posture in the "man in linen" when Daniel asked for clarity as to when the prophecy given to him would occur:

> … he held up his right hand and his left hand unto heaven and sware by him that liveth forever that it shall be for a time, times, and a half, and when he shall have

accomplished to scatter the power of the holy people, all these things shall be finished…. Go thy way, Daniel: for the words are closed up and sealed till the time of the end. (Dan.12:7-9, KJV)

This time prophecy, as well as the 1,290 and 1,335-day prophecies, were "sealed" until the "time of the end." But Daniel was promised that these prophecies would be understood by the wise at the "end of the days" (Dan. 12:10, 13, KJV). When did the "end of the *days*" occur? The Bible links this time period to 1844, the completion of the historical 2,300-*day* prophecy (Dan. 8:14). Therefore, Daniel 12's "time, times, and a half," 1,290, and 1,335-day prophecies likely began in 1844 and would be understood just before Christ's second coming. This timing is further explained in Revelation 10:5-7 (KJV, italics added):

And the angel which I saw stand upon the sea and upon the earth lifted up his hand to heaven and sware by him that liveth for ever… that there should be time no longer: But in the days of the voice of the *seventh angel, when he shall begin to sound,* the mystery of God should be finished, as he hath declared to his servants the prophets.

This verse refers back to the previously discussed seven trumpets (Rev. 8-9). It points to the time periods occurring just before the seventh trumpet is blown. At this time, the thunderous horsemen from the second to the fourth seals likely repeat their attack on God's people (Rev. 9:14-19; 6:4-8) who are symbolized in the first seal of the white horse (Rev. 6:1-2). Revelation 10:3-4 (KJV) may also reference this powerful repetition of the seven seals by calling them "seven thunders" (compare Rev. 6:1; Is. 29:6):

(He) cried with a loud voice, as when a *lion* roareth: and

when he had cried, *seven thunders* uttered their *voices*. And when the *seven thunders* had uttered their *voices*, I was about to write: and I heard a voice from heaven saying unto me, "*Seal* up those things which the seven *thunders* uttered, and write them not. (italics, underlining, & parenthesis added)

In this text, the seven thunders are "*sealed*" after a cry goes out "as when a *lion* roareth" (Rev. 10:3-4). By comparing Revelation 6:1 to Revelation 10:3, one finds that when Jesus, the Lion of Judah, opened the first seal containing His white horse kingdom ("beast" [Dan. 7:23]), He spoke with a "*voice like thunder*" (Rev. 6:1; 4:7; 5:5, NKJV; compare Job 37:2-5). Moreover, the Bible states that horses are clothed with "*thunder*," tying thunder back to the first four seals (Job 39:19, KJV). When did the thunder of this white horse seal occur? It likely began after 1798 when Protestantism was unleashed and went forth unhindered by papal persecution, swelling during the Midnight Cry in 1844 and continuing today.

Specifically, from that time until the present, the last three symbolic horsemen of the second through the fourth seals have continually attacked God's white horse kingdom of Protestant Christianity (Rev. 6:2-8). These horsemen, the red horse of paganism/spiritualism (Rev. 12:3, 9), the black horse of humanistic government, and the pale horse of Catholicism have continued to repeat their assaults on God's people, especially in the United States. For example, the red horse of spiritualism exploded during the Civil War when the "sword" of deadly conflict divided America (Rev. 6:4). Additionally, the pagan worldview of "Social Darwinism" and the "survival of the fittest" rose in 1864 with Spencer's book, *Principles of Biology*.[174] Then, Pentecostalism

---

[174] https://www.smithsonianmag.com/science-nature/herbert-spencer-survival-of-the-fittest-180974756/

followed, beginning in the 1860s with Edwin Irving, and formalizing in the early 1900s.[175] Furthermore, the black horse of secular humanistic government mixed with spiritual darkness galloped forward after the Civil and World Wars to become the primary philosophy behind postmodern views, gaining prominence in 1967,[176] and heralding the Hippie Movement, the drug culture, and "free sex."[177] Finally, the pale horse of Catholicism and the ecumenical movement propelled in 1994 with the signing of *Evangelicals and Catholics Together*[178] continued its rise, heralding the "end" of the Protestant Reformation in 2017[179] when the martyr's cry of the fifth seal likely began its thunderous repetition (Rev. 6:10-11). In addition, modern omens of the soon-coming sixth seal include the Northridge earthquake of 1994, the "states' most destructive" quake "since San Francisco's in 1906 and the costliest one in U.S. history,"[180] the four blood moons occurring on Jewish feast days in 2014-2015,[181] as well as the Great American Eclipse in 2017 (Rev. 6:12-17; compare Is. 24:18-23; 29:6)[182] Repeated as "thunders" increasing in intensity, such wakeup calls were "sealed" in John's day, but would be revealed before Christ's return (Rev. 10:4-7, KJV; Dan. 12:7-9, 13).

Furthermore, Revelation 10:6 (NKJV) states that just before the sounding of the seventh trumpet, the mystery of God would

---

[175] http://s-media.nyc.gov/agencies/lpc/lp/2077.pdf

[176] https://www.christianitytoday.com/ct/1967/may-12/trouble-with-humanism.html

[177] https://theweek.com/articles/713202/sex-drugs-summer-love

[178] https://www.firstthings.com/article/1994/05/evangelicals-catholics-together-the-christian-mission-in-the-third-millennium

[179] https://www.ncronline.org/news/world/reformed-churches-endorse-catholic-lutheran-accord-key-reformation-dispute

[180] https://www.britannica.com/event/Northridge-earthquake-of-1994

[181] https://uscatholic.org/news_item/blood-moon-sets-off-apocalyptic-debate-among-some-christians/

[182] https://en.wikipedia.org/wiki/Solar_eclipse_of_August_21,_2017

no longer be "delayed." To what delay was the Angel referring? Again, one must go back to Daniel when he prays, "O Lord, hear! O Lord, forgive! O Lord, listen and act! *Do not delay* for your own sake, my God, for Your city and Your people are called by Your name" (Dan. 9:19, NKJV; italics added). In direct answer to this prayer, the Lord gave Daniel the event that would signal the beginning of the 2,300-day prophecy (Dan. 9:25; 8:14). According to Revelation 10:7, the context of this delay would end when the investigative judgment would commence at the close of this prophecy in 1844 in preparation of the sounding of the seventh angel. Likely the prophetic timing of a day-for-a-year used historically to figure the 2300-day prophecy is what the Angel referenced when He stated that "there shall be time (delay) no longer" (Rev. 10:6, KJV; parenthesis added). However, the Angel did not say that all time prophecies had ended in 1844 since the Bible cites additional time prophecies afterward (i.e. Rev. 18:10; 20:2, 7). Instead, a complete understanding of the fulfillment of time prophecies, such as the 2,300-day prophecy, had just been *delayed* (Rev. 10:6, NKJV). Instead, Daniel was promised that the wise would understand these time prophecies when they would become unsealed at "the time of the end" (Dan. 12:9-10, KJV).

Just as John saw the covenant posture of the Angel in Revelation 10, Daniel saw this same posture in chapter 12, but in Daniel's vision, he was given "a time, times, and a half" as the answer to his question, "How long?" (vs. 7-8, KJV). If one uses the timing found in Leviticus 25:8 and inserts forty-nine-year periods for each "time" in this prophecy, it totals 171.5 years (compare Is. 29:1). Then if these years are added to 1844 (the end of the 2,300-day prophecy), they end in 2015. Amazingly, on Sept. 24, 2015, *for the first time in history*, the pope met with the U.S. Congress in a formal session, urging governmental leaders to take action on climate change. Just months later, the U.S. joined the Paris Agreement in submission to the pope's promptings. President Biden also confirmed this agreement in 2021.[183] Could these historic events signal a repetition of the time when the "mystery" would be "finished" and these prophecies would be understood? (Rev. 10:7, KJV).

Paul gives further evidence of this possibility of repetition by speaking of a mystery that would end just before Christ's second coming. He explains that Jesus would not return until the "mystery of lawlessness" would be revealed:

> And now you know *what is restraining*, that he may be *revealed in his own time*. For the *mystery of lawlessness* is already at work only He who now restrains will do so, until He is taken out of the way. And *then the lawless one will be revealed*, whom the Lord will consume with the breath of His mouth and destroy with the brightness of His coming. The coming of the lawless one is according to the working of Satan, with all power, signs, and lying wonders, and with all unrighteous deception among those who perish, because they did not receive the love of truth, that they may be saved. (2 Thess. 2:6-10, NKJV; italics added)

This text declares that God "restrains" the "mystery of lawlessness" until the time he is revealed, causing him to rise to world recognition. The Greek word for "restrains" is *"katecho,"* which means *"to detain,"* the same meaning as *"delay."* When would this delay end? According to this text, the delay would end at the time that the "lawless one" would "be revealed" or is no longer "restrained" (delayed). Therefore, the mystery, referred to in Revelation 10, may also be speaking of the time when the

---

[183] https://www.whitehouse.gov/briefing-room/statements-releases/2021/01/20/paris-climate-agreement/

delay would end and the "lawless one" would rise to power.

Paul continues his description of the "lawless one" by referring to him as the "man of sin" and the "son of perdition":

> … for that day shall not come, except there come a falling away first, and that *man of sin* be revealed, the *son of perdition*, who opposeth and exalteth himself above all that is called God or that is worshiped; so that he as God sitteth in the temple of God, shewing himself that he is God. (2 Thess. 2:3-4, KJV; italics added)

Clearly, this text is a description of the pope because he is the only one on Earth that claims to be the "Vicar of Jesus Christ" with the feigned religious authority to change God's law (specifically the second and fourth commandments [Dan. 7:25). So could the return of the pope's political and religious world power, specifically in Protestant America, be a signal that this "delay" is ending?

Revelation 13:5 (KJV) also describes a "mouth speaking great things and blasphemies; and power was given unto him to continue forty and two months." In this text, the word, "to continue" in Greek is *"poieo,"* and can mean *"to delay."* This forty-two-month delay is reminiscent of Revelation 10:6-7 (NKJV), "… that there should be *no delay any longer* but in the days of the sounding of the seventh angel, when he is about to sound the mystery of God would be finished as he declared it to his servants the prophets" (italics added). Again, this "mystery of God" would likely be finished when the "mystery of lawlessness," or the "man of sin," would rise to power (2 Thess. 2:3).

To understand this forty-two-month delay, one must go back to the breaking of the seventh seal in 1844, when Jesus moved into the Most Holy Place to start the investigative judgment (Dan.

7:9-14, 22; Mal. 3:1-3; Heb. 9;24-28). At that time, God's people on the earth experienced the Great Disappointment that Christ had not returned, yet they were directed to the specific text in Habakkuk 2:3-4, KJV:

> "For the vision is yet for an *appointed time ("mow'ed")*, but at the end, it shall speak and not lie: though it *tarry (delay)*, wait for it; because it will surely come, it will not *tarry (delay)*. Behold, his soul which is lifted up (proud- NKJV) is not upright in him…" (parentheses and italics added).

This text seems to indicate that at an appointed time, a proud man would rise to power. But when would this occur? According to Revelation 13:5, this would likely happen after a forty-two-month delay. If forty-two months are multiplied by forty-nine (the principle found in Deuteronomy 16:9 and Leviticus 25:8), the total is 2,058 months, which then can be divided by twelve months in a year, equaling 171.5 years. If these 171.5 years are added to 1844, the sum ends in 2015, the *exact year that Pope Francis addressed the U.S. Congress for the first time in history*. This prophecy in Revelation 13 simply confirms Daniel 12's "time, times, and a half" prophecy, both likely ending in 2015 at the pope's rise to political prominence in the United States government which would be delayed "no longer!" (Rev. 10:6-7).

With this turn of events trumpeting Christ's imminent return, why would God's people be reluctant to share the prophetic importance of these great signs? Perhaps a clue lies in the explanation given in the following verses of Revelation 10:8-11. John was instructed to take the "little book" (the book of Daniel and its prophecies), which was opened (unsealed), and "eat it up; and it shall make thy belly bitter, but it shall be in thy mouth sweet as honey" (Rev. 10:8-9, KJV; compare Eze. 3:1-3; Jer. 15:16; Lam 3:15). Historically, at the close of the 2,300-day prophecy when the seventh seal opened in 1844, the Advent message was as "sweet as honey" because it was based upon the immediate coming of Christ. However, when Jesus did not return, many Millerites' faith in Daniel's prophecies wavered, and ever since then, Satan has been transforming the Bible's sweet Living Water into bitter wormwood (Rev. 8:10-11). Could God's people today be repeating the Millerites' hesitancy to share these biblical truths that attack Satan's deceptions of spiritualism/Pentecostalism, secular humanistic government, and false papal teachings combined with apostate Protestantism?

Instead, Jesus commands His faithful followers to study the teachings of Daniel and Revelation and allow them to "stand... at the end of the days" and "prophesy AGAIN!" This final plea beckons us to share these bittersweet prophecies that are repeating today before our very eyes! (Dan. 12:13, KJV; Rev. 10:11; KJV). May we boldly proclaim their urgent, end-time messages to all "peoples, and nations, and tongues, and kings!" (Rev. 10:11, KJV).

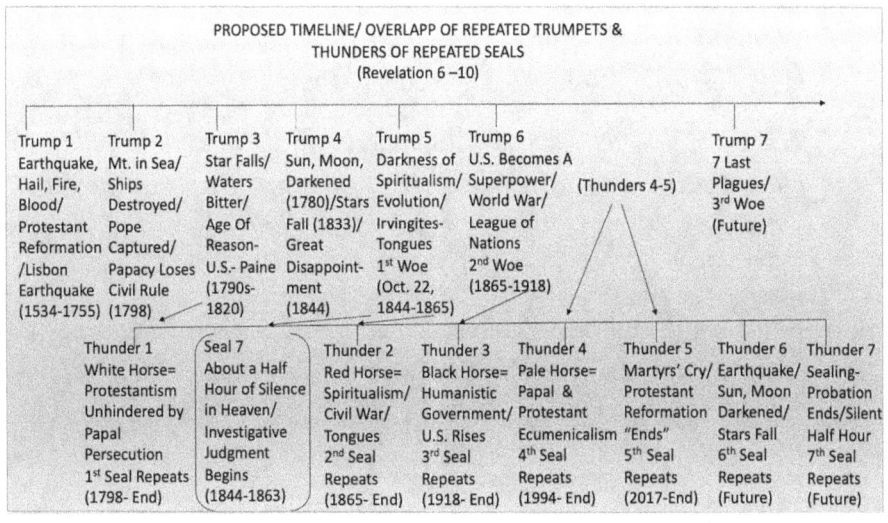

PROPOSED TIMELINE/ OVERLAPP OF REPEATED TRUMPETS & THUNDERS OF REPEATED SEALS
(Revelation 6 –10)

| Trump 1 | Trump 2 | Trump 3 | Trump 4 | Trump 5 | Trump 6 | | Trump 7 |
|---|---|---|---|---|---|---|---|
| Earthquake, | Mt. in Sea/ | Star Falls/ | Sun, Moon, | Darkness of | U.S. Becomes A | | 7 Last |
| Hail, Fire, | Ships | Waters | Darkened | Spiritualism/ | Superpower/ | (Thunders 4-5) | Plagues/ |
| Blood/ | Destroyed/ | Bitter/ | (1780)/Stars | Evolution/ | World War/ | | 3rd Woe |
| Protestant | Pope | Age Of | Fall (1833)/ | Irvingites- | League of | | (Future) |
| Reformation | Captured/ | Reason- | Great | Tongues | Nations | | |
| /Lisbon | Papacy Loses | (1790s- | Disappoint- | 1st Woe | 2nd Woe | | |
| Earthquake | Civil Rule | 1820) | ment | (Oct. 22, | (1865-1918) | | |
| (1534-1755) | (1798) | | (1844) | 1844-1865) | | | |

| Thunder 1 | Seal 7 | Thunder 2 | Thunder 3 | Thunder 4 | Thunder 5 | Thunder 6 | Thunder 7 |
|---|---|---|---|---|---|---|---|
| White Horse= | About a Half | Red Horse= | Black Horse= | Pale Horse= | Martyrs' Cry/ | Earthquake/ | Sealing- |
| Protestantism | Hour of Silence | Spiritualism/ | Humanistic | Papal & | Protestant | Sun, Moon | Probation |
| Unhindered by | in Heaven/ | Civil War/ | Government/ | Protestant | Reformation | Darkened/ | Ends/Silent |
| Papal | Investigative | Tongues | U.S. Rises | Ecumenicalism | "Ends" | Stars Fall | Half Hour |
| Persecution | Judgment | 2nd Seal | 3rd Seal | 4th Seal | 5th Seal | 6th Seal | 7th Seal |
| 1st Seal Repeats | Begins | Repeats | Repeats | Repeats | Repeats | Repeats | Repeats |
| (1798- End) | (1844-1863) | (1865- End) | (1918- End) | (1994- End) | (2017-End) | (Future) | (Future) |

# Discussion Questions Over Revelation 10

1. Who likely is the "mighty angel" coming down from Heaven who appeared to John in Revelation 10:1, and what was His appearance? (Rev. 10:1; 1:13-16; Ex. 14:19; 13:21; Gen. 9:16; Mal. 4:2)

2. What did this Angel have in His hand? (Rev. 10:2; Dan.12:9; Rev. 5:1) What might this have contained? (Zech. 5:1-4; Eze. 2:9-10; 20:23-25)

3. What is Christ's covenant with His people, and which commandment of God's law is specifically exemplified in His seal? (Rev. 10:2, 5-6; Heb. 10:16; Ex. 20:11; 31:16-18; Rev. 14:7)

4. Why does Satan viciously attack the faithful who obeys God's commandments, specifically at the end of time? (Rev. 12:9, 12, 17)

5. Until the close of probation, why do we still have hope if we break our covenant with God and fail to keep His commandments? (II Chron. 7:14; I John 1:9; Gal. 3:13)

6. What does Christ promise to do for those who desire to keep His law? (Deut. 4:29-31; Heb. 10:16-17; Phil. 4:13)

7. What do "thunders" possibly symbolize in the book of Revelation? How are the seven thunders (likely the repetition of the seven seals) being seen in the United States today? (Rev. 10:3-4; 6:1; Job 39:19)

8. What has likely been "delayed," and how is this delay ending? (Rev. 10:6-7; 2 Thess. 2:6-8; Dan. 12:9-10; Hab. 2:3-4)

9. What is symbolized when John ate the little book and it was bitter in his stomach? How is Satan causing bitterness toward Bible prophecy today? (Rev. 10:8-11; Lam 3:15 compare Rev. 8:11; Is. 5:20)

10. What is God calling His church to do in response to Satan's demonic attack of turning the sweet truths of God's Word into bitterness, especially the prophecies of Christ's soon return? (Rev. 10:11; Jer. 15:16; Ps. 19:10; Eze. 3:1-3)

# Revelation 11 (KJV)

*¹ And there was given me a reed like unto a rod: and the angel stood, saying, Rise, and measure the temple of God, and the altar, and them that worship therein. ² But the court which is without the temple leave out, and measure it not; for it is given unto the Gentiles: and the holy city shall they tread under foot forty and two months. ³ And I will give power unto my two witnesses, and they shall prophesy a thousand two hundred and threescore days, clothed in sackcloth. ⁴ These are the two olive trees, and the two candlesticks standing before the God of the earth. ⁵ And if any man will hurt them, fire proceedeth out of their mouth, and devoureth their enemies: and if any man will hurt them, he must in this manner be killed. ⁶ These have power to shut heaven, that it rain not in the days of their prophecy: and have power over waters to turn them to blood, and to smite the earth with all plagues, as often as they will. ⁷ And when they shall have finished their testimony, the beast that ascendeth out of the bottomless pit shall make war against them, and shall overcome them, and kill them. ⁸ And their dead bodies shall lie in the street of the great city, which spiritually is called Sodom and Egypt, where also our Lord was crucified. ⁹ And they of the people and kindreds and tongues and nations shall see their dead bodies three days and an half, and shall not suffer their dead bodies to be put in graves. ¹⁰ And they that dwell upon the earth shall rejoice over them, and make merry, and shall send gifts one to another; because these two prophets tormented them that dwelt on the earth. ¹¹ And after three days and an half* the spirit of life from God entered into them, and they stood upon their feet; and great fear fell upon them which saw them. ¹² And they heard a great voice from heaven saying unto them, Come up hither. And they ascended up to heaven in a cloud; and their enemies beheld them. ¹³ And the same hour was there a great earthquake, and the tenth part of the city fell, and in the earthquake were slain of men seven thousand: and the remnant were affrighted, and gave glory to the God of heaven. ¹⁴ The second woe is past; and, behold, the third woe cometh quickly. ¹⁵ And the seventh angel sounded; and there were great voices in heaven, saying, The kingdoms of this world are become the kingdoms of our Lord, and of his Christ; and he shall reign for ever and ever. ¹⁶ And the four and twenty elders, which sat before God on their seats, fell upon their faces, and worshipped God, ¹⁷ Saying, We give thee thanks, O Lord God Almighty, which art, and wast, and art to come; because thou hast taken to thee thy great power, and hast reigned. ¹⁸ And the nations were angry, and thy wrath is come, and the time of the dead, that they should be judged, and that thou shouldest give reward unto thy servants the prophets, and to the saints, and them that fear thy name, small and great; and shouldest destroy them which destroy the earth. ¹⁹ And the temple of God was opened in heaven, and there was seen in his temple the ark of his testament: and there were lightnings, and voices, and thunderings, and an earthquake, and great hail.

# Death of the Two Witnesses

Have you ever been to a funeral of a loved one? The sadness of the occasion is overwhelming! Now just imagine how heart-wrenching it would be if God's people realized that they were responsible for the spiritual death of the two most important witnesses of Christ in history! This is precisely what John discovered in his vision recorded in Revelation 11.

First, an angel gave John a measuring rod and told him to *"measure the temple of God,* and the altar, and *them that worship therein"* (Rev. 11:1, KJV; italics added). In figurative language, the angel likely referred to judgment because God often compares measuring to judging: "For with what *judgment* you judge, you will be judged: and with the same *measure* you use, it shall be measured back to you" (Matt. 7:2, NKJV; italics added). God also says, "I will make justice the measuring line and righteousness the plummet" (Is. 28:17, NKJV). Also, the definition of "temple" in Revelation 11:1 may be explained in the phrase, *"them that worship therein"* because the Bible refers to God's people as "the temple of God" (I Cor. 3:16). So, "measuring," could symbolize the investigative judgment of God's followers (1 Pet. 4:17).

Furthermore, John was told to "leave out the court, which is outside the temple, and do not measure it for it has been given to the Gentiles" (Rev. 11:2, NKJV; compare Luke 21:24). They would trample the holy city for forty-two months, during the time that God's two witnesses would be clothed in sackcloth, the garb of mourning (Rev. 11:2-3; Gen. 37:34). If the historical day-for-a-year method of time prophecy is used to figure forty-two months in Revelation 11:2 (42 X 30), it would equal 1,260 years (Num. 14:34; Eze. 4:6). During these 1,260 years, from 538 AD to 1798 AD, the papacy squelched public access to the Scriptures. Moreover, towards the end of this time period, the French Revolution raged against God and His Word. Churches became properties of the state; Bibles were burned; and Christianity, as a whole, was "crucified." Voltaire's motto, "Crush the Wretch"—referring to Christ, Himself—became the rallying cry of this horrific time.[184] Amazingly, the revolutionary leaders were not content with mere dechristianization;[185] instead, they attempted to replace traditional faith with their own state-sponsored cult of Reason.[186] These outrageous atrocities, resulting from the national death of God's Word, left a bloody legacy that stained French history forever! During this political "earthquake," France was shaken to its core (Rev. 11:13). Tragically, throughout the French Revolution, Christianity was "tread underfoot" by the Gentiles (Rev. 11:2), and many Christians lost their lives because the wicked masses refused to listen to God's Two Witnesses.

But who, specifically, are the Two Witnesses that prophesy in sackcloth and get trodden underfoot? (Rev. 11:3-7). The Greek

---

[184]

https://books.google.com/books?id=sbAIAAAAQAAJ&pg=PA39&lpg=PA39&dq=crush+the+wretch+voltaire+quote&source=bl&ots=kvSguWLrzs&sig=ACfU3U3C sNGxs7sHaxcEx5csPHr8icoF_g&hl=en&sa=X&ved=2ahUKEwiezdO7vM3vA-hUMWs0KHci4Bk04ChDoATAIegQICBAD#v=onepage&q=crush%20the%20wretch%20voltaire%20quote&f=false

[185] https://www.iwp.edu/articles/2018/01/12/the-dechristianization-of-france-during-the-french-revolution/

[186] https://thehumanist.com/commentary/storming-of-the-cults-a-revolutionary-remembrance

word for "witness" is *"martys,"* the origin of the English word, *"martyrs."* Few would argue that the lives and deaths of God's faithful followers throughout history certainly have been a powerful witness to the world! The symbols in Revelation 11:4 of the "two olive trees and the two lampstands" could represent God's people in the Old and New Testaments. For example, Israel is referred to as an olive tree in the Old Testament [Hosea 14:5-6], and lampstands are symbols of Christ's church, specifically in the New Testament [Rev. 1:20]). Yet, the fourth chapter of Zechariah associates God's Word with both olive trees and lampstands (Zech. 4:2-6, NKJV). Moreover, in Revelation 11:5-6, an allusion to the prophetic power of God's Word is manifested in the lives of Moses, who told Pharaoh that Egypt would be struck with plagues (Ex. 7:14-20), and Elijah, who predicted that the Lord would shut the heavens so that no rain would fall (I Kings 17:1). Therefore, the Two Witnesses described in Revelation 11 seem likely to symbolize more than just God's faithful followers throughout history.

Additionally, no human being has ever lived 1,260 years (Rev. 11:3; Eze. 4:6) or fully manifested Christ's perfect witness to the world (I Jn. 5:9). The Bible states that the Lord Jesus, Himself, is the "faithful and true Witness," portrayed through the pages of His Holy Word (Rev. 3:14, KJV; 1:5; Jn. 1:14; I Jn. 5:7). In fact, it proclaims that Jesus is the Word made flesh who "was with God and the Word was God" (John 1:1, KJV). Therefore, God's Word, depicted in the Old and the New Testaments, is the BEST witness of Christ (John 5:39).

Furthermore, Exodus 31:18 speaks of God's law contained in the Ten Commandments as being the two tablets of the *"Testimony."* The Hebrew word for "testimony" is *"eduwth,"* meaning *"witness."* Additionally, in the New Testament, John saw the tabernacle of the *"testimony"* *("martyrion"),* meaning both *"Deca-logue"* (the Ten Commandments) and *"witness"* (Rev. 15:5). Paul also states that the "righteousness of God" is *"witnessed by the law and the prophets"* (Rom. 3:21, KJV; italics added). Since both the Old and the New Testaments portray the Lord's laws and prophets, they are both God's witnesses—*God's Two Witnesses!* Each of these testaments gives testimony of Christ and stands as a witness of His mercy and justice. Therefore, the Old and New Testaments of the Bible are the best fulfillment of the Two Witnesses of Revelation because they perfectly reveal Christ's character that is displayed in His law and demonstrated in His prophets' lives (Rev. 11:6).

Sadly, however, these Two Witnesses have been under direct attack over the years but are specifically targeted at the close of time. Prophecy predicts that *"the beast from the bottomless pit"* will make war against them, overcome them, and kill them" (Rev. 11:7, NKJV; italics added). Who is this "beast" from the "bottomless pit?" The apostle, John, states, "... I saw a *star* (an angel [Rev. 1:20]) *fallen from heaven to the earth;* and to him was given the key (authority [Matt. 16:19) to the bottomless pit" (Rev. 9:1; italics added). Revelation 9:11 further implies that the Devil is "the *angel of the bottomless pit,"* named in Hebrew, *"Abaddon"* (meaning *"a destroying angel")* and in Greek, *"Apollyon"* (meaning, *"the De-stroyer").* Moreover, Revelation 9:1 states that this "star" (Satan) is fallen to the *"earth,"* similar to Revelation 12:9 (KJV): "And the great dragon was cast out, that old serpent, called the Devil, and Satan, which deceiveth the whole world: he was cast out *to the earth,* and his angels were cast out with him" (italics added). Additionally, in Hebrew, the earth before creation is called an *"abyss" (deep-"thowm,"),* which has the same meaning as the Greek word, *"abyssos,"* the word used for the "bottomless pit" in

Revelation (Gen. 1:2; Rev. 9:1-2, 11; 11:7; 17:8; 20:1, 3). So the "beast" (nation/kingdom [Dan. 7:23]) "of the bottomless pit" likely symbolizes the earth in control of Satan and his angels. Moreover, a specific nation, or the earth "beast," is described in Revelation 13:11-14 that makes war against God's people (Rev. 11:7). Therefore, the Bible implies that the "bottomless pit" is the earth, and the *beast* may represent a specific nation of the earth under the control of demonic rulership (Dan. 7:23; Is. 24:1, 3, 21-22).

Furthermore, God's Word warns that this beast from the bottomless pit will make *"war"* against the Two Witnesses (the Old/New Testaments), overcome them, and kill them, and "their dead bodies" will lie in the "streets of the great city...." (Rev. 11:7-8, KJV; parentheses added). Additionally, the prophecy states that this great city will rule "over the kings of the *earth*," usurping Christ's leadership and becoming a counterpart to "Mystery Babylon the Great" (Rev. 17:4, 5, 18; 1:5, KJV). So, in what great city today do the Two Witnesses of God's Word "lie in the streets?" The Bible affirms that it is speaking in symbolic language by stating that the great city is *"spiritually* called Sodom and Egypt, where also our Lord was "crucified" (Rev. 11:8, KJV). This means that this great city will display the same characteristics as ancient Sodom, Egypt, and Jerusalem where Christ was crucified (Jer. 23:14; Is. 30:2-3; Lk. 24:18-20). From this biblical description, this modern nation will be sexually immoral like Sodom (Gen. 19; Jude 1:7; Jer. 23:14), challenge God's commandments like Egypt (Ex. 5:2), and not only be a professedly Christian nation like Jerusalem (Jer. 3:17; Heb. 12:22) but also be responsible for "crucifying" the principles of Christ found in His Word (Zech. 12:10). The Bible further describes this country as one that contains a "woman," specifically, a "harlot," which symbolizes an apostate church (Rev. 17:5, 18; Jer. 3:8, 20). Additionally, this apostate Christian nation will celebrate the passage of national laws against God's people because it cannot tolerate the teachings of the prophets that "tormented them that dwelt on the earth" (Rev. 11:10, KJV).

Moreover, the Bible states that this religious deterioration would occur during the 1,260 days when the Two Witnesses of God's Word would prophesy in the sackcloth of mourning (Rev. 11:3). As shown previously, these historical 1,260 days/years refer to the time that the papacy ruled politically during the Dark Ages, leading up to the French Revolution. However, could this prophecy repeat after 1798 and refer to a modern Christian country ruling at the end of time? Revelation 12:6 (NKJV) seems to infer such an interpretation: "Then the woman (church [Jer. 6:2]) fled into the wilderness, where she has a place prepared by God, that they should *feed* her there a thousand two hundred and sixty days." The Greek word for *"feed"* in this passage is *"trepho"* and means, *"to nourish, support, fatten, and bring up."* Since the church was severely persecuted during the historical 1,260-year time period, this prophecy likely repeats during a time when the church is protected, specifically from governmental interference (Eze. 34:25-30). Only one primary Protestant Christian country rising to world power after 1798 AD has "nourished" the growth of God's church and provided its citizens with religious freedom—the United States of America! (Rev. 12:14). Yet, sadly, Satan's deceptions and false teachings have crept into this great nation without many Christians even realizing it! In recent years, the U.S., founded upon godly principles, has been quickly losing its spirituality through humanism, materialism, and immorality. Moreover, its biblical bedrock is being chipped away by ecumenical compromises between Catholics and Protestants.

Returning to the prophecy in Revelation 11, the Bible states that the witnesses of the Old and New Testament would preach in sackcloth for 1,260 days (Rev. 11:3). If this prophecy were to repeat and 1,260 days are multiplied by forty-nine (the timing found in Deut. 16:9; compare Lev. 25:8), the total is 61,740 days. Then, if this number is divided by 365 days in a year, the quotient equals 169 years. If 169 years are added to 1844 (the context of Rev. 11:1-2, the end of the 2,300-day prophecy and the start of the investigative judgment [Dan. 7:9-10; 8:14]), its sum is 2013. This is the revolutionary year that the joint declaration, *"From Conflict to Communion,"* was published, which promotes global Protestant and Catholic unity.[187] It is also the same year that Pope Benedict XVI mysteriously resigned, something that had not occurred in more than *six hundred years* in the Catholic Church.[188] Inaugurated as Benedict's replacement, Pope Francis has trumpeted his liberal political views in the U. S. with one source declaring: "through his activism, Francis has significantly raised the Church's profile on issues with which it wasn't previously associated in American politics—issues chiefly championed by Democrats."[189] In fact, in 2013, according to Gallup polls, liberal self-identification rose to its highest level since 1992.[190] Furthermore, a Pew Research study found an increasing polarization between Democrats and Republicans,[191] with one prominent New York source comparing the country's division to a "cold, civil

---

[187] https://www.vaticannews.va/en/vatican-city/news/2021-01/catholics-and-lu-therans-reaffirm-commitment-to-communion.html
[188] https://www.theguardian.com/world/2013/feb/11/pope-benedict-shock-resigna-tion-taboo
[189] https://www.theatlantic.com/politics/archive/2015/09/why-pope-francis-sounds-like-a-democrat/407023/
[190] https://news.gallup.com/poll/166787/liberal-self-identification-edges-new-high-2013.aspx
[191] https://www.pewresearch.org/politics/2014/06/12/political-polarization-in-the-american-public/

war."[192] Sadly, civil unrest in the U.S. would continue to multiply, despite the efforts of either political party.

Biblical prophecy may have hinted at a modern repetition of such political turmoil when it states that the holy city would be trampled underfoot by the Gentiles for forty-two months (Heb. 10:26-30; Rev. 11:2). If forty-two months are multiplied by forty-nine (the principle found in Lev. 25:8 and Deut. 16:9), the product equals 2,058 months or 171.5 years. In comparison, the prophet Daniel might have also referred to this same total of years when he was told that after a "time, times, and half a time," the "power of the holy people" would be "completely shattered" (Dan. 12:7, NKJV). The Hebrew word for "time" in Daniel 12:7 is *"mow'ed,"* meaning an *"appointed time."* If revolutions of forty-nine years are inserted into "time, times, and half," it equals 171.5 years (Lev. 25:8), mirroring the forty-two months of Revelation 11:2. Then if these 171.5 years are added to 1844, the year that the investigative judgment began (Dan. 7:9-10; 8:14; Rev. 11:1-2), the total ends in the middle of the year of 2015.

Did America experience a moral and spiritual shaking in 2015? It was precisely in the middle of this very year that the Supreme Court made a historic ruling which denied the authority of God's Word, like ancient Egypt, and legalized sexual immorality, like Sodom (Rev. 11:8; Jer. 23:14). Amazingly, on June 26, 2015, in direct opposition to the biblical definition of marriage between one man and one woman (Gen. 2:24-25), the United States Supreme Court voted that "same-sex couples" could marry nationwide.[193] This unprecedented ruling permitted *"sodomy,"* which the online Encyclopedia of Britannica defines as *"denoting any homosexual practices... in allusion to the biblical story of*

---

[192] https://nymag.com/intelligencer/2016/10/8-years-in-obamas-america.html
[193] https://www.cnn.com/2013/05/28/us/same-sex-marriage-fast-facts/index.html

*Sodom"* (Gen. 19:5)[194] Yet, in national celebration of this biblically amoral decision, the White House was lit up in rainbow colors, and "scenes of jubilation from coast to coast" appeared "as campaigners, politicians and everyday people–gay, straight and in-between–hailed 'a victory of love.'"[195] This is exactly what the Bible predicts: "And those who dwell on the earth will rejoice over them, make merry… because the two prophets (the Old and New Testaments) tormented those who dwell on the earth" (Rev. 11:10, NKJV; parenthesis added). Such disregard for the biblical definition of marriage has been further confirmed with the passage of the "Respect for Marriage Act" in 2022,[196] which directly opposes God's Word (Gen. 2:24).

However, this national rebellion against Christ and His Word didn't just end there! Returning to the year 2015, as previously stated, the United States Congress, in formal session, sought the political counsel of a Roman Catholic pope for the first time in history. Just a few months later, on April 22, 2016, the American government pursued the pope's political agenda, outlined in his encyclical, *"Laudato Si,"* by signing the Paris Agreement, a global pact of 190 nations concerning climate change.[197] Amazingly, if 171.5 years are added to October 22, 1844 (the actual date of the close of the 2,300-day/year prophecy), one arrives on the *exact same day* as the signing of the global climate compact—*April 22, 2016!* By the government of the U.S. aligning itself with the leadership of the Roman pontiff (a mere human being who claims to

---

[194] https://www.britannica.com/topic/sodomy
[195] https://www.theguardian.com/society/2015/jun/26/gay-marriage-legal-supreme-court
[196] https://www.whitehouse.gov/briefing-room/statements-releases/2022/11/29/statement-from-president-joe-biden-on-bipartisan-senate-passage-of-the-respect-for-marriage-act/
[197] https://obamawhitehouse.archives.gov/the-press-office/2015/12/12/us-leadership-and-historic-paris-agreement-combat-climate-change

be the Vicar of Christ and covets the title of "His Holiness"),[198] this country has in all practicality turned away from its Protestant heritage, spiritually "crucifying" Christ and the principles of His Word (Rev. 11:8; Is. 28:15). Instead of the motto, *"sola scriptura"* ("the Bible only") that so many reformers died to uphold, Protestant America has followed a "strong delusion" disguised in climate change, pursuing the political/spiritual manipulation proposed by the pope of Rome "who sits as God in the temple of God, showing himself that he is God" (2 Thess. 2:4, 11, NKJV).

Continuing its prophecy, Revelation 11:13 states that after "3.5 days," an "earthquake" would occur. Interestingly, if 3.5 days are multiplied by forty-nine (Deut. 16:9; Lev. 25:8), it totals 171.5 days or approximately six months. For six months, the United States, in alliance with the majority of the world, rejoiced together in the signing of the Paris Agreement. Then in November 2016, an ideological "earthquake" occurred. The Greek word for "earthquake" comes from the verb, *"seio,"* which can refer to a shaking *"of men, to be thrown into a tremor, to quake in fear, to agitate the mind."* This shaking would occur when "the breath of life from God," would "enter" God's Two Witnesses of His Word, and they would stand "on their feet" (Rev. 11:11). The word, "entered" (*"eiserchomai,"*), in this text can mean *"to come before the public, enter into society."* So, America's population would be shaken when God's Word would rise in popularity.

On November 9, 2016, a political "earthquake" likely erupted when U.S. citizens awoke to one of the biggest election upsets in history—Trump winning the presidency over Hilary Clinton.[199]

---

[198] http://w2.vatican.va/content/francesco/en/letters/2018/documents/papa-francesco_20180820_lettera-popolo-didio.html
[199] https://www.usatoday.com/story/news/politics/onpolitics/2018/06/27/alexandria-ocasio-cortez-big-upsets-u-s-history/737592002/

This swing from the liberal left of Obama's presidency to the conservative right thrilled most American evangelicals! Many attributed Trump's success as a direct answer to prayer! Some Christians even reported having dreams or visions of Trump winning before the election ended.[200] This "very strong" evangelical backing for Trump's national leadership was manifested in the record percentage of supporters, with "more than 80% of white born-again voters casting their ballot for Trump."[201] It was reported that "thousands of Christians" prayed and fasted three days before the outcome of the 2016 election.[202] Overnight, Trump's victory at the polls suddenly breathed a "breath of life" into biblical values being manifested within the government of the United States, and evangelical leadership would later become prominent during Trump's presidency.

Yet, sadly, this reemergence of Christian principles within the United States government would not bring about the spiritual revival needed for national repentance and would be, instead, eventually overturned. In 2016, nearly half of Americans reported being "afraid" at the shocking switch of events at the polls,[203] and many were skeptical of any true reform. A full ten percent did not vote in the elections.[204] Interestingly, Rev. 11:11 predicts that "great fear fell upon them which saw them" and "a tenth part of the city fell" in the earthquake, and the "remnant were affrighted and gave glory to the God of Heaven" (Rev. 11:13, KJV; compare Is. 6:13). Tragically, the evangelicals' victory at the 2016 election

---

[200] https://time.com/4565010/donald-trump-evangelicals-win/

[201] ibid

[202] ibid

[203] https://news.gallup.com/poll/197375/trump-victory-surprises-americans-four-afraid.aspx

[204] https://thehill.com/hilltv/what-americas-thinking/407787-more-than-10-percent-say-they-wouldnt-vote-for-trump-again

would not save the U.S. from its rapid national and spiritual deterioration.

Fearful skepticism may have been prophetically well-founded since Americans currently are divided between two opposing political sides—*neither of which is biblically grounded!* On the liberal left, the United States is repeating the same abandonment of Christian principles which occurred in Egypt, Sodom, and more recently, during the French Revolution. By passing a national law in direct opposition to the biblical definition of marriage, which is one of the only two institutions God set up in Eden before sin (Gen. 2:21-25), the U.S., as a whole, has rebelled against its Creator. These anti-biblical, cultural overtures are gaining unprecedented support, especially among today's youth, decimating America's godly heritage (compare Hos. 5:7). Likewise, on the right, ecumenical unity of doctrine between the papacy and many Protestant churches of the United States have corrupted biblical truth. Sadly, the teachings of God's Word have largely been forsaken! Just as prophecy has predicted, both the secular liberal left and the ecumenical conservative right who are united with the papacy are falling like stars in the night sky, becoming eclipsed by satanic darkness because they are responsible for "crucifying" Christ and the Two Witnesses of His Word (Dan. 12:3; Rev. 6:13; 11:3, 7-8; Jn. 1:14).

After seeing this overt rebellion against God, John was told that the second woe was passed. "Behold the third woe cometh quickly" (Rev. 11:14, KJV). As mentioned previously, the three "woes" generally mirror the timing of the Three Angels' Messages in Revelation 14:6-11. Although the first two messages heralded the close of the 2,300-day/year prophecy in 1844 (Dan. 8:14), they also repeated after 1844 with the additional Third

Angel's Message after the breaking of the seventh seal. Revelation 11:19 continues:

> Then the temple of God was opened in heaven, and the ark of His covenant was seen in His temple. And there were *lightnings*, noises, thunderings, an earthquake, and great *hail*. (Italics added)

This chapter closes much like it began. It covers the time period of the investigative judgment and the sounding of the Three Angels' Messages that began in 1844 (*"lightnings"* of God's Word [Rev. 11:1-2, 19; Dan. 7:9-12]) and spans to the outpouring of the seven last plagues (*"hail"*- plagues [Rev. 11:15, 18-19; 16:1, 17-21]) and Christ's second coming. It outlines the events that would repeat just prior to the close of Earth's history. Fortunately, Christ has raised a movement that can explain Bible prophecy and its current impact on today's life. In the next chapter, we will discover more about the identity of this remnant church, and Satan's war against it.

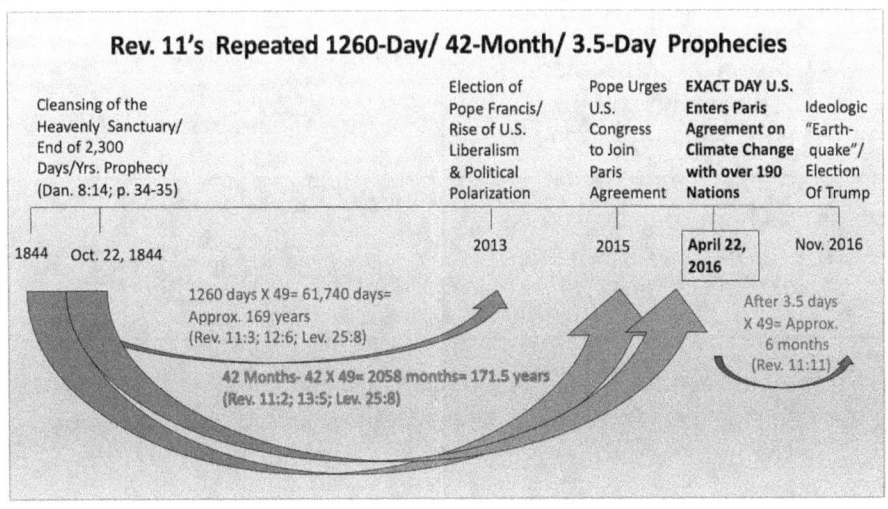

Rev. 11's Repeated 1260-Day/ 42-Month/ 3.5-Day Prophecies

# Christ Takes Our Curses Upon Himself—
# Triumphs for Our Salvation
*(Comparison of Christ's Life and the Seals/Trumpets/Woes)*

| Christ Overcomes for His People | Revelation Seals, Trumpets, Woes & Curses |
|---|---|
| Jesus takes the world's woes upon Himself (Gal. 3:13, Is. 53:4-5) | Woes are pronounced on Babylon/Earth (Rev. 8:13; 12:12; 18:10, 16, 19) |
| Jesus drinks the "cup" of God's wrath for His people (Matt. 26:42) | Babylon drinks the "cup" of God's wrath (Rev. 14:10; 18:6-8) |
| Jesus's body is anointed— bitter myrrh (Jn. 19:39); The box contained bitter myrrh (Matt. 26:7-9) | Book is bitter in John's stomach (Rev. 10:9) Trumpet contains bitter water (Rev. 8:11) |
| Jesus is betrayed because of money (Matt. 26:14-16) | Babylon is betrayed by merchants' wealth (Rev. 18:3, 9, 11, 15-19) |
| Jesus "crushed" in the Garden of Gethsemane; Gethsemane= oil press (Matt. 26:36-39; Lk. 22:63) | Grapes (wicked) are crushed in winepress (Rev. 14:14-20; Rev. 19:15) |
| Jesus's hour of betrayal nears Disciples sleep (Matt. 26:45) | Hour of trial falls upon the world (Rev. 3:10) Kings & beast rule 1 hour (Rev. 17:12) |
| Jesus pleads for Father to take the hour from Him; The hour of darkness (Mark 14:35; Luke 22:53) | Babylon is judged in one hour (Rev. 14:7; 18:10, 17, 19) |

| | |
|---|---|
| Jesus's side is pierced by a sword (John 19:34) | Beasts die by the sword (Rev. 19:15, 19-21) |
| Jesus is condemned by the testimony of two false witnesses (Matt. 26:60) | Death of God's Two Witnesses (Rev. 11:3, 7-9; 1:5; Jn. 1:1, 14) |
| Jesus is said to destroy the temple Will build in 3 days (His body) (Matt. 26:60-61; Mark 14:58) | Destruction of Two Witnesses for 3.5 days (Rev. 11:7-8; 1:5; Jn. 1:1, 14) |
| Jesus is blasphemed & accused of blasphemy (Matt. 26:65-68; 27:39) | Wicked blasphemes God at the end (Rev.16:11) |
| Jesus is judged guilty though innocent (Lk. 23:4, 14, 22-24) | Babylon is judged guilty by God (Rev. 18:5-6) |
| Jesus's death is demanded by the crowd (Matt. 27:22-25) | Prayers of saints cry for vengeance of their deaths (Rev. 6:10) |
| Jesus is struck (Matt. 26:31, 67) | Sun, moon, & stars are struck (Rev. 8:12) (symbols of God's people) (Ps. 89:35-37; Gen. 15:5; Dan. 12:3) |
| Jesus is stripped and clad with a scarlet robe (Matt. 27:28); Jesus is clothed with a robe dipped in blood (Rev. 19:13) | Woman/church is clothed in scarlet (Rev. 17:4; 18:16) |
| Jesus is blindfolded (Luke 22:64) | Laodicean church is blind, poor, and naked (Rev. 3:17) |

| | |
|---|---|
| Jesus prophecies<br>Women's children will cry out<br>(Lk. 23:28-31);<br>Christ cries out<br>(Lk. 23:46) | Wicked cry for mountains<br>to fall on them<br>(Rev. 6:15-16) |
| Jesus dies<br>Darkness over the land<br>(Matt. 27:45) | Darkness falls on the beast<br>(Rev. 16:10)<br>Sun, moon, & stars dark<br>(Rev. 8:12; 9:2) |
| Jesus dies and is resurrected<br>Earthquake occurs<br>(Matt. 27:51; 28:2) | Earthquakes at the first trumpet<br>The 2nd woe/the 7th plague<br>(Rev. 8:5; 11:13; 16:18) |
| Jesus is crucified in Jerusalem<br>(Matt. 20:18-19) | Two Witness' dead bodies lie<br>where the Lord was crucified<br>(Rev. 11:8) |
| Jesus's body is hidden in a rock<br>(Matt. 27:59-60) | Wicked hide in caves & rocks<br>(Rev. 6:15-16) |
| Jesus is dead in the grave<br>for three days<br>(Matt. 27:63; Jn. 2:19-21) | Two Witnesses are dead<br>for 3.5 days<br>(Rev. 11:8-9) |
| Jesus's tomb is sealed<br>Jesus breaks seals<br>(Matt. 27:66; 28:2; Rev. 5:5-6) | No human/angel worthy to<br>break the curses contained<br>in the seven-sealed scroll<br>(Rev. 5:1, 5) |

| Christ Earns the Reward for Righteous | Saints Rewarded for Christ's Sacrifice |
|---|---|
| Jesus is condemned by the High Priest (Matt. 26:65) | Jesus mediates as High Priest & Judge (Heb. 8:1-2, 6; 9:24-28; Jn. 5:22) |
| Jesus confirms His covenant in communion which represents His death (Matt. 26:28) | Christ confirms His covenant with His people (Dan. 10:5-6; 12:7-9; Heb. 10:12, 16-17) |
| 3X Jesus prays for the "cup" of suffering to pass (Matt. 26:42-44) | 3.5 times the church is "nourished" in the wilderness (Rev. 12:14) |
| Jesus dies—resurrected after 3 days (Matt. 27:63; 28:6) | Two Witnesses are resurrected after 3.5 days (Rev. 11:11); Some saints resurrected at cross; Saints resurrected at 2nd Coming (Matt. 27:52-53; Dan. 12:2; I Thess. 4:16) |
| Jesus conquerors death & ascends to Heaven in a cloud (Acts 1:9) | Two Witnesses rise from death (Rev. 11:11) Every eye will see Jesus return in the clouds (Rev. 1:7) |
| Jesus's robe is given to the soldiers (Jn. 19:23-24); Jesus's body is wrapped in clean, white linen (Matt. 27:59) | White robes are given to saints (Rev. 3:5; 6:11); Saints are clothed in clean, white linen (Christ's righteousness) (Rev. 7:9, 14; 19:8, KJV) |
| Jesus is "King of the Jews"- sign on the cross (Matt. 27:37) | King of Kings/Lord of Lords (Rev. 19:16); Christ makes His people kings (Rev. 1:5) |
| Jesus is given a crown of thorns (Matt. 27:29) | God's people are given crowns of victory (James 1:12; Rev. 2:10) |

## PROPOSED CHRONOLOGICAL TIMELINE OF REVELATION

| CHURCHES | Ephesus | Smyrna | Pergamos | Thyatira | Sardis | Philadelphia | Laodicea |
|---|---|---|---|---|---|---|---|
| DESCRIPTION | Apostolic | Persecuted | Compromising | Corrupt | Dead | Faithful Few | Lukewarm |
| Approx. Dates (AD) | 31-100 | 100-323 | 323-538 | 538-1534 | 1534-1750s | 1755-1844 | 1844-End |
| SEALS | White Horse | Red Horse | Black Horse | Pale Horse | Martyrs' Cry | Signs of 2nd Coming | Silence |
| DESCRIPTION | Crown/Bow (Christianity) | Sword (Paganism) | Scales/Famine Gentile Rule Spiritually Dark | Rider- Death Dark Ages (Papacy) | Protestant Reformation | Earthquake Sun, Moon Dark/ Stars Fall | (1844-1863) Disappointment Judgment Starts |
| TRUMPETS (Previous Historical Soundings) | | | | | 1. Hail/Blood (Reformation) | 2. Mt. Falls/Papal Rule Lost (1798) 3. Bitter Water (Age of Reason) 4. Sun, Moon, Stars Struck (1833/1844) | 5. Scorpions/Woe (1844-1865) 6. Horses/2nd Woe (1865-1918) 7. 7 Last Plagues 3rd Woe- Future |
| THUNDERS (Seals Repeated) | White Horse | Red Horse | Black Horse | Pale Horse | Martyrs' Cry | Signs | Sealing & Silence |
| | Protestant Christianity/ Remnant (1798- END) | Spiritualism /Evolution/ Tongues (1865- END) | Humanistic Government/ Spiritually Dark (1918- END) | Catholicism & Apostate Protestantism (1994- END) | Protestant Reformation "Ends" (2017- END) | Earthquake/ Sun, Moon Dark/Stars Fall (Future) | Close of Probation Silence Before Punishment (Future) |

# Discussion Questions for Revelation 11

1. What does "measuring" in Rev. 11:1-2 possibly refer to? (Matt. 7:2; Is. 28:17)

2. What do the "Two Witnesses" likely symbolize? Why are they the best witnesses of Christ? (Rev. 11:3-6; Rom. 3:21; John 5:39; Rev. 1:5 compare Jn. 1:1, 14)

3. What does the "bottomless pit" probably represent? (Rev. 11:7; 9:1-2, 11; 20:1, 3; Is. 24:1, 3, 21-22)

4. What three ancient locations does Revelation 11:8 mention, and what specific characteristics do these ancient places likely symbolize? (Ex. 5:2; Gen. 19:4-5; Zech. 12:10)

5. Why does it seem reasonable to conclude that the 1,260 days in Rev. 11:3 might be repeated sometime after 1798? (Compare Rev. 12:6 to Rev. 12:14)

6. What modern Christian nation formally "nourished" Christianity and seems to fit the description of the "great city" in Rev. 11:8? Recently, how has this great country displayed the same characteristics as ancient Egypt and Sodom by "crucifying Christ" (like Jerusalem's religious leaders) with its apostasy? (Rev. 11:8; 12:14)

7. How has humanism fought against Protestantism in America? (Rev. 11:7; Hosea 5:7)

8. What specific attacks happened in the United States against Protestantism and the truths of God's Word in 2015? (Rev. 11:7-10)

9. *What kind of political shaking occurred in November of 2016, and how did many Americans respond? (Rev. 11:13; compare Is. 6:11-13)*

10. *How are both liberals and conservatives attacking Protestant Christianity today in the United States and around the world? (Dan. 11:27)*

11. *How did Jesus overcome Satan and the judgments of the seals/trumpets/woes? (Gal. 3:13; compare Is. 53:4)*

# Revelation 12 (KJV)

¹ *And there appeared a great wonder in heaven; a woman clothed with the sun, and the moon under her feet, and upon her head a crown of twelve stars:* ² *And she being with child cried, travailing in birth, and pained to be delivered.* ³ *And there appeared another wonder in heaven; and behold a great red dragon, having seven heads and ten horns, and seven crowns upon his heads.* ⁴ *And his tail drew the third part of the stars of heaven, and did cast them to the earth: and the dragon stood before the woman which was ready to be delivered, for to devour her child as soon as it was born.* ⁵ *And she brought forth a man child, who was to rule all nations with a rod of iron: and her child was caught up unto God, and to his throne.* ⁶ *And the woman fled into the wilderness, where she hath a place prepared of God, that they should feed her there a thousand two hundred and threescore days.* ⁷ *And there was war in heaven: Michael and his angels fought against the dragon; and the dragon fought and his angels,* ⁸ *And prevailed not; neither was their place found any more in heaven.* ⁹ *And the great dragon was cast out, that old serpent, called the Devil, and Satan, which deceiveth the whole world: he was cast out into the earth, and his angels were cast out with him.* ¹⁰ *And I heard a loud voice saying in heaven, Now is come salvation, and strength, and the kingdom of our God, and the power of his Christ: for the accuser of our brethren is cast down, which accused them before our God day and night.* ¹¹ *And they overcame him by the blood of the Lamb, and by the word of their testimony; and they loved not their lives unto*

the death. [12] *Therefore rejoice, ye heavens, and ye that dwell in them. Woe to the inhabiters of the earth and of the sea! for the devil is come down unto you, having great wrath, because he knoweth that he hath but a short time.* [13] *And when the dragon saw that he was cast unto the earth, he persecuted the woman which brought forth the man child.* [14] *And to the woman were given two wings of a great eagle, that she might fly into the wilderness, into her place, where she is nourished for a time, and times, and half a time, from the face of the serpent.* [15] *And the serpent cast out of his mouth water as a flood after the woman, that he might cause her to be carried away of the flood.* [16] *And the earth helped the woman, and the earth opened her mouth, and swallowed up the flood which the dragon cast out of his mouth.* [17] *And the dragon was wroth with the woman, and went to make war with the remnant of her seed, which keep the commandments of God, and have the testimony of Jesus Christ.*

# The Dragon's Attack

Most of us have heard stories about a brave knight in shining armor fighting a ferocious, fire-breathing dragon to save the life of a beautiful maiden. John saw a similar story unfolding before his eyes. He beheld a "great sign" — "a woman" (church [Jer. 6:2; 2 Cor. 11:2; Eph. 5:23-27]), "clothed with the sun" (Christ/NT Church [Mal. 4:2; I Thess. 5:5; Matt. 13:43]), "and the moon under her feet" (OT Church/Israel [Ps. 89:35-37; Gen. 37:9-10]), "and upon her head a crown of twelve stars" (apostles [Rev. 12:1, KJV; 21:14]). This woman (church) had previously gone through tribulation because she was seen "in labor and in pain to give birth" (Rev. 12:2, NKJV; Is. 66:7-9; Micah 4:9-10). This representation of a woman in travail who gives birth likely symbolizes God's "pure church" which reemerged during the Protestant Reformation, restoring the doctrinal truths of the Bible that were lost during the papal persecution of the Dark Ages.

With such potential devastation to the Devil's kingdom, it is no wonder, then, that immediately after seeing the woman (church), John beheld a "great fiery red dragon" (Rev.12:3, NKJV). This dragon is identified as the "old serpent, called the Devil, and Satan" (Rev. 12:9, KJV). Since a dragon is a beast, it also represents Satan's kingdom, including his demons and his earthly followers (Dan. 7:23; Eze. 29:3, KJV). Additionally, the Bible associates the dragon with pagan nations such as Babylon and Egypt (Jer. 51:34-35, KJV; Eze. 29:3, KJV). Interestingly, Revelation 12:3 states that the dragon is "fiery red" in appearance, the same two words that describe the horse of the second seal (Rev. 6:4, NKJV) and one of the colors of the breastplates of the horsemen in the sixth trumpet (Rev. 9:17). These symbolic horsemen have already been identified as false teachers rising from the serpent (Satan) and its offspring (Is. 14:29). By these three, one-third of mankind is spiritually killed, the same fraction as the stars that were cast down from Heaven by the dragon's tail of deception (Rev. 9:18; 1:20; 12:4; Dan. 12:3; Is. 9:14-15). Therefore, the dragon represents Satan and his kingdom—his angels and his worldly followers.

Moreover, the great fiery red dragon had "seven heads and ten horns and seven crowns upon his heads" (Rev. 12:3, KJV). Revelation 17:9-10 states that these "seven heads" are "seven mountains." Mountains in biblical prophecy symbolize kingdoms/nations, both godly and ungodly (Eze. 36:4; Zech. 8:3; Jer. 51:24-25; Dan. 9:16), and kingdoms and kings are referred to interchangeably (Dan. 7:17, 23). Crowned heads, then, would represent the rulers of the world kingdoms that have exercised control over God's people throughout history (Eze. 21:25-26), and horns are symbolic of a kingdom's/country's powers (Ps. 75:10; Zech. 1:21).

Looking back over time, God's people were first conquered by Egypt from the South and then Assyria from the North (Ex. 1:13; 2 Kings 17:23). After that, four world kingdoms around the Mediterranean Sea ruled Israel—Babylon, (symbolized by a lion [Dan. 7:4]), Medo-Persia, (represented by a bear [Dan. 7:5]), Greece (portrayed by the four-headed leopard absorbing the "heads" of Egypt, Assyria, Babylon, and Medo-Persia [Dan. 7:6]), plus the terrible beast of Rome (Dan. 7:7). Then pagan Rome evolved into the Holy Roman Empire, the "little horn" (Dan. 7:8), which fiercely persecuted Protestant Christians under papal leadership during the Dark Ages.

Overlapping this history of God's people under Rome's devastating rule, Revelation 12:5 (KJV) states that the woman would bear "a man child" (compare Micah 5:2-4). However, Isaiah 66:7 prophesies that this "man child" would be born *before* the woman (church [Jer. 6:2]) was in labor (tribulation, likely the Protestant Reformation [Matt. 24:29]). Therefore, in figurative language that alludes to Christ's birth and heavenly ascension, Revelation 12:4-5 (NKJV) says:

> ... And the dragon (Satan/followers [Rev. 12:9]) stood before the woman (church [Jer. 6:2]) who was ready to give birth to devour her Child as soon as it was born (Jesus/the "Word" [Matt. 2:13; Is. 9:6-7; Jn.1:1, 14; Rev. 19:11-16]). She bore a male Child, who was to rule the nations with a rod of iron (seized from the "iron" kingdom of Rome [Dan. 2:40; Rev. 19:13, 15]). And her Child was caught up to God and to His throne and sat with God upon His throne (Jesus sat with His Father in the Holy Place of the heavenly sanctuary following His ascension [Heb. 12:2; 1:3; Rev. 3:21; Dan. 7:9, 13-14; parentheses added]).

From this time of Christ's ascent to Heaven, the Devil relentlessly persecuted God's people throughout Rome's iron rule. Even today, the Devil continues to specifically target the Protestant doctrine of justification by faith in Christ's sacrifice for sin, which is the very core of the gospel (Rom. 5:8-9). However, Satan's attempts could not stop the Protestant Reformation founded on the Bible and the Bible alone: "... and they overcame him by the blood of the Lamb, and by the word of their testimony; and they loved not their lives unto the death" (Rev. 12:11, KJV). Nevertheless, God's faithful church had to flee into the wilderness during the papacy's historical reign of 1,260 years (from 538 to 1798 AD), when thousands of innocent Protestants were martyred: "Then the woman (the Protestant church) fled into the wilderness, where she had a place prepared by God that they should feed her there one thousand two hundred and sixty days" (Rev. 12:6, NKJV; Is. 66:12).

Mercifully, Jesus rewarded these faithful martyrs, and the pope finally lost his political control when he was taken captive in 1798. Christ, as an answer to prayer, gave Christians a welcomed escape from papal persecution by granting them freedom in the United States, the primary world power rising just before the political fall of the Holy Roman Empire: Miraculously, the United States became the religious haven for the world! However, Satan was enraged at this turn of events and declared war against this nation protecting the freedom of God's people (Rev. 12:7-9). Revelation 12:13-14 (NKJV) expounds on this conflict:

> Now when the dragon (Satan/his hosts [Rev. 12:9]) saw that he had been cast to the earth (U.S./earth beast [Rev. 13:11), he persecuted the woman (God's church [Jer. 6:2]) who gave birth to the male Child (Jesus/the Word [John 1:1,14]). But the woman (the Protestant church) was given two wings of a great eagle (symbol of United States), that she might fly into the wilderness ("uninhabited land" [Deut. 32:9-11]) to her place, where she is *nourished* (fed [Rev. 12:6]) for *a time, times, and half a time* (Dan. 12:7) from the presence of the serpent (Satan [Rev. 12:8, 14]; italics & parentheses added).

The "time, times, and a half" prophecy in this text likely corresponds with Revelation 12:6's 1,260 days, occurring after the Protestant Reformation when the devil came down to the earth (beast [Rev. 13:11]; U.S.), knowing he had but a "short time" (Rev. 12:12, KJV). Interestingly, the word for "time," "*kairos*," means "*a fixed or definite time; the time when things are brought to crisis; and* "*the decisive epoch waited for*," which is a similar meaning of the word, "time," ("*mow'ed*" = "*appointed time*") in the "time, times, and a half" prophecy found in Daniel 12:7 (compare Acts 17:26). Both prophecies in chapter 12 of Daniel and Revelation seem to point to an end-time context, taking place after Daniel's prophecies were unsealed at the "time of the end" (Dan. 12:9). If forty-nine-year increments are inserted into Revelation 12's prophecy like it was in Daniel's (Lev. 25:8), the woman (church) would be nourished for "a time" (49 years), "times" (49 + 49 = 98 years), "and a half" (49 divided by 2= 24.5 years), totaling 171.5 years. If 171.5 years are added to 1844 (the close of the 2,300-day prophecy; the beginning of Daniel 12's "time, times, and a half"; and the beginning of the three woes [Rev. 12:12]), it ends the protection of God's people in 2015.

Again, this is the same year that the pope spoke to Congress in formal session for the first time in history, urging the U.S. to join the Paris Agreement, which propelled the papacy's political influence in America. Moreover, if 171.5 years are added to October 22, 1844, the precise date that Christ entered the Most Holy Place to start the investigative judgment, the total ends on April 22, 2016, the **exact day** that the U.S. heeded the pope's urgings to join the Paris Agreement![205] Could the Lord be warning His people that the papacy's political power has begun its predicted

---

[205] https://www.un.org/sustainabledevelopment/blog/2016/04/parisagreementsinga-tures/

comeback at this precise time in history?

Moreover, Bible prophecy cautions God's people that the Devil has constantly spewed out a flood of deception upon the Lord's church so that it might be carried away by Satan's false teachings: "And the earth (specifically the U.S. as the earth beast [Rev. 13:11]) helped the woman (the church [Jer. 6:2]), and the earth opened her mouth, and swallowed up the flood which the dragon cast out of his mouth" (Rev. 12:16, KJV; parentheses added). This deluge of deception from false teachers continues today, buffeting Protestantism's biblical foundation that had previously been founded by God's faithful followers during the Protestant Reformation (Rev. 12:16; 2 Sam. 22:4-5; Dan. 9:26).

Such doctrinal truths, illustrated in the sanctuary service, have gradually been reestablished throughout Protestant church history. For example, the Lutherans spearheaded the belief of justification by faith, which was illustrated in the sacrifice made in the outer court of the temple (Rom. 5:1). The Baptists brought out the truth of baptism by immersion, represented by the laver, also located in the outer courtyard of the sanctuary (Jn. 3:23; Matt. 3:16). The Presbyterians proclaimed the priestly mediation of all believers, represented by the altar of incense, found in the Holy Place of the temple (1 Pet. 2:5, 9). The Methodists emphasized the application of God's Word in righteous living, prefigured in the table of shewbread (Jn. 6:27, 35; Rev. 10:8-11). Plus, several Protestant churches began the American Bible Society that spread the light of God's Word worldwide, symbolized in the seven-branched candlestick (Matt. 5:14). Finally, after each of these truths had been restored, Christ moved from the Holy Place into the Most Holy Place in 1844, where the Ark of the Covenant contained the Ten Commandments (Rev. 11:19). Ministering in this last compartment, Jesus raised a remnant church, which would incorporate all of these Protestant beliefs and add the blessing of obeying God's Law (Rom. 6:11-13; 8:3-4; Phil. 4:13), particularly found in the fourth commandment that God told His followers *to remember* (Ex. 20:8-11; Is. 58:13-14).

Unfortunately, throughout history, the Sabbath commandment has been forgotten by many of God's people, even though Sunday-keeping has no biblical evidence. Instead, it originated when Constantine combined paganism with Christianity in 321 AD.[206] Later, the Catholic Church claimed that the solemnity of the Sabbath was transferred to Sunday. *The Catholic Record*, Sept. 1, 1923, declares:

> We have in the authoritative voice of the Church, the voice of Christ Himself. The Church is above the Bible, and this transference of Sabbath observance from Saturday to Sunday is proof positive of that fact."[207]

Additionally, Peter Geiermann's *Convert's Catechism of Catholic Doctrine*, p. 50, states:

> Q. Which is the Sabbath Day?
>
> A. Saturday is the Sabbath day.
>
> Q. Why do we observe Sunday instead of Saturday?
>
> A. We observe Sunday instead of Saturday because the Catholic Church transferred the solemnity from Saturday to Sunday.[208]

Therefore, the Catholic Church, by its own ecclesiastical power, without biblical backing, claims to have changed the day of worship to Sunday, instead of Saturday, which is the Lord's

---

[206] https://grbs.library.duke.edu/article/viewFile/4491/5515
[207] https://amazingdiscoveries.org/S-deception-Sabbath_Sunday_Catholic_Church#!
[208] http://www.jlfoundation.net/papacy.html

seventh-day Sabbath according to the Bible (Ex. 20:8-11; Dan. 7:25).

However, after the papacy's long rule ended, a great spiritual awakening took place, bringing God's Sabbath truth to light. Beginning in 1863, the Seventh-day Adventist Church became the most prominent worldwide denomination to uphold the scriptural, seventh-day Sabbath and the restoration of Protestant doctrines lost during the Dark Ages of papal persecution. It was no coincidence, then, that just before this occurred, Jesus had moved into the Most Holy Place of the heavenly sanctuary where God's Law was located. Through the proclamation of this movement, the Ten Commandments, contained in the Ark of the Covenant in the Most Holy Place, were brought to the world's attention and testified of the Lord's glorious character (James 2:12; Rom. 7:12). It was by the observance of this holy law and faith in Christ's testimony (the spirit of prophecy [Rev. 19:10]) that God's people would be identified in the last days (Rev. 12:17; Rev. 14:12). Therefore, the Lord lovingly restored His Sabbath truth by raising a remnant movement that would proclaim to the world the sanctity of the Lord's law in preparation of His soon return.

The emergence of this godly woman (church [Jer. 6:2]), clothed with the sun, moon, and stars, was the first *"great sign"* of the nearness of Christ's second coming, mentioned in the book of Revelation (Rev. 12:1, NKJV). The word, "sign" must have triggered John's memory of the conversation he and the other disciples had had with Jesus when they asked what would be the signs of His coming and the "end of the age?" (Matt. 24:3). Jesus answered them by saying:

> Immediately after the tribulation of those days shall the sun be darkened, and the moon shall not give her light, and the stars shall fall from heaven, and the powers of the

heavens shall be shaken: And then shall appear the sign of the Son of Man in heaven…." (Matt. 24:29-30, KJV).

What could this sign of Christ's second coming be? Revelation 12:1-2 seems to imply that it is the appearance of the "woman," the Protestant church, giving birth to the "remnant of her seed" (Rev. 12:17, KJV). Christ associates this event, foretold in Matthew 24, happening after the closure of the historic 1,260 days/years of the "tribulation" and the signs in the heavens. Therefore, this remnant would likely arise after the Protestant Reformation, the Dark Day in 1780, and the Great Leonid Shower of 1833 (Matt. 24:29-30). Also, the "powers of heaven" would be shaken—the sun, moon, and stars (God's people [Gen. 37:9-10; Dan. 12:3; Ps. 89:36-37]), which could have figuratively taken place during the Great Disappointment in 1844.

What remnant church arose from the combination of many Protestant denominations in the U.S. soon after these signs occurred? It was the Seventh-day Adventist Church, formed in 1863 with only 3,500 members.[209] This infant church would proclaim Christ's mediatory work in the heavenly sanctuary (Heb. 9:24-28), a personal relationship with Jesus (Rev. 14:12), the importance of keeping God's law/Sabbath (Rev. 12:17), and an understanding of biblical prophecy (Rev. 19:10). It would grow from its small beginnings (Zech. 4:10) to become a worldwide movement, spreading the Three Angels' Messages (Rev. 14:7-12).

Currently, the Seventh-day Adventist Church is in 213 of the 235 countries recognized by the United Nations and is rapidly expanding,[210] "making it probably the most widespread Protes-

---

[209] https://news.adventist.org/en/all-news/news/go/2017-03-01/propelled-by-total-member-involvement-adventist-church-tops-20-million-members/
[210] https://www.adventist.org/en/information/statistics/article/go/-/seventh-day-adventist-world-church-statistics-2016-2017/

tant denomination."[211] The Lord has blessed this remnant church by adding over one million members annually from 2004-2019.[212] Moreover, according to *USA Today*, the Seventh-day Adventist Church was the fastest-growing Protestant denomination in all of North America in 2011.[213] With the occurrence of this sign of Christ's soon coming, the dragon became enraged with the woman (the Protestant church) and "went to make war with the *remnant of her seed* (the Seventh-day Adventist Church) which keep the *commandments of God* (the Ten Commandments) and have the *testimony of Jesus Christ*," which is the *"spirit of prophecy"* (Rev. 12:17; 19:10, KJV; parentheses & italics added).

However, the Bible predicts that God's people will overcome the dragon "by the blood of the Lamb and by the word of their testimony" (Rev. 12:11, KJV). Christ's remnant church will gain victory despite the warning: "Woe to the inhabitants of the earth and the sea! For the Devil has come down to you having great wrath because he knows that he has a short time" (Rev. 12:12, NKJV). Jesus has promised that if His children draw near to Him and resist the Devil, Satan will flee! (James 4:7). Moreover, God's Word states that Christ will "crush Satan under your feet shortly!" (Rom. 16:20, NKJV). Also, the Bible assures us that God is greater than the Devil, and we have the power to overcome him (1 Jn. 4:4; Rev. 12:11): "for the accuser of our brethren is cast down" (Rev. 12:10, KJV). Therefore, victory in Christ is certain!

---

[211] https://en.wikipedia.org/wiki/Seventh-day_Adventist_Church
[212] https://www.adventistreview.org/church-news/story4262-adventist-church-membership-reaches-195-million; https://www.adventist.org/statistics/
[213] https://www.nadadventist.org/sites/default/files/inline-files/Updated_Strategic%20Report_BestPractices_SinglePages-ScreenResolution_0.pdf

# Discussion Questions for Revelation 12

1. What "great sign" did John behold, and what might it represent? (Rev. 12:1-2; Jer. 6:2)

2. How was the woman described, and what do the symbols of the sun, moon, and the garland of twelve stars symbolize? (Rev. 12:1-2; 21:14; Mal. 4:2; Ps. 89:35-37; Gen. 37:9-10)

3. What is meant by the woman crying out "in labor and in pain"? (Rev. 12:2; Is. 66:7-9; Micah 4:9-10; Matt. 24:29)

4. Whom does the dragon represent? (Rev. 12:3, 8; 20:2; Dan. 7:23)

5. How is the fiery red dragon described, and what do these symbols mean? (Rev. 12:3; 17:9-10; Jer. 51:24-25; Zech. 1:21)

6. To what "Child" does the woman figuratively give birth? (Rev. 12:4-5; Micah 5:2-4; Is. 9:6-7; Jn. 1:1, 14; Rev. 19:13-16)

7. Where and how is the woman likely "nourished" for a "time, times, and half a time?" (Rev. 12:13-14, 16; 13:11; Dan. 12:7; Deut. 32:9-12)

8. What specific truths, symbolized in the sanctuary, were lost during the papacy's rule through the Dark Ages, and how were they restored in the Protestant movement? (Rom. 5:1; Jn. 3:23; Matt. 3:16; 1 Pet. 2:5, 9; Jn. 6:27, 35; Rev. 10:8-11; Matt. 5:14; Rom. 6:11-13; 8:3-4; Ex. 20:8-11; Is. 58:13-14)

9. What identifying characteristics does the remnant church display? (Rev. 14:12) What worldwide church fits this description? (Rev.12:17; Rev. 19:10; Ex. 20:8-11) How has the Devil responded to this remnant church? (Rev. 12:12, 17)

# Revelation 13 (KJV)

*¹ And I stood upon the sand of the sea, and saw a beast rise up out of the sea, having seven heads and ten horns, and upon his horns ten crowns, and upon his heads the name of blasphemy. ² And the beast which I saw was like unto a leopard, and his feet were as the feet of a bear, and his mouth as the mouth of a lion: and the dragon gave him his power, and his seat, and great authority. ³ And I saw one of his heads as it were wounded to death; and his deadly wound was healed: and all the world wondered after the beast. ⁴ And they worshipped the dragon which gave power unto the beast: and they worshipped the beast, saying, Who is like unto the beast? who is able to make war with him? ⁵ And there was given unto him a mouth speaking great things and blasphemies; and power was given unto him to continue forty and two months. ⁶ And he opened his mouth in blasphemy against God, to blaspheme his name, and his tabernacle, and them that dwell in heaven. ⁷ And it was given unto him to make war with the saints, and to overcome them: and power was given him over all kindreds, and tongues, and nations. ⁸ And all that dwell upon the earth shall worship him, whose names are not written in the book of life of the Lamb slain from the foundation of the world. ⁹ If any man have an ear, let him hear. ¹⁰ He that leadeth into captivity shall go into captivity: he that killeth with the sword must be killed with the sword. Here is the patience and the faith of the saints. ¹¹ And I beheld another beast coming up out of the earth; and he had two horns like a lamb, and he spake as a dragon. ¹² And he exerciseth all the power of the first beast before him, and causeth the earth and them which dwell therein to worship the first beast, whose deadly wound was healed. [13] And he doeth great wonders, so that he maketh fire come down from heaven on the earth in the sight of men, [14] And deceiveth them that dwell on the earth by the means of those miracles which he had power to do in the sight of the beast; saying to them that dwell on the earth, that they should make an image to the beast, which had the wound by a sword, and did live. [15] And he had power to give life unto the image of the beast, that the image of the beast should both speak, and cause that as many as would not worship the image of the beast should be killed. [16] And he causeth all, both small and great, rich and poor, free and bond, to receive a mark in their right hand, or in their foreheads: [17] And that no man might buy or sell, save he that had the mark, or the name of the beast, or the number of his name. [18] Here is wisdom. Let him that hath understanding count the number of the beast: for it is the number of a man; and his number is Six hundred threescore and six.*

# The Beast and Its Image

When twins look into a mirror, what do they see? Nearly the same image! Similarly, John saw two beast kingdoms (Dan. 7:23): a composite beast with seven heads and ten horns rising from the sea (populated area [Rev. 13:1; 17:15]) and a lamb-like beast rising from the earth (unpopulated area) that spoke like the dragon (Rev.13:11; 12:3). Both of these kingdoms would mirror each other in the pursuit of destroying God's people globally (Rev. 12:17; 13:7, 14-15).

## The Dragon's Sea Beast

First, John describes the sea beast as having "seven heads and ten horns…" (Rev. 13:1, KJV), and the dragon gave him his "power, throne, and great authority" (Rev. 13:2, NKJV). The sea beast has the same number of heads and horns as the pagan red dragon (Rev. 13:1; 12:3). Also, Revelation 13:2 describes this sea beast as a combination of the beast kingdoms of Daniel 7. It has the appearance of a leopard-like beast (Greece [Dan. 7:6]), with feet like a bear (Medo-Persia [Dan. 7:5]) and a mouth like a lion (Babylon [Dan. 7:4]). This description hints that the first six heads of the sea beast likely symbolize the world kingdoms ruling God's people throughout history: Egypt, Assyria, Babylon, Medo-Persia, Greece, and Rome, with its little horn, the papacy and the horns of divided Europe. The remnants of the ten horns may also include additional political powers during the last days.

Interestingly, the Psalmist declares that God "brakest the heads of the *dragons* in the waters... the heads of the leviathan in pieces" (Ps. 74:13-14, KJV). In these texts, the dragon and the sea beast are interchangeable. The Hebrew word for "dragon" is *"tanniyn,"* meaning a *"marine or land monster"* (Deut. 32:33, KJV). The book of Job reveals the name of this sea beast as *"Leviathan,"* meaning in Hebrew, *"dragon, serpent, sea monster"* (Job 41:1, KJV). Job refers to this symbolic beast as the "king over all of the children of pride" (Job 41:34, KJV). Isaiah 27:1 states that God will "punish Leviathan, the fleeing serpent" (NKJV), and will "slay the dragon that is in the sea" (KJV; compare Rev. 12:9). Therefore, the sea beast is rooted in Satan's serpent/dragon kingdom, specifically in the terrible beast of pagan Rome; however, it has grown from a horn (a country's political and religious powers [Dan 7:24; 8:21-22; Zech. 1:18-19; Rev. 17:12; Eze. 34:1, 21]) to its own beast (kingdom [Dan. 7:23]), disguised in the religious garb of the Roman Catholic papacy (Rev. 13:2-6; 12:9; Dan. 7:7-8, 19-25).

Revelation 13:3 (KJV) further states that this sea beast has a head that is "wounded to death," and "his deadly wound was healed." History proves that a deadly wound was inflicted upon the head of the Holy Roman Empire in 1798 when the pope was taken captive by Napoleon's general, Berthier. The last head of the sea beast, then, would likely occur after the fall of the Holy Roman Empire in 1798. Only one major world nation arose during this time: *the United States of America.* Prophecy predicts that the pope's subsequent gain of political/religious influence would return by stating his deadly wound would be healed, and "all the world," including Protestant America, would follow the beast (Rev. 13:3-4, 7-8, KJV).

Interestingly, two additional details are added to the description of the sea beast as compared to the dragon: instead of its heads, its horns are crowned, and it also has a blasphemous name upon its heads (Rev. 13:1). Crowns represent kingly rulership (Eze. 21:26-27; Jer. 2:14, 16; Lam. 5:6, 16), and horns symbolize power. Therefore, the fact that the sea beast's crowns have slipped from its heads to its horns (which will be broken [Ps. 75:10; Zech. 1:21; Lam. 2:3]) most likely means that the sea beast's authority will be manifested in the powers of individual states/countries instead of a single worldwide kingdom.

Secondly, along with its power resting upon its horns, the sea beast has a blasphemous name upon its heads, and it opens its mouth in blasphemy against the Lord (Rev. 13:1, 6; compare 2 Thess. 2:3-4). The definition of blasphemy is claiming the "rights or qualities of God," which would apply to the false pagan religions of the dragon's heads.[214] However, could this text include a so-called Christian religion, as well? According to the Bible, a person claiming the ability to forgive sin is blaspheming (Matt. 9:2-3). For example, the New Testament records that Christ forgave the paralytic's sins and was accused of blasphemy: "Who is this which speaketh blasphemies? Who can forgive sins, but God alone?" (Luke 5:21, KJV). God's Word clearly states that forgiveness is of the Lord: "If Thou, Lord, shouldest mark iniquities, O Lord, who shall stand? But there is forgiveness with thee, that thou mayest be feared" (Ps. 130:3-4, KJV). However, prophecy warns that this sea beast "opened his mouth, in blasphemy against God, to blaspheme his name, and his tabernacle, and them that dwell in heaven" (Rev. 13:6, KJV).

Is there a modern Christian religion that has leaders who claim the right to forgive sins? Yes, indeed! The Roman Catholic

---

[214] https://www.dictionary.com/browse/blasphemy

Church unabashedly claims this authority, and it is a well-known fact that confessions are made to Catholic priests instead of going directly to Christ.[215] Even more flagrant, Pope Francis recently granted the selling of indulgences, which permitted sinners to *buy* forgiveness during the "Year of Mercy" of 2016.[216] The pope decreed:

> During the jubilee year, not only can pilgrims who cross through the special Holy Door in St. Peter's Basilica or other Roman churches obtain an indulgence—that was always the tradition—but for the first time each diocese around the world will also have a Holy Door in one or more churches to make it easier for those who cannot afford to travel to get an indulgence.[217]

This same article further states that Pope Francis promised "all those attending World Youth Day in Brazil in July 2013, would merit indulgences if they also went to confession, took Communion at Mass, and prayed for the pope's prayer intentions."[218] Also, at that time, the pope declared that those who could not make the event in Rio, "could obtain an indulgence if they followed the events on television or radio or 'by the new means of social communication'—such as Twitter."[219] However, the Bible states that forgiveness is a *gift* and cannot be purchased as an indulgence: "For all have sinned, and come short of the glory of God; *Being justified freely by his grace* through the redemption that is in Christ Jesus" (Rom. 3:23-24, KJV; italics added). Yet the pope claims the ability to forgive sin which is blasphemy according to the Bible.

---

[215] https://www.cnn.com/2016/11/21/europe/pope-francis-absolve-abortion/index.html

[216] https://www.ncronline.org/news/vatican/francis-announces-wide-indulgences-mercy-jubilee-grants-lefebvrites-faculties

[217] https://www.ncronline.org/news/vatican/pope-francis-too-indulgent-indulgences

[218] ibid

[219] ibid

Tragically, the pope's popularity has continually increased, both in America and in the world. A motion picture of Pope Francis's life grossed 4.6 million worldwide and was rated sixth place for the highest box office results for documentaries produced in 2018.[220] America's audience response was a "92 percent overall positive score and an 82 percent "definite recommend."[221] Additionally, the Washington Post gave this film a three-star rating, summarizing its contents by stating, "An absorbing, inspiring movie… that introduces viewers to a swashbuckling global SUPERHERO" (capitalization added).[222] Proclaiming Pope Francis's political/spiritual leadership, the Vatican further declared that he has gained "the trust of people of all faith traditions and cultures across the world."[223] Amazingly, the majority of Americans seem to agree! According to a recent Pew Research survey, "among the U.S. public as a whole (including both Catholics and non-Catholics), roughly six-in-ten say they have a favorable view of Pope Francis."[224] Additionally, "two-thirds (67%) of white mainline Protestants and 58% of religiously unaffiliated adults have positive views of Francis."[225] These statistics show that not only the majority of Christians, but even the majority of Americans that don't claim to be religious, think positively of the pope.

---

[220] https://www.the-numbers.com/movie/Pope-Francis-A-Man-of-His-Word-(Documentary)#tab=summary; https://www.the-numbers.com/market/2018/genre/Documentary

[221] https://en.wikipedia.org/wiki/Pope_Francis:_A_Man_of_His_Word

[222] https://www.washingtonpost.com/goingoutguide/movies/pope-francis-a-man-of-his-word-is-an-inspiring-thoroughly-engrossing-portrait/2018/05/16/57c41de8-53f5-11e8-9c91-7dab596e8252_story.html

[223] https://www.vaticannews.va/en/pope/news/2018-03/pope-francis-_-a-man-of-his-word.html

[224] https://www.pewresearch.org/fact-tank/2021/06/25/americans-including-catholics-continue-to-have-favorable-views-of-pope-francis/

[225] ibid

However, the papacy's "healing" has been most clearly demonstrated by the Lutherans, as well as many other mainline Protestant churches, in their declaration of unity with the Catholic Church on the doctrine of justification in 2017. Both Protestant and Catholic leaders summarized this confederation by stating, "We begged forgiveness for our failures and for the ways in which Christians have *wounded* the Body of the Lord and offended each other during the 500 years since the beginning of the Reformation until today" (italics added).[226] Furthermore, the assistant general secretary for Ecumenical Relations of the Lutheran World Federation summarized this joint declaration by stating, "We are witnessing a certain momentum in our shared ecumenical journey. This consultation is meant to appreciate and to use that gift, *to heal the wounds in the body of Christ*" (italics added).[227] The pope, himself, speaking of bringing Protestants back into agreement with the Catholic Church, stated that "it is the favorable time *to heal wounds*" (italics added).[228]

## "Healing the Wounds"

This is an interesting choice of words—"to heal wounds," considering that Bible prophecy uses these same words to describe what happens to the sea beast's head:

> … the dragon (Satan/paganism [Rev. 12:9]) gave him (the sea beast- papacy [Rev. 13:1-10]) his power, his throne, and great authority. And I saw one of his heads (Rome) as if it had been mortally *wounded* (1798- pope taken captive, loses civil authority), and his deadly *wound was healed* (religious/political power restored to the papacy [Rev. 13:2-3, NKJV; italics & parentheses added]).

[226] https://www.bbc.com/news/world-europe-41817418
[227] https://www.lutheranworld.org/news/healing-wounds-body-christ
[228] https://catholicexchange.com/year-of-mercy-time-to-heal-wounds-8-ways

But when would these things transpire? The prophecy states, "And there was given unto him a mouth speaking great things and blasphemies; and power was given unto him to continue *forty and two months"* (Rev. 13:5, KJV; italics added). As stated previously, the historical forty-two-month period occurred when the papacy ruled over God's people (Rev. 11:2). If these days (42 X 30) are figured in years (Num. 14:34; Eze. 4:6), then this time period spans 1,260 years. Also, the forty-two-month time prophecy could span the same period as the "time, times, and a half" prophecy found in Daniel 7:25 (KJV; 3.5 X 360). Therefore, the forty-two months and the "time, times, and a half" prophecies historically refer to the 1,260 years that the papacy ruled during the Dark Ages, from 538 until 1798 AD.

However, could this forty-two-month period be repeated in modern times? Revelation 13:5 (KJV) states that he was given power "to continue for forty and two months." The Greek word for "to continue" is *"poieo,"* which can mean both *"without delay"* and *"to raise up."* Therefore, this text could also mean that he was given power *without delay* or *to raise up* after forty-two months. This reference to delay is similar to Christ vowing to John in Revelation 10:6, NKJV: "by Him who lives forever" that "there should be delay no longer." Likewise, in Daniel 12:7 (KJV), Jesus swears, "… it shall be for a time ("mow'ed"), times, and a half, and when he shall have accomplished to scatter the power of the holy people, all these things shall be finished." If one uses God's method of forty-nine-year time periods, implied in the Hebrew word, *"mow'ed,"* meaning *"appointed time,"*(Lev. 25:8), the sum totals 171.5 years (time= 49, + times= 98, + a half = 24.5 years; compare Is. 29:1). Similarly, if the forty-two-month prophecy found in Revelation 13:5 is multiplied by forty-nine, it equals 2,058 months (compare Ps. 104:19, KJV-"appointed the "moon" [*month*] for "seasons" [*"mow'ed"*]). Then if 2,058 months is divided by twelve months in a year, the quotient is 171.5 years, exactly the same as Daniel 12:7's "time, times, and a half" prophecy. Furthermore, this same 171.5-year-period is likely referred to in Revelation 12:14's (KJV), "time, times, and a half" (*"kairos"* [Gal. 4:10]) prophecy, when the woman (church) would be "nourished" from the "face of the serpent" and the papacy's rule of God's people would be delayed, allowing for church growth.

Moreover, Daniel 11:35-37 (NKJV) states, "… it is still for the *appointed time ("mow'ed")*. Then the king shall… magnify himself above every god, shall speak blasphemies against the God of gods, and… regard neither the God of his fathers nor the desire of women… for he shall exalt himself above them all" (italics added). The apostle, Paul, echos this description by calling this proud soul the "man of sin," "who opposeth and exalteth himself above all that is called God, or that is worshiped; so that he as God sitteth in the temple of God, shewing himself that he is God" (2 Thess. 2:4, KJV). This description can only refer to the papacy because the pope, alone, claims to be infallible and Christ's vicar. But when would the pope regain his political world influence that was formally lost? Did something happen in Protestant America 171.5 years after 1844, the end of the 2,300-day/year prophecy? Yes!

Once again, Bible prophecy seems to repeat the importance of the year 2015! (1844 + 171.5). It was in this year that the U.S. Congress, for the first time in history, formally sought the spiritual and governmental counsel of the Roman pontiff. Only a few months later, this blatant disregard of biblical warnings would result in the United States' shocking adherence to much of Pope Francis's socialistic, political agenda, which is outlined in his encyclical, "Laudato Si."[229] Stealthily growing since the Second

---

[229] https://www.smh.com.au/world/pope-francis-challenges-congress-to-heal-worlds-open-wounds-20150925-gjui8b.html

Vatican Council in the 1960s, this disturbing rise of papal power in the U.S. was prompted by evangelicals uniting with Catholics on common points of doctrine in 1994. Since that time, the pope's influence in both America and the world has rapidly compounded.[230] In 2016, the Roman pontiff's rising political power propelled the unity of more than 190 countries to sign the Paris Agreement, including the United States.[231] This unity of the world's nations is unprecedented in modern history, reflecting the pope's popularity with over 40 million followers on social media.[232]

Prophecy declares that all the world will marvel and follow the beast: "… power was given him over all kindreds, and tongues, and nations. And all that dwell upon the earth shall worship him, whose names are not written in the book of life.…" (Rev. 13:7-8, KJV). This world unity, instigated by the papacy, will eventually result in the persecution of God's people because the Bible predicts: "it was given unto him to make war with the saints, and to overcome them" (Rev. 13:7, KJV). However, God gives hope to His people through this promise: "He that leadeth into captivity shall go into captivity: he that killeth with the sword must be killed with the sword. Here is the patience and the faith of the saints" (Rev. 13:10, KJV).

## The Earth Beast Rises

Then, after seeing the sea beast, John beheld another beast kingdom coming from the earth with two horns *like a lamb*, but it spoke *like a dragon* (Rev. 13:11). Opposite of the sea beast which

---

[230] https://www.huffpost.com/entry/pope-francis-world-politics_n_5448134

[231] https://www.washingtonpost.com/world/2018/10/11/few-countries-are-meeting-paris-climate-goals-here-are-ones-that-are/; https://www.theguardian.com/environment/2019/jun/14/pope-francis-declares-climate-emergency-and-urges-action

[232] https://insidethevatican.com/news/pope-francis-40-million-twitter-followers-counting/

had risen from water (the populated area around the Mediterranean Sea [Rev. 17:15; Dan. 7:2]), this earth beast was predicted to appear in a continent with few people (Rev. 13:11). In review, the Lamb-like beast is a symbol of the Lord's kingdom (Hosea 4:16), and its two horns without crowns represent its government by the people (Rev. 5:6; John 1:29; Dan. 7:24). This earth beast with its Lamb-like horns seems reminiscent of the ram and its two horns from Daniel 8:3, which likely represents God's leadership of His people (Jer. 50:7-8, 11). This young Christian country would arise after the wound of the papacy in 1798 AD, begin in a previously unpopulated part of the world, and have a representative government without a king (portrayed in its two horns lacking any crowns). However, it would eventually speak like the pagan dragon through the passage of secular national laws by its courts (Rev. 13:11; compare Eze. 20:23-25). Over time, this Protestant Christian nation would acquire worldwide influence and "exerciseth all the power of the first beast," causing "the earth and them which dwelleth therein to worship the first beast, whose deadly wound was healed" (Rev. 13:12, KJV). What Protestant Christian nation arose after 1798 in an unpopulated area of the world with a representative form of government and would become a world-renowned superpower? Only one modern nation fits this description: *the United States of America*. Sadly, this country was destined to become the last "head" of the scarlet beast, adding its two horns to Rome's remaining eight (Dan. 7:7-8; Rev. 13:1, 11; 17:3).

Additionally, prophecy predicts that this "false prophet" (apostate Protestant America united with the papacy [Rev. 16:13]), would "perform great signs," and like Elijah, make "fire come down from heaven on the earth in the sight of men" (Rev. 13:13, NKJV). This miracle would be done to:

… deceive those who dwell on the earth (specifically the U.S. "earth beast" [Rev. 13:11]) by those signs which he was granted to do in the sight of the beast (the papacy or "sea beast" [Rev. 13:1-7]) telling those who dwell on the earth to make an image to the beast who was wounded by the sword and lived. (Rev. 13:14, NKJV; parentheses added)

What does fire coming down from Heaven symbolize in the New Testament? Referring to Pentecost, Acts 2:3-4 (KJV) describes the descent of the Holy Spirit "as of fire," and the disciples "began to speak with other tongues, as the Spirit gave them utterance" (languages [Acts 2:4-11; 1 Cor. 14:4-33]). Therefore, the fire could represent the workings of the Holy Spirit.

Today, a modern counterfeit of this spiritual gift of the Holy Spirit likely occurred in 2014 when the pope sent a videoed message via Tony Palmer to the American evangelical leader, Kenneth Copeland, asking for Protestant and Catholic unity during a charismatic event. Palmer, at this time, declared that the Protestant "protest was over."[233] Both Catholics and Protestants joined together in speaking in tongues after hearing the pope's appeal for brotherhood.[234] This ecumenical event propelled the movement for unity, climaxing in 2017 and reconfirming in 2021.[235] Amazingly, many Protestant denominations joined the papacy on the doctrine of justification, the *very doctrine* cited in the pope's appeal to the evangelicals in 2014!

---

[233] https://www.youtube.com/watch?v=uA4EPOfic5A; https://www.ncregister.com/news/we-are-brothers-pope-declares-in-heartfelt-message-to-pentecostals

[234] ibid

[235] https://www.vaticannews.va/en/vatican-city/news/2021-01/catholics-and-lutherans-reaffirm-commitment-to-communion.html

Prophecy predicts that civil legislation persecuting God's people will be passed, which is exactly what is happening today: "He was granted power to give breath to the image of the beast, that the image of the beast should both speak and cause as many as would not worship the image of the beast to be killed" (Rev. 13:15, NKJV). The national passage of laws against religious freedom with their resulting economic impact, and finally, the death penalty, will become the stimulus for Americans and the rest of the world to receive the beast's mark:

> And he causeth all, both small and great, rich and poor, free and bond, to receive a mark in their right hand, or in their foreheads: And that no man might buy or sell, save he that had the mark, or the name of the beast, or the number of his name. (Rev. 13:16-17, KJV)

These texts indicate that the mark of the beast relates to its name (character [Rev. 2:17; 3:12; 14:1; 19:12; 22:4; Is. 62:2]). But what is the beast's name? Revelation 17:5 (KJV) states that the beast's name is "Mystery Babylon," the worldwide conglomerate of church and state causing massive religious confusion at the end of time. Moreover, to understand the beast's mark and name, one must *calculate the number* of the beast, for it is the *number of a man. His number is 666"* (Rev. 13:18, NKJV; italics added). Many people have wondered what this mysterious number means, and recently some have attributed it to a tattoo or a bar code. However, for years, Protestants have believed that the number, 666, is a reference to the pope because the numerical value of the letters, "Vicarius Filii Dei"[236] equals 666.[237] Even a

---

[236] "Answers to Readers' Questions," Our Sunday Visitor, Nov. 15, 1914; https://amazingdiscoveries.org/S-deception_beast_666_Vicarius-Filii-Dei

[237] H Grattan Guinness, Babylon and the Beast: 141, as quoted in S. Svensson, Kyrkans Strid Och Slutliga Streger (Stockholm: 1908): 126, 128; Richard Shimeall, *Our Bible Chronology—Historic and Prophetic, Critically Examined and Demonstrated* (New York: A. S. Barnes and Co., 1867): 180.

footnote for Revelation 13:18 in some Catholic Douay versions of the Bible states, "The numeral letters of his name shall make up this number."[238] However, could God have given even a greater clue in the number, 666, of the timing when this false teacher would arise?

The Bible says to "calculate the number" of this beast or man (Rev. 13:18). The Greek word for "calculate" is *"psephizo"* which means both to *"compute"* and *"to decide by voting."* In addition, the Greek word for "number" (*"arithmos"*) contains a root word, *"airo,"* that means *"to raise up"* or *"to take away from another what is his or what is committed to him."* Therefore, this prophecy could be speaking of the time when a man (specifically the "man of sin" [2 Thess. 2:3-4]) would "rise up," and many Protestant churches would vote to "take away" their historical Protestant beliefs (i.e. justification by faith) that have been "committed to them" by their forefathers. Case in point: If the number, 666, is multiplied— 6 X 6 X 6, it equals 216. If 216 years are added to 1798 (when the papacy lost its political power), one arrives in 2014, the same year that Pope Francis sent Tony Palmer to America to appeal for Catholic/Protestant unity during a tongue-speaking event. This historic event later spurred U.S. evangelicals to travel to the Vatican to propel ecumenical relations with the papacy,[239] possibly referred to in Revelation 13:13-14.

Sadly, even the understanding of this biblical warning will not prevent the eventual demise of religious freedom in the United States. Prophecy is clear—Protestant America has already begun forming an image of the papacy, and it will continue its ecumenical journey in uniting under the pope's mark of authority

---

[238] http://www.drbo.org/chapter/73013.htm
[239] https://www.ncronline.org/news/vatican/pope-francis-meets-us-televangelists-and-first-ever-papal-high-five-follows

(further discussed in the next chapter). The vital decision that all must make is—will we accept the papacy's "mark" in our foreheads or our hands to escape persecution (Rev. 13:7, 16), or will we consciously choose to be sealed by God's Spirit and trust Him to preserve us until the day of our redemption? (Eph. 1:12-14; 4:30).

### Rev. 13's 42-month Prophecy Compared to Rev. 11's 42-month Prophecy & Rev. & Dan. 12's "Time, Times, & Half a Time" Prophecies

| Investigative Judgment Begins (Dan. 8:14) Referred to as "Measuring" in Rev. 11:1-2 | The Exact Date of the End of 2,300-Day/Yr. Prophecy, Occurring on the Day of Atonement (Dan. 8:14; p. 34-35) | National Same-Sex Marriage Law Passes in U.S./ Pope Francis Addresses U.S. Congress, Urges U.S. to Enter Paris Agreement on Climate Change | EXACT DAY U.S. Heeds Pope's Counsel & Enters Paris Agreement with over 190 World Nations |
|---|---|---|---|
| 1844 | Oct. 22, 1844 | 2015 | April 22, 2016 |

42 months X 49= 2,058 months= 171.5 yrs./Time (49), Times (98), Half a Time (24.5)= 171.5 yrs.
(Rev. 13:5; 11:2; Lev. 25:8)            (Dan. 12:7; Rev. 12:14; Lev. 25:8; see p. 74)

*Woman (Church) "Nourished" in the U.S. (Rev. 12:14-17)*
*Despite Attacks from Dragon (Satan/Humanistic Government)*
*Delay of Papal Power, Ending in 2015/2016*

# Discussion Questions for Revelation 13

1. *From where does the first beast arise? (Rev. 13:1) What do "sea" and "waters" represent in prophecy? (Rev. 17:15) In contrast, from where does the second beast rise?*

2. *How are the dragon of Revelation 12 and the sea beast of Revelation 13 similar? What might this similarity imply? (Rev. 13:1-2; Rev. 12:3; Is. 27:1, KJV)*

3. *What entity is symbolized by the sea beast? (Rev. 13:6-8; Dan. 7:23, 25)*

4. *What is the definition of "blasphemy" or "pompous" words? (Rev. 13:6; Luke 5:20-21) How does the pope fit the description of "a man, and a mouth speaking pompous words" outlined in Rev. 13:6? (Dan. 7:8 compare 2 Thess. 2:3-4)*

5. *What does the sea beast continue to do after a forty-two-month delay that likely corresponds to the "time, times and half a time" prophecies in Revelation 12:14 and Daniel 12:7? How does the world respond? (Rev. 13:4-8)*

6. *What is happening as a result of the sea beast's head being healed today? (Rev. 13:3, 6-8;)*

7. *Where does the second beast of Revelation 13 appear? (Rev. 13:11) Why is its location a clue to the beast's identity?*

8. *How is the earth beast described? (Rev. 13:11) What does a Lamb-like beast represent? (Rev. 5:6; John 1:29; compare Hosea 4:16; Dan. 7:23)*

9. *What does "speaking like a dragon" symbolize? (Rev. 13:11; Rev. 12:9) How is this happening today in the United States?*

10. *What does the fire possibly represent that comes down from Heaven in Revelation 13:13? How has a counterfeit of this phenomenon occurred in modern times that has encouraged ecumenical unity between Catholics and Protestants? (Acts 2:3-4)*

11. *What does Bible prophecy predict that the earth beast will do to those who do not worship the image of the beast? (Rev. 13:15) How is religious freedom being stripped away from American citizens today?*

12. *How might the number 666 point to the papacy? (Rev. 13:18)*

# Revelation 14 (KJV)

*¹ And I looked, and, lo, a Lamb stood on the mount Sion, and with him an hundred forty and four thousand, having his Father's name written in their foreheads. ² And I heard a voice from heaven, as the voice of many waters, and as the voice of a great thunder: and I heard the voice of harpers harping with their harps: ³ And they sung as it were a new song before the throne, and before the four beasts, and the elders: and no man could learn that song but the hundred and forty and four thousand, which were redeemed from the earth. ⁴ These are they which were not defiled with women; for they are virgins. These are they which follow the Lamb whithersoever he goeth. These were redeemed from among men, being the firstfruits unto God and to the Lamb. ⁵ And in their mouth was found no guile: for they are without fault before the throne of God. ⁶ And I saw another angel fly in the midst of heaven, having the everlasting gospel to preach unto them that dwell on the earth, and to every nation, and kindred, and tongue, and people, ⁷ Saying with a loud voice, Fear God, and give glory to him; for the hour of his judgment is come: and worship him that made heaven, and earth, and the sea, and the fountains of waters. ⁸ And there followed another angel, saying, Babylon is fallen, is fallen, that great city, because she made all nations drink of the wine of the wrath of her fornication. ⁹ And the third angel followed them, saying with a loud voice, If any man worship the beast and his image, and receive his mark in his forehead, or in his hand, ¹⁰ The same shall drink of the wine of the wrath of God, which is poured* out without mixture into the cup of his indignation; and he shall be tormented with fire and brimstone in the presence of the holy angels, and in the presence of the Lamb: [11] And the smoke of their torment ascendeth up for ever and ever: and they have no rest day nor night, who worship the beast and his image, and whosoever receiveth the mark of his name. [12] Here is the patience of the saints: here are they that keep the commandments of God, and the faith of Jesus. [13] And I heard a voice from heaven saying unto me, Write, Blessed are the dead which die in the Lord from henceforth: Yea, saith the Spirit, that they may rest from their labours; and their works do follow them. [14] And I looked, and behold a white cloud, and upon the cloud one sat like unto the Son of man, having on his head a golden crown, and in his hand a sharp sickle. [15] And another angel came out of the temple, crying with a loud voice to him that sat on the cloud, Thrust in thy sickle, and reap: for the time is come for thee to reap; for the harvest of the earth is ripe. [16] And he that sat on the cloud thrust in his sickle on the earth; and the earth was reaped. [17] And another angel came out of the temple which is in heaven, he also having a sharp sickle. [18] And another angel came out from the altar, which had power over fire; and cried with a loud cry to him that had the sharp sickle, saying, Thrust in thy sharp sickle, and gather the clusters of the vine of the earth; for her grapes are fully ripe. [19] And the angel thrust in his sickle into the earth, and gathered the vine of the earth, and cast it into the great winepress of the wrath of God. [20] And the winepress was trodden without the city, and blood came out of the winepress, even unto the horse bridles, by the space of a thousand and six hundred furlongs.

# The Final Warning

Have you ever been roused from a sound sleep by the blast of a siren warning of a coming storm, and the urgency of quick and immediate action suddenly seizes your heart? Perhaps John might have felt a similar conviction as he beheld the impending mark of the beast. God's people must be awakened to warn the world of this great deception and prepare the way for the second coming of Christ! Mercifully, the Lord did not leave John in this state of anxiety, just as He does not leave us today without hope.

Instead, John's attention was directed to the Lamb (Christ [Jn. 1:29]), standing on Mount Zion (Rev. 14:1; Rev. 5:6). In review, a "mountain" in Bible prophecy represents a kingdom or nation, either righteous or wicked (Zech. 8:3; Eze. 36:4; Dan. 9:16; Jer. 51:24-25). The Bible teaches that Zion is the place where God and His kingdom dwell (Ps. 9:11; 125:1-2). It is referred to as the "city of the great King" and the "joy of the *whole earth*" (Ps. 48:2, KJV; italics added). Additionally, God's Word says, "the Lord has founded Zion, *and the poor of His people shall take refuge in it*" (Is. 14:32, NKJV; italics added). However, Zion is also compared to a "wilderness" and means *"parched place"* in Hebrew ("Tsiyown"), a fitting description of a spiritually struggling Christian nation at the end of time (Is. 64:10, KJV). Whom might Zion represent today? Likely it is a symbol of Protestant America, the primary country offering religious freedom to the world, also referred to in Revelation as the beast with lamb-like horns that speaks as a dragon (Rev. 13:11-17; 5:6; Jn. 1:36; Dan. 7:23).

As John beheld Christ (the Lamb) with His kingdom (spiritual Mt. Zion [Ps. 74:2]), he saw God's faithful religious leaders, referred to as the 144,000, who have "the Father's name written upon their foreheads" (Rev. 14:1). These loyal ones have made a conscious decision to allow Christ to seal His law in their minds so that they can represent His character to the world (Is. 8:16; Heb. 8:10). The 144,000 are also "redeemed from the earth" (Rev. 14:3, KJV) and sing a "new song" of Moses and the Lamb in Revelation 15:3-4 (KJV):

> Great and marvelous are thy works, Lord God Almighty; just and true are thy ways, thou King of saints.
>
> Who shall not fear thee, O Lord, and glorify thy name? for thou alone art holy; for all nations shall come and worship before thee; for thy judgments are made manifest.

Moreover, the 144,000 are described as "firstfruits unto God and to the Lamb," and "redeemed from among men," "not defiled with women" (false churches [Jer. 5:7; 6:2]), and they "follow the Lamb whithersoever he goeth" (Rev. 14:4, KJV). The Lord refers to them as "firstfruits," "aparche," meaning "persons superior in excellence to others of the same class" (Rev. 14:4; compare James 1:18). The Greek root words for "firstfruits" and "redeemed" give further clues that the 144,000 are the godly leaders of the remnant. For example, the Greek root word for "firstfruits" is "archomai," meaning "to be chief, leader, ruler" (Rev. 14:4). Its Hebrew counterpart is "re'shiyth" meaning "chief," taken from "ro'sh" meaning "captain, chief, priest" (Jer. 2:3). Both in the Old and New Testaments, the word for "firstfruits" has the connotation of leadership. Moreover, Revelation 14:4 describes the 144,000 as being "redeemed from among men." The root word for "redeemed" ("*agorazo*") is "*agora*," likely from "*egeiro*" meaning, "*to arouse from the sleep of death*," "*to bring before the public*," to "*collect one's faculties*," to "*stand*." Therefore, by combining these two meanings, the 144,000 appear to consist of God's leaders that are "awakened" from the sleep of spiritual death (similar to the five wise virgins [Matt. 25:7-10]), and bring the prophecies of God's Word "before the public" in the last days of Earth's history (Rev. 12:17; 19:10). These faithful spiritual messengers are contrasted with the false ones because "in their mouth was found no guile: for they are without fault before the throne of God" and stand blameless through the Lord's power (Rev. 14:5, KJV; 2 Peter 3:14; Ps. 34:13-14; Jude 1:24).

These godly church leaders give a specific warning to the world before Christ returns, outlined in the Three Angels' Messages of Revelation 14:6-12. This threefold directive contains the "everlasting gospel," the "gospel of the kingdom," to preach to the world, and "then shall the end come" (Rev. 14:6; Matt. 24:14, KJV). The Greek word for "gospel," "*euangelion*," stems from the Greek word, "*angelos*," which is translated as "*angel*." Along with including life-or-death warnings, the Three Angels' Messages trumpet the gospel's good news that Jesus, our Creator and Redeemer, is coming back to take His people home! Moreover, these proclamations continually build in force and importance as the "spirit of prophecy," which is a distinguishing characteristic of Christ's true followers in the last days (Rev. 12:17; 19:10). These messages likely correspond to the timing and events of the three woes (Rev. 8:13).

The first angel's message focuses on the "everlasting gospel" embedded in God's covenant seal, symbolically written on the foreheads of the remnant (Rev. 14:1, 6; 7:3; 22:4). This seal is a conscious decision to obey the Lord's law, especially the fourth commandment of the seventh-day Sabbath which commemorates Christ as the Creator (Rev. 7:3; Heb. 10:15-16; Is. 8:16). It is found in the first angel's message: "Fear God, and give glory to Him, for the hour of His judgment is come; and worship Him *that made heaven, and earth, and the sea,* and the fountains of waters" (Rev. 14:7, KJV; italics added). This directive is nearly identical to the fourth commandment, "Remember the sabbath day to keep it holy… For in six days the Lord made *heaven and the earth, the sea,* and all that in them is, and rested the seventh day: wherefore, the Lord blessed the sabbath day, and hallowed it" (Ex. 20:8, 11, KJV; italics added). Both of these heavenly mandates are based upon the importance of time required to develop a deep relationship with God. As a result of the Holy Spirit's work, God's people are sealed for "the day of redemption" with His law (Rev. 14:12; Eph. 4:30; Is. 8:16). The Sabbath, this seal of time in God's law, points His followers back to creation and the Creator's recreating power in their lives.

However, just as the first angel's message went forth to restore the vital Sabbath truth that had been largely lost during the Dark Ages of the papacy's rule, Satan counterattacked by introducing Darwin's theory of evolution, written as an essay in 1844.[240] Because this theory eradicates a literal six-day creation, it subsequently eliminates the weekly seventh-day Sabbath as God's creation's memorial. The belief in evolution is in direct opposition to the first angel's message to *"worship him that made heaven and earth…"* (Rev. 14:7; italics added), yet it has continued to gain popularity, even among Bible-believing Christians. In 1968, the U.S. Supreme Court ruled in Epperson v. Arkansas that the refusal of teaching evolution in public schools was unconstitutional.[241] This court ruling resulted in evolution replacing

---

[240] https://pubmed.ncbi.nlm.nih.gov/29623486/

intelligent design as the foundation of science in the American educational system.[242] Similarly, the Bible states that the "people of the prince that shall come shall destroy the city and the sanctuary" (Dan. 9:25, KJV). Could this national downfall be exactly what is happening today, partially as a result of the theory of evolution rescinding Christ's commandment to worship the Creator on His Sabbath?

Amazingly, Daniel 12:7 (KJV) also predicts "the power of the holy people" would be scattered after "a time, times, and a half." Again, if forty-nine-year periods are inserted for a "time," beginning in 1844, one arrives in 2015 (Lev. 25:8; Is. 29:1). This is the very year that the pope, who supports the theory of evolution,[243] came to the United States and urged Congress to join the world in the Paris Agreement.[244] His message to Congress followed his speech to the United Nations Convention on Climate Change in 2014, where he insisted that global warming requires a united worldwide effort and "is a clear, definitive and ineluctable imperative to act... *a grave ethical and moral responsibility*" (italics added).[245]

The pope's emphasis on the "moral" and "ethical" obligation to control climate change is further expounded in his encyclical, *Laudato Si*, which proclaims worship on Sunday as a day centered on the Eucharist that "motivates us to greater concern for nature and the poor":

> Sunday, like the Jewish Sabbath, is meant to be a day which heals our relationships with God, with ourselves, with others and with the world. Sunday is the day of the

---

[241] https://www.oyez.org/cases/1968/7

[242] ibid

[243] http://www.usnews.com/news/articles/2014/10/28/pope-francis-backs-the-big-bang-theory-evolution

[244] https://www.theguardian.com/world/2015/sep/24/pope-francis-congress-speech

[245] https://zenit.org/articles/pope-s-message-to-un-convention-on-climate-change/

Resurrection, *the "first day" of the new creation,* whose first fruits are the Lord's risen humanity, the pledge of the final transfiguration of all created reality. It also proclaims "man's eternal rest in God... And so the day of rest, centered on the Eucharist, sheds it light on the whole week, and motivates us to *greater concern for nature* and the poor. (italics added)[246]

Interestingly, the pope's directive of worshipping on Sunday, commemorating the *"first* day of the new *creation,"* completely counters his endorsement of the theory of *evolution*[247] and is in direct opposition to God's fourth commandment to rest on the *seventh* day in honor of the Creator (Ex. 20:8-11). Yet, Pope Francis's urging of united, climate-based, global government mandates continues to gain political and religious popularity within the United States,[248] a probable result of the indoctrination of the theory of evolution. In direct contrast to the pope's counsel, the first angel's message calls Protestant America to worship their *Creator,* echoing God's fourth commandment to remember His *seventh-day* Sabbath (Rev. 14:7; Ex. 20:8-11).

Because of this flagrant disobedience to the Lord's law, the second angel's message proclaims, "Babylon is fallen, is fallen" (Rev. 14:8, KJV). Spiritual Babylon (God's church in apostasy [Jer. 51:35, 49; Eze. 23:4, 17-19; Rev. 17:4-5; 18:2-7]) has repeatedly fallen throughout history (Rev. 14:8). For example, Christ's church fell prey to the papacy's corruption during the Dark Ages. Then many of God's people fell again in 2017 when many American Protestant churches united back with the papacy and its false

---

[246] *Laudato Si',* 237

[247] http://www.usnews.com/news/articles/2014/10/28/pope-francis-backs-the-big-bang-theory-evolution

[248] https://www.ncronline.org/news/earthbeat/us-catholics-join-pope-press-more-ambitious-climate-action-cop23

doctrines. The timing related to this second fall can likely be seen in Daniel 9's proposed repeated sixty-nine-week prophecy (483 years), starting in 1534 and ending in 2017, the exact year that most of the mainline Protestant churches covenanted with the papacy on the pivotal doctrine of justification. Revelation 18:2-3 (KJV) further adds:

> Babylon the great *is fallen, is fallen,* and is become the habitation of devils… for all nations have drunk of the *wine* of the wrath of her *fornication, and the kings of the earth* have committed fornication with her…. (italics added).

In biblical symbolism, wine can represent false teachings (Deut. 32:32-33; Jer. 51:7), and fornication is a symbol of spiritual idolatry (Eze. 23). Therefore, just as the prophecy predicts, American Protestant leaders, as well as U.S. governmental representatives (the "kings of the earth" [Rev. 18:2-3; 13:11-12]) are uniting under the pope's corrupt religious and political leadership by seeking his counsel instead of following the unadulterated truths of God's Word.

As a result of the previous two messages, the third angel's message declares the impact of this unholy alliance:

> … If any man worship the beast and his image, and receive his mark in his forehead, or in his hand, The same shall drink of the wine of the wrath of God, which is poured out without mixture into the cup of his indignation…. (Rev. 14:9-10, KJV)

Interestingly, the beast's mark of authority is located in the forehead *or the hand,* unlike God's seal which is located *only* in the *forehead* (Rev. 7:3). This distinction is likely emphasized because the mark of the beast can occur from a deliberate decision made in the forehead or as the result of compliance of action, represented by the mark in the hand (Eccl. 9:10). God's seal, in contrast, is located only in the forehead, symbolizing a firm decision. This final warning given to the world, specifically at the close of the investigative judgment, is God's last appeal for His people to come out of Babylon's religious confusion and refuse the beast's mark.

What is the mark of the beast's authority? (Rev. 13:15-18). As previously discussed, the sea beast and its image represent the papacy and the apostate Protestant churches in the U.S. respectively. What specific doctrine do both the papacy and the mainline Protestant churches hold in common that marks the authority of the Roman Catholic Church? Catholic leaders, themselves, answer this question: "Sunday is our MARK of authority... the church is above the Bible, and this transference of Sabbath observance is proof of that fact,"[249] and "of course the Catholic Church claims that the change was her act... and the act is A MARK of her ecclesiastical power" (capitalization added).[250]

Catholics further boast that by keeping Sunday, mainline Protestant churches are a mere image of their mother church:

> But since Saturday, not Sunday, is specified in the Bible, isn't it curious that non-Catholics, who claim to take their religion directly from the Bible and not from the Church, observe Sunday instead of Saturday? Yes, of course, it is inconsistent; but this change was made about fifteen centuries before Protestantism was born, and by that time the

---

[249] https://www.sabbathtruth.com/sabbath-history/denominational-statements-on-the-sabbath/id/catholic; *Catholic Record of London*, Ontario Sept 1, 1923: http://www.canadiana.ca/view/oocihm.8_06663_2342/1?r=0&s=1

[250] Letter written by Chancellor H. F. Thomas, from the office of Cardinal Gibbons, November 11, 1895; https://www.seventh-day.org/historians.htm

custom was universally observed. They have continued the custom even though it rests upon the authority of the Catholic Church and not upon an explicit text in the Bible. That observance remains as a reminder of the Mother Church from which the non-Catholic sects broke away—like a boy running away from home but still carrying in his pocket a picture of his mother or a lock of her hair.[251]

This sinister deception is identified in Daniel 7:25 (NKJV): "He shall speak pompous words against the Most High... and shall *intend to change times and law*" (italics added). Only the papacy has claimed to change God's Law, specifically the fourth commandment that focuses on *time*—*the only one that God specifically said to remember!* As a result, Christ warns:

> ... The same shall also drink of the wine of wrath of God, which is poured out without mixture into the cup of his indignation; and he shall be tormented with fire and brimstone in the presence of the holy angels, and... the Lamb. And the smoke of their torment ascendeth up for ever and ever: and *they have no rest day nor night*, who worship the beast and his image, and whosoever receiveth the mark of his name. (Rev. 14:10, KJV; (italics added)

No *Sabbath rest*, day or night, is given to those who receive this papal mark of the beast!

How, then, did the tradition of worshipping on Sunday come into the church originally? History reveals that the Roman emperor, Constantine, issued an edict in 321 AD that declared that the "day of the sun" (Sunday) was the "universal day of rest."[252]

---

[251] John A. O'Brien, *The Faith of Millions: the Credentials of the Catholic Religion Revised Edition* (Our Sunday Visitor Publishing, 1974): 400-401.
[252] https://www.historychannel.com.au/this-day-in-history/constantine-decrees-sunday-as-day-of-rest/

This decree was designed to combine the worship of Christians and pagans into one day—Sunday—which was named after the pagan sun god, Invictus, who was already worshipped in ancient Rome. Slowly, the majority of Christians succumbed to peer pressure, and the Christian worship day was changed from the seventh-day Sabbath to Sunday, the first day of the week. This purely political change, not found anywhere in Scripture, was embraced by the papacy and continued throughout the Dark Ages and even during the Protestant Reformation without much serious consideration of its pagan origins. According to the *Catholic Mirror*, "The Catholic Church, for over one thousand years before the existence of a Protestant, by virtue of her divine mission, changed the day from Saturday to Sunday...."[253] Additionally, Catholics believe that Protestant Sunday observance is bowing to their authority: "If Protestants would follow the Bible, they should worship God on the Sabbath day. In keeping Sunday, they are following a law of the Catholic Church."[254]

However, in the late 1800s, the Sabbath truth was rediscovered and loudly proclaimed by the Seventh-day Adventist Church (although there has always been a small Sabbath-keeping remnant throughout history). Today, God continues calling His children to honor His seventh-day Sabbath according to the fourth commandment and separate themselves from worshipping on Sunday, the day commemorating the sun (Ex. 20:8-11; Eze. 8:15-16). Fortunately, there is still time to refuse this papal mark of the beast and be saved!

---

[253] *Catholic Mirror*, Sept. 23, 1893; reprinted in *Rome's Challenge*, p. 244; https://www.libertymagazine.org/article/who-really-changed-the-sabbath
[254] Albert Smith, Chancellor of the Archdiocese of Baltimore, replying for the Cardinal, in a letter dated February 10, 1920; https://www.sabbathtruth.com/sabbath-history/denominational-statements-on-the-sabbath/id/catholic

Along with changing God's holy Sabbath day to Sunday, the Catholic Church repeatedly boasts in her supposed right to also adopt many other pagan rituals by disguising them as sacred church ceremonies:

> The use of temples, and these dedicated to particular saints, and ornamented on occasions with branches of trees; incense, lamps, and candles; votive offerings on recovery from illness; holy water; asylums; holy days and seasons... are all of pagan origin and sanctified by their adoption into the Church.[255]

By endorsing these pagan traditions, in addition to Sunday observance, God's church has been corrupted by many "abominations" (Eze. 16:15-59).

Today, the third angel's message warns of final judgment upon those who trample the unadulterated teachings of God's Word and receive the papacy's unbiblical "mark" of authority. However, the Lord promises blessings on all who keep God's seventh-day Sabbath holy:

> If thou turn away thy foot from the sabbath, from doing thy pleasure on my holy day; and call the sabbath a delight, the holy of the Lord, honourable; and shalt honour him, not doing thine own ways, nor finding thine own pleasure, nor speaking thine own words: Then shall thou delight thyself in the Lord; and I will cause thee to ride upon the high places of the earth and feed thee with the heritage of Jacob thy father for the mouth of the Lord hath spoken it. (Is. 58:13-14, KJV)

---

[255] Cardinal John Newman, *An Essay on the Development of Christian Doctrine* (London: Basil Montague Pickering, 1878): 373: https://wacaworldwide.org/multimedia-archive/the-sabbath-catholic-and-protestant-stunning-admissions/

Will Christ's followers choose to be sealed by observing God's seventh-day Sabbath and obeying His law? (Is. 8:16). Or will they choose the papacy's mark of authority, worshipping on Sunday and honoring pagan, papal rituals? Fortunately, no one has received the mark of the beast because mandatory Sunday-keeping has not yet been enforced by civil law (Rev. 13:15-17). Before the seven last plagues are poured out, all will have the opportunity to decide whether to obey God or man (Acts 5:29). The faithful ones that are saved at the end will observe the Lord's seventh-day Sabbath (Ex. 20:8-11) and become part of Christ's remnant identified in Revelation 14:12 (KJV) who "keep the commandments of God" by having "the faith of Jesus," which is the "everlasting gospel" (Rev. 14:6), encapsulated in the Three Angels' Messages.

These messages, then, are Heaven's final call to bring repentance and reformation to God's people! They go forth as three separate warnings, integrated into one complete whole:

> **Fear God and give glory to him;** *(love God and glorify Him through words and actions)* **for the hour of his judgment is come:** *(the current investigative judgment where God is judging His people and the world is judging God by His people's lives [Rom. 3:4; Rev. 18:10])* **and worship him that made the heaven, and the earth, and the sea, and the fountains of water** *(worship God as the Creator on His holy Sabbath day, which is the memorial of His creation [Ex. 20:8-11], and don't be deceived by the theory of evolution)...* **Babylon is fallen, is fallen,** *(God's church has fallen into religious confusion: specifically through the papacy's rule during the Dark Ages and then by many mainline Protestant churches uniting back with the papacy's false doctrines)* **that great city** *(America: God's*

*blessed nation of religious freedom for the world)*, **because she made all nations drink of the wine of the wrath of her fornication** *(America's Protestant leaders are teaching the wine of the pope's unbiblical doctrines and leading the whole world into false worship)*... **If any man worship the beast** *(the papacy)* **and his image** *(apostate Protestant America)*, **and receive his mark in his forehead, or in his hand** *(consciously making a decision or simply complying with the pope's false teachings, enshrined in Sunday-keeping, which is the mark of papal authority)*, **the same shall drink of the wine of the wrath of God, which is poured out without mixture into the cup of his indignation** *(the wicked will suffer the seven last plagues that will be poured out without mercy [Hab. 2:15-16], but God's faithful people will not be harmed because Christ drank this cup of wrath so that His followers would not have to [Matt. 26:42])*; **and he shall be tormented with fire and brimstone in the presence of the holy angels, and in the presence of the Lamb: And the smoke of their torment ascendeth up for ever and ever** *(Fire and brimstone will rain down from Heaven bringing the wicked's complete destruction, just as it did with Sodom and Gomorrah [Luke 17:29; 2 Peter 2:6; 3:10; Jude 7; Mal. 4:1, 3])*: **and they have no rest day nor night, who worship the beast and his image, and whosoever receiveth the mark of his name** *(All false Christians will not have peace or rest of God's holy Sabbath because they worship on Sunday, the mark of papal authority, the day commemorating the sun [Ex. 20:8-11; Heb. 4:1-5; Matt. 11:28-30])*. **Here is the patience of the saints: here are they that keep the commandments of God, and the faith of Jesus** *(Patiently God's people, out of their love for Jesus, will keep the commandments of the Lord's holy law, written upon their* *hearts, according to Christ's New Testament covenant [Heb. 8:10])...* **Blessed are the dead which die in the Lord from henceforth: Yea, saith the Spirit, that they may rest from their labours; and their works do follow them** *(Happy are faithful Sabbath-keeping Christians who die during the investigative judgment before the Time of Trouble but have the privilege of being resurrected to see Jesus come [Dan. 12:1-2]) (Rev. 14:7-13, KJV; parentheses added)*

Heeding these three messages is vital for salvation, especially for those living in the last days!

Then John beheld the Son of Man in Heaven at the close of the investigative judgment. The sealing of God's people was finished (Is. 8:16; Eze. 9:4-6), and the Latter Rain had done its work upon the earth (Rev. 14:15; Jer. 5:24). After all have had an opportunity to choose whom they will worship, the righteous will be vindicated during the punishment of the wicked in the seven last plagues (Rev. 14:16-20). However, true Christians are assured, "For God hath not appointed us to wrath, but to obtain salvation by our Lord Jesus Christ" (I Thess. 5:9, KJV). Nevertheless, John saw the three angels thrust their sickles into the earth (a symbol of judgment [Matt. 13:30; Mark 4:29; Jer. 51:33]). The Bible declares:

> ... he shall give a shout, as they that tread the grapes, against all the inhabitants of the earth... for the Lord hath a controversy with the nations, he will plead with all flesh; he will give them that are wicked to the sword, saith the Lord (Jer. 25:30-31, KJV)

Blood came out of the winepress "to the horses' bridles, for one thousand six hundred furlongs" (Rev. 14:20, NKJV). This reference to horses likely ties back to the first four seals, specifically to the last pale horse seal, representing the papacy's political rule. Interestingly, in the Greek language, the word for "furlongs," "*stadion*," in Revelation 14:20, refers to the *"distance of a race course."* The apostle Paul also compares his life to running a course: "I have fought a good fight, I have finished my course… " (2 Tim. 4:7, KJV). In this text, a "course" refers to the days of Paul's life. Therefore, if 1,600 furlongs are converted into days and then multiplied by forty-nine, the total is 78,400 days (Deut. 16:9; compare Lev. 25:8). If this product is divided by 365 days in a year, it equals approximately 215 years. If 215 years are added to 1798 (the date that the pope was taken captive, inflicting the deadly wound to papal power [Rev. 13:3]), the total ends in 2013, the year that Pope Benedict XVI suddenly resigned, and Jorge Bergoglio became Pope Francis. Furthermore, this is the exact same year that the proposed repeated 1,260-day prophecy ends! (Rev. 11:3). Unsurprisingly, this pope, elected in this very year, would lead in unprecedented ecumenical unity, purportedly ending the Protestant Reformation, and winning papal political prominence throughout the entire world.

Lovingly, Jesus has given His people the Three Angels' Messages that expose the papacy's deceptions (Rev. 14:7-12). He does not want any to perish, but all to come to repentance and be saved! (2 Peter 3:9; John 10:28; I Thess. 5:9). The life-or-death question is—will we heed the Lord's merciful warnings before it is forever too late?

**Rev. 11's 1260-day Repeated Prophecy**
**Rev. 13's 666** (Rev. 13:18)
**Rev. 14's 1,600 Furlongs** (Rev. 14:20)

| Pope Taken Captive/ End of Historical 1,260-Day Prophecy/ Fall of Papacy/ Beginning of Seals Repeated as Thunders (p. 141, chart) | Beginning of Investigative Judgment: End of 2300-day Historical Prophecy | | Pope Francis Elected 1st Jesuit American Pope/Encourages Unity-"From Conflict to Communion" Published (pp. 147-148) | Pope's Plea for Ecumenicalism/ Evangelicals & Catholics Unite & Speak in Tongues/ (Rev. 13:13-18; pp. 171-173) |
|---|---|---|---|---|
| 1798 AD | 1844 | Repetition of 1260-day Prophecy (1260 X 49= 61,740 days= 169 yrs. [Rev. 11:3]) | 2013 | 2014 |

1,600 X 49 (Lev. 25:8) = 78,400 days or approx. 215 years (Rev. 14:20) "Furlongs"= Distance of a Race, Repetition of the Four Horseman Seals as Thunders (Rev. 6:1-8; 10:4)

6 X 6 X 6 = 216 Years (Rev. 13:18)
Number of Beast & Man (Sea Beast/Papacy [Rev. 13:1-7, 18; 2 Thess. 2:3-4])

# Discussion Questions for Revelation 14

1. Who did John see on Mount Zion, and how is Mount Zion described? (Rev. 14:1; Jn. 1:29; Ps. 48:2; 125:1; Is. 14:32)

2. Who might be the 144,000? How are they described? (Rev. 14:1, 3-5; 12:17; James 1:18; Jer. 2:3; Heb. 8:10; 2 Pet. 3:14; Ps. 34:13-14; Jude 1:24)

3. Upon what does the first angel's message focus? (Rev. 14:7; Ex. 20:11; Is. 8:16; Rev. 7:3; Heb. 10:16)

4. How does the theory of evolution specifically counter the first angel's message concerning the worship of the Creator on the Sabbath? (Rev. 14:7; Ex. 20:8, 11)

5. What is the message of the second angel, and how has Babylon repeatedly fallen in recent history? (Rev. 14:8; 17:4-6; 18:2-3; Jer. 51:7-8, 49)

6. Summarize the third angel's message in your own words. How does "their smoke of their torment ascends forever and ever" compare to Sodom and Gomorrah's complete destruction? (Rev. 14:9-11; Luke 17:29; Jude 7; 2 Peter 2:6; 3:10; Mal. 4:1, 3)

7. What is the "mark" of the beast, and how is it contrasted with the "seal" of God? (Rev. 14:9; 13:15-18; Dan. 7:25; Is. 8:16)

8. What do the Three Angels' Messages call God's people to do in the last days? (Rev. 14:12; Is. 58:13-14)

9. What is the result of the "harvest," the close of Christ's investigative judgment? What hope is offered? (Rev. 14:14-20; Jer. 25:30-31; 5:24; I Thess. 5:9; John 10:28)

| PROTESTANT REFORMATION | 2ND GREAT AWAKENING- U.S. | INVESTIGATIVE JUDGMENT | JUST BEFORE 2ND COMING |
|---|---|---|---|
| **Church of Sardis** (Rev. 3:3) (1534-1750s) | **Philadelphia**- (Rev. 3:10) (1755-1844) | **Laodicea** (Rev. 3:21) (After 1844 to Christ's Coming) | |
| **5TH Seal**- Martyr's Cry for Justice/Retribution for Deaths (Rev. 6:9-10) | **6th Seal**- Earthquake (1755) Sun, Moon Dark (1780); Stars Fall (1833) (Rev. 6:12-17) | **7th Seal**- Silence- Great Disappointment/Sealing (judgment) Begins (Rev. 8:1; 7; Is. 41:1; Zech. 2:13; Hab. 2:20) | |
| **1st Trumpet**- Protestant Reformation (Rev. 8:7) | **2nd Trumpet**- Papal "Mount" Falls- 1798 (Rev. 8:8-9) **3rd Trumpet**- Bitter Water -U.S. Age of Reason (Rev. 8:10-11) **4th Trumpet**- Sun, Moon, Stars Dark/Great Disappointment-1844 (Rev. 8:12; 10:9-10) | **5th Trumpet**- "Locusts"- False Teachers/Spiritualism in U.S. (Rev. 9:10-11); **6th Trumpet**- "Army"- World War/League of Nations/ Spiritual Deaths of 1/3 (Rev. 9:13-19) | **7th Trumpet**- Kingdom of God- Given in 1844 to Christ (Start of Investigative Judgment); Manifested on Earth at the Close of the Judgment & His 2nd Coming (Rev. 11:15-19; Dan. 7:14) |
| | (Seals Repeat as Thunders) **1st Thunder**- God's Remnant Movement (1798- End) (Rev. 10:4; 6:2) | **2nd Thunder**- Spiritualism/ Occult; Evolution; Tongues (Rev.10:4; 6:4) **3rd Thunder**- Secular Darkness; Humanistic Government (Rev. 10:4; 6:5-6); **4th Thunder**- Papal/Protestant Ecumenicalism (Rev. 10:4; 6:8) | **5th Thunder**- Martyrs' Cry for Retribution (Rev. 10:4; 6:9-11) **6th Thunder**- Earthquake, Sun, Moon Darkened, Stars Fall/ **7th Thunder**- Sealing- Close of Probation (Rev. 6:12-17; 7); Silence Before Execution of Judgment (Rev. 10:4; 8:1; ) |
| | **1st Sign**- Woman- Protestant Church (Rev. 12:1); **1st & 2nd Angels' Messages**- Worship Creator; Flee sin (Rev. 14:7-8); **3 Woes Announced** (Rev. 8:13) | **2nd Sign**- Dragon- Satan (Rev. 12:12:3-17); Sea Beast- Papacy Revives (Rev. 13:1-10); **1st & 2nd Angels' Messages** Rep. (3rd); **1st & 2nd Woe** (Rev. 9:12; 11:14) | **3rd Sign**- Prelude to 7 Plagues (Rev. 15:1); **Emphasis of 3rd Angel's Message**- Papal Mark of Beast (Rev. 14:9-11) **3rd Woe** (7 Plagues- Rev. 16) |

# Revelation 15 (KJV)

*[1] And I saw another sign in heaven, great and marvellous, seven angels having the seven last plagues; for in them is filled up the wrath of God. [2] And I saw as it were a sea of glass mingled with fire: and them that had gotten the victory over the beast, and over his image, and over his mark, and over the number of his name, stand on the sea of glass, having the harps of God. [3] And they sing the song of Moses the servant of God, and the song of the Lamb, saying, Great and marvellous are thy works, Lord God Almighty; just and true are thy ways, thou King of saints. [4] Who shall not fear thee, O Lord, and glorify thy name? for thou only art holy: for all nations shall come and worship before thee; for thy judgments are made manifest. [5] And after that I looked, and, behold, the temple of the tabernacle of the testimony in heaven was opened: [6] And the seven angels came out of the temple, having the seven plagues, clothed in pure and white linen, and having their breasts girded with golden girdles. [7] And one of the four beasts gave unto the seven angels seven golden vials full of the wrath of God, who liveth for ever and ever. [8] And the temple was filled with smoke from the glory of God, and from his power; and no man was able to enter into the temple, till the seven plagues of the seven angels were fulfilled.*

# The Close of the World's Probation

Some years ago, there was a game show on television that quizzed the contestants with trivia questions. If they did not know the answer, they could use a "lifeline" or call a friend. But after that, their final decision had to be made, and it could not be changed. John had just seen the investigative judgment in Heaven nearing completion. Then his attention focused on the irreversible decision of Earth's inhabitants—whether they had chosen to obey God's law, which is His covenant, or worship the sea beast (the papacy [Rev. 13:1-7; 2 Thess. 2:3-4]) and its image (apostate Protestantism unified with the papacy [Rev. 13:11-17]). Patiently, the Lord had waited for all to make their final decision, but at last, Earth's probation was about to close, which would result in the outpouring of the seven last plagues.

However, not all had chosen to be lost. John then saw something like "a sea of glass mingled with fire," possibly symbolizing those who have gotten "the victory over the beast, and over his image, and over his mark, and over the number of his name" (Rev. 15:2, KJV; 17:15). They stood before God, praising Him for His miraculous deliverance in their lives, just like Moses and the Hebrews had done during the exodus from Egypt (Ex. 15). They sang the song of the Lamb, glorifying Jesus for His great sacrifice for their salvation. Joyfully, they acknowledged their Redeemer's works as "great and marvelous" and His ways as "just and true"

(Rev. 15:3). Vindicating God's character by their loving obedience to His law, they declared, "For thou only art holy: for all nations shall come and worship before thee; for thy judgments are made manifested" (Rev. 15:4, KJV). What a beautiful picture of God's remnant!

Simultaneously, John beheld the door of the Most Holy Place in the heavenly sanctuary open a second time, which released the seven angels with the seven last plagues (Rev. 15:5-6). Sadly, step by step, the apostate Protestant church had broken its covenant with the Lord and His holy Sabbath and participated in idolatry. God had pled with His people to return to their former devoted relationship with Him and obey His commandments. This "testimony" of God's law would have resulted in a multitude of blessings! (Lev. 26:1-13; Rev. 15:5; Ex. 25:21-22; 26:33-34; 31:18). Likewise, the Lord had repeatedly warned them of the curses that would follow if they persisted in separating themselves from Him (Lev. 26:14-39). The prophet, Daniel, refers to these judgments in his prayer: "… the curse is poured upon us, and the oath that is written in the law of Moses, the servant of God, because we have sinned against him" (Dan. 9:11, KJV). However, Christ's warnings had been stubbornly ignored, and now, the consequence of forsaking the Lord was about to be realized (Is. 22:12-14).

Interestingly, one of the first biblical results of rebellion is a "wasting disease" (Lev. 26:16, NKJV). The Hebrew meaning of these words includes: *"consumption, a disease of the lungs, inflammation, and a burning fever."* Amazingly, these symptoms are very similar to the Covid 19 virus that has caused so much worldwide havoc, rising to prominence in the U.S. in 2020, the very year that Daniel 9's proposed repeated "middle-of-the-week" prophecy predicts (Dan. 9:27). Could this virus be a warning that judgments against America are beginning, which will eventually usher in the seven last plagues? (Deut. 28:58-62; Micah 6:13).

Furthermore, the angels that John saw, clothed as priests in white linen (righteousness [Rev. 19:8, KJV]), were holding seven bowls filled with God's wrath, designed to deliver His people (Rev. 15:6-7; Rev. 16). Up to this time, God's judgments had been mixed with mercy to bring repentance (Is. 26:9), but after Jesus departs from the sanctuary, no more atoning blood washes away sin, so the lost must suffer the full impact of their separation from God (Rev. 14:14-16). The wicked are left to bear the consequences of their final decision. The passage of global laws decreeing the death penalty for all who do not worship according to the dictates of the papal/Protestant leaders corresponds with the close of probation (Rev. 13:15-16; 14:19; 16:5-6; 22:11-12). As a result, no one was allowed to enter the temple until the seven last plagues were completed (Rev. 15:8).

However, the outpouring of the seven last plagues will finally bring deliverance and hope for God's remnant people because they know that this is the last sign of Jesus's return. Although the lost will suffer tremendously from the plagues, the Lord's true followers have been sealed by the Holy Spirit for their day of redemption (Eph. 4:30). These faithful ones will pass through the seven last plagues safely under Christ's protection because God promises:

> Thou shalt not be afraid for the terror by night, nor for the arrow that flieth by day; Nor for the pestilence that walketh in darkness; nor for the destruction that wasteth at noonday. A thousand shall fall at thy side, and ten thousand at thy right hand; but it shall not come nigh thee.

Only with thine eyes shalt thou behold and see the reward of the wicked. Because thou hast made the Lord, which is my refuge, even the most High, thy habitation; There shall *no evil shall befall thee, neither shall any plague come nigh thy dwelling.* For he shall give his angels charge over thee, to keep thee in all thy ways. (Psalm 91:5-11, KJV; italics added)

Praise the Lord! The great controversy between Christ and His followers versus Satan and his captives is drawing to an end! Only Satan's adherents must reap the consequences of their final decision and suffer the results of the seven last plagues. Those who have chosen to worship God sing songs of His mighty deliverance: "In thy name shall they rejoice all the day: and in thy righteousness shall they be exalted" (Ps. 89:16, KJV).

# Discussion Questions for Revelation 15

1. *How are God's people described who have obtained victory over the beast? What could the "sea of glass" possibly symbolize? (Rev. 15:2; 17:15)*

2. *What songs of deliverance do the 144,000 sing, and for what specific characteristics do they praise God? (Rev. 15:3-4; 14:3)*

3. *What does the door to the Most Holy Place, which is opened a second time, signal, and what is the result for Earth's inhabitants? (Rev. 15:5-8; 16:1; compared to Rev. 22:11-12)*

4. *What have the ungodly done throughout the investigative judgment and the final days of its closing? (Lev. 26:14-15; Is. 22:12-14; 24:4-5)*

5. *How is the Covid 19 virus similar to the "wasting disease" described in Leviticus 26:16, and what might be the implications of this similarity? (Deut. 28:58-62; Micah 6:12-13)*

6. *What brings about the close of probation? (Rev. 13:15-16; 14:15-19; 22:11)*

7. *What do the seven bowls (plagues) of God contain, and why are they poured out? Upon whom do they NOT fall? (Rev. 15:1-2, 4; 16:1, 5-7; 11:18; Dan. 12:1)*

8. *Why don't Christ's true followers need to fear this time of trouble and the outpouring of the seven last plagues? (Ps. 91:5-11; Eph. 4:30)*

9. *Why do God's people praise Him specifically during this time? (Ps. 89:14-18)*

# Revelation 16 (KJV)

[1] *And I heard a great voice out of the temple saying to the seven angels, Go your ways, and pour out the vials of the wrath of God upon the earth. [2] And the first went, and poured out his vial upon the earth; and there fell a noisome and grievous sore upon the men which had the mark of the beast, and upon them which worshipped his image. [3] And the second angel poured out his vial upon the sea; and it became as the blood of a dead man: and every living soul died in the sea. [4] And the third angel poured out his vial upon the rivers and fountains of waters; and they became blood. [5] And I heard the angel of the waters say, Thou art righteous, O Lord, which art, and wast, and shalt be, because thou hast judged thus. [6] For they have shed the blood of saints and prophets, and thou hast given them blood to drink; for they are worthy. [7] And I heard another out of the altar say, Even so, Lord God Almighty, true and righteous are thy judgments. [8] And the fourth angel poured out his vial upon the sun; and power was given unto him to scorch men with fire. [9] And men were scorched with great heat, and blasphemed the name of God, which hath power over these plagues: and they repented not to give him glory. [10] And the fifth angel poured out his vial upon the seat of the beast; and his kingdom was full of darkness; and they gnawed their tongues for pain, [11] And blasphemed the God of heaven because of their pains and their sores, and repented not of their deeds. [12] And the sixth angel poured out his vial upon the great river Euphrates; and the water thereof was dried up, that the way of the kings of the east might be*

*prepared.* [13] *And I saw three unclean spirits like frogs come out of the mouth of the dragon, and out of the mouth of the beast, and out of the mouth of the false prophet.* [14] *For they are the spirits of devils, working miracles, which go forth unto the kings of the earth and of the whole world, to gather them to the battle of that great day of God Almighty.* [15] *Behold, I come as a thief. Blessed is he that watcheth, and keepeth his garments, lest he walk naked, and they see his shame.* [16] *And he gathered them together into a place called in the Hebrew tongue Armageddon.* [17] *And the seventh angel poured out his vial into the air; and there came a great voice out of the temple of heaven, from the throne, saying, It is done.* [18] *And there were voices, and thunders, and lightnings; and there was a great earthquake, such as was not since men were upon the earth, so mighty an earthquake, and so great.* [19] *And the great city was divided into three parts, and the cities of the nations fell: and great Babylon came in remembrance before God, to give unto her the cup of the wine of the fierceness of his wrath.* [20] *And every island fled away, and the mountains were not found.* [21] *And there fell upon men a great hail out of heaven, every stone about the weight of a talent: and men blasphemed God because of the plague of the hail; for the plague thereof was exceeding great.*

# God's People Vindicated

When the innocent are released and the guilty punished, all should agree that justice has been served. Perhaps John might have come to this conclusion as he watched the consequences of the wicked's decision to separate themselves from God's protective power that shields the righteous (Lev. 26:21; Deut. 28:59-62). This tragic choice leaves all who have received the papacy's mark of authority in full control of Satan and his demonic forces and propels the outpouring of the seven last plagues. Like the calamities that fell upon ancient Egypt (Ex. 7-12; 14:13-14), these "vials of wrath" are the very means of bringing God's people freedom from the persecution of their captors, destroying many wicked (Rev. 16:1; Zech. 14:12-13). Moreover, the plagues enrage the ungodly, and they blame the righteous for their tragic plight. Helplessly, the lost search from one end of the earth to the other trying to find physical and spiritual relief, but it is too late! Amos 8:12 (KJV) states, "And they shall wander from sea to sea, and from the north even to the east, they shall run to and fro to seek the word of the Lord, and shall not find it." In condemning God's people to death through a global decree, the wicked have sealed their destiny (Rev. 13:15). Their final decision and its consequences are irreversible! During the seven last plagues that fall upon the ungodly, Christ's followers are miraculously preserved and unharmed because they have been sealed by their conscious decision to obey God's commandments instead of following man's mandates (Ps. 91:10; Eph. 1:12-13). As the plagues begin to fall all around them, the righteous claim Ps. 9:9 (KJV): "The Lord also will be a refuge for the oppressed, a refuge in times of trouble."

The wicked, in contrast, suffer greatly as the seven last plagues strike the earth. The first plague is a physical manifestation of the result of receiving the mark of the beast: a "foul and loathsome sore" comes upon those that have "the mark of the beast" and who have "worshipped his image" (Rev. 16:2, NKJV). The Greek word, *"kakos,"* translated as *"foul"* is similar in meaning to the Hebrew word, *"ra,"* which is used to describe the boils that fell upon Job when Satan was granted permission to smite him (Job 2:7). Interestingly, the word, *"malignant,"* is used to define the latter. God's people were warned in Deuteronomy 28:27 that these boils and tumors would be a sure result if they did not "observe to do all his commandments…" (Deut. 28:15, KJV). This first plague of sores is also similar to the sixth plague that fell on Egypt (Ex. 9:9). Because the wicked are no longer under God's protection, demonic forces are granted permission to "mark" their prey—those who have chosen to worship the beast and its image.

The next two plagues fall upon the sea, rivers, and springs of water, bringing vindication to God's people. The second plague is nearly identical to the first one in Egypt—the ocean becomes blood and the living creatures in it die (Rev. 16:3; Ex. 7:17-21). Although this plague will likely affect the physical waters of the earth and be attributed to "climate change," it may also indicate massive deaths among the wicked because water can represent "peoples, and multitudes, and nations, and tongues" (Rev. 17:15, KJV). Likewise, in the third plague, rivers and springs of water turn to blood, yet the Lord's righteousness and justice are praised. The wicked have "shed the blood of saints and prophets," and God has "given them blood to drink" (Rev. 16:5-7, KJV). These judgments against the lost are similar to the second and third warning trumpets and vindicate those who have given up their lives as martyrs, the answer to the saints' prayers in the fifth seal (Rev. 6:9-10; 8:8-11). Revelation 11:18 (KJV) further expounds:

> And the nations were angry, and thy wrath is come, and the time of the dead, that they should be judged, and that thou shouldest give reward unto thy servants the prophets, and to the saints, and them that fear thy name, small and great, and shouldest destroy them which destroy the earth.

The fourth plague contrasts the sounding of the fourth trumpet by increasing the sun's brightness instead of darkening it (Rev. 16:8-9; compare Rev. 8:12). Moreover, God's people are assured:

> "… the light of the moon shall be as the light of the sun, and the light of the sun shall be sevenfold, as the light of seven days, in the day that the Lord bindeth up the breach of his people, and healeth the stroke of their wound" (Is. 30:26, KJV).

Also, Christ promises, "The sun shall not smite thee," "nor any heat" (Ps. 121:6; Rev. 7:16, KJV). However, since the wicked have rejected Jesus, the Light of the World (Jn. 8:12) and the "Sun of righteousness" (Mal. 4:2), permission is given to "scorch men with fire" (Rev. 16:8). Concerning this awful time, God says:

> The earth mourneth and fadeth away, the world languisheth and fadeth away, the haughty people of the earth do

languish. The earth also is defiled under the inhabitants thereof; because they have transgressed the laws, changed the ordinance, broken the everlasting covenant. Therefore hath the curse devoured the earth, and they that dwell therein are desolate: therefore the inhabitants of the earth are burned, and few men left. (Is. 24:4-6, KJV)

Despite this "great heat," men "blasphemed the name of God," and "they repented not to give him glory" (Rev. 16:9, KJV). The wicked's rebellion is clearly displayed in this verse, and even if the Lord gave them more time, they would not humble themselves in repentance! They have chosen to worship on the day honoring the sun instead of God's Sabbath, and they suffer physically and spiritually from the sun's intense heat of global warming (Joel 1:15-20).

Symbolic of their rejection of God's Light (John 8:12; Mal. 4:2), darkness follows the scorching of the sun in the fifth plague (Rev. 16:10). This darkness, again, is similar to the ninth plague that fell upon Egypt. The Bible compares this Egyptian plague to "thick darkness" that could even "be felt," yet "the children of Israel had light in their dwellings" (Ex. 10:21-23, KJV). Likewise, the Lord makes a distinction between His people and the lost in the fifth plague because it only falls on the "seat of the beast and his kingdom" (Rev. 16:10, KJV; Micah 7:8-9). This difference symbolizes that the wicked have chosen darkness instead of the light of God's Word (Ps. 119:105; Jn. 3:19-20). However, the righteous are promised light, and God's glory is risen upon them (Is. 60:1-2, KJV; Judges 5:31).

Unlike the Egyptian plagues that ended before the next one began, at least some of the seven last plagues compound. The wicked's reaction to the fifth plague demonstrates this: "… and they gnawed their tongues for the pain, and blasphemed the God of heaven because of their pains *and their sores*, and repented not of their deeds" (Rev. 16:10-11, KJV; italics added). This text indicates that the results of the first plague of sores are still felt in the fifth plague (Rev. 16:2). However, the response of the lost remains the same—total rebellion against God!

In the sixth plague, John records more details than in the previous ones. First, God strikes the great Euphrates River "and the water thereof was dried up, that the way of the kings of the east might be prepared" (Rev. 16:12, KJV). The Lord states through the prophet, Isaiah: "The brooks of defense shall be emptied and dried up…" (Is. 19:6, KJV; compare Jer. 51:36-37). This is exactly what happened during the fall of ancient Babylon. History shows that the Euphrates River ran directly through Babylon, and Cyrus and his soldiers diverted its waters and were able to seize the city by going through the open gates of the dry riverbed (Is. 44:27-28). This turnover of rulership was a result of King Belshazzar's command to profane the Lord's temple vessels and praise the gods of *"gold, and of silver, of brass, of iron, of wood, and of stone"* (Dan. 5:4, KJV; italics added). The sixth trumpet predicts a similar type of rebellion which would cause the downfall of spiritual Babylon:

> And the rest of mankind, which were not killed by these plagues, did not repent of the works of their hands, that they should not worship demons, and idols of *gold, silver, brass, stone, and wood,* which can neither see nor hear nor walk. And they did not repent of their murders or their sorceries or their sexual immorality or their thefts. (Rev. 9:20-21, NKJV; italics added)

Along with a physical manifestation,[256] the drying of the Euphrates may symbolize the Holy Spirit's withdrawal from the

---

[256] https://phys.org/news/2021-08-euphrates-threatens-disaster-syria.html

wicked because of their false doctrines (a "dry wind" [Jer. 4:11-13; Acts 2:2; Ps. 107:33-34]). Through this work, God's judgment of the seven last plagues will finally destroy spiritual Babylon and end its followers' support (Rev. 16:12-14; 18:2, 8; Jer. 46:6-10; 51:36-44), heralding Christ's coming (the "kings of the east" [Rev. 16:12; Matt. 2:2; 24:27; Rev. 7:2-3]).

Then John saw "three unclean spirits like frogs" coming out of the mouth of the dragon, the beast, and the false prophet that are "spirits of devils working miracles, which go forth unto the kings of the earth and the whole world, to gather them to the battle of that great day of God Almighty" (Rev. 16:13-14, KJV). These three—the dragon, the beast, and the false prophet—make up a false trinity that destroys the gullible with their lying tongues, like frogs eating flies (Rev. 16:13). The Bible clearly defines the dragon as Satan and his united world kingdom that propels humanism, paganism, and spiritualism (Rev. 12:9; Dan. 7:23). The beast from the sea is described in detail in Revelation 13:1-7 as one main blasphemous religious/political entity—the papacy. Finally, the false prophet likely represents the apostate Protestant leaders who set up the "image of the beast," described in Revelation 13:11-18 because Revelation 19:20 (KJV) states, "And the beast was taken, and with him the *false prophet, that wrought miracles before him*, with which he deceived them that had received the mark of the beast and them that worshiped his image" (italics added). In this text, the false prophet is identified as the one who worked *"miracles before him"* (the beast). Revelation 13:12-13 (KJV) identifies the image of the beast as the one who "exerciseth all the power of the first beast *before him,"* and *"doeth great wonders, so that he maketh fire come down from heaven on the earth*... and deceiveth them that dwell on the earth *by the means of those miracles..."* (italics added). Therefore, this false prophet likely represents the apostate religious leaders of the Lamblike Earth beast that speak with the spirits of devils like frogs coming from their mouths (Rev. 13:11; Rev. 16:13-14). Already identified as Protestant America, this earth beast is led astray by these apostate leaders, possibly speaking in false tongues.

The Bible predicts that this fraudulent trinity (the dragon, beast, and false prophet) will "go out to the kings *of the earth and of the whole world*" (likely indicating two different locations—the U.S. and other world nations); they will "gather them to the battle of that great day of God Almighty..." to the place "called in the Hebrew tongue Armageddon" (Rev. 16:14, 16, KJV; italics added). The Greek word, *"Armageddon,"* means *"the hill or city of Megiddo," "a place of crowds,"* or *"rendezvous."* It is the physical place where the Canaanite kings fought against the children of Israel (Judges 5:19-31). Plus *"Armageddon"* may stem from the word, *"mow'ed,"* meaning *"appointed time/place," "assembly,"* or *"mount of the congregation"*—the same word for the mount (king-dom) that Lucifer aspired to attain (Is. 14:13). The battle of Arma-geddon, then, is likely symbolic of the spiritual war between Satan/his captives and God/His people, initiated by the gathering of nations at an *appointed time,* just before Christ's coming.

After John saw the bleak destiny of the nations during the plagues, he abruptly heard these words, "Behold, I come as a thief. Blessed is he that watcheth, and keepeth his garments, lest he walk naked, and they see his shame" (Rev. 16:15, KJV). These words echo Christ's admonition to the church of Sardis: "Re-member therefore how thou hast received and heard, and hold fast, and repent. If therefore thou shalt not watch, I will come on thee as a thief, and thou shalt not know what hour I will come upon thee" (Rev. 3:3, KJV). Moreover, Paul exhorts:

But concerning the times and seasons, brethren, you have no need that I should write to you. For you yourselves know perfectly that the day of the Lord so comes as a thief in the night. For when they say, 'Peace and safety' then sudden destruction comes upon them as labor pains upon a pregnant woman, and they shall not escape. But you, brethren, are not in darkness that this Day should overtake you as a thief. You are all sons of light and sons of the day. We are not of the night, nor of darkness. Therefore let us not sleep, as others do, but let us watch and be sober. (I Thess. 5:1-6, NKJV)

So when John heard that Jesus was coming "as a thief," he would have understood that this phrase describes those who do not "watch," such as the wicked that he had just been shown. It is *not* referring to God's people who do not need an explanation of the "times and seasons" of Christ's coming because they are aware of the signs predicted in Bible prophecy. Although Jesus told His disciples that no one knows "the day or hour" of His return (Matt. 24:36, NKJV) or even the "times or the seasons which the Father hath put in his own power" (Acts 1:7, KJV), He rightly assumes that Christians should be watchful of the "signs of the times" (Matt. 16:3, KJV).

Unfortunately, even amidst God's church today, a vast majority who claim to be watching are asleep on duty! Christ counsels these, "Remember therefore how thou hast received and heard, and hold fast, and repent. If therefore thou shalt not watch, I will come on thee as a thief, and thou will *not know what hour I will come upon thee*" (implying that they *should have known*—Rev. 3:2, KJV; italics added). Moreover, Jesus promises a blessing to everyone who "watcheth and keepeth his garments..." (Rev.

16:15, KJV; compare Rev. 19:8). This blessing is poured out upon all of God's people who are diligently looking for the Lord's return by confessing their sins and developing a Christ-like character while sharing with others the signs of His soon coming.

The seventh and final plague occurs when Jesus proclaims that "It is done" (Rev. 16:17, KJV; 21:6). This declaration mirrors His final words on the cross, "It is finished" (John 19:30, KJV). This solemn proclamation declares that Christ's work in the Most Holy Place has ended. At the utterance of these words, the world is thrown into a state of chaos. A great earthquake occurs, unlike any previous one (Rev. 16:18). This terrible quake is the physical manifestation of the spiritual shaking that has already taken place which awakens humanity to the reality of Christ's return. At this time, "every island" flees away, and the "mountains" (possibly kingdoms) are "not found" (Rev. 16:20, KJV). This final plague is further described in the thunderous repetition of the sixth seal:

> … And, lo, there was a great earthquake; and the sun became black as sackcloth of hair, and the moon became as blood; And the stars of heaven fell unto the earth, even as a fig tree casteth her untimely figs when she is shaken of a mighty wind. And the heaven departed as a scroll when it is rolled together, and every mountain and island were moved out of their places. (Rev. 6:12-14, KJV)

This terrible plague divides spiritual Babylon into "three parts" causing the "cities of the nations" to fall, and the Lord gives great Babylon its "cup of the wine of the fierceness of his wrath" (Rev. 16:19, KJV). These three groups may be symbolically described in Isaiah 19:24: "In that day, shall Israel (God's true followers) be the third with Egypt (the South—probably

apostate Protestants, specifically in the U.S.) and with Assyria…
" (the North—likely Catholics). Although a remnant will be
saved from all of these groups (Zech. 10:9-10), the fate of each
may be foretold in Ezekiel 5:12 (KJV): "A third part of thee shall
die with the pestilence, and with famine… a third part shall fall
by the sword… and I will scatter a third part into all the winds,
and I will draw out a sword after them." These judgments could
also be prefigured in the first four trumpets, with trumpet calls
for each of these groups (Rev. 9:5-13). The large cities specifically
suffer from these plagues, similar to Sodom and Gomorrah, because of their wickedness (Gen. 18:20; 19:24-25; Rev. 11:8). Desperately, their inhabitants cry for the rocks to hide them "from
the wrath of the Lamb" (Rev. 6:16, KJV).

However, throughout the plagues, God's people are miraculously delivered from the wicked because they have been sealed
for redemption (Eph. 4:30; Rev. 7:3; Dan. 12:1-2; Ps. 91:8-11). The
remnant's supernatural shielding from the plagues will enrage
the lost and cause them to blame their sufferings upon God's
people. "Great hail" will fall upon men, each hailstone "about
the weight of a talent" (about 120 lbs),[257] "and men blasphemed
God because of the plague of the hail" which is "exceeding great"
(Rev. 16:21, KJV). This devastating hailstorm casts the earth into
its final state of chaos, heralding Jesus's return (Is. 30:30).

The next two chapters confirm the tragic fall of apostate
Christianity and give the reasons for the seven last plagues, specifically outlining the sixth and seventh. God has suffered long
with humanity, but at last, those remaining in spiritual Babylon,
who insist on eliminating freedom of choice, must suffer the terrible consequence of their own final decision!

---

[257] https://www.biblestudytools.com/dictionary/talent/

| DANIEL 2 | DANIEL 7 | DANIEL 8 | DANIEL 11 | REV. 2-3 | REV. 6 |
|---|---|---|---|---|---|
| **Head- Gold** Nebuchadnezzar (**Babylon**/Jews) (605-539 B.C.) | **Lion** Eagle's Wings Plucked Stood/Man's Heart | | | **7 CHURCHES** (Apostle John the Revelator) | **7 SEALS** |
| **Shoulders/Arms** Silver **Medo-Persia** (539-331 B.C.) | **Bear** Side Raised 3 Ribs in Mouth Told to Devour | **Ram** Medo-Persia Abraham's Seed God's Kingdom | 3 More Kingdoms of Persia; Then 4th Richer & Stronger | | |
| **Belly & Thighs** Brass- **Greece** (331-168 B.C.) | **Leopard** 4 Heads/4 Bird Wings Given Dominion | **Goat** Greece/Gentiles Satan's Kingdom | Mighty King Great Dominion Kingdom Divided into 4 & Uprooted (Greece) | **Ephesus** (31-100 AD) **Smyrna** (100-323 AD) **Pergamos** (323-538 AD) | **White Horse** Christianity **Red Horse** Paganism **Black Horse** Civil Law |
| **Two Lower Legs** Iron- Rome (168 B.C. – 476 A.D.) | **Terrible Beast** Iron Teeth/Brass Nails Ten Horns Tramples Remnant | From 1 of 4 Divided Kingdoms of Greece (Rome) | From 1 of 4 Divided Kingdoms of Greece (Rome) | **Thyatira** (538-1534 AD) **Sardius** (1534-1750s AD) | **Pale Horse** Papacy (Church & State) Martyr's Cry |
| **Feet** Iron & Clay Papacy & USA (476 A.D. - 2nd Coming) | **Little Horn** Defeats 3 Other Horns Wars Against Saints | **Little Horn** Sly, Proud King Destroys Saints (Roman Papacy) | **King of North** (Roman Papacy) **King of South** (USA) | **Philadelphia** (1750s-1844 AD) **Laodicea** (1844 AD- End) | Earthquake & Heavenly Signs Silence ½ Hour |

| REV. 2-3 | REV. 6 | REV. 8-9 | REV. 10 | REV. 16 |
|---|---|---|---|---|
| **7 Churches** | **7 Seals** | **7 Trumpets** | **7 Thunders (Seals Repeated)** | **7 Last Plagues (Future)** |
| **Ephesus** (31-100 AD) | **White Horse** (Christianity) | Earthquake/Hail/ Blood (Protestant Reformation) | Protestantism Unhindered (Pope Captive-1798) | Sores- Mark of the Beast |
| **Smyrna** (100-323) | **Red Horse** (Paganism) | Mt. in Sea (Papacy Loses Power- 1798) | Spiritualism/ Tongues/Evolution (1844) | Sea to Blood (Loss of Life) |
| **Pergamos** (323-538) | **Black Horse** (Civil Law) | Star Falls on Waters (Age of Reason- USA) | Humanistic Government (USA) | Rivers to Blood (Retribution of Saints' Deaths) |
| **Thyatira** (538- 1534) | **Pale Horse** (Papacy) (Church & State) | Sun, Moon, Stars Darkened (1780-1844) | Papal/Protestant Ecumenicalism (1994-End) | Scorching Sun (Climate Change) |
| **Sardis** (1534-1750s) | Martyr's Cry for Justice/Reformation | Scorpions/Locusts Released on Earth (Spiritualism/Tongues) | Martyr's Cry (Protestant Reformation Ends/2017-End) | Darkness (Spiritual & Physical) |
| **Philadelphia** (1750s-1844) | Earthquake/Sun, Moon Dark/Stars Fall | War Horses/World War (1918-End) | Earthquake/ Heavenly Signs (Future) | Dragon (Spiritualism), **Beast** (Catholicism), & **False Prophet** (Protestantism) **Deceive Nations for War** |
| **Laodicea** (1844-End) | Silence About ½ Hour | Judgment/ 2nd Coming (Future) | Silence, Then Judgment Executed | Earthquake/Islands & Mts. Sink/Great Hail |

# Discussion Questions for Revelation 16

1. What is the result of the wicked's decision to separate themselves from God's protection? (Lev. 26:21; Deut. 28:59-62)

2. How do the seven last plagues affect the righteous? (Ex. 14:13-14; Ps. 91:10-11)

3. For what do the wicked search the land? (Amos 8:11-12)

4. Describe the first plague. Upon whom does it fall? (Rev. 16:2; Deut. 28:27)

5. Describe the second and third plagues. (Rev. 16:3-6) How might they be the response to the fifth seal? (Rev. 6:10; 17:15) As well as likely being literal, what might they symbolize? How are they similar and different from the second and third trumpets and the first Egyptian plague? (Rev. 8:8-9; Ex. 7:17-21)

6. Describe the fourth plague and the wicked's reaction. (Rev. 16:8-9) How does it contrast the sounding of the fourth trumpet (Rev. 8:12), and to what might the fourth plague be attributed? (Is. 30:26)

7. Describe the fifth plague. (Rev. 16:10-11) How does it contrast with the fourth? (Rev. 16:8-9) How is it similar to the ninth Egyptian plague? (Ex. 10:21-23) How can we know that at least some of the seven last plagues compound? (Rev. 16:11, 2) Upon whom or what does the fifth plague fall? (Rev. 16:10)

8. Describe the sixth plague. (Rev. 16:12-14) What unrighteous act caused ancient Babylon's downfall? (Dan. 5:4) How is this repeated in the last days with spiritual Babylon? (Rev. 9:20-21) Who consists of the false trinity? (Rev. 16:13) What happens to this false trinity? (Rev. 19:20; 20:2) To whom does Christ come as a "thief?" (Rev. 16:15) What are we to do to be ready for Christ's coming? (1 Thess. 5:1-6; Matt. 16:3)

9. Describe the seventh plague. (Rev. 16:17-21) How is it similar to the earthquake described in Rev. 6:12-14? What likely happens to each third of spiritual Babylon? (Rev. 16:19; Is. 19:24; Eze. 5:12)

10. What promises are given for the protection of God's people during these plagues? (Dan. 12:1; Ps. 9:9; 91:8-11)

# Revelation 17 (KJV)

*[1] And there came one of the seven angels which had the seven vials, and talked with me, saying unto me, Come hither; I will shew unto thee the judgment of the great whore that sitteth upon many waters: [2] With whom the kings of the earth have committed fornication, and the inhabitants of the earth have been made drunk with the wine of her fornication. [3] So he carried me away in the spirit into the wilderness: and I saw a woman sit upon a scarlet coloured beast, full of names of blasphemy, having seven heads and ten horns. [4] And the woman was arrayed in purple and scarlet colour, and decked with gold and precious stones and pearls, having a golden cup in her hand full of abominations and filthiness of her fornication: [5] And upon her forehead was a name written, Mystery, Babylon The Great, The Mother Of Harlots And Abominations Of The Earth. [6] And I saw the woman drunken with the blood of the saints, and with the blood of the martyrs of Jesus: and when I saw her, I wondered with great admiration. [7] And the angel said unto me, Wherefore didst thou marvel? I will tell thee the mystery of the woman, and of the beast that carrieth her, which hath the seven heads and ten horns. [8] The beast that thou sawest was, and is not; and shall ascend out of the bottomless pit, and go into perdition: and they that dwell on the earth shall wonder, whose names were not written in the book of life from the foundation of the world, when they behold the beast that was, and is not, and yet is. [9] And here is the mind which hath wisdom. The seven heads are seven mountains, on which the woman sitteth. [10] And*

there are seven kings: five are fallen, and one is, and the other is not yet come; and when he cometh, he must continue a short space. [11] And the beast that was, and is not, even he is the eighth, and is of the seven, and goeth into perdition. [12] And the ten horns which thou sawest are ten kings, which have received no kingdom as yet; but receive power as kings one hour with the beast. [13] These have one mind, and shall give their power and strength unto the beast. [14] These shall make war with the Lamb, and the Lamb shall overcome them: for he is Lord of lords, and King of kings: and they that are with him are called, and chosen, and faithful. [15] And he saith unto me, The waters which thou sawest, where the whore sitteth, are peoples, and multitudes, and nations, and tongues. [16] And the ten horns which thou sawest upon the beast, these shall hate the whore, and shall make her desolate and naked, and shall eat her flesh, and burn her with fire. [17] For God hath put in their hearts to fulfil his will, and to agree, and give their kingdom unto the beast, until the words of God shall be fulfilled. [18] And the woman which thou sawest is that great city, which reigneth over the kings of the earth.

# Church and State United

Have you ever gone horseback riding and wondered if the massive beast would buck you off at any moment? At such times, one might question the wisdom of getting on the back of such a powerful animal with a mind all its own! In Revelation 17, John saw a harlot who had committed spiritual fornication with the "kings of the earth" (Rev. 17:1-2, KJV). She was sitting on a scarlet-colored beast with seven heads and ten horns and ruling over the sea of waters, symbolizing "peoples, and multitudes, and nations, and tongues" (Rev. 17:1, 3, 15, KJV). One of the angels that had the seven bowls of God's wrath, likely the seventh, told John that he would show him "the *judgment* of the great harlot," which refers back to why the seven last plagues had been poured out and upon whom they had fallen (the harlot and her followers) (Rev.16:1; 17:1, NKJV). Then John saw a symbolic picture of the combination of church and state and how this coalition will persecute God's people in the last days, but in the end, it will finally be overthrown.

In review, a harlot in Bible prophecy often symbolizes a church in apostasy (Jer. 3:20). Most likely, John would have contrasted this harlot with the pure woman (church) of Revelation 12:1 and recognized the Protestant church's disastrous downfall from a godly woman to an idolatrous harlot united back with her apostate mother—the papacy (Rev. 17:5; Is. 1:21-23). Moreover,

John saw the harlot and the scarlet beast in the *wilderness* (likely the USA), the same place where he had previously beheld the glorious woman (church [Jer. 6:2; Rev. 12:1, 14]), escaping the red dragon (Satan and his kingdom [Rev. 12:3-4, 9; 17:3]). Why had God's church, as a whole, lost its purity? It was supposed to be the "voice of one crying in the wilderness: prepare ye the way of the Lord" (Matt. 3:3, KJV). However, the fiery red dragon had spewed out a flood of deceptions through its false teachers (Rev. 12:15; 17:15). As a result, most religious leaders had become drunk with the wine of papal teachings and shared it with the kings of the earth (Rev. 17:2; Jer. 51:7; Deut. 32:33; Rev. 12:9). The plagues, then, were largely the tragic outcome of the apostate Protestant churches' demand for worldwide civil enforcement of the papacy's false teachings, including Sunday observance (Rev. 17:5, 16-17; 13:15-17).

Furthermore, the harlot's sinful nature is demonstrated by the jewels and scarlet/purple clothes that she wore, matching the scarlet beast and the garb of the pope and his cardinals (Rev. 17:4; Eze. 23:5-6). This tragic transformation is described in Revelation 17:4-6 (KJV):

> And the woman was arrayed in purple and scarlet color, and decked with gold and precious stones and pearls, having a golden cup in her hand full of abominations and filthiness of her fornication. And upon her forehead was a name written, "Mystery, Babylon the Great, the Mother of Harlots and of the Abominations of the Earth." And I saw the woman drunk with the blood of the saints, and with the blood of the martyrs...

This appalling description is the bitter consequence of the fallen Protestant churches, mirroring their mother, the papacy, in the persecution of God's people (Rev. 13:15; Eze. 16:44). The beast's name is seen on the Protestant daughter's forehead, signifying her conscious decision to enforce Sunday-keeping, the papal mark, instead of God's Sabbath (Rev. 17:5; 13:16-17; Jer. 3:3). Moreover, the woman is called *Mystery Babylon*, that "great city which reigneth over the kings of the earth" (Rev. 17:5, 18, KJV). The name, "Babylon" means confusion (Gen. 11:9), which rightly describes America's Protestant churches mixing biblical doctrine with the teachings of the pope, the "*mystery* of lawlessness" (2 Thess. 2:3-7, NKJV). This amalgamation is further manifested today in the Protestant church's embracement of not only the papacy (the sea beast [Rev. 13:1) but also the modern secular philosophies promoted by the U.S. (the earth beast [Rev.13:11). This confederacy of leadership will, at last, unify the world's wicked nations in the destruction of God's people, triggering the seven last plagues (Rev. 17:6; 13:15; 18:6-8; Jer. 50:28-29).

Then John's attention was turned towards the great scarlet beast. In review, a beast represents a world kingdom (Dan.7:23), in this case, Satan's unified world nations enforcing church and state, causing persecution of God's people (Rev. 17:8; 13:15). John stared at this seven-headed, scarlet beast that had engulfed the papal sea beast and the American earth beast (Rev. 17:3; 12:3, 9; 13:1-3, 11-12). Its civil heads, portrayed as mountains & kings (Rev. 17:9-10; Jer. 51:24-25), are symbolic of the world nations that have ruled over God's people throughout history.[258] At the time that John was given this vision, five of the seven kingdoms had fallen from power: Egypt, Assyria, Babylon, Medo-Persia, and Greece. One was currently ruling in John's time (Rome), and one was yet to come—the United States of America—and when it came, it would rule a short time (Rev. 17:10). The beast that "was,

---

[258] https://ssnet.org/blog/wednesday-seven-heads-of-beast/

and is not, even he is the eighth, and is of the seven" refers to the pagan dragon's (Satan's [Rev. 12:9]) united political/religious world kingdom, which includes the wicked characteristics of all seven kingdoms before it (Rev. 17:11, 12:3; Dan. 7:3-8, 11-12, KJV). This conglomeration, fueled by the apostate American religious/civil leaders, will attack God's people worldwide (Rev. 17:16).

In addition to its political rulership, the scarlet beast is also a false religious power because it is full of "names of blasphemy," meaning that it demands worship and/or the ability to forgive sin, which is rightfully God's (Rev. 17:3; 13:6; 2 Thess. 2:4; Matt. 9:2-3). Like the sea beast, it has a blasphemous name upon its governmental heads (Rev. 13:1). The return of a unified civil/religious kingdom persecuting God's people is referred to as the beast that "was, and is not, and shall ascend out of the bottomless pit (the "earth," likely the U.S.) and go into perdition" (Rev. 17:8; compare 1:7; 13:2; Dan. 7:17, KJV). Historically, this combination of church and state occurred during the 1,260 years when Rome had both religious and civil power over God's people, tyrannizing His faithful followers throughout the Dark Ages (Dan. 7:25). Likewise, the papacy's deadly power will rise again in the scarlet beast. This time it will be fueled by the U.S. Protestant churches and their political influence, resulting in global persecution of all who do not adhere to Catholic doctrine.

Even now, many Protestant churches that originally split from the Catholic Church have reunited with the papacy on common points of doctrine in 2017. Additionally, the United States has predominantly Catholic leadership in many of its primary civil offices (i.e. the Supreme Court), and the papacy is insisting on worldwide political unity. This solidarity was highlighted in

Pope Francis's 2020 address to the United Nations when he declared, "The world has a duty to rethink the future of the world, with strengthened multilateralism and cooperation between States."[259] Slowly, Protestant America is surrendering its governmental head to the scarlet beast's united nations under papal leadership (Rev. 17:3; 13:1-4, 11-12; 12:9). As the result of this future church and state coalition, Satan and his unified dragon kingdom will gain political/religious rulership over the entire world: "… and those who dwell on the earth will marvel whose names are not written in the Book of Life … when they see the beast that was, and is not, and yet is" (Rev. 17:8; compare Rev. 13:3-4, KJV).

Additionally, the ten horns that John saw on the scarlet beast symbolize its combined civil/religious forces, just as horns empower an animal (Rev. 17:3; Zech. 1:21). Moreover, Revelation 17:12 refers to these ten horns as ten kings. These "kings of the *earth*" (Rev. 17:2, 18) should trigger the memory of the beast from the *earth* (Rev. 13:11), referred to separately from the world (Rev. 16:14), which likely represents the United States. America's political leaders will be of "one mind" (unified) and give their "power and strength to the beast," the united world nations (Rev. 17:13, 17, KJV). Just as prophecy has predicted, today the United State's powerful horns are joining Europe's in gaining papal authority "over every kindreds, and tongues, and nations" (Rev. 13:7, 11-12, KJV). The Bible predicts that these civil horns will "hate the harlot" (apostate Christianity) and "make her desolate and naked" (Rev. 17:16, NKJV). Through the passage of national laws, the U.S. government will lead the world in mandating false worship on Sunday and prohibit all who do not comply from buying or selling (Rev. 13:17). Finally, a global death decree of

---

[259] https://news.un.org/en/story/2020/09/1073772

God's faithful followers will be passed as a result of popular demand (Rev. 13:15). This decree will be cloaked in the disguise of religious piety through forced worship. However, God never forces worship! Instead, Christ died so that all people would have the freedom to choose whether or not they wanted to believe in Him and be saved (John 3:16). Yet, prophecy predicts that this freedom of choice, engrained in the United States Constitution, will be sabotaged by the kings of the earth, and the American government will mandate worship, leading all the other world nations to do likewise.

These same ten horns "which have received no kingdom as yet" (referring to John's day) will gain "power as kings one hour with the beast" (Rev 17:12, KJV). If the same method of timing is used to figure the approximate half an hour of silence in Revelation 8:1 (a day for a 1,000 years [Ps. 90:4; 2 Peter 3:8), one hour could equal roughly forty-one years (1,000 divided by 24). This approximate forty-year time period in the Bible is very significant for symbolizing a time of testing (Ps. 95:8-10). For example, Moses spent forty years in the wilderness, as did the children of Israel (Acts 7:30; Num. 14:33-34). Interestingly, the United States, through President Reagan, began formal diplomatic relations with the Vatican in 1983.[260] If forty-one years are added to 1983, the total ends in 2024, *the exact same year that Daniel 9's proposed repeated seventy-week prophecy closes,* possibly completing the time period for Protestant America as God's favored nation. Could the end of this prophecy predict the termination of the U.S. ruling as "kings" with the papacy and usher in religious persecution from the world's united nations? (Rev. 17:13-14; 13:7; 18:10). Only time will tell!

---

[260] https://www.mtsu.edu/first-amendment/article/975/vatican-city-u-s-recognition-of

The entire seventeenth chapter of Revelation predicts the downfall of the apostate Protestant/papal churches (harlot) in alliance with the world's nations under satanic rule (the scarlet beast) through the enforcement of church and state. Moreover, the civil powers (horns) of these nations will try to destroy God's people through the passage of anti-Christian legislation (Rev. 13:15). However, Jesus will defeat the beast, its horn, and the harlot: "... and the Lamb shall overcome them, for He is Lord of lords and King of kings" (Rev. 17:14, KJV; compare 18:8; Ps. 75:10). God's people, the "called, and chosen, and faithful" (Rev. 17:4, KJV) will claim victory in Christ and "keep the commandments of God and have the testimony of Jesus Christ" (the "spirit of prophecy" [Rev. 12:17; 19:10, KJV]). Then the saints will defeat the devil's church/state conglomerate "by the blood of the Lamb, and by the word of their testimony!" (Rev. 12:11).

---

### Chart of Symbols of Revelation 17

**Great Harlot-** Church in apostacy- Protestantism united with Catholicism (Rev. 17:1-6; 19:2; Is. 1:2, 21-23; Jer. 3:20; Eze. 20:30; Jer. 3:1, 20; Eze. 16:15-49; Hosea 4:9-15; see *Mystery Babylon the Great* below)

**Many Waters-** Multitudes, nations, and tongues (Rev. 17:1, 15; Num. 24:7; Is. 17:12-13; Jer. 51:55)

**Kings of the Earth-** Civil leaders, specifically of the United States as the "Earth Beast," enforcing the dictates of the state churches (Rev. 17:2; 13:11-12; 16:14; 18:3, 9; 6:15-16; 19:19; Is. 24:21-22; see *Ten Horns* below)

**Wine of Fornication-** Idolatry/false worship & teachings (Rev. 17:2; 14:8, 18:3; Deut. 32:32; Prov. 4:17; Is. 28:7; Jer. 51:7)

**Scarlet Beast-** Red Dragon/Satan's united world nations combining church & state that rule and persecute God's people (Rev. 17:3; 12:3, 9; 11:7-8; 13:1)

**Seven Heads/Mountains/Kings -** World kingdoms, specifically ruling and persecuting God's people throughout history- Egypt, Assyria, Babylon, Medo-Persia, Greece, Rome, United States (Rev. 17:9-10; Dan. 7:3-8, 11-12, 17, 23; Rev. 12:3; 13:1-3, 7; Jer. 51:24-25)

**Ten Horns/Kings-** Civil powers enforcing state churches (Rev. 17:12; Dan. 7:20-21, 23-24; Zech. 1:21; see *"Kings of the Earth"*)

**Lamb-** Christ (Rev. 17:14; 5:6, 8, 12-13; 13:11; 14:1, 4, 10)

**Mystery Babylon the Great** – A system of mixed religious confusion (Rev. 17:5-6, 18; 14:8; 18:2; Jer. 51:41-49; Gen. 11:9)

# Discussion Questions for Revelation 17

1. Who is figuratively portrayed as the great harlot? How have God's people throughout the ages acted like a harlot spiritually? (Rev. 17:1-6; Jer. 3:20-21; Is. 1:21-23)

2. What do "many waters" symbolize? What is meant by the harlot sitting on them? (Rev. 17:1, 15; compare Acts 12:21-22)

3. What political/religious system does the scarlet beast symbolize? In what ways are the nations of the modern world unifying today under the papacy? (Rev. 17:3; Dan. 7:23; Rev. 12:3, 9; 13:1, 3-7; 2 Thess. 2:3-4)

4. In John's time, what five kingdoms (represented as heads/mountains/kings) had fallen, what kingdom was in power in John's day, and what last world-influential nation after John's time would rule God's people for a "short time?" (Rev. 17:9-10; Dan. 7:3-7; Rev. 13:2, 11)

5. Who, specifically, are the "kings of the earth"? How does the beast from the earth give us a possible clue to their identity? (Rev. 17:2; 18; Rev. 13:11-12) What do the ten "horns" (kings [Dan. 7:24]) likely represent? (Rev. 17:3, 12-14; Zech. 1:21;)

6. How are the nations' civil horns today displaying that they "hate the harlot" (apostate Christianity) and are trying to "make her desolate and naked" to destroy her? (Rev. 17:16)

7. What will happen to the scarlet beast and its horns that make war with the Lamb? (Rev. 17:14; Ps. 75:10)

# Revelation 18 (KJV)

*¹ And after these things I saw another angel come down from heaven, having great power; and the earth was lightened with his glory. ² And he cried mightily with a strong voice, saying, Babylon the great is fallen, is fallen, and is become the habitation of devils, and the hold of every foul spirit, and a cage of every unclean and hateful bird. ³ For all nations have drunk of the wine of the wrath of her fornication, and the kings of the earth have committed fornication with her, and the merchants of the earth are waxed rich through the abundance of her delicacies. ⁴ And I heard another voice from heaven, saying, Come out of her, my people, that ye be not partakers of her sins, and that ye receive not of her plagues. ⁵ For her sins have reached unto heaven, and God hath remembered her iniquities. ⁶ Reward her even as she rewarded you, and double unto her double according to her works: in the cup which she hath filled fill to her double. ⁷ How much she hath glorified herself, and lived deliciously, so much torment and sorrow give her: for she saith in her heart, I sit a queen, and am no widow, and shall see no sorrow. ⁸ Therefore shall her plagues come in one day, death, and mourning, and famine; and she shall be utterly burned with fire: for strong is the Lord God who judgeth her. ⁹ And the kings of the earth, who have committed fornication and lived deliciously with her, shall bewail her, and lament for her, when they shall see the smoke of her burning, ¹⁰ Standing afar off for the fear of her torment, saying, Alas, alas that great city Babylon, that mighty city! for in one hour is thy judgment come. ¹¹ And the merchants of* the earth shall weep and mourn over her; for no man buyeth their merchandise any more: [12] The merchandise of gold, and silver, and precious stones, and of pearls, and fine linen, and purple, and silk, and scarlet, and all thyine wood, and all manner vessels of ivory, and all manner vessels of most precious wood, and of brass, and iron, and marble, [13] And cinnamon, and odours, and ointments, and frankincense, and wine, and oil, and fine flour, and wheat, and beasts, and sheep, and horses, and chariots, and slaves, and souls of men. [14] And the fruits that thy soul lusted after are departed from thee, and all things which were dainty and goodly are departed from thee, and thou shalt find them no more at all. [15] The merchants of these things, which were made rich by her, shall stand afar off for the fear of her torment, weeping and wailing, [16] And saying, Alas, alas that great city, that was clothed in fine linen, and purple, and scarlet, and decked with gold, and precious stones, and pearls! [17] For in one hour so great riches is come to nought. And every shipmaster, and all the company in ships, and sailors, and as many as trade by sea, stood afar off, [18] And cried when they saw the smoke of her burning, saying, What city is like unto this great city! [19] And they cast dust on their heads, and cried, weeping and wailing, saying, Alas, alas that great city, wherein were made rich all that had ships in the sea by reason of her costliness! for in one hour is she made desolate. [20] Rejoice over her, thou heaven, and ye holy apostles and prophets; for God hath avenged you on her. [21] And a mighty angel took up a stone like a great millstone, and cast it into the sea, saying, Thus with violence shall that great city Babylon be thrown down, and shall be found no more at all. [22] And the voice of harpers, and musicians, and of pipers, and trumpeters, shall be heard no more at all in thee; and no craftsman, of whatsoever craft he be, shall be found any more in thee; and the sound of a millstone shall be heard no more at all in thee; [23] And the light of a candle shall shine no more at all in thee; and the voice of the bridegroom and of the bride shall be heard no more at all in thee: for thy merchants were

*the great men of the earth; for by thy sorceries were all nations deceived.*
[24] *And in her was found the blood of prophets, and of saints, and of all that were slain upon the earth.*

# The Downfall of an Apostate Nation

Have you ever been in a cave when the lights were turned off? Darkness completely engulfs you! But then, with a flip of a switch, the light suddenly appears and fills the room with such brightness that it is almost blinding! Most likely the apostle, John, also squinted and covered his eyes at the appearance of a mighty angel coming down from Heaven to Earth, radiating God's glory through the outpouring of the Holy Spirit (Rev. 18:1). John saw that this event was to occur just before the close of probation. At this time, the Lord's faithful followers will be granted wisdom to explain Bible prophecy clearly and simply so that all can understand (Is. 60:1-3; Dan. 12:3; 1 Pet. 3:15). Moreover, they are imbued with tremendous power to proclaim the Three Angels' Messages of Revelation 14 to the world in preparation of Christ's imminent return.

Through this second loud cry, Jesus calls His wayward people out of spiritual Babylon, giving this special message to the fallen Protestant/Catholic churches holding political sway (Rev. 18:2-4; 14:8). This international conglomerate of church and state, represented by the harlot riding on the beast in Revelation 17 and "Babylon the great" in Revelation 18, "is fallen, is fallen" and has become the "habitation of devils" and a cage of "every unclean and hateful bird" (Rev. 18:2, KJV; Jer. 5:26-27). It has forced all nations to drink the "wine" of its corrupted doctrines and commit spiritual fornication against God (Rev. 18:3; Is. 28:7). The Lord calls His people to reject Sunday worship, the beast's mark of authority, and obey His law "that ye be not partakers of her sins," and "receive not of her plagues" (Rev. 18:4, KJV; Rev. 14:9-10; Jer. 50:13). The corruption within the Protestant/Catholic churches from the amalgamation of church and state has caused Babylon's fall. Christ decrees that His apostate church and its false spiritual leaders are cursed "*double* according to her works" (Rev. 18:6, KJV). Against mother (the Catholic Church) and her daughters (apostate Protestant churches), God declares:

> "In the measure that she glorified herself and lived luxuriously in the same measure give her torment and sorrow; for she says in her heart, 'I sit as queen and am no widow and will not see sorrow.' Therefore her plagues will come in one day (or "moment" [Is. 47:9])—death and mourning and famine. And she will be utterly burned with fire for strong is the Lord God who judges her." (Rev. 18:7-8, NKJV; compare Is. 47:7-9)

This terrible pronouncement of guilt upon apostate Christianity is finally followed by the outpouring of the seven last plagues in Revelation 16. Revelation 17 describes apostate Protestantism as a harlot, and why the plagues are poured out, outlining specifically the details of the sixth and seventh plagues (Rev. 17:1; 16:12-21). Chapter 18, then, details the fall of Babylon (Rev. 18:8-10), the conglomerate of church and state, especially in the United States. As tragedy after tragedy occurs, it becomes apparent that God's mercy is being withdrawn from this once-prosperous nation where Heaven's blessings are no longer found. Final conscious decisions are made—either to accept the mark of the beast or to obey the Lord's commandments, which are included in the New Testament covenant (Heb. 10:16). However, the rebellious Protestant leaders who refuse to repent and stubbornly cling to the Roman Catholic Church's unbiblical traditions suffer twice as much as the wicked who have never claimed to be Christians (Rev. 18:6). As these disasters increase in intensity and extent, climaxing in the outpouring of the seven last plagues, the whole world watches in horror as the United States' prosperity is shattered like a broken clay pot (Note: "plague" means *"to strike"* and is related to the word, *"plasso"* to *"mould, shape like clay,"* similar to the crushing of the clay feet and toes in Nebuchadnezzar's dream [Rev. 18:7-8; Dan. 2:34; Rom. 9:19-22]). Prophecy denounces all who fight against God's law:

> "Because ye despise this word, and trust in oppression and perverseness, and stay thereon: Therefore this iniquity shall be to you as a breach ready to fall, a swelling out in a high wall, whose breaking cometh suddenly, in an instant. And he shall break it as the breaking of the potter's vessel, that is broken in pieces; he shall not spare..." (Is. 30:12-14, KJV)

The Lord watches as Protestant America, which He formed as a religious refuge for the world, is destroyed by "death and mourning and famine" and "utterly burned with fire... strong is the Lord God who judgeth her" (Rev. 18:8, KJV). He weeps, brokenhearted! (Jer. 9:10; 13:16-17; 14:17).

A mighty angel takes a great millstone and throws it into the sea and then declares: "Thus with violence shall that great city Babylon be thrown down, and shall be found no more at all" (Rev. 18:21, KJV; compare verse 24). This angel simply echos Christ's teaching that it is better to have a millstone hung around the neck and be thrown into the sea than to offend one of His children (Luke 17:2). Tragically, the religious and civil authorities of the United States have not only offended God's true followers, but they have mandated the death penalty for faithful Christians and blamed them for the disasters! In like manner, the other nations of the world have followed the United States' leadership in passing national Sunday laws, compelling their citizens to break God's fourth commandment or be killed (Ex. 20:8-11; Rev. 13:15). The Lord condemns this worldwide enforcement of ecumenical unity:

> "Because ye have said, 'We have made a covenant with death, and with hell are we at agreement; when the overflowing scourge shall pass through, it shall not come unto us, for we have made lies our refuge, and under falsehood have we hid ourselves... Your covenant with death will be disannulled, and your agreement with hell shall not stand; when the overflowing scourge shall pass through, then ye shall be trodden down by it." (Is. 28:15, 18, KJV)

No trace of remorse is found in these proud, defiant souls as God withdraws His protection, allowing demons to wreak devastation (Is. 23:8-9). If the lost were given more time, none would repent. Probation has closed, and the plagues only fuel their hatred of God (Rev. 18:7; 22:11).

In horror, the kings of the earth (beast [Rev. 13:11]), specifically the American civil leaders, "lament for her, when they shall see the smoke of her burning" (Rev. 17:1-2; 18:3, 9-10, KJV). Moreover, the merchants "mourn over her, for no man buyeth their merchandise any more" (Rev. 18:11, 19, KJV; compare Eze. 27:32-36). They stand at a distance for fear of her torment, wailing and saying, "Alas (Woe), alas (woe), that great city, that was clothed in fine linen, and purple, and scarlet, and decked with gold and precious stones and pearls! For in one hour, so great riches is come to naught" (Rev. 18:16-17, KJV; parentheses added; compare Eze. 27:24-31). Ironically, this is the same list of papal adornment that the harlot church (Babylon) wore to entice the U.S. civil leaders to enforce state churches (Rev. 18:16; 17:4). Now the glory of this once proud Protestant nation has been stripped away, and she is left desolate, both physically and spiritually (Rev. 18:19). No merriment of music is found in her streets, nor buying or selling in the marketplace (Rev. 18:22-23; Is. 24:8; Jer. 7:34; 25:10).

Tragically, "all the things which are rich and splendid" have disappeared from the United States and its unified Protestant/papal churches because they have persecuted God's faithful remnant, and in their solidarity, the "blood of prophets and saints" was found (Rev. 18:14, NKJV; compare Jer. 51:47-49). This once flourishing Christian nation is brought to its knees as calamity after calamity decimates America, rippling to all the earth. Christ's warnings have not been heeded in the United States, the example for the entire world, and He sadly declares:

> "This is a nation that obeyeth not the voice of the Lord their God, nor receiveth correction: truth is perished, and is cut off from their mouth.... they have set their abominations in the house which is called by My name..." (Jer. 7:28, 30, KJV)

The Lord has pronounced this judgment upon apostate Christianity because by its "*sorceries* were all the nations deceived" (Rev. 18:23, KJV; compare Rev. 22:15; italics added). The word for "sorceries" in this text is the same word found in Revelation 9:21 where it lists the sins of which mankind did not repent. Interestingly, this Greek word, "*pharmakeia,*" is the modern predecessor of the word, "*pharmacy,*" meaning "*medication,*" "*the use of administering drugs,"* and *"poisoning."* Could this prophetic warning be a clue that medical mandates may play a primary role in deceiving the entire world?

Furthermore, the "light of the lamp" (God's Word [Ps. 119:105]) will no longer shine in the United States, and the "voice of the bridegroom" (Jesus [Luke 5:33-34]) will not be heard (Rev. 18:23, NKJV). Additionally, the Lord states through His prophet, Jeremiah:

> "Moreover I will take from them the voice of mirth and the voice of gladness, the voice of the bridegroom and the voice of the bride, the sound of the millstones, and the light of the lamp. And this whole land shall be a desolation and an astonishment, and these nations shall serve the king of Babylon seventy years. Then it will come to pass, when seventy years are completed, that I will punish the king of Babylon and that nation... for their iniquity... and I will make it a perpetual desolation'" (Jer. 25:10-12, NKJV).

The seventy years spoken of in this passage means seventy *"shaneh"* or years as *"revolutions of time"* (compare Ps. 102:24). Interestingly, if seventy is multiplied by seven years, it totals 490 years, the same time period allotted for the Jews in the seventy-week prophecy of Daniel 9, along with its proposed repetition for the Protestant churches (Dan. 9:24).

Moreover, the ending date for this modern repetition of Daniel 9's seventy-week prophecy likely corresponds to the ending date of the "hour" of time spoken of in Revelation 18: "... for in one hour is thy judgment come" (Rev. 18:10, KJV; Rev. 14:7), "for in one hour so great riches is come to naught" (Rev. 18:17, KJV), and in "one hour is she made desolate" (Rev. 18:19, KJV). If an hour is calculated the same way it was figured in Revelation 8:1 and 17:12 (Heaven's timing of a day for a thousand years [2 Peter 3:8; Ps. 90:4]), one hour is forty-one years of Earth time. Interestingly, if forty-one years are added to 1983 when the USA began formal political relations with the Vatican,[261] the total ends in 2024, the exact same year as Daniel 9's proposed repeated seventy-week prophecy for the Protestant church and the "hour" predicted for the ten kings to rule with the beast (Rev. 18:10; 17:12).

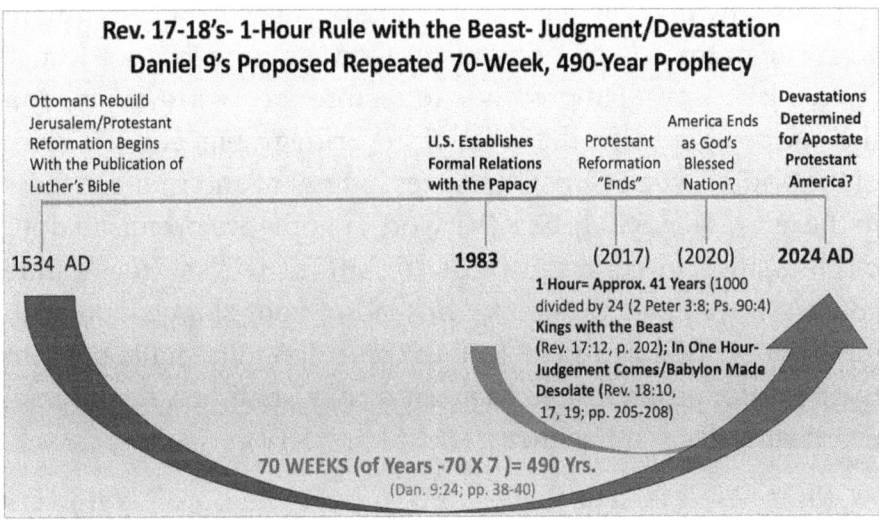

Why have such terrible judgments fallen upon this once-blessed country and its apostate state churches at this time? Perhaps the answer can be found in Jesus's own words: "… much is given, much will be required" (Lk. 12:48, NKJV). The Bible predicts that after the voice of gladness and the voice of the bridegroom has ceased (Hos. 2:11), the people will cry out, "Why has the Lord pronounced all this great disaster against us?… Or what is our sin that we have committed against the Lord our God?"

---

[261] https://www.mtsu.edu/first-amendment/article/975/vatican-city-u-s-recognition-of

(Jer. 16:10, NKJV). Then the Almighty One will answer:

> "Because your fathers have forsaken Me," says the Lord; "they have walked after other gods and have served them and worshipped them, and have forsaken Me and not kept My law. And you have done worse than your fathers, for behold, each one follows the dictates of his own evil heart, so that no one listens to Me." (Jer. 16:11-12, NKJV)

Nevertheless, Christ will not leave His faithful followers hopeless during this terrible global apostasy! To His remnant who "keep the commandments of God, and the faith of Jesus" (Rev. 14:12, KJV), He promises to restore the "voice of joy, and the voice of gladness, the voice of the bridegroom, and the voice of the bride," when Christ "executes judgment and righteousness in the land" (Jer. 33:11, 15, KJV). God's people are promised double blessings in contrast to the unfaithful who suffer double curses! (Rev. 18:6). He states, "Instead of your shame, you shall have double honor; and instead of confusion they shall rejoice in their portion: therefore in their land they shall possess double: everlasting joy shall be theirs" (Is. 61:7, NKJV).

Praise God for His justice and mercy! The Lord's followers have nothing to fear during this time of awful destruction! Jesus covers them under the shelter of His wings: "The Lord also will be a refuge for the oppressed: a refuge in times of trouble. And they that know thy name will put their trust in thee. For thou, Lord, hast not forsaken them that seek thee" (Ps. 9:9-10, KJV).

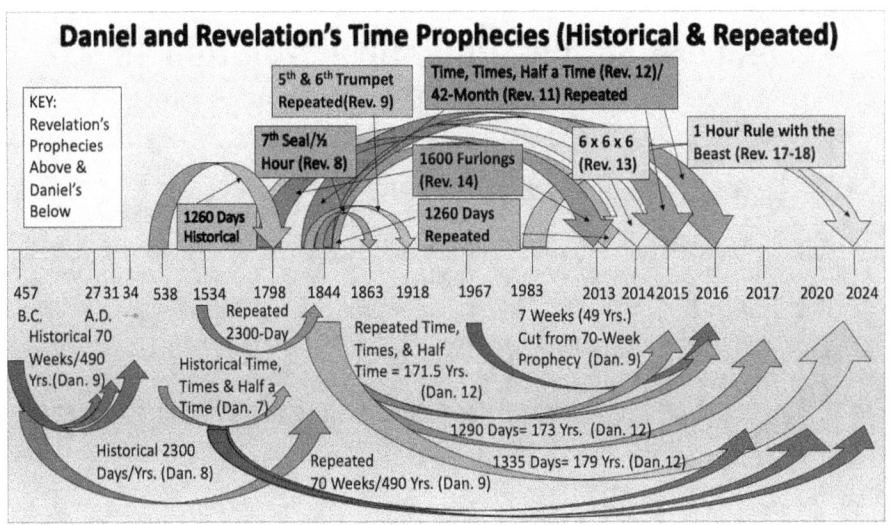

# Discussion Questions for Revelation 18

1. What special message does the mighty angel give to God's people? (Rev. 18:2-4; Rev. 14:8-10)

2. Why has Babylon fallen? (Rev. 18:2-3; 14:8; Is. 28:7)

3. What judgments will God bring against spiritual Babylon? (Rev. 18:5-8; Is. 47:7-9; Jer. 50:13)

4. Why is God's nation, "called by His name," broken like a shattered clay pot? (Jer. 7:28, 30) What is God's response? (Jer. 9:10; 13:16-17; 14:17)

5. Why is Babylon thrown down? (Rev. 18:21, 24; 13:15; Is. 28:15, 18) Why doesn't our merciful Lord wait longer? (Rev. 18:7; 22:11)

6. In all likelihood, who, specifically, are the "kings of the **earth**"? (Rev. 18:3; 9-10; 17:1-2; 13:11-12)

7. How do the merchants react to the fall of Babylon? (Rev. 18:11, 19; Eze. 27:30-36)

8. How is Babylon described? (Rev. 18:16-17; 17:4)

9. What might the word, "sorcery," in Rev. 18:23, Rev. 9:21, and Rev. 22:15 contain in its Greek meaning that may play a primary role in deceiving the nations?

10. What will not be found in Babylon any longer? (Rev. 18:22-23; Is. 24:8; Jer. 7:34; 25:10)

11. Why have plagues specifically fallen upon the once-blessed Protestant United States and its people? (Luke 12:48; Jer. 16:9-12)

12. What is God's promise to His faithful followers during this time? (Jer. 33:10-11; Is. 61:7; Ps. 9:9-10)

# Revelation 19 (KJV)

*¹ And after these things I heard a great voice of much people in heaven, saying, Alleluia; Salvation, and glory, and honour, and power, unto the Lord our God: ² For true and righteous are his judgments: for he hath judged the great whore, which did corrupt the earth with her fornication, and hath avenged the blood of his servants at her hand. ³ And again they said, Alleluia And her smoke rose up for ever and ever. ⁴ And the four and twenty elders and the four beasts fell down and worshipped God that sat on the throne, saying, Amen; Alleluia. ⁵ And a voice came out of the throne, saying, Praise our God, all ye his servants, and ye that fear him, both small and great. ⁶ And I heard as it were the voice of a great multitude, and as the voice of many waters, and as the voice of mighty thunderings, saying, Alleluia: for the Lord God omnipotent reigneth. ⁷ Let us be glad and rejoice, and give honour to him: for the marriage of the Lamb is come, and his wife hath made herself ready. ⁸ And to her was granted that she should be arrayed in fine linen, clean and white: for the fine linen is the righteousness of saints. ⁹ And he saith unto me, Write, Blessed are they which are called unto the marriage supper of the Lamb. And he saith unto me, These are the true sayings of God. ¹⁰ And I fell at his feet to worship him. And he said unto me, See thou do it not: I am thy fellowservant, and of thy brethren that have the testimony of Jesus: worship God: for the testimony of Jesus is the spirit of prophecy. ¹¹ And I saw heaven opened, and behold a white horse; and he that sat upon him was called Faithful and True, and in righteousness he doth judge and make war. ¹² His eyes were as a flame of fire, and on his head were many crowns; and he had a name written, that no man knew, but he himself. ¹³ And he was clothed with a vesture dipped in blood: and his name is called The Word of God. ¹⁴ And the armies which were in heaven followed him upon white horses, clothed in fine linen, white and clean. ¹⁵ And out of his mouth goeth a sharp sword, that with it he should smite the nations: and he shall rule them with a rod of iron: and he treadeth the winepress of the fierceness and wrath of Almighty God. ¹⁶ And he hath on his vesture and on his thigh a name written, King Of Kings, And Lord Of Lords. ¹⁷ And I saw an angel standing in the sun; and he cried with a loud voice, saying to all the fowls that fly in the midst of heaven, Come and gather yourselves together unto the supper of the great God; ¹⁸ That ye may eat the flesh of kings, and the flesh of captains, and the flesh of mighty men, and the flesh of horses, and of them that sit on them, and the flesh of all men, both free and bond, both small and great. ¹⁹ And I saw the beast, and the kings of the earth, and their armies, gathered together to make war against him that sat on the horse, and against his army. ²⁰ And the beast was taken, and with him the false prophet that wrought miracles before him, with which he deceived them that had received the mark of the beast, and them that worshipped his image. These both were cast alive into a lake of fire burning with brimstone. ²¹ And the remnant were slain with the sword of him that sat upon the horse, which sword proceeded out of his mouth: and all the fowls were filled with their flesh.*

# Rescued by the Hero on the White Horse

If you have ever watched an old-fashioned Western, you have probably noticed that invariably the bad guys on black horses are defeated by the gallant, dashing hero riding on a strong white steed. What may be more surprising is that John saw a similar scene at Christ's second coming, and like the old-time movies, the Hero on the white horse arrives just in time to save the day!

During the fall of the United States, the entire world is devastated by the seven last plagues. However, John beheld a great multitude (Rev. 7:9), praising God and saying:

> "Alleluia! Salvation and glory and honor and power belong to the Lord our God! For true and righteous are His judgments, because He has judged the great harlot (the apostate Protestant/Catholic Church) and He has avenged on her the blood of His servants shed by her." (Rev. 19:1-2, NKJV; parenthesis added)

Jesus has honored the cry of the martyrs in the fifth seal, pleading, "How long?" and vindicated their blood and rewarded their great sacrifice (Rev. 6:10). His faithful remnant now rejoice and give the Lord glory for their salvation! As the wicked suffer and die all around them, God's people realize that the "marriage of the Lamb is come, and his wife hath made herself ready" (Rev. 19:7, KJV). The saved have been clothed in the wedding garments of "fine linen" which is Christ's "righteousness" (Rev. 19:8, KJV; 2 Cor. 5:21). Moreover, they have been protected through the great time of trouble because their sins have been confessed, forgiven, and cleansed before the close of probation (I John 1:9; Eph. 5:25-27). The righteous have escaped the terrible plagues unscathed, and not one has perished during their outpouring (Ps. 91:10). Now, at last, Jesus comes to their rescue to take them home with Him!

Then John saw the heavens open. A white horse appeared, "and he that sat upon him was called Faithful and True, and in righteousness he doth judge and make war" (Rev. 19:11, KJV). "And the armies which were in heaven followed him upon white horses, clothed in fine linen, white and clean" (Rev. 19:14, KJV). These white horses are symbolic of Christ's kingdom found in the first seal and specifically refer to the angelic armies of Heaven that will come down to gather the Lord's earthly kingdom of saints (Rev. 6:2; 19:14; Rom. 8:37). Also, the way John describes the white horse's Rider in Revelation 19 is similar to Christ's description outlined in other Bible passages:

> His eyes were like a flame of fire (Rev. 1:14; Dan. 10:6), and on His head were many crowns (representing the conquering of all earthly kingdoms [2 Sam. 12:29-30 compare Ps. 132:17-18]). He had a name written that no one knew except Himself. He was clothed with a robe dipped in blood (Is. 63:2-6), and His name is called, "The Word of God (John 1:1, 14)... Now out of His mouth goes a sharp sword, that with it He should strike the nations (God's Word [Rev. 1:16; Heb. 4:12]). And He Himself will rule them with a rod of iron (Ps. 2:8-9).... And He has on His robe and on His thigh a name written: King of Kings and Lord of Lords. (Rev. 19:12–13, 15-16, NKJV; parentheses added)

This magnificent description of Jesus echos the beginning of John's vision and illustrates Christ's words when He declares: "I am the Alpha and Omega, the beginning and the end, the first and the last" (Rev. 22:13; 1:13-18, KJV). Jesus is truly the "author and finisher" of our faith! (Heb. 12:2, KJV). "He which hath begun a good work in you" will be faithful to complete it! (Phil. 1:6, KJV). Christ has come back to the earth, not in humility as He did the first time when He gave His life for man's salvation, but this time, as the mighty King in all His magnificence with a host of heavenly angels at His side: "When the Son of man shall come in his glory, and all the holy angels with him, then shall he sit upon the throne of his glory" (Matt. 25:31, KJV).

The Bible describes Christ's second coming as a literal event in the heavens that is like lightning, flashing from the east to the west (Matt. 24:27). Interestingly, He returns in the *same manner as He left* (Acts 1:9-11), coming in the sky *with clouds* (Rev. 1:7, KJV). His feet never touch the Earth at His second coming, and the saints will meet Him *in the air* (I Thess. 4:17, KJV). Moreover, the Lord returns with *a body of flesh and bones,* not just in spirit (Luke 24:36-43, 50-51). The Bible also states that His return is *loud:* "For the Lord himself shall descend from heaven with a *shout,* with the *voice* of the archangel, and with the *trump of God*" (I Thess. 4:16, KJV; italics added). It is not a secret! Every living being will see Jesus returning in the sky: "Behold, he cometh with clouds, and *every eye shall see him…* and all kindreds of the earth shall wail because of him" (Rev. 1:7, KJV; compare Matt. 24:30; 26:64; 1 Thess. 4:17; italics added). Therefore, Christ's coming in the heavens is *literal, loud,* and *visible* to everyone on Earth, including the saints and the wicked.

In one last desperate attempt, the beast (the united world nations under satanic power), the kings of the earth (specifically the

U.S. leaders), and the world's armies gather to make war with Christ and His heavenly hosts (Rev. 19:19). However, they are destined to fall helplessly at His Word: "… the Lord shall consume with the spirit of his mouth and shall destroy with the brightness of his coming" (2 Thess. 2:8, KJV), and "… he shall smite the earth with the rod of his mouth, and with the breath of his lips shall he slay the wicked" (Is. 11:4, KJV).

The beast (the united world nations) and the false prophet (apostate Christianity) are then captured and "cast alive into a lake of fire burning with brimstone" (Rev. 19:20, KJV). These lost souls who have received the mark of the beast (mandated false worship) are not able to bear to look upon the face of the One who "treadeth the winepress of the fierceness and wrath of the Almighty God" (Rev. 19:15, KJV). They are part of the "sorcerers and sexually immoral and murderers and idolaters, and whoever loves and practices a lie" (Rev. 22:15, NKJV). Jesus, Himself, speaks of this judgment against lawbreakers: "… so it will be at the end of the age. The Son of Man will send out His angels, and they will gather out of His kingdom, all things that offend, and those who practice *lawlessness* and will cast them in the furnace of fire" (Matt. 13:40-42, NKJV; italics added).

Sadly, the wicked have ignored the Ten Commandments and the warning that Christ is coming quickly to "give to everyone according to his works" (Rev. 22:12, NKJV). Therefore, as a tragic result, these lost souls are slain by the sword (God's Word [Heb. 4:12]) which proceeds from the mouth of Him who sat on the horse (Rev. 19:15), and their dead bodies are left unburied for the birds to eat (Rev. 19:17-21; Eze. 39:17-20). The righteous, not the wicked, are promised eternal life, so the wicked do not burn forever (John 3:36; 5:24; 6:40, 47). Instead, they simply perish, according to John 3:16 (KJV): "For God so loved the world that he gave his only begotten Son, that whosoever believeth in him should not *perish,* but have everlasting life" (compare Ps. 37:20; 92:9; Prov. 10:28-29; Is. 26:14). God is merciful, even to the lost, and His everlasting love is manifested in the wicked's complete destruction. The prophet, Jeremiah, describes their demise at Christ's second coming by stating:

> And the slain of the Lord shall be at that day from one end of the earth even unto the other end of the earth: they shall not be lamented, neither gathered, nor buried; *they shall be dung upon the ground.* (Jer. 25:33, KJV; compare Is. 24:1-3; italics added)

The wicked have refused Christ's wedding garment of righteousness by rejecting God's holy law (Rev. 19:8; KJV; Matt. 22:11-13). They have repeatedly ignored Christ's gracious invitation: "And the Spirit and the bride say, 'Come!' And let him who thirsts come" (Rev. 22:17, NKJV). So, the Lord simply honors their final decision to separate themselves forever from the Source of Life, and they are utterly destroyed (Is. 34:2-3).

In contrast, the righteous dead are resurrected and rise in the clouds to meet their Lord in the sky with the faithful remnant alive on the earth:

> For the Lord himself shall descend from heaven… and the dead in Christ shall rise first. Then we which are alive… shall be caught up together with them in the clouds, to meet the Lord in the air: and so shall we ever be with the Lord. (I Thess. 4:16-17, KJV)

Along with the righteous living, the resurrected have glorified bodies like Christ: "We also eagerly wait for … the Lord Jesus Christ, who will transform our lowly body that it may be conformed to His glorious body" (Phil. 3:20-21, NKJV); "… we shall

all be changed ... and the dead shall be raised incorruptible... For ... this mortal must put on immortality" (I Cor. 15:51-53, KJV). Both the resurrected and the living saints will sing praises to Jesus as they hear His voice roll like thunder throughout the heavens (Job 40:9). With a great shout, they cry, "Alleluia: for the Lord God Omnipotent reigneth! Let us be glad and rejoice, and give honour to him: for the marriage of the Lamb is come, and His wife hath made herself ready" (Rev. 19:6-7, KJV). At last, those who have kept God's commandments through the power of the Holy Spirit "may have the right to the tree of life" (Rev. 22:14; compare Heb. 8:10). They hear the Lord's words, "Well done, thou good and faithful servant; thou hast been faithful over a few things, I will make thee ruler over many things; enter thou into the joy of thy lord" (Matt. 25:21, KJV). What a glorious day!

At last, all of God's people receive rest from their battle with evil, similar to the rest God gives on the Sabbath during Creation's weekly cycle (Gen. 2:1-3). The war with Satan and his followers has raged upon the earth for approximately 6,000 years,[262] but at Christ's return, the seventh millennium begins. The saints reign in Heaven with Jesus during this time, while the wicked are dead, and Satan and his angels wander the desolate earth, alone (Rev. 20:6; further explained in the next chapter). Since a thousand years is as one day to God (2 Pet. 3:8; Ps. 90:4), Christ will have completed His work of redemption of mankind in six "heavenly" days (6,000 years), and on the seventh "day" (millennium), the "Sabbath" rest will begin for His saints in Heaven. Furthermore, God's redemption of mankind will be memorialized each weekly Sabbath as the saints worship before the Lord (Is. 66:23). Therefore, today we have the privilege of honoring Christ's seventh-day Sabbath as we look forward to celebrating

---

[262] https://www.icr.org/biblical-age

it each week in Heaven when our Hero on the white horse comes to take us home!

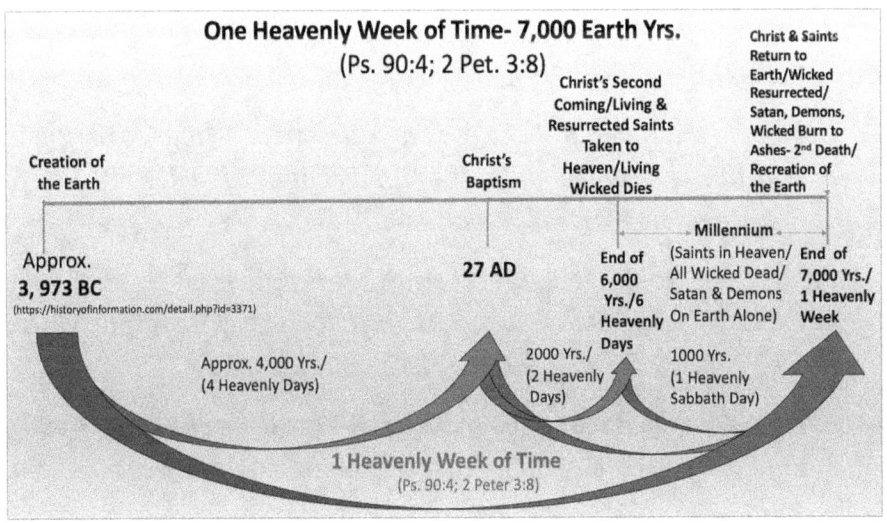

# Discussion Questions for Revelation 19

1. What is the "marriage of the Lamb?" (Rev.19:7-9; 21:2-3; Eph. 5:25-27)

2. How is the Rider of the white horse described? How do we know that this is a symbol of Jesus and His kingdom? (Rev. 19:11-16; 6:2; Rom. 8:37; 1:13-16; John 1:1, 14)

3. How is Christ's return to the earth different from the first time He came? Why is the name, "Alpha and Omega" so fitting? (Rev. 19:11, 16; 1:8, 18; 22:12-13; Heb. 12:2; Phil. 1:6)

4. How does the Bible tell us that Christ's second coming is a literal, loud, and visible event? (Luke 24:39, 51; Acts 1:9-11; I Thess. 4:16; Matt. 24:27; Rev. 1:7)

5. How are the wicked destroyed at Christ's second coming? Who specifically is named as being lost and destroyed in the fire? (Rev. 19:18-21; 2 Thess. 2:8; Is. 11:4)

6. Why are the wicked lost, and what becomes of them? (Rev. 19:15, 20-21; 22:12; Matt. 13:40-42; Jer. 25:33; Is. 34:2-3)

7. Why are God's people ready for the coming of Jesus? (Rev. 19:6-8, KJV; Rev. 22:14; Heb. 8:10; Matt. 25:21)

8. What happens to the righteous dead at the second coming of Christ? (1 Thess. 4:16-17; Phil. 3:20-21; 1 Cor. 15:51-54)

9. How is God's Sabbath rest for His people manifested, both now and in Heaven? (Gen. 2:1-3; Rev. 20:6; Ps. 90:4; Is. 66:23)

# Revelation 20

*¹And I saw an angel come down from heaven, having the key of the bottomless pit and a great chain in his hand. ²And he laid hold on the dragon, that old serpent, which is the Devil, and Satan, and bound him a thousand years, ³And cast him into the bottomless pit, and shut him up, and set a seal upon him, that he should deceive the nations no more, till the thousand years should be fulfilled: and after that he must be loosed a little season. ⁴And I saw thrones, and they sat upon them, and judgment was given unto them: and I saw the souls of them that were beheaded for the witness of Jesus, and for the word of God, and which had not worshipped the beast, neither his image, neither had received his mark upon their foreheads, or in their hands; and they lived and reigned with Christ a thousand years. ⁵But the rest of the dead lived not again until the thousand years were finished. This is the first resurrection. ⁶Blessed and holy is he that hath part in the first resurrection: on such the second death hath no power, but they shall be priests of God and of Christ, and shall reign with him a thousand years. ⁷And when the thousand years are expired, Satan shall be loosed out of his prison, ⁸And shall go out to deceive the nations which are in the four quarters of the earth, Gog, and Magog, to gather them together to battle: the number of whom is as the sand of the sea. ⁹And they went up on the breadth of the earth, and compassed the camp of the saints about, and the beloved city: and fire came down from God out of heaven, and devoured them. ¹⁰And the devil that deceived them was cast into the lake of fire and brimstone, where the beast and the false prophet are, and shall be tormented day and night for ever and ever. ¹¹ And I saw a great white throne, and him that sat on it, from whose face the earth and the heaven fled away; and there was found no place for them. ¹² And I saw the dead, small and great, stand before God; and the books were opened: and another book was opened, which is the book of life: and the dead were judged out of those things which were written in the books, according to their works. ¹³ And the sea gave up the dead which were in it; and death and hell delivered up the dead which were in them: and they were judged every man according to their works. ¹⁴ And death and hell were cast into the lake of fire. This is the second death. ¹⁵ And whosoever was not found written in the book of life was cast into the lake of fire.*

# The Dragon Chained

Throughout history, prisoners have been tethered to heavy metal balls so that they could not escape. How terrible it would be to lose your freedom to a ball and chain! However, freedom can also be lost through a "chain" of circumstances. Interestingly, this kind of bondage is similar to what John beheld happening to the dragon in his vision:

> And I saw an angel come down from heaven, having a great chain in his hand. And he laid hold of the dragon, that old serpent, which is called the Devil, and Satan, and bound him a thousand years. (Rev. 20:1-2, KJV)

From the preceding verses in chapter 19, this event occurs soon after Jesus, who possesses the master "key" of authority, returns and destroys the wicked upon the earth, the "bottomless pit" (Is. 24:1, 3, 21-22; Matt. 16:19). Satan is bound by a figurative "chain" of circumstances because there is no one left in the world to tempt (Rev. 20:3; 19:20-21; 2 Peter 2:4; Jude 1:6). He is sealed for a thousand years ("*etos,*" meaning a literal year) by being left to wander the desolate earth with his demons, empty of humanity (Rev. 20:3; Is. 9:19; 24:1-3). All of the wicked have perished by the fire of Christ's breath at His second coming (Rev. 19:15; 2 Thess. 1:8-9; Ps. 68:2), and the unsaved dead are left in their graves until after the thousand years are expired (Rev. 20:3, 7).

During Satan and his demons' thousand-year proverbial "time-out" on the earth, both the resurrected righteous and the faithful remnant who were alive at Christ's second coming enjoy the splendors of Heaven. However, they are not idle, for each of them has a specific work to do: "… they shall be priests of God and of Christ" (Rev. 20:6, KJV). John beheld these saints upon thrones, "and *judgment was given unto them…* and they lived and reigned with Christ for a thousand years" (Rev. 20:4, KJV). Throughout this time, the righteous vindicate God's verdict for the Devil and his wicked followers and confirm their punishment (Dan. 7:22, KJV). The apostle, Paul, speaks of this work by stating: "Do you not know that the saints shall judge the world?… Know ye not know that we shall judge angels?" (I Cor. 6:2-3, KJV). The saints must understand that God's ways are just and true to ensure that rebellion never occurs a second time (Rev. 15:3; Nahum 1:9). John describes this heavenly judgment by the saints: "And I saw the dead, small and great, stand before God…. And the dead were judged out of those things which were written in the books, according to their works" (Rev. 20:12, KJV). By the end of the thousand years, all the saints will come to the same conclusion—Jesus, in His great love for mankind, had done everything He possibly could to save lost humanity! Everyone had made their final decision for or against God, and Christ had simply honored their choice of eternal life or death (Rom 6:23).

At the close of the thousand years when the saints' task of judgment is completed, John saw the heavenly hosts with God's people descending to Earth in the New Jerusalem (Rev. 21:2; 20:3, 5). At this time, the wicked are resurrected, and Satan is released from his circumstantial bondage and goes out to deceive them (Rev. 20:7-8; compare Is. 24:22). He gathers the lost for battle from the four corners of the earth; then they surround the New

Jerusalem, planning a last-ditch attack against Christ and His kingdom (Rev. 20:9). However, before the battle can begin, every knee is forced to bow, and every tongue confesses that Jesus Christ is Lord (Rom. 14:11; Phil. 2:10-11). Then fire from God out of Heaven devours them (Rev. 20:9, KJV). The "cowardly, unbelieving, abominable, murderers, sexually immoral, sorcerers, idolaters, and all liars" are cast into the lake of fire and brimstone (Rev. 21:8, NKJV), including the Devil and his angels whom the lake of fire was primarily intended (Matt. 25:41; Rev. 20:10).

They are "tormented day and night for ever and ever" as they are consumed by fire, some suffering longer "according to their works" (Rev. 20:10, 13, KJV; 2 Thess. 1:9; Obadiah 15). The Greek word, *"aion,"* translated as *"for ever"* in this text, means *"end of an age"* or a specific *"period of time."* The Bible states, "Let the sinners be *consumed* out of the earth," and "… the wicked shall *be no more*" (Ps. 104:35, KJV; 37:10; italics added). Additionally, the Lord mercifully proclaims that the lost "shall be as nothing" and "perish," "as though they had never been" (Is. 41:11, KJV; Obadiah 16). In fact, the Bible compares the destruction of Satan and his hosts to Sodom and Gomorrah who suffered "the vengeance of *eternal fire"* (Jude 7, KJV; Gen. 19:24, 28-29; italics added). These two cities burned for a period of time until nothing more was left to burn, and they became ashes (2 Peter 2:6; Ps. 37:20). God's Word verifies that Satan, his angels, and "all that do wickedly shall be stubble," leaving "them neither root nor branch;" they shall be *"ashes under the soles of your feet"* (Mal. 4:1, 3, KJV; Eze. 28:18-19; italics added).

Because God, alone, is immortal (1 Tim. 1:17; 6:15-16), and the righteous, not the wicked, are promised eternal life (Jn. 3:16; I Cor. 15:52-54), no immortal sinners are burning forever in hell;

instead, the wicked perish (Ps. 9:3). The apostle Peter describes this final destruction: the "elements shall melt with fervent heat, the earth also and the works that are therein shall be *burned up*" (2 Peter 3:10, KJV). The fire cleanses the earth from all traces of sin so that it can be recreated into its original Edenic state (Rev. 21:1; Is. 66:22; 2 Pet. 3:12-13). Only after sin and sinners are completely gone can God wipe away all tears; Christ's wonderful promise will, at last, be fulfilled: "… no more death, neither sorrow, nor crying, neither shall there be any more pain, *for the former things are passed away*"—FOREVER! (Rev. 21:4, KJV).

# Discussion Questions for Revelation 20

1. How is Satan bound by a "chain" of circumstances for a literal thousand-year period? (Rev. 20:1-3; 2 Peter 2:4; Jude 1:6)

2. What is the condition of the world throughout the thousand years following Christ's second coming? (Rev. 20:1; Is. 24:1, 3)

3. What has happened to all the wicked that were alive at Christ's coming? (Rev. 19:20-21; 2 Thess. 1:8-9; Ps. 68:2)

4. Why must the saints participate in the judgment process? (Rev. 20:4; 15:3; Rom. 14:11; Phil. 2:10-11; Nahum 1:9)

5. What happens to the resurrected wicked, the Devil, and his angels at the end of the thousand years? (Rev. 20:3, 5, 7-10; 21:8; Matt. 25:41)

6. How are Sodom and Gomorrah an example of "the vengeance of eternal fire?" (Jude 6-7; Jer. 49:18; 2 Peter 2:6)

7. How does the Bible confirm that the wicked, the Devil, and his angels are completely destroyed in the lake of fire and do not keep burning forever in hell? (Rev. 20:9; Ps. 104:35; 37:10; Mal. 4:1, 3)

8. What is the result of the "lake of fire" upon the earth's surface? (2 Pet. 3:10-13; Rev. 21:1; Ps. 104:30)

9. What are God's promises to His faithful people during this time? (Rev. 7:17; 21:4; Is. 25:8; 35:10; 65:17-19)

# Revelation 21 (KJV)

[1] *And I saw a new heaven and a new earth: for the first heaven and the first earth were passed away; and there was no more sea.* [2] *And I John saw the holy city, new Jerusalem, coming down from God out of heaven, prepared as a bride adorned for her husband.* [3] *And I heard a great voice out of heaven saying, Behold, the tabernacle of God is with men, and he will dwell with them, and they shall be his people, and God himself shall be with them, and be their God.* [4] *And God shall wipe away all tears from their eyes; and there shall be no more death, neither sorrow, nor crying, neither shall there be any more pain: for the former things are passed away.* [5] *And he that sat upon the throne said, Behold, I make all things new. And he said unto me, Write: for these words are true and faithful.* [6] *And he said unto me, It is done. I am Alpha and Omega, the beginning and the end. I will give unto him that is athirst of the fountain of the water of life freely.* [7] *He that overcometh shall inherit all things; and I will be his God, and he shall be my son.* [8] *But the fearful, and un-believing, and the abominable, and murderers, and whoremongers, and sorcerers, and idolaters, and all liars, shall have their part in the lake which burneth with fire and brimstone: which is the second death.* [9] *And there came unto me one of the seven angels which had the seven vials full of the seven last plagues, and talked with me, saying, Come hither, I will shew thee the bride, the Lamb's wife.* [10] *And he carried me away in the spirit to a great and high mountain, and shewed me that great city, the holy Jerusalem, descending out of heaven from God,* [11] *Having*

the glory of God: and her light was like unto a stone most precious, even like a jasper stone, clear as crystal; <sup>12</sup> And had a wall great and high, and had twelve gates, and at the gates twelve angels, and names written thereon, which are the names of the twelve tribes of the children of Israel: <sup>13</sup> On the east three gates; on the north three gates; on the south three gates; and on the west three gates. <sup>14</sup> And the wall of the city had twelve foundations, and in them the names of the twelve apostles of the Lamb. <sup>15</sup> And he that talked with me had a golden reed to measure the city, and the gates thereof, and the wall thereof. <sup>16</sup> And the city lieth foursquare, and the length is as large as the breadth: and he measured the city with the reed, twelve thousand furlongs. The length and the breadth and the height of it are equal. <sup>17</sup> And he measured the wall thereof, an hundred and forty and four cubits, according to the measure of a man, that is, of the angel. <sup>18</sup> And the building of the wall of it was of jasper: and the city was pure gold, like unto clear glass. <sup>19</sup> And the foundations of the wall of the city were garnished with all manner of precious stones. The first foundation was jasper; the second, sapphire; the third, a chalcedony; the fourth, an emerald; <sup>20</sup> The fifth, sardonyx; the sixth, sardius; the seventh, chrysolyte; the eighth, beryl; the ninth, a topaz; the tenth, a chrysoprasus; the eleventh, a jacinth; the twelfth, an amethyst. <sup>21</sup> And the twelve gates were twelve pearls: every several gate was of one pearl: and the street of the city was pure gold, as it were transparent glass. <sup>22</sup> And I saw no temple therein: for the Lord God Almighty and the Lamb are the temple of it. <sup>23</sup> And the city had no need of the sun, neither of the moon, to shine in it: for the glory of God did lighten it, and the Lamb is the light thereof. <sup>24</sup> And the nations of them which are saved shall walk in the light of it: and the kings of the earth do bring their glory and honour into it. <sup>25</sup> And the gates of it shall not be shut at all by day: for there shall be no night there. <sup>26</sup> And they shall bring the glory and honour of the nations into it. <sup>27</sup> And there shall in no wise enter into it any thing that defileth, neither whatsoever worketh abomination, or maketh a lie: but they which are written in the Lamb's book of life.

# All Things New

Have you ever tried to imagine what it would be like to live in an ideal world—a world full of joy and harmony beyond your wildest imagination? John must have held his breath as he saw the desolate, dark earth recreated back into its original dazzling beauty and complete perfection (Rev. 21:1; Is. 66:22). In admiration, he likely gazed awestruck at the new Heaven and new Earth (Rev. 21:2, 9-10; Is. 61:10-11). There was no more sea (Rev. 21:1) because sin had been cast "into the depths of the sea" (Micah 7:19, KJV), and affliction would never again "rise up the second time" (Nahum 1:9, KJV). Nothing abominable remained (Rev. 21:8, 27). Moreover, God promises, "... behold, I create new heavens and a new earth: and the former shall not be remembered, nor come into mind" (Is. 65:17, KJV; compare 2 Peter 3:10-13).

Then, John saw the New Jerusalem coming down out of Heaven "as a bride adorned for her husband" (Rev. 21:2, 9-10, KJV; compare Is. 61:10). It shone with the glory of God, and the city's gates, wall, and foundation sparkled, clear as crystal (Rev. 21:11). Twelve angels sat at its twelve gates. Each gate was inscribed with the name of one of the twelve tribes of Israel, each tribe equaling 12,000, which totals 144,000 (Rev. 21:12; 7:5-8). Three gates faced east, three faced north, three faced south, and three faced west—twelve gates total (Rev. 21:13). Likewise, the city's wall had twelve foundations, each with the name of the twelve apostles (Rev. 21:14). Paul further describes this foundation in Ephesians 2:19-22 (KJV):

> Now therefore, ye are no more strangers and foreigners, but fellowcitizens with the saints, and of the household of God; And are *built upon the foundation of the apostles and prophets, Jesus Christ himself being the chief corner stone;* In whom all the building fitly framed together growth unto an holy temple in the Lord: *In whom ye also are builded together for an habitation place of God through the Spirit.* (italics added)

Therefore, the New Jerusalem will not only be a literal city, but it is also a symbol of God's people, built on the teachings of the apostles, prophets, and Christ, Himself (Heb. 12:22-24).

The beauty of this glorious city will be like none other! John saw all kinds of precious stones sparkling in its foundation: the first layer was jasper, the second, sapphire, the third, a chalcedony, the fourth, an emerald, the fifth, sardonyx, the sixth, sardius, the seventh, chrysolite, the eighth, beryl, the ninth, a topaz, the tenth, a chrysoprasus, the eleventh, a jacinth, and the twelfth, an amethyst (Rev. 21:19-20). In comparison, these jewels were similar to the stones that were on the high priest's breastplate in the Old Testament which represented the twelve tribes of Israel (Ex. 28:15, 17-21). Moreover, each gate was made of one giant pearl (Rev. 21:21), and the city's golden streets glistened as clear as glass (Rev. 21:21). Also, a crystal river flowed from God's throne, and on each of its sides, the tree of life bore twelve fruits, a different fruit each month for the saints to enjoy (Rev. 2:7; 22:1-2; Eze. 47:12). Inside the city, the righteous, called God's jewels, lived in dazzling mansions (Mal. 3:17; Jn, 14:1-3). All in all, the New Jerusalem was beyond description!

As John watched, an angel measured the city, its gates, and its wall. Perfectly laid out in a square, the New Jerusalem covered 12,000 furlongs (about 1,500 miles/375 miles on each side [Rev. 21:16]). Additionally, its jasper wall was 144 cubits (216 feet [Rev. 21:18]) "according to the measure of a man, that is, of the angel (*"angelos"= "messenger"* [Rev. 21:17, KJV]). These figures are similar to the 144,000 leaders of the living who were saved when Christ returned to Earth (Rev. 7:4, 14:1). Furthermore, this measuring may represent the completion and reward of the judgment (Rev. 11:1; Matt. 7:2). The prophet Zechariah states:

> Then I raised my eyes... and behold, a man with a measuring line in his hand. So I said, "Where are you going?" And he said... "To measure Jerusalem, to see what is its width and what is its length.... Jerusalem shall be inhabited... 'For I,' says the Lord, 'will be a wall of fire all around her, and I will be the glory in her midst.'" (Zech. 2:1-5, NKJV)

God's splendor will encompass His saints, who have been "measured," or judged righteous through Christ, and His glorious presence will be their best reward!

In fact, there is no need for a temple there because the presence of the "Lord God Almighty and the Lamb are the temple of it" (Rev. 21:22, KJV). Also, the city will require no illuminance of the sun or moon (although they will likely still shine [Is. 24:23]) because its light radiates from the glory of the Lamb (Rev. 21:23; Is. 60:19-20). Also, no darkness will ever descend upon the new Jerusalem because there is no night, and the gates are left open for all to enjoy the presence of the "Sun of Righteousness" (Rev. 21:25; 22:5; Zech. 2:4; Mal. 4:2). The Lord's glory will constantly shine, radiating His magnificent grace to His beloved: "Behold, the tabernacle of God is with men, and he will dwell with them, and they shall be his people, and God himself shall be with them, and be their God" (Rev. 21:3, KJV; 2 Cor. 6:16; Eze. 37:27).

The reward of the righteous is more splendid than anyone can imagine! Jesus promises that there will be no more death, sorrow, crying, or pain (Rev. 21:4; Is. 25:8; 65:17-19); all the universe is in perfect harmony under God's holy law (Rev. 22:14; Is. 119:142-144; Rom 7:12). Each Sabbath the saints will come to worship the Lord and cast their crowns at His feet in humble adoration (Is. 66:23). Only the scars on Christ's hands and side will remain as a constant reminder of the costly price of salvation (Is. 49:16). God's love will forever unfold! Truly, the Lord will fulfill His promise: "Eye hath not seen, nor ear heard, neither have entered into the heart of man, the things which God hath prepared for them that love him" (I Cor. 2:9, KJV)

# Discussion Questions for Revelation 21

1. *How are Heaven and Earth described? Why is there "no more sea?" (Rev. 21:1; Is. 65:17-19; 66:22; Micah 7:19)*

2. *What promise is given to God's people concerning the eradication of sin? (Nahum 1:9; Is. 65:17; 2 Peter 3:10, 13; Rev. 22:3)*

3. *What are the New Jerusalem and its occupants compared to? Why do you think the Lord chose to describe His people in this way? (Rev. 21:2, 9-10; Is. 61:10)*

4. *What will NOT be present in this city forevermore? (Rev. 21:8, 27; 22:15)*

5. *How is the New Jerusalem described? What is most striking to you? (Rev. 21:10-21)*

6. *To what is the measurement of the New Jerusalem similar? (Rev. 21:16-17; 7:4)*

7. *What could "according to the measure of a man" possibly symbolize? (Rev. 21:17; 11:1; Matt. 7:2; Zech. 2:1-2)*

8. *Why is there no need for a temple in the New Jerusalem? (Rev. 21:3, 22; 2 Cor. 6:16)*

9. *Why will there be no night or darkness in this holy city? (Rev. 21:23-26; 22:5; Mal. 4:2)*

10. *By what standard shall the righteous live throughout eternity, and how is this exemplified on each Sabbath? (Rev. 22:14; Ps. 119:142-144; Rom 7:12; Is. 66:23)*

11. *What promise are we given concerning our life in the New Jerusalem? What will be the only reminder of sin? (Rev. 21:4; Is. 49:16; 65:19; 1 Cor. 2:9)*

12. *What is the best part of living on the new earth? What are those who overcome promised? (Rev. 21:3, 7; 3:21)*

# Revelation 22 (KJV)

*¹ And he shewed me a pure river of water of life, clear as crystal, proceeding out of the throne of God and of the Lamb. ² In the midst of the street of it, and on either side of the river, was there the tree of life, which bare twelve manner of fruits, and yielded her fruit every month: and the leaves of the tree were for the healing of the nations. ³ And there shall be no more curse: but the throne of God and of the Lamb shall be in it; and his servants shall serve him: ⁴ And they shall see his face; and his name shall be in their foreheads. ⁵ And there shall be no night there; and they need no candle, neither light of the sun; for the Lord God giveth them light: and they shall reign for ever and ever. ⁶ And he said unto me, These sayings are faithful and true: and the Lord God of the holy prophets sent his angel to shew unto his servants the things which must shortly be done. ⁷ Behold, I come quickly: blessed is he that keepeth the sayings of the prophecy of this book. ⁸ And I John saw these things, and heard them. And when I had heard and seen, I fell down to worship before the feet of the angel which shewed me these things. ⁹ Then saith he unto me, See thou do it not: for I am thy fellowservant, and of thy brethren the prophets, and of them which keep the sayings of this book: worship God. ¹⁰ And he saith unto me, Seal not the sayings of the prophecy of this book: for the time is at hand. ¹¹ He that is unjust, let him be unjust still: and he which is filthy, let him be filthy still: and he that is righteous, let him be righteous still: and he that is holy, let him be holy still. ¹² And, behold, I come quickly; and my reward is with me, to give every man according as his work shall be.* <sup>13</sup> *I am Alpha and Omega, the beginning and the end, the first and the last.* <sup>14</sup> *Blessed are they that do his commandments, that they may have right to the tree of life, and may enter in through the gates into the city.* <sup>15</sup> *For without are dogs, and sorcerers, and whoremongers, and murderers, and idolaters, and whosoever loveth and maketh a lie.* <sup>16</sup> *I Jesus have sent mine angel to testify unto you these things in the churches. I am the root and the offspring of David, and the bright and morning star.* <sup>17</sup> *And the Spirit and the bride say, Come. And let him that heareth say, Come. And let him that is athirst come. And whosoever will, let him take the water of life freely.* <sup>18</sup> *For I testify unto every man that heareth the words of the prophecy of this book, If any man shall add unto these things, God shall add unto him the plagues that are written in this book:* <sup>19</sup> *And if any man shall take away from the words of the book of this prophecy, God shall take away his part out of the book of life, and out of the holy city, and from the things which are written in this book.* <sup>20</sup> *He which testifieth these things saith, Surely I come quickly. Amen. Even so, come, Lord Jesus.* <sup>21</sup> *The grace of our Lord Jesus Christ be with you all. Amen.*

# Come, Lord Jesus!

Do you remember in preschool how excited you were when you could recite the entire alphabet from A to Z, and then, many years later, how much more thrilled you were the day you graduated from high school or college? All of us can relate to beginnings and endings, firsts and lasts. As John's vision of the ending of Earth's history and the beginning of eternity faded from his sight, an angel declared that God's Word is "faithful and true," and these prophecies would "shortly come to pass" (Rev. 22:6; compare 1:1, 3, KJV).

John must have listened with rapt attention as Christ, Himself, proclaimed, "I am the Alpha (A) and Omega (Z), the beginning and the end, the first and the last" (Rev. 22:13, KJV; compare Rev. 21:6; parentheses added). Amazingly, both the book of Revelation and the entire Bible illustrate this circular truth! For example, at the beginning of John's vision, he heard similar words in Revelation 1:8: "I am the Alpha and the Omega, the Beginning and the End, says the Lord, who is and who was and who is to come." Moreover, within chapter 22 of Revelation itself, John began by seeing living water coming out of the throne of God and the Lamb (Rev. 22:1) and ended his vision by referencing this same water, "... let him who thirsts come. Whoever desires, let him take the water of life freely" (Rev. 22:17, NKJV; compare Rev. 21:6). Additionally, the Creation story of Genesis 1 is repeated at the end of Revelation when Jesus recreates the earth, restoring man's access to the tree of life (Rev. 21:1 compare to Gen. 1:1; Gen. 3:24 compare to Rev. 2:7; 22:14). These examples simply illustrate how God's handiwork is completed, and the plan of salvation is perfectly fulfilled from beginning to end!

All of the Godhead—the Father, the Son, and the Holy Spirit—have had an important role from start to finish in the redemption of mankind. The Trinity can be seen in the last chapter of Revelation in verses 1 and 17 which refer to the "throne of God (the Father) and of the Lamb" (Jesus [Rev. 22:1]), and the "Spirit" who says, "Come" (Rev. 22:17, KJV). Additionally, at the beginning of the book of Revelation, the "seven Spirits," (the Holy Spirit's work through the seven churches), Jesus Christ, and God the Father are also present (Rev. 1:4-6). Likewise, in the story of Creation in Genesis 1, the Trinity's roles are exemplified by the "Spirit of God moved upon the face of the waters" (Gen. 1:2), and the Lord saying, "Let *us* make man in *our* image" (Gen. 1:26, KJV). Furthermore, the apostle, Paul, clarifies that both the Father and the Son played a vital part in the creation of this world (Heb. 1:1-3; compare John 1:1-3). Therefore, all of the Godhead have been working since creation for the restoration of mankind!

Specifically, the third person of the Trinity, the Holy Spirit, helps us today to understand and apply Bible prophecy by guiding us "into all truth" and telling us "things to come" (John 16:13, KJV). This is important because "no prophecy of the scripture is of any private interpretation" (2 Peter 1:20, KJV ). Christ closes the book of Revelation with this warning:

> If any man shall add unto these things, God shall add unto him the plagues that are written in this book: And if any man shall take away from the words of the book of this

prophecy, God shall take away his part out of the book of life, and out of the holy city, and from the things which are written in this book. (Rev. 22:18-19, KJV)

Therefore, we must come humbly to the Lord in prayer, seeking *His* wisdom, not our own, when we study Bible prophecy! Fortunately, we are assured that through the Holy Spirit's guidance and carefully comparing scripture with scripture (Is. 28:9-10; I Cor. 2:12-13), we don't need to be afraid of studying the truths found in the book of Revelation. In fact, the Lord promises to reward our search by saying, "Behold, I am coming quickly: *blessed* is he that keepeth the sayings of the prophecy of this book..." (Rev. 22:7, KJV; Rev. 1:3). By asking daily for the Holy Spirit's leading, we can study and heed the counsel specifically written in this book (Jn. 16:13).

Additionally, God's Word reveals that all true prophecy centers around Jesus (Rev. 19:10; I Cor. 1:4-8), and His ability to give all who ask Him power to keep His commandments through the Holy Spirit (I John 3:22, 24). Because of this work, Christ's name is written on His people's foreheads (Rev. 22:4), and we will "be like him" and "see him as he is" (I Jn. 3:2, KJV). Jesus promises, "And, behold, I am coming quickly; and My reward is with Me, to give to every one according to his work" (Rev. 22:12, NKJV). "Blessed are they who do his commandments, that they may have right to the tree of life, and may enter in through the gates into the city" (Rev. 22:14, KJV; compare Rev. 12:17; 14:12; 1 Peter 1:15-17). Moreover, He promises that He will keep us from falling and present us faultless before His presence with exceeding joy (Jude 1:24). Furthermore, the Lord is both the "Root and the Offspring of David" (fulfillment of the OT prophecies of the Messiah) and the "Bright and Morning Star" (the NT Savior [Rev. 22:16; 2:28; Rev. 5:5; Is. 11:1]). Therefore, throughout all of history and eternity, He is both the "author and finisher of our faith" (Heb. 12:2, KJV).

Overwhelmed at such amazing love, John falls at the foot of the angel showing him these marvelous truths but is quickly told to worship God and God alone (Rev. 22:8-9). Interestingly, angels are symbolized as "stars" in Revelation 1:20. Therefore, John was instructed not to worship "stars." This instruction is relevant for us living today, as well. How much time is spent "worshipping" Hollywood stars instead of worshipping God? (especially since the Bible states that God's people are the true stars! [Dan. 12:3]). Satan is quite pleased when this type of idolatry is rampant! Ultimately, the Devil is the author of all false worship, coveting homage from the very beginning when he boldly declared:

> "I will exalt my throne above the *stars of God*. I will sit also upon the mount of the congregation in the sides of the north: I will ascend above the heights of the clouds; I will be like the most High." (Is. 14:13-14, KJV; italics added)

However, worship belongs to God alone (Ex. 34:14), not to people, or even "stars" (angels) like Satan (Matt. 4:10; 2 Cor. 11:14). One does not want to be found in the Devil's kingdom among the "dogs (outcasts of Israel [Is. 56:8-11; Matt. 15:24-27]) and sorcerers (compare Rev. 9:21; 18:23) and sexually immoral (Rev. 21:8; Heb. 13:4) and murderers and idolaters, and whoever loves and practices a lie" (Rev. 22:15, NKJV; parentheses added). In fact, the entire theme of Revelation centers on the idea of whom to worship—God or Satan. It is the theme of the great controversy, and like Joshua of old, we are counseled, "Choose for yourselves this day whom you will serve" (Josh. 24:15, NKJV).

If you would like to choose to give your life to Christ or recommit it today, why not pray this simple prayer right now?

*Dear Jesus,*

*Please fill me with the Holy Spirit so that I might apply the truths of Your Word to my life. Help me understand Your prophecies so I will not be deceived! Please forgive my sins, and give me the power to obey Your commandments. Thank you for dying in my place so I could choose to live forever with You, and give me the courage to tell others about Your soon return!*

*In Jesus's name,*

*Amen*

By praying this prayer, you can be confident "that He who has begun a good work in you will complete it until the day of Jesus Christ" (Phil. 1:6, NKJV).

From the start of the world's history till the climax of the re-created Earth, the Lord is the "Alpha and Omega, the beginning and the end, the first and the last" (Rev. 22:13, KJV). The Bible promises that God will "finish the work, and cut it short in righteousness: because a *short work* will the Lord make upon the earth" (Rom. 9:28). Christ is coming *soon*, and we must be ready! That is why Jesus declares, "Do not seal the words of the prophecy of this book, *for the time is at hand*" (Rev. 22:10, NKJV; italics added). These prophecies are **UNSEALED** for us today because we are living in **the Time of the End**! Jesus promises us, "Surely, I come quickly!" (Rev. 22:20, KJV).

John's vision is finished with this final appeal: "the Spirit and the bride say, 'Come.' And let him that heareth say, 'Come!'" (Rev. 22:17, KJV). May we embrace this invitation today, sharing it with all the world, and then, like the apostle John, exclaim with our whole hearts, *"Even so, come, Lord Jesus!"* (Rev. 22:20, KJV).

# Discussion Questions for Revelation 22

1. How is God portrayed in the book of Revelation and the entire Bible? (Compare Rev. 22:13 to Rev. 1:8, 17; Rev. 22:2, 14 to Gen. 3:24; Rev. 21:1 to Gen. 1:1)

2. How do we see the Trinity active in the salvation of mankind? (Rev. 22:1, 17; 1:4-6)

3. What warning is given to those who study the prophecies of Revelation? Why should we not let this warning stop us from studying Bible prophecy? (Rev. 22:18-19; 22:7; 1:3)

4. How can we understand the prophecies of the Bible, specifically in Daniel and Revelation, and why should we study them? (Is. 28:9-10; John 16:13; Rev. 22:6,10)

5. Why is Bible prophecy centered upon Jesus? (Rev 19:10; Heb. 12:2)

6. Who are blessed that they might have the "right to the tree of life" and may enter the city? (Rev. 2:7; 22:7, 14)

7. How do we obtain the power to keep God's commandments? (1 John 3:22, 24)

8. What assurance of salvation and understanding of prophecy do we have through Christ? (Jude 1:24; Phil. 1:6; I Cor. 1:4-8)

9. Like John, what are we counseled not to do to angels (called "stars" [Rev. 1:20])? Why? Who alone should we worship? How do we sometimes worship "stars" today? (Rev. 22:8-9; 2 Cor. 11:14; Matt. 4:10) Why is this so amazing considering what the righteous are called in Daniel 12:3?

10. Why should we study God's Word and apply the Bible's prophecies to our lives today? (Rev. 1:3; 22:6-7, 10, 20)

11. What loving invitation does Christ extend to His people at the
close of the book of Revelation? (Rev. 22:17)

# Appendices

# Appendix I

## Bible Prophecy Symbols and Their Meanings
## Found in Daniel & Revelation

*(Note: The prophetic terms below may have both a symbolic & literal meaning. This glossary concentrates on the symbolic meaning.)*

## DANIEL 2

**Gold/Silver** — Israel/God's people/purity/faith (Dan. 2:32, 38; Lam. 4:1-2; Mal. 3:3; Zech. 13:9; 1 Peter 1:7)

**Bronze (Brass) and Iron** — Rebellious/corrupters (Dan. 2:32-33, 39-42; Is. 48:4; Jer. 6:28)

**Clay** — Israel/God's people/moldable (Dan. 2:33, 41-43; Lam. 4:2; Is. 64:8; 45:9; Jer. 18:4, 6; Rom. 9:20-21)

**Mountain** — Kingdom (Dan. 2:35, 45; 9:16; Zech 8:3; Joel 3:17; Micah 4:1-2; Is. 2:2-3)

**Stone/Rock** — Christ/Ten Commandments (Dan. 2:45; Deut. 32:4, 18; 1 Cor. 10:4; Ps. 18:46; 31:1-3; Rom. 9:31-33; Matt. 21:42, 44; I Peter 2:4-8; Ex. 24:12; 31:18)

## DANIEL 7

**Four Winds** — Four directions (N, S, E, W)/ corners of heaven/earth (Dan. 7:2; 8:8; 11:4; Jer. 9:26; 49:32, 36; Is. 21:1; Eze.

5:12; 37:9; Zech. 2:6; Rev. 7:1) strife/war (Jer. 4:11-13; 25:31-33; Zech. 7:14); doctrine (Eph. 4:14)

**Great Sea** (*"yam"* meaning *"sea,"* specifically the Mediterranean Sea) — People, nations, densely populated (Dan. 7:2; Rev. 17:15; Is. 17:12-13)

**Beasts** — Kingdoms/nations (Dan. 7:17, 23; Eze. 34:25-28)

**Lion** (beast representing a kingdom [Dan. 7:4, 23]) — Judah (Gen. 49:9); Babylon (Jer. 50:17, 43-44; Joel 1:6) devourer (Hosea 13:8; Jer. 4:7)

**Eagle** — Swift, devouring (Dan. 7:4; Deut. 28:49; Lam. 4:19; Jer. 4:13; Hab. 1:6-8)

**Plucked/Baldness** — Shame, desolation, captivity, grief (Dan. 7:4; Micah 1:16; Amos 8:10; Jer. 48:37)

**Wings** — Extremity (Dan. 7:4, 6; Is. 8:8; 18:1, KJV; Jer. 48:40; 49:22) covering (Ps. 36:7; Is. 18:1)

**Stand on Feet/Man's Heart** — Human reasoning, religious, contrasted with wild, beastly, irrational (Dan. 7:4; 4:15)

**Bear** (beast- kingdom [Dan. 7:5, 23]; *history shows this represents Medo-Persia*) — Violent, devourer (Lam. 3:10-11; Hosea 13:8); wicked ruler (Prov. 28:15)

**Ribs** — Part of a whole (body/kingdom- Dan. 7:5,11; Gen. 2:21)

**Teeth** — Spear and arrows; brute force (Dan. 7:5, Zech. 9:6-7; Ps. 57:4)

**Mouth** — Sword/tool used to destroy (Dan. 7:5; Is. 49:2; Rev. 1:16; 19:15; Hosea 6:5; Is. 9:10, 12; Jer. 5:14)

**Leopard** (beast- kingdom [Dan. 7:23]; *History shows that this represents Greece*) — Enemy (Jer. 5:6; Hosea 13:7) evil doings (Jer. 13:23)

**4 Wings** — Extremities/directions N, S, E, W- worldwide (Dan. 7:6; "Lion" above)

**Heads** — Civil leaders- heads of nations (Ex. 18:25; Num. 1:16; 10:4; 13:3; 30:1, KJV; Deut. 33:5, 21, KJV; Ps. 110:6; Dan. 7:6; Rev. 13:3; 17:9-10) religious leaders (Is. 29:9-10); generational heads of lineage (Ex. 6:14, 25; Micah 3:9) princes (Num. 7:2, KJV); chiefs/captains (Deut. 1:15)

**Terrible "Different" Beast** —(beast- kingdom [Dan. 7:23]; *History shows that this represents Rome*)-Composite of characteristics of former beast kingdoms (Dan. 7:7, 19; Rev. 13:2)

**Horns** — Civil/religious powers/kings (Dan. 7:8, 20, 24; Dan. 8:5-6, 21-22; Micah 4:13; Zech 1:18-21; Ps. 75:4-5, 10; Rev. 5:6; 13:1, 11; 17:12)

**Ten** — Symbolic of a greater number (Dan. 7:7; 1:20; Matt. 25:1-13; Luke 15:8-10; Rev. 2:10)

**Iron teeth** — Strong rebellious corrupter/warrior against God's people (Dan. 7:7); iron (Jer. 6:28; Is. 48:4; Dan. 2:33-45); teeth (Ps. 37:12; Prov. 30:14)

**Breaking in Pieces the "Residue"** (*"shar"= "remnant"*) **Feet** — Tramples God's people—persecution (Dan. 7:7, 19-21, 23; Rev. 13:1, 7)

**Little Horn** — Civil & religious power/king (see above "horns") that rose from the "terrible beast" (Dan. 7:8; *history shows that this represents the papacy*) plucks out three other "horns" (Dan. 7:8; *the Holy Roman Empire conquered the Heruli, Vandals, & Ostrogoths*); eyes of a man, mouth speaking pompous (*"rabrab"= "domineering, captain, chief"*) words (Dan. 7:8, 11, 20, 25; 8:9-12); eyes- prophet, religious leader (Is. 29:10)

**Ancient of Days** — God the Father (Dan. 7:9-10, 13; Rev. 1:4; Is. 44:6-7)

**Son of Man** — Jesus (Dan. 7:13-14; Matt. 18:11)

## DANIEL 8

**Ram** (sheep) — Medo-Persia (Dan. 8:4, 6-7, 20); Christ/Followers (Dan. 8:3-4; Eze. 34:2, 17, 21-22; Matt. 25:32-34; Jer. 50:8, 17; Ps. 95:7)

**Male Goat** *("saiyr"= "shaggy," "devil"* [Dan. 8:21]) — Greece/Gentiles (Dan. 8:5-8, 21; Col. 3:11; Gal. 3:28; I Cor. 10:32); Satan/followers (Lev. 16:8-10, 21-22; Zech. 10:3; Matt. 25:32-33, 41)

**Stars** — God's people (Dan. 8:10; 12:3; Gen. 15:5); Angels (*"angelos"= "messengers"* [Rev.1:20; 12:4, 9])

**Glorious** (*"tsbiy"= "pleasant"*) **Land** — a symbol of where God and His people live (Dan. 8:9, 11:16, 41; Jer. 3:18-19; 12:10; 23:10; Zech. 8:7, 12-14)

**Prince of Princes/ Prince of the Host** — Jesus Christ (Dan. 8:11, 25; 9:25; Is. 9:6; Josh. 5:13)

**Little Horn** — political/religious power/king (see "Horns" & "Little Horn" in Dan. 7; *history shows that this represents the papacy*) from the West (but claims to be from the North [Dan. 8:9; Is. 14:13-14]); Casts down God's people ([Dan. 8:10] see "stars"); exalts himself above Christ, ([Dan. 8:11, 25] see "Prince of the host"); casts down God's sanctuary and sacrifices (Dan. 8:11); is given an army, posses civil power (Dan. 8:12); casts down God's truth (Dan. 8:12); Is a "king" (Dan. 8:23; Rev. 17:12); destroys the "mighty" and God's people (Dan. 8:24-25); deceives (Dan. 8:25) will eventually be broken (completely forever) without human means (Dan. 8:25)

## DANIEL 9

**"People Called by Your Name"** — Gentile Christians/Jews (Dan. 9:19; Is. 43:7; Amos 9:12; Rom.3:29, 9:23-26; I Cor. 12:13)

## DANIEL 10

**Michael** — Jesus Christ (Dan. 10:21; 9:25; Jude 1:9; I Thess. 4:16; Judges 6:22-24; Is. 9:6; Ex. 14:19; 13:21)

**Prince of Persia** *("Parac"* meaning *"pure"* or *"splendid"*) — symbolic of the rulers of God's people (Dan. 10:13; 2 Chron. 36:23; Ezra 1:1-2; 9:9)

**Prince of Greece** — symbolic of Gentile rulers (Dan. 10:20; Zech. 9:13; Rom. 1:14, 16; 1 Cor. 1:24; Gal. 3:28; Col 3:11)

## DANIEL 11

**Kings** — (Dan. 11:2-3) kingdoms or nations (Dan. 7:17, 23)

**Four Winds** — Directions - N, S, E, W (Dan. 11:4; see "four winds" in Dan. 7)

**King of the South** — (Dan. 11:5-8, 11-12, 14, 27, 40, 43) leaders of spiritual Egypt/Sodom/Jerusalem- God's people/nation in apostasy; (Eze. 16:46, 48-49; Jer. 23:14; 46:2, 9; Is. 1:9-10; Deut. 32:28, 32; Ps. 126:1-4; Is. 30:6-7; Zech. 9:14-16; Obadiah 1:19-21; Rev. 11:8)

**King of the North** — (Dan. 11:6-13, 15-32, 36-45) True King of the North is God ruling over His people (Ps. 48:1-3; Is. 14:13)_but the antichrist claims to be the King of the North in God's place ruling over His people/Rome symbolized by iron_ (Dan. 2:40; Jer. 6:22, 28; 15:12; Dan. 7:25; 8:25; 11:22; Is. 14:12-14; 2 Thess. 2:3-4; Rev. 13:4-6)

**Daughter** (Woman) — church [both pure and apostate] (Dan. 11:6; Jer. 6:2; 2 Cor. 11:2; Eph. 5:23-27; Eze. 16:15-59; 23; Hosea 2:5; 3:1)

**Glorious Land** — (Dan. 11:16) see "Glorious Land" in Dan. 8

**Prince of the Covenant** — Jesus Christ (Dan. 11:16; Neh. 9:32; Dan. 9:4; Deut. 29:1, 14-15, 25)

**Appointed Time** *("mow'ed")* — specific time pointed out beforehand; concerning judgment (Dan. 11:29, 35; 12:7; Ps. 75:2; Jer. 8:7); in the North (Is. 14:13); *"an appointment, fixed time or season"* (Gen. 1:14- month [Ps. 104:19]), a feast (of Tabernacles [Hos. 12:9]), *"an assembly, a signal appointed beforehand, sign, time, set time"* (Ps. 102:13); Zion, city of "solemnities" [*"mow'ed"]* (Is. 33:20, KJV); answers, "How long?"( Dan. 12:7; Ps. 74:8-9); time of Zion's favor (Ps. 102:13); forgotten (Lam. 2:6); revolving terrors (Lam. 2:22); time of the end (Dan. 8:19); saint's power scattered (Dan. 12:7)

**Abomination of Desolation** — *"shiqquwts"*= *idol/idolatry* (Dan. 11:31; Matt. 24:15; Jer. 44:22-23)

## DANIEL 12

**Michael** — (Dan. 12:1) see "Michael" in Daniel 10

**Stars** — (Dan. 12:3) see "Stars" in Daniel 8

**Daily** — (*"tamiyd"*= *"continual"* [Dan. 12:11; 8:11-13; 11:31]) continual, relating to daily sanctuary sacrifices, specifically performed in the outer court and the Holy Place (Num. 28:24, KJV; Eze. 46:13-14, KJV; Num. 4:7, margin)

**Abomination of Desolation** — idolatry (Dan. 12:11); see "Abomination of Desolation" in Dan. 11

**Times** *("mow'ed")* — may refer to 49-day/year revolutions of time (Dan. 12:7; Lev. 25:8; Deut. 16:9); *"mow'ed"*= *"seasons"* (Gal. 4:10; Gen. 1:14); see "Appointed Time" in Dan. 11

# REVELATION 1

**Signified** — (*"semaino"*= *"to make a sign"*) written in symbols used to portray the meaning of the prophecies shown to John (Rev. 1:1; Matt. 13:10-16; I Cor. 2;12-14)

**Keys of Hades and Death** — "keys" [authority] (Rev. 1:18; 9:1; 20:1-3; Matt. 16:19) *"Hades"*= *"hell,"* (KJV) the grave (Rev 1:18; Acts 2:31; Rev. 6:8; 20:13-14; Hosea 13:14)

**Seven Stars/Seven Angels** — (*"angelos"*= *messengers*) of the churches; can be heavenly angels or humans (Rev. 1:20; I Peter 1:12; Dan. 8:10; 12:3; Gen. 15:5)

**Seven Spirits of God** — symbolic of the Holy Spirit's work through the seven churches/lampstands (Rev. 1:4; 3:1; 4:5; 5:6: Is. 11:2)

**Seven Golden Lampstands** — seven churches; God's people empowered by the Holy Spirit and cared for by Christ, Himself (Rev. 1:12-13; 20; Matt. 5:14-16; Zech. 4:1-6; Jn. 14:16-18, 23)

**Seven** — (*"sheba"*- *seven times, week, sacred full one* from *"shaba" to swear, take an oath, curse, to adjure;* a symbol of completion, rest (Gen. 2:1-4; Ps. 119:164; Ex. 20:8-11)

> *"... [Seven] occurs 42 times in Daniel and Revelation" i.e. "seven churches, seven spirits, seven golden candlesticks, seven stars, seven lamps, seven seals, seven horns, seven eyes, seven angels, seven trumpets, seven thunders, seven thousand slain in a great earthquake, seven heads, seven crowns, seven last plagues, seven golden vials, seven mountains, and seven kings" (Remnant Bible, p. 1590).*

**Two-Edged Sword** — words/God's Word (Rev. 2:12, 16; 1:16; 19:15, 21; Ps. 55:21; Is. 49:2; Heb. 4:12)

# REVELATION 2

**Seven Golden Lampstands** — churches (Rev. 2:1); see "Seven Golden Lampstands" in Rev. 1

**Nicolaitans** — historical false Christian sect said to have been followers of Nicolas (Acts 6:5); falsely promoted that the deeds of the flesh do not affect the salvation of the soul (Rev. 2:6, 14-15; Gal. 5:13); sexual immorality, and idolatry; symbolic of false teachers who promote cheap grace (see "Doctrine of Balaam/Balak" below); encouraged "a lifestyle of unrestrained indulgence," (*https://www.biblegateway.com resources/encyclopedia-of-the-bible/Nicolaitans*)

**Synagogue of Satan** — hypocrites; symbolic of those claiming to be true Christians but are followers of Satan (Rev. 2:9; 3:9; Is. 60:14; Rom. 2:28-29)

**Second Death** — the final destruction of Satan, his angels, & the wicked (Rev. 2:11; 20:8-14)

**Antipas** — from *"anti,"* meaning *"against,"* & *"pas,"* meaning *"father;"* may be symbolic of faithful Protestants who were martyred for their faith throughout history by Roman Catholic popes—Latin word for "pope," (*"pater"*) means *"father"* (Rev. 2:13)

**Doctrine of Balaam/Balak** — false hypocritical teachings of combining Christianity with paganism; allowing sexual immorality and idolatry in a Christian lifestyle (Rev. 2:14; Num. 31:16; Acts 15:29; 2 Peter 2:12-22; Jude 1:8, 10-11)

**Two-Edged Sword** — words/God's Word (see "Two-edged Sword" in Rev. 1)

**Jezebel** — historical evil queen (harlot) that persecuted God's people (Rev. 2:20-24; I Kings 16:31; 2 Kings 9:7, 22); symbolic of apostate church system steeped in idolatry, sexual immorality, & wickedness ("harlot" [Rev. 17:1, 3-6; 19:2; Jer. 3:20; Eze. 16:2, 30-32])

**Hidden Manna** — Bread of Life/ Christ/His Word (Rev. 2:17; Ex. 16:15; John 6:57-58)

**White Stone** — judgment/vote of innocence (Rev. 2:17); **white**-sinlessness (Is. 1:18); **stone**- Greek method of voting i.e. black stone= guilty, white stone= innocent; Greek word for *"stone"* is *"psēphon,"* which is the same word used in Acts 26:10 to cast a vote

**New Name** — character (Rev. 2:17; 3:12; 14:1; 19:12; 22:4; Is. 62:2)

**Rod of Iron** — mighty rulership; possible inference to Rome & its "iron" rule that broke all other kingdoms (Rev. 2:27; 19:15; 12:5; Ps. 2:7-9; Is. 11:4; Dan. 2:40, 44; 7:7, 19)

**Morning Star** — Christ; may also refer to the dawning of the Protestant Reformation by John Wycliffe, known as the "morning star" of the Reformation (Rev. 2:28; 22:16)

# REVELATION 3

**Seven Spirits of God**- symbolic of the Holy Spirit's work through the seven "stars" ("angels" meaning "messengers" of churches [Rev. 1:20; Rev. 3:1]); see "Seven Spirits of God" in Rev. 1)

**Seven Stars** — angels/messengers to the churches (Rev. 3:1); *"angelos"* meaning *"messengers"* (Rev. 1:20), heavenly or human (see "Seven Stars" in Rev. 1)

**Come as a Thief** — caught unaware—*only applies to the wicked who are not watching and ready for Christ's second coming,*

NOT God's people (Rev. 3:3; 16:15; Matt. 24:43-44; 2 Peter 3:10; 1 Thess. 5:2-6)

**White Garments** — sinless/pure character (Rev. 3:4-5; 16:15; 19:7-8, 14; Is. 1:18; 61:10)

**Key of David** — authority/rulership of literal and/or spiritual Israel (Rev. 3:7; Is. 22:22; 9:6-7)

**Open Door** — a reference to the temple doors of the Holy & Most Holy Place; symbolic of granting opportunity (Rev. 3:8; 4:1; 11:19)

**Synagogue of Satan** — hypocrites; symbolic of those claiming to be true Christians but are followers of Satan (Rev. 3:9; see "Synagogue of Satan" in Rev. 2)

**Pillar in the Temple** — a foundation of truth/doctrine (Rev. 3:12; Prov. 9:1; I Tim 3:15)

**New Name** — character (Rev. 3:12; see "New Name" in Rev. 2)

**Gold Tried in the Fire** — pure character refined by trials (Rev. 3:18; Zech 13:9; I Peter 1:7, 22)

**Eye Salve** — spiritual discernment (Rev. 3:18; Is. 6:9-10)

## REVELATION 4

**Voice-** trumpet — (Rev. 4:1); "lightnings (7 Spirits of God sent out to the earth- churches [Rev. 4:5; 5:6; Job 28:26, KJV]), thunderings (7 seals [Rev. 6:1]), and voices (7 trumpets [Rev. 4:1, 5, KJV])

**Seven Lamps of Fire** — seven churches, seven "Spirits of God," and seven "horns and eyes" of Lamb (Rev. 4:5; 5:6; Zech. 3:9; Is. 29:10; Ps. 89:17); sent out into all the earth (Rev. 5:6)

**Twenty-Four Elders** — divisional leaders of God's people (Rev. 4:4; 5:8-12; Is. 24:23; Joel 1:14; 1 Chron. 24:4-5, 7-18)

**Four Living Creatures/Beasts** (KJV) — 4 kingdoms of God's redeemed led by the angelic hosts (Rev. 5:8-10) with specific characteristics and likely from different time periods of earth's history (Rev. 4:6-9; 5:8-14; 15:7; Dan. 7:23; Eze. 1:5-25); introduces seals (Rev. 6:1-7)

**Like a Lion** — Jewish nation/Jacob's descendants (Rev. 4:7; 6:1; Gen. 49:2, 9-10); introduces the **first seal of the white horse** (**Christianity** [Rev. 19:11])

**Like a Calf** — **martyrs** from persecution (Rev. 4:7; 6:3-4); calf was a sacrificial animal in God's sanctuary services (Lev. 9:3); "calf"-"moschos" meaning *young heifer*, often associated with the color red/blood (Num. 19:2-5); introduces **second seal of red horse;** may refer to Ishmael's/Esau's descendants (Gen. 16:11-12; 28:9), the Edomites (Gen. 27:40-41; 36:9; Mal. 1:2-4); associated with **"red"** (Gen. 25:30; Is. 63:1-2) and a **"sword"** (persecution [Amos 1:11])

**Like a Man** — God's people under **Gentile civil rulership** (Rev. 4:7; Jer. 50:41-42); opens the **third seal of the black horse** (Rev. 6:5)

**Like a Flying Eagle**- Rome/U.S./Catholic/Protestant rule; (Rev. 4:7; Deut. 32:9, 11; Hosea 8:1); opens **fourth seal of pale horse** (Rev. 6:7-9) **swift** (Jer. 4:13; Lam. 4:19; Hab. 1:8; Deut. 28:49); **bald** (Mic. 1:16)

# REVELATION 5

**Scroll Written Inside and on the Back** — judgments/curses against lawbreakers (Rev. 5:1-5; Zech. 5:1-4; Ex. 32:15)

**Seal** — a decree concerning certain events for a specific time period (Rev. 5:1-5, 9; 6:1, 3, 5, 7, 9, 12; 7:2-8; 8:1; 10:4; 20:2-3; 22:10;

Dan. 9:24; 12:4, 9; Esther 8:8-13)

**Lion of the Tribe of Judah** — Jesus (Rev. 5:5; Hosea 4:1; 5:14)

**Root of David** — Jesus's ancestry through David's descendants (the tribe of Judah [Rev. 5:5; 22:16; Is. 11:1, 10; Matt. 1:1-2])

**Lamb** — Jesus (Rev. 5:6; John 1:29)

**Four Living Creatures/Beasts** (KJV) — kingdoms (Rev. 5:6; see "living creatures" in Rev. 4)

**Seven Horns** — civil/religious powers of states or countries/ churches (Rev. 5:6; Ps. 89:17; see "horns" in Dan. 7)

**Seven Eyes** — prophets/leaders of churches (Rev. 5:6; Zech. 3:9); eyes- prophets [Is. 29:10])

**Seven Spirits of God** — the Holy Spirit working through the seven churches in specific time periods (Rev. 5:6; Rev. 3:1; 4:5; 5:6; Is. 11:2)

**Golden Bowls of Incense** — prayers of the saints (Rev. 5:8; 8:4)

# REVELATION 6

**Thunder** (noise) — events occurring or being repeated at a specific time (Rev. 6:1, KJV)

**Seal** — a decree concerning certain events for a specific time period (see "Seal" in Rev. 5)

**First Seal** (Rev. 6:2)

> **White Horse** — Christ's kingdom- Christianity (Rev 6:2; 19:11; Zech. 10:3-4); **horse**/beast- kingdom (Dan. 7:23); **white**- purity (Is. 1:18)

> **Horse/Chariot/Rider** — **rider** (Christ); **chariot/horse** (beast- kingdom [Is. 63:13-14; Jer. 51:19-21; Hag. 2:22])

**Conqueror** — Jesus (Rev. 19:11); God's people (Rom. 8:37)

**Second Seal** (Rev. 6:3-4)

**Red Horse** — Satan's kingdom manifested in paganism/spiritualism/occult (Rev. 6:4; 12:3, 9); **horse-beast/kingdom** (Dan. 7:23); **red/scarlet-** sin (Is. 1:18; Rev. 17:3)

**Sword** — persecution of God's people (Ps. 37:14; Amos 1:11)

**Third Seal** (Rev. 6:5-6)

**Black Horse** — **Gentile kingdoms** ruling God's people through the laws of the land; the combination of culture and religion (Rev. 6:5-6); **Black-** spiritual darkness (2 Peter 2:17-18; Jn. 3:19); **beast-** kingdom (Dan. 7:23)

**Scales/Balances** (KJV) — justice/law (Lev. 19:35-36; Eze. 45:9-10; Micah 6:9-11)

**Wheat/Barley** — God's Word (bread- Jn. 6:51, 63);

**Famine** — lacking biblical truth (Amos 8:11)

**Oil & Wine** — blessings of God's people (Deut. 11:14; Jer. 31:12; Joel 2:23-24; Hos. 2:9)

**Fourth Seal** (Rev. 6:7-8)

**Pale Horse** — kingdom of **apostate Christianity** (Rev. 6:7-8); **pale-** shameful (Is. 29:22; Jer. 30:6; Nahum 2:10; Joel 2:3-6; Hosea 2:6); **horse**/beast- kingdom (Dan. 7:23)

**Rider** — **Death & Hell** (KJV) (Rev. 6:8; "hell" - "hades," can mean "grave" [Hab. 2:5])

**Kill God's People** — (Dan. 8:23-25; Rev. 13:5-7, 11-15; II Thess. 2:3-12; Acts 20:29)

**Fifth Seal** (Rev. 6:9-11)

**Cry of the Souls Under the Altar** — symbolic of **Christian martyrs'** cry for the vindication of their blood/deaths- an allusion to Abel's death, the first martyr (Rev. 6:9; Gen. 4:8-11; Ps. 9:11-12; 79:5, 10); Symbolic of **God's people's protest** against apostate Christianity and the wicked's persecution against them

**Sixth Seal** (Rev. 6:12-17)

**Earthquake, Sun Darkened, Blood Moon, Stars Fall** — symbolic of spiritual darkness (deception) and its effects upon God's people (symbolized as the sun- Ps. 89:35-36; moon- Ps. 89:37; stars- Gen. 15:5; Dan. 12:3) as well as literal signs of Christ's return (Rev. 6:12-13; 8:12; 9:2; 11:13; 16:8-10, 18-20; Matt. 24:29; Mk. 13:24-26; Joel 2:31; Is. 13:8-11; 34:4; Micah 3:6)

# REVELATION 7

**Four Corners/Winds** — 4 Directions—NSEW—4 corners (Rev. 7:1; Is. 11:12; Jer. 9:26)

**Four Winds/Corners** — strife/war (Jer. 4:11-13; 25:31-33; Zech. 7:14); doctrine (Eph. 4:14); 4 directions/corners (see "Four Winds" in Dan. 7)

**Seal on Forehead** — **seal** - declaration concerning a specific time period (see Rev. 5); the result of a conscious decision in the **forehead** to obey God's commandments (Heb. 8:10) through the power of the Holy Spirit, specifically the fourth commandment concerning the time of the Sabbath, bestowed just before Christ's second coming (Rev. 7:2-3; 14:1; Is. 8:16; Dan. 12:4, 9; Eph. 1:13; II Tim. 2:19; I Cor. 6:11; II Thess. 1:12)

**144,000** — godly religious leaders of the remnant at the end of time (Rev. 7:4-8, 14:1-5; 12:17; 19:8; Eph. 2:11-13)

**Great Multitude** — (*"ochlos"* meaning common people opposed to leaders [Rev. 7:9]) innumerable saints saved in God's kingdom (Rev. 7:9-12)

# REVELATION 8

**Seventh Seal** — the beginning & execution of the investigative judgment (8:1; Ch. 7); the sealing of the righteous (Dan. 7:10, 22; Rev. 7:2-8; 11:18)

**Silence in Heaven** — indication of judgment (Rev. 8:1; Hab. 2:20; Is. 41:1; Zech. 2:13; Ps. 50:3-6)

**Prelude & First Trumpet** (Rev. 8:2-7)

> **Smoke/Incense** — prayers of the saints (Rev. 8:4; Ps. 141:2; Eph. 5:2)

> **Fire of the Altar** — Holy Spirit (Rev. 8:5, 7; Acts 2:3-4; Deut. 4:24; 9:3; Heb. 12:29)

> **Voices, Thunderings, Lightning, Earthquake** — voices/noises (trumpets [Rev. 4:1]); thunderings (seals repeated with power [Rev. 6:1; 10:2-3]); lightnings (Spirit of God/Great Awakenings [Rev. 4:5; 5:6; Job 28:26, KJV] ); earthquake- shaking (Is. 29:6; Heb. 12:25-28; Rev. 6:12; 8:5, KJV; 11:13, 19; 14:2; 16:18; Ex. 20:18; Dan. 9:10; Ps. 18:12-13)

> **Hail** — symbolic of the powerful outpouring of God's Word (Rev. 8:7; 7:17; John 4:10-11; Is. 28:17; 30:30; Ps. 18:12-13)

> **Fire** — Holy Spirit (Rev. 8:5; see "Fire of the Altar" above); God's Word (Jer. 23:29)

> **Blood** — Death; can represent Christ's death on the cross

(Rev. 8:7; 6:9-11; 14:20; I John 5:6-7; Matt. 26:28; Rom 3:25)

**Green Grass/Trees** — **green grass** - God's people; **green trees**- godly leaders (Rev. 8:7; Is. 40:7; 61:3; Jer. 17:7-8; Ps. 1:3; 92:12)

**Second Trumpet** (Rev. 8:8-9)

**Great Mountain** — **"great"**- Babylon (Rev. 8:8; 17:5; Jer. 51:24-25); **"mountain"**- kingdom (Dan. 7:23; see "Mountain" in Dan. 2)

**Fire** — Holy Spirit/God's Word (Rev. 8:8; see "Fire of Altar" above)

**Sea** — people (Rev. 8:8; Is. 17:12-3; Rev. 17:15)

**Blood** — death (Rev. 8:8; see "blood" in First Trumpet)

**1/3 of the Living Creatures** — people (Rev. 8:9; Eze. 5:2, 12)

**Died** — Symbol of baptism/conversion into Protestant Christianity (Rev. 8:9; Rom 6:4)

**Ships Destroyed** — Instruments of spiritual warfare destroyed (Rev. 8:9; Is. 43:14-17)

**Third Trumpet** (Rev. 8:10-11)

**Great Star Falls Like a Torch** — angel (Rev. 8:10; 1:20); Satan (Is. 14: 12-13; Lk. 10:18)

**Rivers and Springs of Water** — God's Word (Rev. 8:10; Jn. 4:10-14; Jer. 17:13)

**Wormwood** — meaning *"bitter"* (Rev. 8:11; Is. 5:20); bitter water (Lam. 3:15); deception/false teachings (Amos 6:12; Rev. 12:15-16)

**Fourth Trumpet** (Rev. 8:12-13)

> **Sun, Moon, Stars Darkened** — symbolic of God's people being deceived (Rev. 8:12; see "Sun Darkened, Blood Moon, Stars Fall" in Rev. 6)
>
> **One-Third** — fraction of people affected (Rev. 812; see "1/3 of Living Creatures" in second trumpet; Zech. 13:8-9)
>
> **Three Woes** — a cry of distress (meaning the same as "alas") (Rev. 8:13; 14:6-11; 11:14; 14:8; 18:2, 10, 16, 19; Amos 5:16-18 compare Hab. 2:7, 9, 12, 15, 19)

## REVELATION 9

**Fifth Trumpet** (Rev. 9:1-12)

> **Star *Fallen* from Heaven** — Satan fallen to the earth in the third trumpet (Rev. 9:1; 8:10; see "Great Star" in Rev. 8)
>
> **Sun & Air Darkened** — satanic deception/demonic forces released (Is. 5:20; Eph. 2:2)
>
> **Smoke of a Great Furnace** — judgment of the wicked (Gen. 19:28)
>
> **Key** — authority (Rev. 9:1; see "Keys" in Rev. 1)
>
> **Bottomless Pit** — earth (Rev. 9:1-2, 11; 11:7; 17:8; 20:1-3, 8; Is. 24:1, 3, 21-22; Gen. 1:2-*"deep"* *("thowm")*- *abyss*; Lk. 8:31-33)
>
> **Locusts like Horses/Scorpions** — soldiers/false teachers (Rev. 9:2-3, 7, 9; 6:1-8; Nahum 3:17; Jer. 51:14, 27; Judges 7:12; Joel 1:1-4)
>
> **Scorpions** — satanic forces (men and demons) (Rev. 9:3-

5, 10; Luke 10:19); judgment from God against His unfaith-ful people (I Kings 1:11 margin); persecution of the right-eous by the wicked (Eze. 2:6) **"with stingers in their tails"** — deception/lies (Rev. 9:10, 19; Is. 9:15)

**Green Trees/Grass** — God's people (see "Green Grass/Trees" in the 1st trumpet [Rev. 8])

**Crowns of Gold/Faces** (*"prosopon" - appearance*) **of Men** — symbols of the 1st seal of Christianity becoming apostate (Rev. 9:7-8; crowns [Rev. 4:4, 6:2; 19:10])

**Hair** (covering [Eph. 11:15]) **of Women** — (church [Jer. 3:20; 6:2])

**Teeth like Lions** — devouring (Rev. 4:7; 6:1; Jer. 4:7; Is. 5:26, 29)

**Breastplates of Iron** — heart of Rome/Papacy (Rev. 9:9; **Iron** [Dan. 2:33; 7:19; Jer. 15:12; Ps. 107:16; Is. 45:2])

**Sound of Wings like Sound of Chariots/Horses** — a pos-sible reference to the fourth seal (horse) & speaking in false tongues (sound- *"phone"* which means *"language, noise (of an instrument), voice, speech"*- possibly similar to the babbling noise of glossolalia (tongue-speaking) (Rev. 9:9; 6:1-8; Is. 5:28-30; Acts 2:2-4)

*"Abaddon,"* **or** *"Apollyon,"* — *"the destroyer"* from *"apol-lymi"* meaning *"death"* (Rev. 9:11; compare Rev. 6:8; Jer. 50:10-11); *"son of perdition"* (destruction) *"apologia"* mean-ing *"destroying"* (2 Thess. 2:3)

**Sixth Trumpet** (Rev. 9:13-21)

**Euphrates River**- physically located in ancient Babylon, possibly symbolizing God's Word being polluted by false doctrine (Rev. 9:14; 16:12; Jer. 46:6-10; Rev. 12:15)

**Bound Angels** (*"angelos"-"messengers"*) — evil angels/men (Rev. 9:14; Jude 1:6-8)

**200 Million Horseman** — a symbolic army of false religious teachers inspired by demons (Rev. 9:14-16; Nahum 3:1-4)

**One-Third**- a percentage of fallen mankind, similar to the fallen angels of heaven (Rev. 9:15-17; 8:12; 12:4; Eze. 5:2, 12; Zech 13:8-9)

**Horse Riders' Breastplates of Fiery Red, Hyacinth Blue** (Black), **and Sulphur Yellow** — reference to second seal, **red horse** (paganism/spiritualism/occult), third seal - **black horse** (Gentile government/spiritual darkness), and fourth seal- **pale horse** (papacy/Protestants united) (Rev. 9:9, 17; 6:4-5, 8)

**Head of Lions** — spiritual Babylon- fallen Christianity (Rev. 9:17; 5:5-6; 4:7; 6:1; Is. 5:26, 29; Dan. 7:4)

**Serpent Tails** — false prophets that teach lies (Rev. 9:17-19; 12:9; Is. 9:15)

**Fire/Smoke/Brimstone** — *brimstone ("theion")* meaning *incense (prayers* [Rev. 8:3-4])

**From Their Mouths** — (Rev. 9:18) false teachings/false speaking in tongues (Holy Spirit- fire [Acts 2:3-4]); spiritual darkness (Rev. 9:3, 17-19; 8:3-4)

## REVELATION 10

**Mighty Angel** — "clothed with a cloud," a "rainbow on his head," "his face was like the sun," "his feet like pillars of fire"-

Jesus (Rev. 10:1; 18:1-4; Rev. 1:13-16; Dan. 10:5-6) compare "Angel of the Lord"- Jesus (Judges 6:22-24)

> **Rainbow** — the covenant between God and man (Gen. 9:15-16)

> **Face Like the Sun** — Jesus (Rev. 1:16; Mal. 4:2)

> **Cloud/Pillar/Fire** — description of God (Ex. 14:19; 13:21; Is. 4:5-6)

**Open/Unsealed Little Book/Scroll Likely Written on Both Sides-** unsealed small scroll likely containing judgments and prophecies at certain times against those who break the Law of God, specifically outlined in the book of Daniel (Rev. 10:2, 8-11; 5:1, 4-10; Dan. 12:7-9, 13; Eze. 2:9-10; Zech. 5:1-4; Is. 29:10-13)

**Mystery of God** — prophecies unsealed in the last days concerning the deceptions of the "man of sin"/the "mystery of lawlessness" (Rev. 10:7; 2 Thess. 2:3-9)

**Seven Thunders** — repetition of the seven seals and their corresponding events that occur in the last days before Christ's return (**thunder** [Rev. 10:3-4; 6:1; Job 37:1-5; Eze. 3:12-13] **ties to seals** [Job 39:19; Is. 29:6])

**Sweet/Bitter Eating of the Little Book** — consuming God's Word/prophecy with understanding (Rev. 10:8-9; Eze. 3:1-4, 10, 17-21; Is. 5:20; sweet [Ps. 19:7-10]; bitter [Lam. 3:15, 19])

## REVELATION 11

**Reed and Rod** — Measuring tools- symbolic of the judgment of character (Rev. 11:1; 21:15; Is. 28:17; Matt. 7:2; Jer. 51:13; Micah 6:9-11)

**Two Witnesses** — the Old and New Testament of the Bible/God's

Law (Rev. 11:2-3; 3:14; John 1:1; 5:39; Ex. 32:15-16; Deut. 31:26)

**Two Olive Trees** — Israel (Rev. 11:4; Hosea 14:5-6)

**Lampstands** — God's church of the New Testament (Rev. 11:4; 1:20)

**Fire** — Holy Spirit (Rev. 11:5; see "Fire of the Altar" in Rev. 8)

**Beast that Ascends from the Bottomless Pit** — Dragon - Satan's kingdom on the earth (Rev. 11:7; 9:1, 11); satanic (Rev. 20:1-3; 12:9); beast- kingdom (Dan. 7:23) bottomless pit- earth (see "Bottomless Pit" in Rev. 9)

**Great City which is Spiritually Sodom and Egypt, Where our Lord was Crucified** — spiritual Babylon (Rev. 11:8; 17:4-5, 18) displaying the same characteristics as these ancient places: Sodom- immorality (Gen. 19; Deut. 32:28. 32; Is. 3:8-9; Jer. 23:14); Egypt rebellion against God (Ex. 5:2; Is. 31:1); Jerusalem- location of a professed God-fearing nation (Israel) but responsible for "crucifying" Christ/the principles found in His Word (2 Chron. 6:5-6; Jer. 3:17-20; Zech. 12:10; John 19:37; Heb. 12:22; Rev. 1:7).

**2nd Woe** — Events likely corresponding to the timing of the second angel's message of Babylon falling (Rev. 11:14; see "Woe" in Rev. 8)

**Seventh Trumpet (Last Trump)** — seventh trumpet- judgment begins on the righteous dead (in 1844 [Rev. 11:18; 8:1; Dan. 7:10, 14]); spans to the last trump- execution of judgment/the reward of the saints (the resurrection of the righteous dead and the translation of the living saints & the destruction of those who destroy the earth at the second coming of Christ [Rev. 11:15-18; I Cor. 15:52])

**Lightning, Voices, Thundering, Earthquake, Great Hail** —

lightning- Spirit of God- Great Awakenings (Rev. 5:6; Job 28:26, KJV); voices- trumpet warnings (Rev. 4:1); thundering - 7 seals of events repeated with power (Rev. 6:1; 10:3-4); earthquake- shaking (Is. 29:6; Heb. 12:25-28; Rev. 6:12; 8:5; 11:13, 19; 16:18); hail- the power of God's Word in judgment (Rev. 11:19, KJV; 4:5; 8:5; 14:2; Ex. 20:18; Is. 29:6 11:19; Dan. 7:9)

# REVELATION 12

**First "Great Sign" of the Nearness of Christ's Coming** — woman (church [see following]) coming out of tribulation (Protestant Reformation [Rev. 12:1-2; Matt. 24:29-30])

> **Woman** — church/God's people (Rev. 12:1-2, 4, 6, 13-17; Jer. 6:2; 2 Cor. 11:2)

> **Sun** — Christ, specifically shining through the NT church (Mal 4:2; I Thess. 5:5; Phil. 2:15; Ps. 89:15; Matt. 13:43)

> **Moon** — OT church- Israel- David's "seed" (Ps. 89:35-37)

> **12 Stars** — 12 disciples (Rev. 12:1; 1:20; 21:14)

> **Labor Pains** — great persecution (Rev. 12:2; Jer. 30:5-7; Is. 66:7-9; Micah 4:9-10)

**Second Sign - Fiery Red Dragon/Serpent of Old/ Devil/Satan** — Satan's attack through his followers and false doctrines/pagan philosophies that assail God's church/people (Rev. 12:3; 7-9; 16:13); dragon/beast- kingdom (Dan. 7:23); associated with Babylon (Jer. 51:34-35, KJV) and Egypt (Eze. 29:3, KJV)

**Seven Heads** — seven kingdoms ("mountains"- Rev. 17:9-10; Jer. 51:24-25) of Satan on Earth, symbolizing control of the world, represented by the primary world kingdoms throughout Earth's history (Rev. 12:3; 13:1, 3; Ps. 110:6; Dan. 7:3-8; 17, 19-21, 23); likely Egypt, Assyria, Babylon, Medo-Persia, Greece, Rome, U.S.

**Crowns** — kingly rulership (Eze. 21:26-27; Jer. 2:14, 16; Lam. 5:6, 16)

**Ten** — symbolizing a larger number or whole of a group (Dan. 1:20; Matt. 25:1; Lk.15:8; Rev. 2:10)

**Horns** — symbolizing civil/religious powers/leaders (Rev. 12:3; 17:3; Zech 1:18-21; Ps. 75:4-5, 10; see "Horns" in Daniel 7)

**Male Child** — Jesus/ the "Word" of God (John 1:1, 14; Rev. 12:5, 13) born before the "woman" (church) was in labor/tribulation (Is. 66:7-8) which likely occurred during the Protestant Reformation (great tribulation- Matt. 24:29)

**Michael** — Jesus (Rev. 12:7; see "Michael" in Dan. 10)

**War** (between Christ and Satan) — the great controversy that began in heaven and continues today on earth (Rev. 12:7-12, 17)

**Wilderness** — *("eremos"- desolate, uninhabited place)* likely symbolic of the earth, specifically the beast (nation [Dan. 7:23]) from the earth found in Rev. 13:11 (Rev. 12:6, 9, 12-16; Job 12:24; Is. 14:17; 64:10; Jer. 4:26; 12:12; 31:1-2; 51:43-44; Eze. 20:13-23; 34:25, 30)

**Serpent's** (Satan [Rev. 12:9]) **Water** — false doctrine (Rev. 12:15; 8:10-11; see "Wormwood" in Revelation 9); opposite of "living water" of Christ (Jn. 4:14; Eph. 5:26); people (wicked)(Rev. 17:15)

**Rest of Her Offspring** — God's remnant church/people who keep the Ten Commandments and have the testimony of Jesus, which is the spirit of prophecy (Rev. 12:17; 19:10; 1:1-2)

## REVELATION 13

**Beast from the Sea** — (Rev. 13:1-8) **beast**- nation/kingdom (Dan. 7:23); **sea**- populated area (Rev. 17:15); **"the sea"**- Mediterranean

Sea (see Dan. 7- "Great Sea")

**Seven Heads & Ten Horns** - **7 heads** — 7 world kingdoms; **10 horns**- powers of smaller states/countries (Rev. 13:1; 12:3; Dan. 7:8; "Heads" & "Horns" in Rev. 12; Dan. 7)

**Blasphemous Name** — claiming the power of God, such as the ability to forgive sin (Rev. 13:1, 6; Matt. 9:2-5; Luke 5:20-21)

**Like a Leopard, Feet like a Bear, Mouth like a Lion** (composite) — symbolic of the nations/kingdoms, specifically found in Daniel 7:3-7 (Rev. 13:2; see "Leopard," "Bear," and "Lion" in Dan. 7)

**Power from Dragon** — Satan/his kingdom of angels and people on earth/false doctrines (Rev. 13:2; 12:9, 15; see "Fiery Red Dragon" in Rev. 12)

**Wounded Head/Healed** — **wounded**- Rome/papacy lost civil power over Europe in 1798 AD (Rev. 13:3, 14); **head**- kingdom (see "Head' in Rev. 12 & Dan. 7); **healed** - returns to world influence before Christ's coming (Rev. 13:4-7); last beast kingdom with little horn- a "man speaking pompous words" (Dan. 7:8)

**Given Power Over the Nations of the World** — authority (Rev. 13:7-8)

**Slain Lamb**- Jesus Christ (Rev. 13:8; see "Lamb" in Rev. 5)

**Beast from the Earth** — **beast** - nation/kingdom (Rev. 13:11-18; Dan. 7:23); **earth** *("ge")* likely means a specific country, territory, region within borders; main land (unpopulated area) as opposed to sea or water (populated area [Rev. 17:15]); compare wilderness (Rev. 12:6, 14; see "Wilderness" in Rev. 12); "bottomless pit"- earth (see "Bottomless Pit" in Rev. 9); clay (Is. 45:9, 12; see "Clay" in Dan. 2)

**Two Horns like a Lamb** - **horns** — civil/religious powers of a nation (Rev. 13:11; see "Horns" in Rev. 12, 5; Dan. 7); **lamb**-Christ/Christian (see "Lamb" in Rev. 5)

**Speaks like a Dragon** — false satanic teachings (Rev. 13:11; 12:9; "Dragon" in Rev. 12)

**Fire from Heaven** — symbolic of a counterfeit "sign" (Rev. 13:13-14); possibly false Pentecost/outpouring of spirit/speaking in tongues (Rev. 13:13; Acts 2:3-4; 1 Cor. 14:4-33)

**Image of the Beast** — **image** *("eikon"- "resemblance")* of the **sea beast** (kingdom- Dan. 7:23; Rev. 13:1-7); false worship of an entity claiming divinity; idolatry (Rev. 13:14-18; 14:9-11; 15:2; 19:20; 20:4; Ex. 20:4; 23:24; Is. 41:29)

**Mark of the Beast** — a symbolic seal of loyalty; *"mark"* *("charagma")*= *"stamp"* (Rev. 13:17; 14:9-11) compare *"seal"* *("sphragis")* = *"stamp"* (Rev. 7:2), concerning a change of *"times and law"* (Dan. 7:25) that all who worship the beast and his image receive (Rev. 13:15-18; 14:9; 17:5; 20:4; Eze. 9:4-6) in the right hand (actions [Eccl. 9:10]) and/or in the forehead (decision [Jer. 3:1-3]) compared to God's seal, placed only in the forehead (Rev. 7:3)

**666** — Number of the beast (likely the scarlet beast with the name, "Mystery Babylon" [Rev. 17:5]) required to buy or sell (Rev. 13:17), also the number of the "man of sin" and the "lawless one" (Rev. 13:18; 19:20; 2 Thess. 2:3-8)

## REVELATION 14

**Lamb** — Jesus (Rev. 14:1, 4; see "Lamb" in Rev. 5 & 13)

**Mount** — kingdom (Rev. 14:1; 17:9-10; Eze. 36:4; Zech. 8:3; Dan. 9:16)

**Zion (Sion)** — God's kingdom and dwelling place (Rev. 14:1; Ps. 48:2; 125:1; Is. 2:3; 24:23; 64:10; Micah 4:7-10) often associated with

Judah and Jerusalem (2 Kings 19:31; Is. 8:18; 37:32; 40:9; Ps. 78:68; Joel 2:32; 3:17; Micah 4:2); daughter of Zion- spiritual Israel (Is. 14:32; Joel 2:23, 32; Micah 5:8; Eph. 2:11-19)

**144,000** — leaders of God's remnant church (Rev. 14:1; see "144,000" in Rev. 7)

**Name Written on Their Foreheads** — a conscious decision to worship and obey God and display His character in one's life (Rev. 14:1; 22:4; Heb. 8:10; Ex. 34:5-7; see "Seal on Forehead" in Rev. 7)

**Virgins** — God's people not defiled with spiritual harlotry (Rev. 17:1, 5; 14:4; Matt. 25:1-11; Jer. 6:2)

**Follows the Lamb** — followers of Christ, not the beast (Rev. 14:4; 13:3, 8; Jn. 1:29)

**Firstfruits to God and the Lamb** — *"archomai," (firstfruits)* meaning, *"to be chief, leader, ruler"* (James 1:18; Rev. 14:4; Lev. 23:10; Heb. 12:22-23)

**No Guile in Mouth** — blameless through Christ's power (Rev. 14:5; Zeph. 3:13; 2 Peter 3:14; Jude 24; Col. 1:20-22)

**Four Living Creatures (Beasts-KJV)** — kingdoms (Dan. 7:23; Rev. 14:3; see "Four Living Creatures" in Rev. 4)

**24 Elders** — divisional leaders of God's people (Rev. 14:3; see "Twenty-four Elders" in Rev. 4)

**New Song** — song of the redeemed from the earth, not ever sung by God's angels because they have never sinned; the song of Moses and the Lamb (Rev. 5:9; 14:3; 15:3; Is. 51:11)

**First Angel's Message** — worship the Creator and keep His commandments (especially the fourth that commemorates creation) in order to be sealed (Rev. 14:7, 12; Ex. 20:8-11; Eze. 20:20; Is. 8:16; Heb. 10:16; Eph. 4:30; Col. 1:15-17) because the hour of His judgment has come (Rev. 14:7; 18:10)

**Second Angel's Message** — Babylon (symbol of apostate Christianity) is fallen because of her false doctrines (wine of fornication- idolatry [Rev. 14:8; 17:4-5; 18:2-3; Jer. 51:7-8, 41, 44; Deut. 32:32-33; Eze. 23:13-18, 22-26; Dan. 3:1-6])

**Third Angel's Message** — warning against receiving the mark of the beast and its image (Rev. 14:9-11; 13:15-17; Dan. 7:25; see "Mark of the Beast" in Rev. 13)

**Smoke of Torment Ascends Forever**- the final destruction of those who worship the beast and receive its mark, compared to the destruction of Sodom (Lk. 17:29; 2 Peter 2:6; 3:10; Jude 7; Mal. 4:3)

**No Rest Day or Night** — no rest of God, specifically the rest of His Sabbath day (Heb. 4:1-4; Matt. 11:28-30; Ex. 20:8-11)

**Son of Man in Clouds** (Rev. 14:14; 1:7) — Jesus (Matt. 9:6; 12:8, 40, 13:41); coming in clouds- won't touch the earth (Acts 1:9-11; Matt. 24:30; 26:64; Mk. 13:26; 14:62; 1 Thess. 4:17; Rev. 1:7; Jer. 4:13)

**Sickle** — instrument for reaping a harvest (see "Harvest" below); the implementation of judgment (Rev. 14:14-19; Mk. 4:29; Joel 3:13])

**Harvest of the Earth** — the completion of earth's judgment (Rev. 14:14-20; Dan. 7:9-10, 13; I Thess. 5:9; Matt. 13:30, 36-43; Mk. 4:29; Jer. 51:33)

**Winepress** — symbolic of the judgment of the wicked, finally resulting in their destruction (Rev. 14:19-20; 19:15; Joel 3:13-14; Is. 63:3-4)

**Blood** — persecution/death (Rev. 14:20; 6:9-11; see "Blood" in Rev. 8)

**Horses' Bridles** — a reference to the first four seals (Rev. 14:17-20; 6:1-8)

# REVELATION 15

**Third Sign in Heaven** — seven angels with the seven last plagues (Rev. 15:1; first sign- "woman" (church [Rev.12:1; Jer. 6:2]); second sign - "dragon" (Satan/his kingdom/ [Rev. 12:3, 9])

**Image, Mark, Number of the Beast** — (Rev. 15:1; see "Image," "Mark," & "666" in Rev. 13)

**Sea of Glass Mingled With Fire** — (Rev. 15:2; 4:6) "sea"- a symbol of people, nations, tongues (Rev. 17:15); "glass"- transparent purity (Rev. 21:18, 21); "fire"- Holy Spirit (Acts 2:3-4)

**Song of Moses** — song of deliverance from bondage (Rev. 15:3-4; Ex. 15:1; Deut. 31:30; 32)

**Song of the Lamb** — song of redemption that Christ paid on Calvary (Rev. 15:3-4; 5:12-13; 7:9-10; see "Lamb" in Rev. 5, 13, & 14)

**Temple of the Tabernacle of the Testimony Opened** — the Most Holy Place in the heavenly sanctuary containing the Ark of the Covenant or the ark containing the Ten Commandments which are called the *"Testimony"* (Rev. 15:5; Ex. 25:21-22; 26:33-34; 31:18; 40:20); "opened"- likely indicating the departure of the presence of Christ in the Most Holy Place of the sanctuary in heaven; the completion of the investigative judgment and the closing of Christ's intercessory work for mankind in Heaven/the close of probation for the earth and the outpouring of the seven last plagues (Rev. 15:5; 11:19; Lk. 23:45)

**Pure Bright Linen/Chests Girded with Golden Bands** — heavenly holy priestly attire (Rev. 15:6; 1:13; 19:8)

**Four Living Creatures (Beasts - KJV)** — kingdoms (Rev. 15:7; Dan. 7:23; see Rev. 4, 5)

**Seven Golden Bowls Full of the Wrath of God** — prayers of vindication and justice by the saints manifested in the seven last plagues (Rev. 15:7-8; 5:8; 6:9-11; 16)

**Smoke-filled Temple/No One Can Enter** — indication of intercession for sinners ended/probation closed (Rev. 15:8; Lev. 16:13; Heb. 10:19; Ex. 40:34-35; 2 Chron. 7:1-2)

## REVELATION 16

**Bowls of Wrath of God** — the vindication of the saints' prayers for justice/seven last plagues (Rev. 16:1; 5:8; 6:10; 15:7; 17:1; 21:9; Zech. 14:12-20)

**First Plague** — foul and loathsome sores fall upon those with the mark of the beast and worship his image (Rev. 16:2; Job 2:7; Deut. 28:15, 27; Ex. 9:9)

**Second Plague** — sea becomes blood and sea creatures die (Rev. 16:3; 8:8-9; 17:15)

**Third Plague** — rivers and springs of water become blood (Rev. 16:4-7; 6:9-10; Ex. 7:17-21)

**Fourth Plague** — the sun's heat scorches some of the wicked (Rev. 16:8-9; Joel 1:10-12, 17-20)

**Fifth Plague** — darkness falls upon the throne of the beast (Rev. 16:10-11; Ex. 10:21-23)

**Sixth Plague** — (Rev. 16:12-16)

**Euphrates River** is dried up — God's Word (Living Water- Jn 4:14; Eph. 5:26; Amos 8:11-12;) and the Holy Spirit's influence (Jn. 7:38) is "dried up" in spiritual Babylon, resulting in the loss of people, who can also be represented as waters (Rev. 16:12; 9:14; 17:15; Hosea 13:14-15)

**Kings of the East** — Jesus/the Lord (Is. 41:2-4; Matt. 2:1-2; 24:27)

**Frogs/Unclean Spirits** — the wicked, like frogs, capture their prey with deceitful mouths (Rev. 9:17-18; Lam. 3:46-47); demons empower (Acts 8:7; Mk. 3:11; Gen. 8:7)

**Dragon** — Satan/his kingdom (Rev. 16:13; 12:9; Dan. 7:23)

**Beast** — kingdom of sea beast/"man of sin"/"lawless one" (Rev. 16:13; 13:1-7; 19:20; Dan. 7:23; 2 Thess. 2:3-4, 6-12)

**False Prophet** — false religious teachers from the kingdom of the "earth beast" who do great "signs" and deceives the world into worshipping the sea beast (Rev. 16:13; 13:11-14; 19:20; 1 Kings 18:36-39; Micah 3:5)

**Armageddon** *("mountain of Megiddo")* — meaning *"a place of crowds"* and *"rendezvous"* (Rev. 16:16; 19:20; 20:2, 10; Zech. 12:9-11) or from *"mow'ed" - appointed time/place," "mount of the congregation"* or *"assembly"* (Is. 14:13)

**Thief in the Night** — the close of probation and Christ's coming as a surprise to the wicked, NOT the righteous (Rev. 16:15; 3:2-3; 1 Thess. 5:1-4; Matt. 24:42-44)

**Battle of Armageddon** — war between Christ and His followers and Satan and his followers, ending ultimately with the final destruction of the Devil, his angels, and the wicked (Rev. 16:14-16; 20:7-10; Joel 3:1-3, 9-12)

**Seventh Plague** — great earthquake; islands sink; mountains fall;

cities fall; Babylon divided into thirds; hail falls (Rev. 16:17-21; 6:12-14; 9:5-12; Is. 19:24; Eze. 5:12)

**Voices, Thunders, Lightnings, Great Earthquake, Great Hail** — Voices- seven trumpets repeated (Rev. 4:1; Ex. 19:16); Thunders-seven seals powerfully repeated as thunders (Rev. 6:1; 10:3-4); Lightnings- Spirit of God in churches/Latter Rain- (Rev. 4:5; 5:6; Job 28:26, KJV); Earthquake - shaking (Is. 29:6; Heb. 12:25-28); Hail- 7 Last Plagues/close of probation (Rev. 16:17-18, 21, KJV)

# REVELATION 17

**Great Harlot/Woman** — church in apostasy (Rev. 17:1, 3-6; 19:2; Is. 1:21; 23:16-17; Jer. 3:2-13, 20; Eze. 16:15-49; Hosea 4:6-11)

**Many Waters** — peoples, multitudes, nations, tongues (Rev. 17:1,15; 19:6; Num. 24:7; Is. 17:12-13)

**Wine of Fornication** — false doctrines/idolatry (Rev. 17:2; 14:8, 18:3; Deut. 32:32; Prov. 4:17; Is. 28:7; Jer. 51:7)

**Purple/Scarlet/Pearls/Gold** — symbols of wealth/power of kings/ungodly character (Rev. 17:4; Eze. 23:5-6, 14); idolatry (Jer. 10:8-9); **"scarlet"** (red) - sinful (Is. 1:9); dragon/Satan/his followers (Rev. 17:3; 12:3, 9); (papacy's colors)

**Golden Cup** — (Rev. 17:4, 6; 18:6; Jer. 51:7); utensil of the temple (I Chron. 28:17-18; Dan. 5:2-4); a symbol of fate (Eze. 23:32-33; Matt. 26:39; Ps. 16:5; I Cor. 10:21); often associated with wickedness/wrath of God (Rev. 14:10; 16:19; Ps 75:8; 11:6)

**Kings of the Earth** — the civil authority of the nations, specifically of the American "earth" beast (Rev. 17:2; 13:11-14; 16:14; 18:3, 9; 6:15-16; 19:19; Is. 24:21-22)

**Scarlet Beast** — red dragon beast (Rev. 17:3, 8; 12:3, 9; 11:7-8; 13:1); Satan's kingdom disguised in the religious garb of the papacy that unites the world's kingdoms through the combination of church & state (see "Beast"/"Dragon" in Rev. 12 & 13)

**Wilderness/Bottomless Pit** — earth (Rev. 17:8; 9:2; 12:6, 14, see "Bottomless Pit" in Rev. 9 & "Wilderness" in Rev. 12)

**Names of Blasphemy** — claiming divinity (Rev. 17:3; 13:1, 5-6; see "Blasphemy" in Rev. 13)

**Seven Heads/Mountains/Seven Kings Representing Their Kingdoms** — civil world kingdoms, specifically reigning over God's people throughout history that compose the dragon's (Satan's [Rev. 12:9]) and the sea beast's kingdom (Rev. 17:9-10; Dan. 7:3-8, 11-12, 17, 23; Rev. 12:3; 13:1-3, 7; Jer. 31:23; 51:24-25; Ps. 74:13-14; see "Seven Heads," "Dragon," & "Sea Beast" in Rev. 12-13)

**Ten Horns/Kings** — civil powers (Rev. 17:12; Dan. 7:7-8, 17, 20-21, 23-24; see "Ten Horns"in Rev. 13)

**One Mind** — unified in thought and purpose (Rev. 17:13; Rom. 12:16; 15:6)

**Lamb** — Christ (Rev. 17:15; 5:6, 8, 12-13; 13:11; 14:1, 4, 10; see "Lamb" in Rev. 5, 13, 14)

**Mystery Babylon the Great** — symbols of a false church/state system that persecutes God's people/spiritual confusion (Rev. 17:5-6, 18; 14:8; 18:2; Jer. 51:41-43, 49, 52; Gen. 11:9)

## REVELATION 18

**Babylon the Great** — false church/state system that persecutes God's people; spiritual confusion [Rev. 18:2, 18; see "Babylon the Great" in Rev. 17])

**Prison of every Foul Spirit and a Cage for Every Unclean and Hated Bird** — demonic agencies/evil men (Rev. 18:2, 23;

19:17-18, 21; Mk. 9:25-26; Eze. 39:4,17-21; Jer. 5:26-27; 12:7, 9; 15:3; Rom. 1:22–25)

**Wine of the Wrath of Fornication** — false doctrine (Rev. 18:3; "Wine of Fornication"- Rev. 17)

**Kings of the Earth** — civil authorities of the nations, specifically the "earth" beast of Rev. 13:11-18 (Rev. 18:3, 9; see "Kings of the Earth" in Rev. 17)

**Merchants/Great Men of the Earth** — commerce of the nations, symbolizing spiritual wealth, specifically of the "earth" beast of Rev. 13:11-17 (Rev. 18:3, 11-19, 23; Is. 23:2-3,7-9)

**Fourth Angel's Message** — "Come out of Babylon," repetition of the Second & Third Angels' Messages in Rev. 14:8-11 (Rev. 18:4-8; see the three angels' messages in Rev.14)

**Double Measure in Cup** — double the judgment/punishment (Rev. 18:6-8; Matt. 7:2)

**Alas! Alas!** *("ouai"- woe)* — Woe! Woe! (Rev. 18:10; See "Woe" in Rev. 8)

**Great Millstone Cast into the Sea** — the downfall of a nation/prosperity (Rev. 18:21-23; Jer. 25:10; Matt. 18:6)

## REVELATION 19

**Great Multitude** — saved from the earth (Rev. 19:1; see "Great Multitude" in Rev. 7)

**Four Living Creatures (Beasts- KJV)** — kingdoms (Rev. 19:4; Dan. 7:23; see "Four Living Creatures" in Rev. 4)

**24 Elders** — leaders of the "great multitude" (Rev. 19:4; see "Twenty-four Elders" in Rev. 4)

**Marriage of the Lamb** — uniting of Christ and His wife

441

(people/church/city/kingdom [Rev. 19:7-9; 21:2; Is. 62:5; Jer. 33:11])

**Testimony of Jesus** — Spirit of prophecy (Rev. 19:10; 12:17; 1:1-3)

**White Horse/Rider** — a reference to the first seal of Christ/Christianity in Rev. 6:2 (Rev. 19:11-12; see "White Horse" in Rev. 6)

**Called Faithful and True** — Christ and His Word (Rev. 19:11; 1:5; 3:14; 21:5; Jer. 42:5)

**Eyes Flame of Fire** — eyes of Christ, Son of Man (Rev. 19:12; 1:14; 2:18); symbolic of the Holy Spirit's work in the churches/prophets (Rev. 5:6; Zech. 4:9-10; Is. 29:10)

**Out of Mouth Two-Edged Sword** — Christ/Word (Rev. 19:15, 21; see "Sword"- Rev. 2)

**Rod of iron** — all-powerful civil authority (Rev. 19:15; see "Rod of iron" in Rev. 2)

**Tread the Winepress** — judgment/wrath of God (Rev. 19:15; 14:19; Lam. 1:15; Is. 63:3)

**Birds** — demons (Rev. 19:17-18, 21; 18:2, Jer. 15:3; see "Prison of every Foul Spirit" in Rev. 18)

**Beast** — earthly kingdom of Satan (Rev. 19:19-20; 11:7; 13:1-4; 16:13; 17:3, 8; 20:10; Dan. 7:23)

**False Prophet** — false teachers in God's nation (Rev. 19:20; 16:13; 20:10; 13:11-14; 2 Peter 2:1)

## REVELATION 20

**Bottomless Pit** — earth (Rev. 20:1-3; see "Bottomless Pit" in Rev. 9)

**Chain** — bound for judgment by circumstances (Rev. 20:1-3; Jude 1:6)

**Seal** — events decreed for a certain time period (Rev. 20:3; 22:10; Dan. 12:4, 9)

**Judgment by the Saints**- saints affirm God's judgment against the Devil/demons and the wicked (Rev. 20:4, 11-13; I Cor. 6:2-3)

**1000 Years (Millennium)** — time that the saints are in heaven reviewing the record books of the wicked and affirming God's character of love and justice (Rev. 20:4, 6; 19:1-2; I Cor. 6:2-3); the earth is empty of humans because they have been destroyed at the second coming of Christ and only the Devil and his angels remain on the earth (Rev. 20:1-3, 5; 2 Thess. 2:8-10; Jer. 4:23-26); symbolic of Sabbath rest (6,000 years of sin on earth/seventh thousand - rest in Heaven for righteous (Gen. 2:2-3; Ex. 23:10-11; Lev. 26:32-35; Ps. 90:4; 2 Peter 3:8)

**Gog and Magog** — symbolic of the wicked nations of the earth that will be resurrected after a thousand years and destroyed with Satan and his demons in the lake of fire (Rev. 20:3, 7-10, 13-15; 16:14; Eze. 38:18-23; 39:17-20)

**Second Death** — the final death of the wicked and the complete destruction of Satan and his angels (with the wicked) in the lake of fire (Rev. 20:10, 13-14; 21:8; I Cor. 15:25-26; Is. 11:4; Eze. 28:18-19); everlasting/devouring punishment/fire compared to Sodom's "eternal fire" (Jude 1:6-7; 2 Thess. 1:7-9; Is. 33:11, 14; Matt. 18:8; 25:41, 46; Mark 3:29); the fire consumes the devil, his angels, sinners, and the earth until there is only ashes (Is. 47:14; 5:24; Nahum 1:7-10; Mal. 4:1, 3; Ps. 37:9-10)

**Book of Life** — Lamb's - Christ's (see "Lamb" in Rev. 21) book of life (Rev. 20:15; 13:8; 21:27)

## REVELATION 21

**New Jerusalem** — city of the saints (Rev. 21:2, 10; 3:12; Is. 65:17-19; 66:22; 2 Peter 3:10-13)

**No More Sea** — symbolic of the eradication of sin (Rev. 21:1; Micah 7:19; Nahum 1:9)

**Lake of Fire/Second Death** — the final and complete destruction of Satan, his angels, and the wicked (Rev. 21:8; see "Second Death" in Rev. 20)

**Bowls of Seven Angels** — containing the seven last plagues (Rev. 21:9; see "Bowels of Wrath" in Rev. 16)

**Bride/Lamb's Wife** — Christ's kingdom of saints/the New Jerusalem (Rev. 21:9-10, 14, 22-23, 27; 5:8-9, 12-13; 7:9-10, 17; 12:11; 14:1; 17:14; 19:7, 9; 22:1, 3; Is. 61:10)

**Measurement of a Man** — Jerusalem measures 12,000 furlongs squared, the walls are 144 cubits — "the measure of a man, that is of an angel" (*"angelos"* meaning *"messenger"* [Rev. 21:15-17]). This measurement is similar to the 144,000 (Rev. 7:4; 14:1, 3) and may be symbolic of the completion/reward of the judgment (Rev. 11:1; Zech. 1:16-17; 2:1-5)

**Lamb's Book of Life** — list of saints' names covered by the blood of Christ (Rev. 21:27, see "Book of Life" in Rev. 20)

## REVELATION 22

**River of Water of Life From God's Throne** — a symbol of Christ/His Word- (Rev. 22:1, 17; 21:6; John 4:10,13-14; living waters- Jer. 2:13; 17:13; Zech. 14:8-9; Eph. 5:26)

**Tree of Life** — a symbol of a righteous character/words (Rev. 22:2, 14; 2:7; Prov. 11:30; 15:4)

**God's Name on His People's Foreheads** — God's character/law manifested in His people (Rev. 22:3-4; **name**- character (I Cor. 6:11; 2 Thess. 1:12; 2 Tim. 2:19; Ps. 119:51-56) on **foreheads**- decision in mind (Rev. 14:1, 5; 7:3-4; 3:12)

**No Night or Light of the Sun** — Light from God's presence (Rev. 22:5; 7:16-17; Is. 60:19-20)

# Appendix II
## Confirmation of Repeated Bible Prophecies*

## PROMISED INSIGHT OF PROPHECY DURING THE LAST DAYS

**Jn. 16:13** "…when He, the Spirit of truth, is come, he will guide you into all truth; for he shall not speak of himself; but whatsoever he shall hear, that shall he speak: and *he will shew you things to come.*" (KJV)

**Amos 3:7** "Surely the Lord God will do nothing, but *he revealeth His secret to his servants the prophets.*" (KJV)

**Dan. 12:4, 9-10, 13** "But thou, O Daniel, shut up the words, and seal the book, *until the time of the end:* many shall run to and fro, and *knowledge shall be increased….* for the words are closed up and **sealed** till the **time of the end**. Many shall be purified, and made white, and tried; but the wicked shall do wickedly: and none of the wicked shall understand; *but the wise shall understand…and (thou shall) stand in thy lot at the* **end of the days**." (KJV)

*"Daniel's history is given us for our admonition.…* As in the Jewish age, so in this age, <u>**God reveals his secrets to his servants the prophets.**</u>" *(YI December 1, 1903, par. 3)*

*"[<u>Daniel 12:9, 4, 10, 13 quoted.</u>] The time has come for Daniel to stand in his lot. The time has come for the light given him to go to the world as never before. <u>If those for whom the Lord has done so much will walk in the light, **their knowledge of Christ and the prophecies relating to Him will be greatly increased as they near the close of this earth's history.**</u>" (Ms176-1899.24)*

*"<u>Each period of the fulfillment of prophetic history is a prepara-</u><u>tion for the advanced light which will succeed each period.</u> As the prophecy comes to the end, there is to be a perfect whole."* (Lt8-1895.6)

*"Then we are to get more light from the throne of God, <u>and have an</u> <u>increase of light.... it is the old light brought up and placed in</u> <u>new settings.</u>"* (Ms5-1889.14)

*"<u>When God's people are at ease and satisfied with their present</u> <u>enlightenment, we may be sure that He will not favor them. It is</u> <u>His will that they should be ever moving forward to receive the</u> <u>increased and ever-increasing light which is shining for them.</u> The present attitude of the church is not pleasing to God. <u>There has come</u> <u>in a self-confidence that has led them to feel no necessity for more</u> <u>truth and greater light</u>. We are living at a time when Satan is at work on the hand and on the left, before and behind us, and yet as a people we are asleep. <u>God wills that a voice shall be heard arousing His people to</u> <u>action.</u>"* (5T 708)

*"We must study carefully the old waymarks. <u>These experiences in the</u> <u>past are to be revived. Daniel is to stand out conspicuously with</u> <u>the Revelation</u>...."* (Ms223-**1902**.11)

## HISTORY (PROPHECY) WILL BE REPEATED

Eccl. 1:9-10- **"That which has been is what will be.** That which is done is what will be done. And there is nothing new under the sun... <u>It has already been in ancient times before us</u>." (NKJV)

Eccl. 3:15-**"That which is has already been. And what is to be has already been;** And God requires an account of what is past." (NKJV)

*"Study the Revelation in connection with Daniel; for history will be repeated*.... We are living amid the perils of the last days, and many are insensible to the perils that threaten our world. **We, with all our religious advantages, ought to know far more today than we do know.** 'Watch, and pray,' said Jesus, 'for ye know not when the time is. Be ye therefore ready also: for the Son of Man cometh at an hour when ye think not.'" (SpTA07 55.1)

*"We are standing on the threshold of great and solemn events. Many of the prophecies are about to be fulfilled in quick succession. Every element of power is about to be set to work. **Past history will be repeated; old controversies will arouse to new life, and peril will beset God's people on every side.** Intensity is taking possession of the human family. It is permeating everything upon the earth." (The Review and Herald, August 31, 1897 {Ms142-1901.15})*

*"The Lord has declared that the **history of the past shall be rehearsed as we enter upon the closing work.**" (Manuscript 129, 1905)*

*"Although new and important truths appropriate for succeeding generations have been opened to the understanding, the present revealings do not contradict those (truths rather than beliefs) of the past. **Every new truth understood only makes more significant the old**.... **What is now needed is divine enlightenment, and a more intelligent knowledge of the wonderful dealings of God with His people anciently.**" (RH, March 2, 1886)*

*"Many will discover the **lost links in the chain of truth, and they will see a beautiful harmony in the whole.** They will have a fresh experience, being assured that He whom they trusted has not forsaken them and left them in darkness." (Lt22-1890.4.*

*"Study Revelation in connection with Daniel, **for history will be repeated**.... We, with all our religious advantages, ought to know **far more today than we do know**...." (TM 116)*

## PROPHECY REPEATED IS VITALLY IMPORTANT

*"**Some prophecies God has repeated,** thus showing that importance must be given to them. **The Lord does not repeat things that are of no great consequence.**" (Manuscript 107, 1897, pp. 1, 2 {9MR 7.5})*

## THE OLD TESTAMENT PROPHECIES APPLY TO THE LAST DAYS

*"DANIEL, ISAIAH, EZEKIEL… **reach down to the future** and to what would occur in **the last days.**" Letter 132, 1898 (3SM 419)*

*"The prophecies in the Old Testament are the word of the Lord **for the last days**." (Letter 154, 1906, May 26)*

*"**Each of the ancient prophets spoke less for their time than for ours so that their prophecies is in force for us** (I Cor. 10:11, 1 Peter 1:12).… All the great events and solemn transactions of the Old Testament history **have been and are repeating themselves in the church in the last days**." (CTr 357)*

*"[Daniel 12:8-13]. Daniel has been **standing in his lot since the seal was removed** (Note: in 1844) and the light of truth has been shining upon his visions. He stands in his lot, bearing the testimony **which was to be understood at the end of the days**." (1SAT 225.5)*

*"How dare men teach that the Revelation is beyond human understanding? It is a mystery revealed, a book opened. **Revelation directs the mind to Daniel.** Both present important instruction **concerning***

*events at the close of world history." (HF 213.1)*

"The light that Daniel received direct from God was given **especially for these last days. The visions he saw by the banks of the Ulai and the Hiddekel** (see DANIEL 8:2- Vision found in Daniel 8-9; 10:4- vision found in Daniel 10-12), the great rivers of Shinar, are **now in process of fulfillment, and all the events foretold will soon have come to pass."** (16MR 334.2)

"The burden of Christ's preaching was, 'The time is fulfilled, and the kingdom of God is at hand: repent ye, and believe the gospel.' Mark 1:15. The gospel message as given by the Saviour was based on the prophecies. **The 'time' which He declared fulfilled was the period made known to Daniel. 'Seventy weeks,'** said the angel Gabriel, 'are determined upon thy people and upon thy Holy City, to finish the transgression, and to make an end of sins, and to make reconciliation for iniquity, and to bring in everlasting righteousness, and to seal up the vision and prophecy, and to anoint the Most Holy" Daniel 9:24...." (HLv 147.2)

"As the message of Christ's first advent announced the kingdom of His grace, **so the message of His second advent announces the kingdom of His glory. And the second message, like the first, is based on the prophecies**.... (NOTE: the 70 Week TIME prophecy of Daniel 9). The Jews misinterpreted the Word of God and knew not the time of their visitation. The years of the ministry of Christ and His apostles they spent in plotting the destruction of the Lord's messengers. Earthly ambitions absorbed them. **So today the kingdom of this world absorbs men's thoughts, and they take no note of the rapidly fulfilling prophecies and the tokens of the swift-coming kingdom of God. While we are not to know the hour of our Lord's return, we may know when it is near.** 'Therefore let us not sleep, as do others; but let us watch and be sober' 1 Thessalonians 5:6...." (HLv 149)

## JESUS TAUGHT THAT PROPHECIES REAPPLY AT DIFFERENT TIME PERIODS

*(Matt. 24:3) "In the prophecy of Jerusalem's destruction Christ said, 'Because iniquity shall abound, the love of many shall wax cold. But he that shall endure unto the end, the same shall be saved....'* **This prophecy will again be fulfilled."** *(DA 633.3)*

*"The ruin of Jerusalem was a symbol of the final ruin that shall overwhelm the world.* **The prophecies that received a partial fulfillment in the overthrow of Jerusalem have a more direct application to the last days.**" *(MB 120.2)*

## THE SIGNS OF CHRIST'S COMING WILL BE REACTED OVER AGAIN

*"Time of trouble, it will come right early.* **The signs shall be reacted over again;** *the day and hour will then be known." (1EGWLM 179.3 [Ms6-1849.9])*

## SEVEN THUNDERS UNSEALED (A DELINEATION OF TIMED EVENTS DURING THE LAST DAYS)

*"Seal up those things which the seven thunders uttered."* **These relate to future events which will be disclosed in their order.** *Daniel shall stand in his lot at the end of the days. John sees the little book unsealed.* **Then Daniel's prophecies have their proper place in the first, second, and third angels' messages** *to be given to the world.* **The unsealing of the little book was the message to time... the seven thunders was a delineation of events which would transpire under the first and second angels' messages.**"*(Ms. 59, 1900)*

*"We must understand the doctrines that have been studied out carefully and prayerfully. It has been revealed to me that there is **among our people a great lack of knowledge in regard to the <u>rise and progress of the third angel's message</u>.** There is great need to search the book of Daniel and the book of Revelation and learn the texts thoroughly, that we may know what is written."* (2SM 392.1)

*"There are those now living who, in studying the **prophecies of Daniel and John,** received great light from God as they passed over the ground where **special prophecies were in process of fulfillment in their order.** They bore the **message of time** to the people. The truth shone out clearly as the sun at noonday. **Historical events,** showing the direct fulfillment of prophecy were set before the people, and the prophecy was seen to be a <u>**figurative delineation of events leading down to the close of this earth's history.**</u> <u>The scenes connected with the working of the man of sin are the last features plainly revealed in this earth's history.</u> The people now have a special message to give to the world, <u>**the third angel's message.**</u>"* (2SM 102-104)

## <u>THE BIBLE GIVES MULTIPLE TIME PROPHECIES AFTER 1844:</u>

**Rev. 20- Millennium = 1000 Literal Years**

**Rev. 20:2-** "And he laid hold of the dragon, that old serpent, which is the Devil, and Satan, and bound him for **a thousand years.**" (KJV)

EGW comments on this text in GC 660 and 4SP 475, stating that this is a literal thousand years.

## REVELATION 13 SPEAKS OF "FORTY-TWO MONTHS"/EGW SAYS REPEATED

**Rev. 13:5**- "…there was given unto him a mouth speaking great things and blasphemies; and power was given unto him to continue for forty and two months."(KJV)

*"In the last days Satan will appear as an angel of light, with great power and heavenly glory, and claim to be the Lord of the whole earth. He will declare that the Sabbath has been changed from the seventh to the first day of the week; and as lord of the first day of the week he will present this spurious sabbath as a test of loyalty to him.* **Then will take place the final fulfillment (NOTE: MUST HAVE MORE THAN ONE FULFILLMENT) of the Revelator's prophecy. [Revelation 13:4-18, quoted]**" *(NOTE: EGW quotes the very verse that has the 42-month time prophecy in it!) (19MR 282.1)*

*"He that leadeth into captivity shall go into captivity; he killeth with the sword must be killed with the sword. Here is the patience and faith of the saints" [Rev. 13:10].* **_THIS ENTIRE CHAPTER is a revelation of what WILL SURELY TAKE PLACE._**" *(Ms88- 1897.17)*

## REVELATION 18 SPEAKS OF "ONE DAY" & "ONE HOUR"/IN FUTURE

**Rev. 18:8**- "Therefore her plagues will come in **one day**…." (KJV)

**Rev. 18:10**- " … For in **one hour** is thy judgment come." (KJV)

EGW states, " ... *in the* **_eighteenth chapter of the Revelation_**, *in a message* **_which is yet future_**, *the people of God are called upon to come out of Babylon" (GC88 382.3). "The words of Revelation 18 will be fulfilled." (ST Oct. 9, **1901**)*

## SEALS IN REVELATION REPEATED & TIED TO REVELATION 18

*"The mark of the beast is exactly what it has been proclaimed.... Not all in regard to this matter is yet understood, nor will be understood until **the unrolling of the scroll**...."* (6T 17)

*"The same spirit is seen today that is represented in **Revelation 6:6-8 (3rd & 4th Seal). History is to be repeated.** That which has been will be again."* (20MR 199.1)

*"When the **fifth seal was opened,** John the Revelator in vision saw beneath the altar the company that were slain for the Word of God and the testimony of Jesus Christ. **After this came the scenes described in the eighteenth of Revelation,** when those who are faithful and true are called out from Babylon [Revelation 18:1-5 quoted]."* (Manuscript 39, 1906)

*"The prophecy in the **eleventh of Daniel** has nearly reached its complete fulfillment. **Much of the history that has taken place in fulfillment of this prophecy will be repeated."** (19LtMs, Lt 103, 1904, par. 17)*

*"God has warned His people of the perils before them. John beholds the things which will be in the **last days,** and he sees a people working counter to God. **Read Revelation 12:17; 14:10-13, and chapters 17 and 13."*** (NOTE: These chapters contain TIME prophecies [17MR 18.2])

**"The prophecies... of Revelation, CHAPTERS 12-18, ARE being fulfilled."**

(NOTE: These chapters contain TIME prophecies [Manuscript 75, Sept. 20, **1906**])

*"In these last days the representation made in the twelfth chapter of Revelation will be fulfilled* (NOTE: This chapter contains a time prophecy). Satan will carry on the great conflict that he began in heaven, of which we read, 'And there was war in heaven; Michael and His angels fought against the dragon; and the dragon fought, and his angels, and prevailed not; neither was their place found any more in heaven.'" {Lt165-1903, August 3, par. 16)

"Let all who would understand the meaning of these things **read the eleventh chapter of Revelation** (EGW says that the French Revolution was an example of any nation that would repeat its atrocities [Rev. 11:8- Education, 228]). Read every verse, and learn the things that are **yet to take place in the cities**. Read also the scenes portrayed in the **eighteenth chapter** of the same book." (NOTE: These chapters contain time prophecies [21MR 91.4])

## IT IS SINFUL TO BE INDIFFERENT TO THE SIGNS OF CHRIST'S COMING

"There are in the world today many who close their eyes to the evidences that Christ has given to warn men of His coming. They seek to quiet all apprehension, while at the same time the signs of the end are rapidly fulfilling.... it is **sinful to be indifferent to the signs which are to precede the second coming of Christ**." (AA 260.1)

## WE MUST KNOW WHEN CHRIST IS NEAR OR IT WILL BE FATAL FOR US:

Hos. 4:6- "My people are destroyed for lack of knowledge: because thou hast rejected knowledge, I will also reject thee." (KJV)

*"Point after point of truth should be investigated; for there is <u>no limitation to the truth</u>... For years the voice of God has been saying to us, "Agitate, agitate, agitate."* **<u>Study every point of truth, that you may know for yourselves what is truth</u>** <u>in distinction from error</u>*. Let students search for themselves, that they may <u>know the deep things of God</u>. Let this work be done in the Spirit of Christ. Put no restriction upon the students."* TSS 55.2

*"Every new truth has made its way against hatred and opposition; those who were blessed with its light were tempted and tried.* **<u>The Lord gives a special truth for the people in emergency</u>. <u>Who dare refuse to publish it</u>?"** *GC 609.1*

*"Though no man knoweth the day nor the hour of His coming,* **<u>we are instructed and required to know when it is near</u>**. *We are further taught that to* **<u>DISREGARD HIS WARNING, and REFUSE OR NEGLECT TO KNOW when His ADVENT IS NEAR will be . . . FATAL for us</u>.**" *(GC 370.2; capitalization supplied)*

*\*All references other than the Bible texts are taken from the writing of Ellen G. White (https://egwwritings.org/)*

For the latest prophecy information and more books by this author, please visit
unsealedthetimeoftheend.com

www.ingramcontent.com/pod-product-compliance
Lightning Source LLC
Chambersburg PA
CBHW071131130626
46553CB00004B/1335